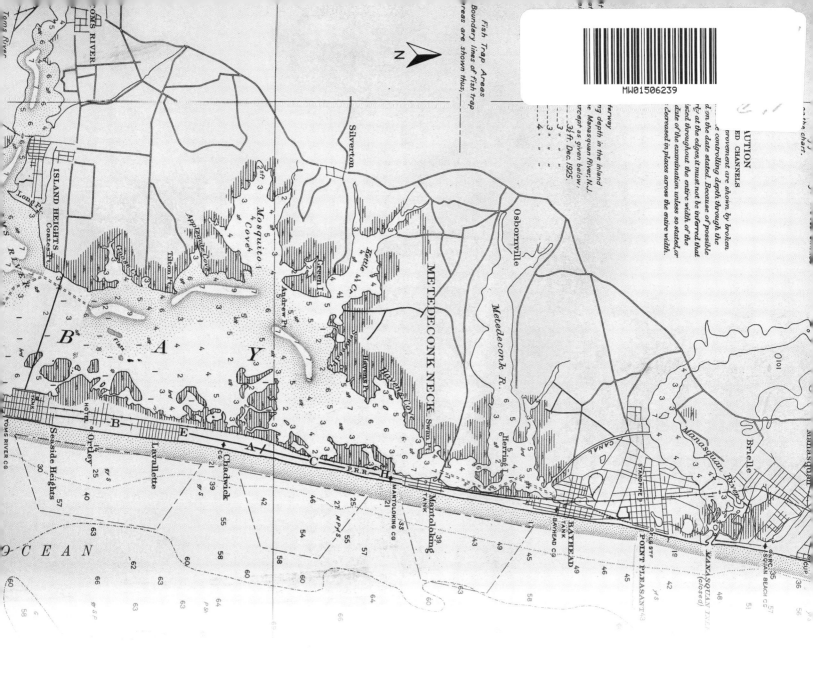

brought it to the boat shop to be reframed. He never got around to it, and the chart hung bare over a workbench where it survived two hurricanes—Irene and Superstorm Sandy, both of which completely flooded the workshop in 2011 and 2012. After this reproduction was made, the chart was reframed and now is displayed at Paul's home in Point Pleasant Beach.

This portion of the chart is to be compared with the modern NOAA version presented on the inside back cover.

Silent Maid

A CATBOAT HISTORY

Silent Maid

A CATBOAT HISTORY

Kent Mountford

The Chronicle of Her Bay, People, and Legacy

ISBN 978-0-692-28975-4

To order additional copies of this book, please contact:
Fishergate, Inc.
2216 Piney Creek Road, Chester, MD 21619
410.643.8646 • vianna@fishergate.com • fishergate.com

Printed in the United States of America

Dedication

This book is dedicated to

PETER RITTENHOUSE KELLOGG

. . . who in 2009 emailed me:

"How about a *Silent Maid* history?"

When I responded with a one-page proposal,
he emailed back:

"Please start now."

Here it is, Peter!

Peter Kellogg at the helm of Silent Maid
off Padenarum, Massachusetts.

Contents

Acknowledgments

Writing this book has been a considerable effort stretching across some four years and dominating 2000 days in my life. The task could not have been completed without the assistance of many people, within and outside the seven families and groups who made their mark on *Silent Maid*'s history.

Many of the participants in this vessel's long life have been dead for decades, and the task of reconstructing people, places, and events long-gone has been challenging. I hope I have done this fairly, respectfully, and have certainly been as honest as the data allowed throughout the process. I hope to have dealt openly with the many characters who played parts in this story.

When I recreated myself as an environmental historian some 30-odd years ago, I quipped that writing about the 17th century Chesapeake Bay offered a great deal of freedom because all the people who could counter my pronouncements had been dead for centuries. That is not the case in the present book, because the *Maid*'s history comes within a decade of the present, and some of my informants changed —well revised— their stories as the book was being written. If the final versions are in error, it is still my fault alone for putting them in print.

Peter R. Kellogg, who saved the original *Silent Maid* and re-created her anew as a modern vessel, both inspired this book and made its writing possible through his unquestioning support, start to finish. I am deeply indebted to him for this opportunity to delve into and re-live the history of this fascinating vessel that occupied so much of my formative years.

Many people who contributed to this tale are acknowledged directly in the text or in the chapters' endnotes. Some bear being called out for special thanks, but please forgive me if individuals are not enumerated among the following listing of five dozen or so people and organizations that is intended to be a representative, not exhaustive, list of those whose valuable information helped me on this journey.

Among sources about the Edwin J. Schoettle family and their interactions with the *Maid* I was started on my quest by Philip Alden Schoettle, Edwin's nephew. I missed the opportunity to talk with William Clarkson Schoettle, who died in 2012, but was already ill when this project started. Ben Kracauer, Curator, and Cathie Coleman of the Bay Head, Mantoloking and Lovelandtown Historical Museum provided advice and images, many from the Bill Schoettle collection; and the late Bob O'Brien, Curator of the New Jersey Museum of Boating, often eased my path and provided access to many images in this book. Roy Wilkins, who with co-author Gary Jobson, wrote the book *A Cats: A Century of Tradition*, taught me all I needed to know about working through this project with its generous sponsor, Peter R. Kellogg.

Suzy Mitchell Davis, Edwin's granddaughter and her cousin Sally Randolph provided constant feedback and access to many of the Schoettle family images used here. She also opened lines of communication to many other Schoettle descendants including Karl, Michael, Will, the late Andy (Ferdinand) Schoettle, Polly Schoettle Miller, and Jack LaFleur, who was actually Edwin Schoettle's dock boy in the late 1930s.

Many people provided context and helped set the tone of times past. Among these were:

- Alicemay Weber-Wright, Toms River Yacht Club historian, who permitted use of images and maps she owns and her mother Dorrie Snyder's wonderful paintings from around Island Heights.

- Eileen Fancher (of Island Heights)

- The late Runyon and Betsy Colie

- Tommy Beaton, owner, and Paul Smith, shipwright at David Beaton and Sons, Boat Builder. Nor can I ignore all Tom's father Lachlan and grandfather David Beaton taught me over several decades.

- Bill DeRouville

- Jimmy Glenn (of Chestertown, MD)

- Lorna Chadwick Shinn

- Russ Manheimer

- Kathy Marr

- Evelyn (Gillie) Ogden

- Janet Jessel

- Dan Crabb, President in 2013 of the Toms River Seaport Society (which archives and has provided ideas, memories, and copies of many documents, plans and images of *Silent Maid*)

- Morton Johnson Bell and his sister Suzanne Patton who helped make *Silent Maid*'s shipwright Morton Johnson come alive

- Reilly (Snapper) Applegate and the folks at the Toms River Seaport Society

- Clinton Trowbridge, who sailed Schoettle's *Scat* for decades

- The Ocean County Historical Society, especially Janis Gibson, for images and paintings published herein

- Art dealer and collector Roy Pedersen graciously opened his wonderful collection of New Jersey historical paintings some of which appear here
- Brian Dibble supplied the image of WW-II bandoleer cardboards
- Barnegat Bay historian Robert Jahn allowed me use of several of his images before his death
- Ben Kracauer, then Curator for the Bay Head Historical Society Museum, offered resources and encouragement

Among owners and their families interviewed as I gathered information were Nancy and Clifford Hogan, my parents Stan and Dot Mountford (interviewed before their deaths in 1981 and 2003), Sally Schneider (before her death), Marie Darling, Gerald Darling, Esq., Karen Palmer, Peter R. Kellogg, M.W. "Rusty" Kellogg, Thacher Brown, Bill Chandlee, and Jody and Alan Fitts. I've drawn many times on the expertise of John Brady, President, Philadelphia Independence Seaport Museum, who, with his professional and volunteer staff, including Newt Kirkland, restored the *Maid* uncovering her many flaws and who built her replica, which now sails the Atlantic Coast. The Seaport Museum's then-librarian Megan Good provided many archived documents and images donated by *Silent Maid* families. Judson Smith and his brother Fred shared memories of their repeated unsuccessful attempts to own *Silent Maid*.

Marguerite Gorman, Peter Kellogg's Administrative Assistant, kept this project alive with her prompt attention. At Fishergate, Inc., the late Tony Drummond saved my six decades of journals from extinction, while Susan Vianna, President, and Roy Jones made this book a reality.

Finally, my wife (of 43 years) Nancy Kirk Mountford, who joined my life six years after our family sold *Silent Maid*, was still able to sail with me aboard her (and on each of our four subsequent boats together). She has been supportive, encouraging, and suitably critical of me throughout this project's long and arduous course.

—*Kent Mountford PhD*
August 2014

Introduction

"They say we never die as long as one thinks of us—reveres us."
—Mary Schoettle (1867–1933) writing in 1930 when *Silent Maid* was in her ninth year[1]

This is a book about an old catboat, a traditional type with one mast and one sail. There were hundreds of catboats on Barnegat Bay in the early 20th century, but none quite like *Silent Maid*. She was built in 1924 at Bay Head, New Jersey, for a Philadelphia businessman, Edwin J. Schoettle. This book traces *Silent Maid's* progress through her eighty-odd years of sailing.

The history of this ship is as much about the people who sailed her and where they came from as it is about the wood, iron, bronze, cordage, and canvas that fleshed out her frames. This has been the one unique opportunity to write such a detailed history of *Silent Maid*, and I have tried to make the account complete. I have presented as much detail as is available from and about the seven principal families who owned her. It was through their lives she moved, and I seek to recount how they came to shape, nurture, and, ultimately, preserve her. It is also about how she influenced their lives in return.

Two thousand days were spent researching and writing this book. It has been an interesting time, but often puzzling, where memories and opinions contradict and written records fail to fill the voids. Most of the complicated people who took *Silent Maid* through her halcyon years are long dead, and I will never know their true inner thoughts. Survivors, descendants, and scores of allied sources have been clawed and pestered for their stories, opinions, and disagreements. Each has viewed time with the *Maid* through different prisms of experience, sometimes with dark or contradictory recollections, sometimes through varying lenses of happy or nostalgic colors.

Cutlery and a Spode 'Camilla' Copeland English dinner plate made in December 1939, one of eight aboard *Silent Maid* in 1953 and believed to be from the Schoettles' use 1924–1944. A single plate in 2013 sold for $50.

I've tried to remain true to the stories as people recounted them to me. Many tales writ simply here have taken half a dozen revisions, submitted to the participants before clarity—even humor—emerged. If I failed in this endeavor, then the fault, of course, is mine. All authors of nonfiction are supposed to say this, but I have done my best to make the *caveat* unnecessary, and the hundreds of references inserted at the ends of my chapters document what I have found and what I have been told. Many of these notes are worth close attention because they explain or amplify the text. There will always be enough spaces amongst my lines for the reader to insert interpretations, as their own lights dictate.

I expect few users of this volume will read the book *in toto* so I have endeavored to make each chapter intelligible as a stand-alone. This means you will find some events and anecdotes appearing more than once, with a particular slant tailored to each of the *Maid*'s "family" chronologies. I beg forgiveness from those who take note of this repetition.

Text boxes are pulled out to highlight items and stories that would interrupt the flow of the main narrative. This book is also full of pictures, which help interpret the *Maid*'s life and times and the personalities that came aboard. Most of these images, from family archives or arcane sources, would never be seen by more than a few people without this book.

Since my family was among those fortunate enough to own *Silent Maid*, my personal logbooks provide extraordinary detail. The *Maid* was also the platform from which I launched my timid childhood nautical adventures, now stretching well beyond 50,000 nautical miles. Aboard the *Maid*, I learned about the marine life, marshes, winds, and tide of Barnegat Bay. This long coastal lagoon slowly revealed to me its history and led eventually to my first published book *Closed Sea*. In a real sense, by holding me close to the water all those years, *Silent Maid* cradled and shaped my half-century career as scientist, sailor, historian, and writer.

I have shared more of my environmental perspective than some readers may wish, because *Silent Maid* is inseparable from Barnegat Bay upon which she sailed. This book will tell you something about this bay and its history, and how this natural and human environment laid the groundwork for the time in which this famous old catboat was built and sailed.

—*Kent Mountford, PhD*

ENDNOTE

1. Mary Schoettle, 1930. Account of Ferdinand Ehrhardt Schoettle. Courtesy of Phillip A. Schoettle, 2009.

***Silent Maid*'s Battle Flag.** By the end of this volume you will find *Silent Maid* has been born anew to be sailed and raced for generations to follow. Graphic designer Bev Vienckowski designed this flag for owner Peter R. Kellogg.

FIGURE 1-1. A catboat and sloop grace this 1917 painting by E.B. Rowaski.

Roy Pedersen collection, with permission

1

Silent Maid's Barnegat Bay

To understand *Silent Maid's* history I want to introduce geology, history, aquatic conditions, and meteorology to show how people came to harvest, enjoy, and, more recently, abuse Barnegat Bay. This background will set the conditions under which an eager sailing community built and raced those first specialized catboats from the mid-19th century to the 1920s.

From conception and as a sailing vessel, *Silent Maid* spanned a significant fraction of recent Barnegat history, from a time when the region was still a mostly rural, undeveloped chain of sand dunes, seacoast farming settlements, and pine-woods fishing camps.

In 1928, Edwin Schoettle, *Silent Maid's* first owner, wrote about his own earliest times on Barnegat Bay, which embraced the last two decades of the 1800s. He reminisced that during his youth ". . . workboats of small size were entirely propelled by sail or steam. The gasoline engine was not known, and the necessity of sails with the corresponding ability to handle them produced a picturesque and interesting type of waterman. . . . Up to the end of the [19th century] one of the greatest pleasures [for boaters] consisted of seeking the haunts of professional fisherman and sailors, listening to their interesting yarns and discussing the various problems of sailing."[1]

Barnegat Bay was also part of a complex natural system that enabled and, in some ways, controlled the life-ways and industries, which eventually flourished around its shorelines. Schoettle, we shall see, appreciated this environment, but he had no clue about how the natural ecosystem worked to support the human endeavors that surrounded him.

The bay was backed by vast pine woods, towering white cedar (*Chamecyparis thyoides*) swamps, and underlying deposits of bog iron ore—all of which proved to be the source of materials for naval stores and artisanal boatbuilding. Felling these tall

FIGURE 1-2. *(Top)* Sand road behind Mosquito Cove on upper Barnegat Bay about 1953. Hundreds of miles of these tracks spider-webbed the Pine Barrens until the mid-20th century and some still remain. The sand drained well enough that they were rarely muddy and carried the wheels of even heavily loaded wagons wheeled with wide iron tires *(bottom)* without bogging down.

Kent Mountford photographs

straight cedars was done inwards from the outside of the swamp, the smaller saplings being used as fishnet stakes and slowly the long, straight sawtimber was felled. When the swamp was clear, level wet meadows were exposed, which, as cranberry bogs, became part of an economy served by sand roads and then a few tenuous railroad tracks. One of Schoettle's close associates, Edward Crabbe, was in the cranberry business . . . and very successful at it.

On Barnegat Bay in the early 19th century only the dreams of builders and land speculators looked ahead to a future of small, close-knit seacoast communities (grazing upon the wallets of visiting "sports"!). These dreams devolved into a harsher reality with the rampant development that has since occurred. The stories preserved from *Silent Maid*'s builders, owners, crews, and by-standers are bright lines that parallel the difficult course of growth, over-development, and ecological decline that the bay has since experienced. It will take a great effort to stem these problems and reverse long decline.

GEOLOGY UNDERPINS BARNEGAT BAY

Sailing this coastal estuary today, with blazing summer sun, salt spray coming over the bow, and the lee rail awash, it seems impossible that 14,000 years ago this entire region was a freezing cold coastal plain—a semi-desert. With billions of tons of water locked up in the world's icecaps, the actual coastline was over a hundred miles to the east of today's beaches.

Standing on this icy plain, some modern scientists speculate that one could have looked north in clear weather and seen the great ice wall of the Wisconsin glacier.[2] At its southernmost extent, the advance of this great ice sheet had ploughed up a ridge of soil and stony debris called a terminal moraine. Today this remnant line of hills still persists, bisecting New Jersey near Holmdel on the Garden State Parkway. This moraine continued northeast to the tip of today's Long Island and the remnant tips of Block and Nantucket Islands. All the surrounding landscape now lies under the salt waters of a sea risen from ancient melt waters. From the sea floor, offshore trawl fishermen still recover the teeth of the woolly mammoth and other ancient creatures that once roamed where today we sail.

From atop the great glacier, which covered thousands of square miles, deeply cold air, much heavier than normal, literally spilled down from the ice wall at its terminal moraine. Accelerating as it came, this flow generated violent katabatic winds roaring across the sandy plain, whipping loose soil (what geologists call loess) from atop the permafrost, in some places scouring out, or deflating, deep circular indentations. Over broad areas, dunes of windborne sand and loess moved and reformed crescent, or sickle shapes much as in modern deserts. Some were 50 to 80 feet high, and they can be traced well into modern Delaware hidden under today's unaware landscape.

Remnants of these structures still remain on today's landscape as high banks along the Manasquan River and, significant to this story, at Island Heights on Toms River where *Silent Maid* made her home for many years. The banks there rise an unusual 60 feet above the current river level. Man's efforts here since the 1930s have hardened the shoreline, established vegetation on the banks, and limited erosion.[3]

The ancient and fierce winds of the glacial period swept across a broad coastal plain to where the continental shelf lies today. Clouds of dust were swept so far out to sea that layers of mainland loess were laid down on distant Bermuda where, on a friend's schooner, *Silent Maid*'s owner Edwin J. Schoettle would someday sail. Around Pine Barrens depressions back on mainland America, small stones too heavy to be rolled by the wind faced the icy blasts and were bombarded with millions of sand particles. Over years, this eroded their upwind sides into distinctive shapes, which geologists call ventifacts. Bits of iron oxide on the sand grains slowly coated these surfaces with a dark reddish brown deposit recognized by geologists as desert varnish.

In the New Jersey Pine Barrens today, circular ponds called spungs (after a pouch in men's pants common during the 1600s) still remain—relics of that wind-stripped environment. These were originally places where loose sand and dust were blown out and long afterwards filled by rain and groundwater. Along the rims of these ponds one can still find the reshaped, desert-varnished stones that are remnant evidence of those violent winds many thousands of years ago[4] in a world unrecognizable to us.

When the great glacier was finally in retreat and its melt waters poured across the surface of frozen landscape into the sea, permafrost, where the Pine Barrens are today, prevented streams from deeply incising the land. In the last hundred years or so in south New Jersey, these broad shallow and damp valleys were called cripples by the indigenous "Piney" residents. Thus spungs and cripples are relics of glacial times still among us.

The sands that underlie today's Pine Barrens still have iron oxides on their surfaces, which is why most inland New Jersey sands have a yellow or orange cast. It is all washed away from the sugary seacoast quartz sands for which New Jersey beaches have been famous for 140 years. Rainwater, percolating through piney soils and made acidic by the plants that occupy them, also helped dissolve this iron into solution. Once underground and away from oxygen in the atmosphere, the water interacted with specialized bacteria, which turned the iron back into oxide and precipitated it amongst groundwater-soaked sand and gravel.

The iron compounds precipitated under New Jersey's surface soils became consolidated into hard deposits of the mineral limonite. These deposits were recognized as a source of rich iron ore by colonial explorers, and they became important as the young United States struggled to attain its own industrial footing. Thousands of tons of these iron deposits had formed beneath many square miles of the Pines. This "bog ore" could be as much as 40% elemental iron by weight, and thus an extraordinarily rich ore for extraction. It was also a renewable resource because the process of formation was continuous. Lying under the forest, these solid layers (sometimes a foot or so thick) formed in and around the lace-like network of Pine Barrens streams. In the 19th century, furnaces, casting floors, and forges dotted the pinelands helping to fuel America's industrial revolution.

Three natural resources needed to come together for this iron industry to flourish: clean-burning charcoal to fuel a smelting furnace; abundant shells for flux, which removed impurities; and the bog ore itself. Once fired and hot, the furnace was charged with layers of charcoal, oyster or other calcified shell, and broken-up bog iron ore. These were added continually when the furnace was in blast, a continuous roaring fire of tremendous heat sustained by bellows, which forced air through a side tube called the tuyere. Simplifying a complex industrial process, heavy and relatively pure molten iron and a glassy waste product called slag, drained out the bottom and the slag was discarded

Furnaces sprang up throughout the Barrens wherever streams would allow damming for water power. Operations like those at Allaire (just several miles by road from Bay Head) and Batsto (up the Mullica River from Egg Harbor) each required something like 25,000 acres of pine forest to supply charcoal for their bog-iron furnaces and forges.

FIGURE 1-3. Ventifacts are small stones sculpted by violent winds sweeping down from the ancient glacier across a frozen plain. This ventifact shows the characteristic keel-shaped edges formed by the impact from billions of sand grains and the brownish coating of desert varnish. Now, some 12,000 years later, this severe, long-gone environment has been partially inundated by Barnegat Bay.

Mark Demitroff photograph with permission

The Barnegat Connection to Early Steamships

In a coincident historical sidelight, New Jersey bog iron formed the cylinders, pistons, and shafting for one of the earliest marine engines. Engine components for Robert Fulton's landmark steamship *Clermont* were made at John Paul Allaire's iron works on the Manasquan River. Fulton, a family friend, honeymooned in the foreman's cottage, which still stands at Allaire's village, now a state park.

Fulton and some of his innovative contemporaries started an historic bifurcation in naval architecture. Large ships, workboats, and yachts began to be divided into the categories of "sail" and "power."

This juncture in history has a unique Barnegat connection. When Fulton inaugurated commercial traffic on the Hudson with his first steamship *Clermont*, his partner Robert Livingston had obtained a monopoly for steamship service from the New York State Legislature. They were able to grant such things in those days, but might one make an analogy with today's cable service provider monopolies? Accordingly, John Stevens, who almost simultaneously built his 1807 steamship *Phoenix* with an eye to provide the New York area with cargo and passenger service from head of tide and terminus of the

FIGURE 1-5. In 1807, John Stevens' steamer *Phoenix*, while enroute to Philadelphia became the first ocean-going steamship in the world. She lay over in Barnegat Bay during a storm, probably before the first catboats ever reached the Bay.

Delaware-Raritan Canal at New Brunswick, was literally and legally driven out of town.[5]

Stevens had an open ferry market awaiting him between Philadelphia and Trenton, but he had to get there with his vessel, and before that time no steamship had ever navigated in the open ocean. Pundits of the time predicted that as soon as *Phoenix* encountered wind and waves at sea, her feeble machinery would be overcome.

Stevens had no choice but to move his ship. His Captain, Moses Rogers, took Stevens' 21-year-old son Robert, who was mechanic enough to keep the steam engine running, and hired a schooner as tender to carry emergency supplies and bail them out in the event of unmanageable trouble.[6] They departed June 10, 1809, and headed south past Sandy Hook, bound for Cape May.

Weather forecasting was solely by eye in those times, and they were not far on their way, at the vessel's flank speed of about three miles per hour, when they were overtaken by an intensifying storm—likely a nor'easter. By the time conditions became unmanageable, they were apparently some 50 nautical miles out and already south of Cranberry Inlet, which would still have been open as a possible

FIGURE 1-4. *(Left)* Allaire furnace in ruins (1957) and *(right)* with its casting floor and a discovered iron pipe as exhibited in 2007.

Kent Mountford photographs

refuge for another four years. They were probably faced with fading daylight and the task of entering hazardous Barnegat Inlet. Their tender (the schooner) abandoned *Phoenix* and ran offshore to escape foundering and was not seen for several days.[7]

In 1809, there were few accurate charts besides those in the heads of pilots with local knowledge. It would be 27 years before the first rickety Barnegat Lighthouse would be erected and 57 years before the first decent chart was laid out. We can only guess at the temerity Moses Rogers had to make that entrance with an unwieldy, underpowered, and storm-tossed ship.

In this irony of ironies, the steamship *Phoenix* stayed several days weathered in behind the barrier islands in Barnegat Bay some 47 years before the first proper catboat supposedly arrived from New York! When calm weather let her continue and, once at Philadelphia, *Phoenix* began a stellar commercial career.

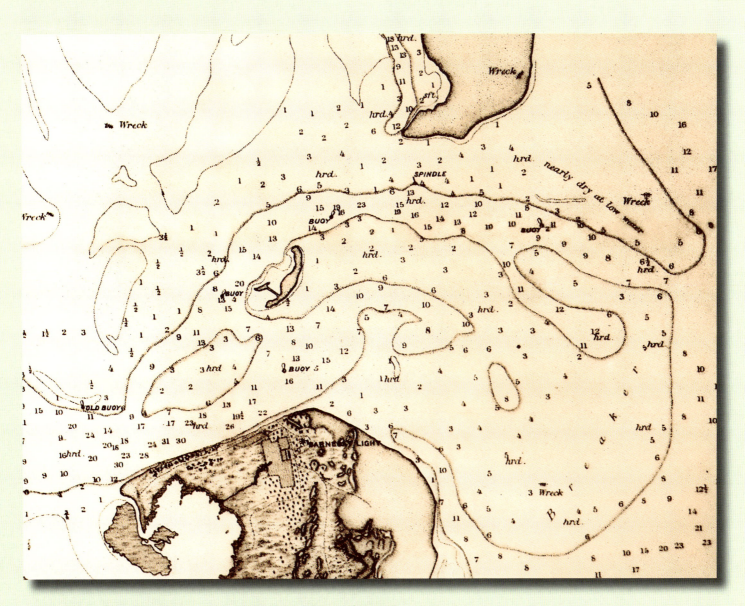

FIGURE 1-6. Barnegat Inlet charted in 1866, then resurveyed in 1867.

U.S. Coast Survey A.D. Bache, C. Fendall and R.E. Halter 1:20,000. Owned by AliceMay Weber-Wright, Island Heights

During charcoal production much of the volatile combustible material in wood is lost, leaving light, fragile relatively purified carbon (charcoal). Many thousands of tree-covered acres were required to assure sustainability. Large tracts meant that aggressive wood cutting and charcoal production could be made up by years of natural regeneration in the pine forests. Charcoaling was a serious business, and a trade-off against natural fires, which ravaged the pines once escaped from man's control. *Silent Maid* was twice threatened by uncontrolled fires during her decades of sailing.

It's been estimated that in the natural—unmanaged—state, each area of the pine forests was burnt over on average every 25 years or so. In some areas, like those transected by NJ Route 72, from Barnegat west into New Jersey's midlands, repeated burning so depleted the soil nutrients nitrogen and phosphorus that the trees remained stunted, and no matter how old, never reaching the height of a man. These several areas were called, in local Piney parlance, "The Plains."

I heard the story once of a hunter who stood on a small rise in this stunted forest (likely where today's State Rt. 72 runs out to the coast), where he could see a great distance. He was (illegally) jacklighting with a spotlight or car headlights and his eye picked up what he thought was the momentary reflected glint of a deer's eye, which is usually a slightly greenish-white. He was ready with his gun, and some seconds later seeing the flash he instantly fired, only to realize he was trying to extinguish Barnegat Light's repeated flashing beam many miles distant! He was looking, and shooting, over the tops of the tiny forest of trees that intervened. Protected from fire for many years, these once dwarf-forests are slowly growing taller, as soil nutrients rebuild.

Fires and poor, sandy, excessively drained soils engendered a mostly scrubby, gnarled forest, which did not yield the long straight timber that boat and house builders wanted. The thousands, many tens of thousands, of acres of Pine Barrens forest did produce enough wood for short cordwood logs, and any amount of this large supply of cellulose fiber, including branches, could be piled in kilns (sod covered mounds that were ignited allowing only minute amounts of air to help roast the wood of volatile organics). These kilns were burnt for charcoal and in the process large amounts of pine sap were melted out of the logs and collected.

When a carefully burnt kiln finally went out and cooled with no oxygen being admitted for combustion, the result was a large pile of charcoal. A byproduct of charcoal production was a class of materials called Naval Stores like turpentine and pine tar, which were vital to the maritime trades. Using tubes and collecting vessels, these could be drained off from the heated wood.

Charcoal burning was hard and exacting work that involved stacking and sodding the kilns. This required laying pads of hand-cut sod over the entire kiln surface to exclude combustion oxygen. There was also boredom from tending them 24 hours a day. But if some of the sod collapsed and too much air got into the kiln, it would burn brightly like a campfire and convert all of the charcoal, wood, and hard work to fine white ash.

Those tending the kilns were not recruited from society's brain surgeon population, and fire from many kilns got loose and burnt through the pines. Pine Barrens historian Mark Demitroff showed me old aerial photographs in which the landscape was dotted with the clear circles of charcoal kilns burnt decades before. These photos also showed the paths of wildfires running downwind from kiln sites, which had escaped. Soil nutrient complexes and organic compounds were destroyed by the intense heat, and ecosystem scars from these events remained on the landscape, visible after decades and revealed in the different hardy herbaceous plant species that re-colonized the incinerated landscape. Charcoal was an absolutely necessary ingredient for the extraction of bog iron deposits.

The molten iron from the furnace was either directly cast or allowed to cool in heavy pig-iron ingots, which were sent to forges, casting floors, and smithies for working. The cast iron ware, fasteners, cannons, and shot helped fuel our nation's War for Independence against England. In peacetime, the economy required iron nails, drift rods, chainplates, pintles and gudgeons, masthead and bowsprit hoops, and naval stores for the region's ship and boat-building industry. Like many of the catboats built around Barnegat Bay, *Silent Maid* was fastened with iron nails and her gooseneck spreaders and other hardware were also of galvanized iron.

THE MARCH TO CREATE BARNEGAT BAY

Today's Barnegat–Manahawkin–Egg Harbor complex of bays is protected from the open Atlantic Ocean by barrier islands. These sheltered habitats are called estuaries, where freshwater from the land and seawater from the inlets mix together. Of earth's coastal ecosystems, estuaries are the most productive environments for plants, animals, and fish and are thus extremely important in nature—and extremely attractive to humankind.

In 2011, professors Orrin Pilkey and Matthew L. Stutz attempted to determine how many barrier-built estuaries there are in the world. They used conventional maps and satellite imagery to survey the entire planet and found 657 new barrier islands that had simply been missed or ignored in previous surveys. Their work establishes that there are 2,149 barrier islands, which, if chained together, would stretch 12,914 miles (20,783 kilometers).[8] The United States has the largest number of these islands along its coasts, and because of human activity and abuse, they are among the most populated and the most troubled of our landscapes and seascapes.

These islands were not always there. About 12,000 years ago when the great glacier was in retreat and its melt waters poured across the surface of frozen landscape and into the sea, permafrost (where the Pine Barrens are today) prevented streams from deeply incising the land. In the last hundred years or so in south New Jersey, these broad shallow and damp valleys were laced by cripples or creeks by "Piney" residents. But those thousands of years ago, the sea was rising—sometimes a yard in less than a century—and surf on the shores alternately piled, withdrew, and redistributed offshore bars of sand—analogs to the coast that would be there in future. These early barrier islands were far eastward of those witnessed when the first colonists came to settle here.

Each sequence of islands was in turn altered and submerged by the advancing sea and recreated, with their inlets, vegetated habitats, peaty salt marshes, and wildlife positioned farther towards the continent. This happened again and again as the sea migrated towards the ever setting sun over thousands of years.

In the late 19th century, inhabitants on some New Jersey beaches would find marsh peat exposed on the ocean face by eroding sand dunes. In those peats, on their way to being wiped out by the encroaching surf, were the hoof prints of cattle that once grazed on the backsides of barrier islands. Early settlers had deposited cattle here—too far for them to swim the bay and escape—on a landscape where they could forage and reproduce unmolested.

FIGURE 1-7. **A 19th century cedar swamp behind the barrier islands in South Jersey.**

Collection of Roy Petersen, with permission

Sea-level rise and the inexorable natural forces driving this erosional migration of the islands westward still continues and will do so forever in spite of our development, post-storm rebuilding, and damage mitigation efforts.

Much of Barnegat's historically rich estuarine life—its clams, oysters, fish, and crabs—relied on a functioning ecosystem atop the surrounding landscape, i.e., the supply of organic material from surrounding forests and the spongy labyrinth of estuarine marshes that ringed the shorelines, both on the islands and mainland. This entire ecosystem was virtually intact at the start of the 20th century, but it was a dynamic system, with rising sea level slowly killing forest in the west and replacing it with new marshland.

Slade Dale of Bay Head displayed the trunk of an ancient Atlantic white cedar found buried under marshes in 1959 where the Garden State Parkway crossed the Mullica River. He erected it at his Bay Head boatyard. There were enough of these ancient tree trunks found in the 19th century that they were literally mined and found especially stable wood for splitting house shingles, which resisted weathering and checking better than those from freshly cut trees.

Simultaneously, the barrier islands on the east side of Barnegat Bay were being slowly inundated by storm erosion and rising sea levels. Storm surges would breach the dunes and wash sand over to the west shore, where it was deposited atop the marshes there. The marshes slowly grew out into the bay, migrating the entire barrier beach sequentially westward, and sea-grass beds covered the deposited sandy bottom across the shallow flats.

The system thus attained a dynamic equilibrium. For the first century or two of European habitation, the resources of this system were harvested sustainably. Underwater grasses (eelgrass *Zostera marina* near the inlets and *Ruppia maritime* in fresher waters) covering the bay's shallows supported a myriad of living things: billions of worms, clams, and baitfish, which fed larger species harvested by baymen. The sheltering grasses hid juvenile fish species and were themselves grazed by millions of visiting seasonal waterfowl.

Seasonally, masses of eelgrass washed ashore as the plants shed their blades, were leached of salt by the rain, then dried naturally and raked up for harvesting. Wagonloads of it were collected annually, and it was a popular material for stuffing upholstered furniture. My old Barnegat catboat *Spray*, bought in 1970, still had cabin mattresses stuffed with eelgrass. It was also used with paper backing to manufacture wall insulation

FIGURE 1-8. A New Jersey salt hay barge grounded at low tide with a catboat sailing by in the background.

John Frederick Peto, oil on canvas, undated.
Collection of Roy Petersen, with permission

FIGURE 1-9. Salt hay barges sailing to market on upper Barnegat Bay. Men, giving scale, are just visible atop the sailing barge. Note that the schooner rig enabled sliding the boom goosenecks up the mast, "reefing" the sail, but making room for the massive deck cargo!

Runyon Colie photograph,
with permission

in buildings and even to stuff the decorative linings of caskets for the dead!

The marsh grasses (called salt hay) were first grazed by feral cattle allowed to roam, but were later harvested by horse-drawn mowing machines. The horses wore wide wooden plaques secured to their hooves to keep them from sinking into the soft peat. The cut grass, when baled, was sold as a mineral-rich fodder for inland animals, avoiding the need to supply stock with supplemental salt. In one unusual application, the marsh grasses were used at Harrisville in the pines to manufacture a kind of butcher paper for several years early in the 20th century. Baled salt hay is still a valuable product. In 1982, Joseph Shisler[9] reported that salt hay was being sold for $12 a bale, versus $3 for common straw.[10]

FIGURE 1-10. Eelgrass (*Zostera marina*) along the west shore of the Island Beach Peninsula was piled on racks to dry, then taken away by horse-drawn wagons.

George Chase photograph, with permission

INLETS PIERCE BARNEGAT BEACHES

The earliest maps show apparent radical changes in the geography of what came to be called the Squan Beach peninsula. As time progressed, several inlets are shown piercing the barrier chain at different points. The shoreline today has shape-shifted so much that it masks what the landscape was like hundreds of years ago.

However, inlets on the coast form with repeatable patterns, which develop shallow complex shoals inside the bay where rapid current flows slow and deposit sand that they have scoured on the rising tide (a flood-tide delta). There is one down at the heel of Island Beach State Park called "Winter Anchorage" in *Silent Maid*'s time, but labeled "Johnny Allen's Cove" on later charts.

Offshore, where inlet tides spill out into the sea, deposits of sand are similarly left by scouring currents on the ebbing tide (an ebb-tide delta), which indeed formed the hazardous breaking shoals for Henry Hudson's first visit in 1609. These complex sandbars extend some distance to sea and many ships were wrecked on Barnegat Shoals from the 17th through 20th centuries. The huge tonnages of sand on the ebb-tide delta, however, are further distributed back and forth along the coast by perennial coastal currents, prevailing winds, constant surf, and northeast gales.

The sandbars that were created (shifting at the whim of weather, tide, and season) were the bane of navigators and a source of income for clever local inlet pilots with knowledge of these shifts. It was only with this local knowledge that mariners could use these inlets frequently—until massive, modern federal-dollar infusions for jetties and dredging. While these inlets tend to migrate along the shoreline (Barnegat is still trying to do that in spite of engineering!) the wide sand expanses are eventually colonized by plant life and whole, well-adapted barrier island ecosystems, stable on a generational time-scale.

Little Egg Inlet to the south of Long Beach Island has received no such infusions of money and, while buoyed today for navigation, it remains and behaves much as it did four hundred years ago when Cornelius Jacobsen Mey probed its entrance or when, during the American Revolution, the British Navy lost its warship, HMS *Zebra*, after grounding her at the inlet.[11]

Sailing off the mouth of Little Egg Inlet, you can feel the seas lump up as they respond to the shoaling bottom beneath, see the white of heavy breakers on the bars, and the surf plunging against the uninhabited beaches of Brigantine. Such is the scene in light weather and one can fairly shiver at the thought of making an entry there in a storm. The

FIGURE 1-11. This is probably what Barnegat Inlet looked like from its European discovery in 1609 until the middle 19th century.

Kent Mountford photograph along North Carolina's coast, 2003

FIGURE 1-12. The shoreline along Island Beach where wind-tortured cedars contend with tides and winter ice at the juncture of bay and barrier island.

Kent Mountford photograph

sight of these apparently impenetrable breaking bars is equally daunting as boaters today swing out of the Mullica River and head across to the toe of Long Beach Island.

One can view another one of these old inlet flood-tide delta sites today (probably from the 18th–19th century Cranberry Inlet's piercing of the peninsula) just below where Island Beach State Park begins. Parking on the west side of the road, just across from the old Coast Guard Lifesaving Station, which serves as maintenance depot for the park, one can walk trails and shorelines through scores of acres with undisturbed dune lands and maritime forest. The visitor will pass wind-tortured copses of trees, sunny hollows scattered in spring with blooming bayberry, and beach plum shrubs and later strewn with a virtual golden carpet of low, flowering poverty grass (*Hudsonia tomentosa*).

Forethought many decades ago could have preserved more large areas of these habitats elsewhere on the barrier islands and helped sustain a healthy Bay. Such planning would have spared the cluttered, paved over, often sweltering, and storm-vulnerable development that today covers almost everything north of this fine park.

Farther north on the coast there are old tales—and the geology of the area suggests this—of another inlet that entered Barnegat Bay through the barrier island long ago near today's Mantoloking. The opening of each of these inlets brought a massive flow of highly saline, full-strength seawater into the bay and radically affected the plants and animals that lived there. Where the water was saltier, the seagrass meadows were primarily eelgrass (*Zostera marina*) and delectable critters (like bay scallops and oysters) grew in abundance, creating a harvestable resource for both Native American and later for the English settlers.

When inlets like the upper bay inlet closed during storms and remained closed, the freshwater flows from the Metedeconk and smaller streams eventually lowered salinity so that eelgrass could not survive. It was replaced by other aquatic meadow grasses, such as the more freshwater-tolerant widgeon grass (*Ruppia maritima*) and horned pond weed (*Zannachellia palustris*). For shipwrights in the 18th and 19th centuries, this low salinity also meant that boats in the water were spared the annoyance of barnacles and the ravages of destructive shipworms in their timbers.

FIGURE 1-13. Horned pond weed (*Zannichelia palustris*). Inset top: The small horned seeds that gave it its name. Inset bottom: Its tiny springtime flowers.

Kent Mountford photographs

The formation of wider beach areas by moving sands around the inlet mouths permitted pocket wetlands to develop along with freshwater ponds and swamps, as they have continued to do on the modern Island Beach peninsula. In low areas with freshwater close to the surface, bog plants, like the cranberry (*Vaccinium sp.*), could prosper. The fruit of cranberry is high in vitamin C and, like the consumption of lime juice used by 18th and 19th century British merchantmen, was capable of remedying scurvy, a debilitating ailment afflicting sailors on long sea voyages without fresh foods. The ability to gather these berries ashore led to the inlet opposite Toms River being called Cranberry Inlet.

In 1812, a violent northeast storm swept up the Atlantic coast, ironically just as another war with England was breaking out and more busy traffic in privateers was set to resume. David Mapes, a young African-American boy, was camping on the barrier beach near Cranberry Inlet. He was there to manage a herd of cattle grazing on the salty marsh grasses and sheltering from severe weather using Island Beach's interior maritime forest. Mapes awoke after the storm and found that Cranberry Inlet had been closed. He quickly crossed the bay and reported this to his employers at Toms River. Toms River's time as a busy seaport had ended.

Several attempts to re-open the inlet and reclaim Toms River's maritime status were made over the following decades. Once Cranberry Inlet was closed, however, there were no further navigable breaks sustained through Squan (or Island) Beach north of Barnegat[12] and the more freshwater that came in from Toms River, Cedar Creek, and other Upper Barnegat drainages, the fresher the water became in Upper Barnegat Bay.

River herrings, which migrated up bay in commercial quantities, came through Barnegat Inlet and followed, from generation to generation, the *scent* of this water to their natal freshwater spawning grounds in the tributaries.

The boats that baymen used to intercept and harvest these living resources were adapted to the environment in which they had to work. They were shaped by the geography and shallow bottomed meadows of the estuary, shaped by the hands of the men who built the boats, and defined by the materials from the land available to construct them.

Over thousands of years, it has been geology that has determined where modern bridges are built across the bay and where the remnant flood-tide deltas remain as islands inside former inlets. This is true at Mantoloking, at Seaside (the Rt. 37 spans), for the old railroad bridge at Goodluck Point, and at Manahawkin where the wooden causeway, and now the high concrete bridge, made its dramatic leap to Long Beach Island.

BARNEGAT BAY'S MARITIME HISTORY

Native Americans and Pine Barrens Land Use

Native Americans occupied New Jersey's coastal landscape for millennia before Europeans intruded. Their impact on the land did not leave it pristine or without impact, but their use of resources was sustainable; their numbers being too few and their technology just enough to take what they required year after year.

Indian peoples hunted and fished as hard as they could to wrest sustenance from the forests, swamps, marshes, and bays. They gathered abundant shellfish and used the purple shell discards from the hard clam (*Mercenaria mercenaria*) to turn out thousands of tiny colored beads. Woven into ornamental belts, these were a sort of tribal currency and extremely valued as bonds of treaty.

FIGURE 1-14. **A cranberry and its vines on Island Beach. Their keeping qualities are exceptional. This berry is picked in March of the year after it grew, making the fruit ideal for carrying to sea.**

Kent Mountford photograph

FIGURE 1-15. **A herring (*Alosa aestivalis*) caught migrating in through Manasquan Inlet from the Atlantic Ocean.**

Kent Mountford photograph

The History of Toms River and Dillons Island

The origin of the name Toms River is shrouded in history; variously reported to be named after a Native American man locally called Indian Tom, an 18th century settler Captain William Tom, and the (also 18th century) ferryman Tom Luker. Tom Luker arrived in America aboard *Falcon* with two brothers in 1685. By 1712, he had settled along Goose Creek and offered ferry service across the river. Until then there had been virtually no roads in the region, and commerce had been primarily by small boat. For a rider whose course was blocked by the creek, a ferry was indispensable. Tom was in the right place at the right time; and Goose Creek was soon called Tom's River. (The apostrophe was dropped some years ago by the Board of Geographic Names). Tom married an Indian woman named Ann and became known as Indian Tom and she as Indian Ann. That's how two of the stories come together.[13]

In 1690, a large parcel of land around Toms River had been patented to a Dr. John Johnstone. The high island along Toms River's northern bank became known for the next decade or so as Dr. Johnstones Island,[14] but the land remained undisturbed and in its natural state. By 1748, the island was referred to as Toms River Island.

About 1758, a stroke of fortune came in the shape of a violent storm that overtopped the barrier beach almost opposite the mouth of Toms River and opened an inlet there.[15] Tides inside Barnegat Bay lag behind those in the neighboring ocean. It takes some hours for the incoming tide to fill up the bay and by the time the process is completed, the ocean tide had already fallen for some hours. This disparity meant that once the barrier island was breached tides would pour in and out in both directions.

As sometimes happens, the new inlet deepened and widened, and soon provided a navigable channel for Toms River merchants and smugglers and, when the Colonies rebelled, for privateers. The inlet remained unnamed as late as 1765, while Toms River developed its trade. As the American Revolution churned on, the port of Toms River became an important refuge for privateers who ventured out under Letters of Marque to harass British shipping. Society in America became bitterly divided into Patriot and Loyalist camps. The British administrators considered Toms River nothing more than a nest of pirates.

In 1762, the William Dillon family took over this land, and the island became known as Dillons Island. They built a house there, which still stood in 2000.[16] In 1778, Dillon was tried by a Patriot Court as a Loyalist sympathizer. He and a friend, Robert McMullen, were just barely reprieved from hanging at Freehold.

Militiamen in Dover Township (where Toms River was then located) were unsatisfied with McMullen's reprieve from hanging and pursued him on horseback to the north bank of Toms River where, to escape, he spurred his mount into the river at Coates Point. Wading in some at start and again as soon as depth permitted on the far side, his steed swam the entire way across the river with McMullen shouting "Good Luck!" back at his pursuers. He landed and escaped to the salt marshes of the south bank, which are still named Goodluck Point today.[17]

The American Revolution had effectively ended with Cornwallis' surrender at Yorktown in 1781. Despite this, still-Loyalist William Dillon had a run-in that eventually resulted in bloodshed. In March of 1782, cargo from Dillon's boat the *Lucy* was confiscated by Whig (Patriot) Americans and sold at Toms River. Dillon protested to the British colonial government in New York, which was then amidst the process of packing up to leave for England.

There was enough bad feeling among Whigs and Loyalists that British General Sir Henry Clinton sent redcoats, as well as Loyalist troops aboard HMS *Arrogant* to Toms River hoping to deal a final vengeful blow to American militia there. His target at Toms River Village was a small defensive blockhouse manned by Captain Joshua Huddy and about two dozen men. *Arrogant* sailed through Cranberry Inlet and disembarked her complement at Coates Point on the north bank from where they marched seven miles to the village. They were guided by William Dillon, who was thus considered a spy by the Americans. The attack was launched in the morning on Sunday, March 14. The defense was valiant, but the blockhouse was overwhelmed. At least nine Toms River men were killed; some fled and others were captured, including Captain Huddy. Ships in port and on the stocks were burnt along with most of the village and likely the town's historical records.

Captain Huddy should have been made a prisoner of war and treated as an officer, but he was handed off several times, eventually to Monmouth County Loyalist Captain Richard Lippincott and six of his men. At Gravelly Point on the Navesink River about a mile from the Highlands lighthouse, they erected three long fence rails and hanged Huddy, ostensibly in revenge for the earlier death of Loyalist Phil White, with whom Huddy had no connection. A document was pinned on the breast of Huddy's corpse concluding: "Up goes Huddy for Phillip White."

The incident became an international dust-up and young British Officer Captain Charles Asgill, drawn by lot from among British captives, was sentenced to death in retaliation. Negotiations in Paris for the peace between

England and the new American nation were suspended. Asgill was, of course, totally innocent and pleas by his mother Lady Asgill, wife of London's former Lord Mayor, resulted in a pardon signed by General George Washington in September 1782. For Toms River, the war was finally over.[18]

The Dillon family fled to Canada, and the 320-acre Dillons Island was divided into three parcels. By 1878 it was called Island Heights, by which name it is known today. The Schoettles would settle there in a then-bucolic community and, eventually, they built *Silent Maid*.

FIGURE 1-16. Toms River showing Toms River Village, Island Heights (Dillons Island), Coates Point and Goodluck Point where Robert McMullen swam his horse across the deep channel between shallows to escape the militiamen who were chasing him. *Inset:* Island Heights, showing how it was originally separated from mainland (arrow) by channels, which in the 18th century supposedly concealed privateers and smuggler's boats.

U.S. Coast and Geodetic Survey Chart, 1924; inset from New Jersey Museum of Boating exhibit, Bob O'Brien, Curator.

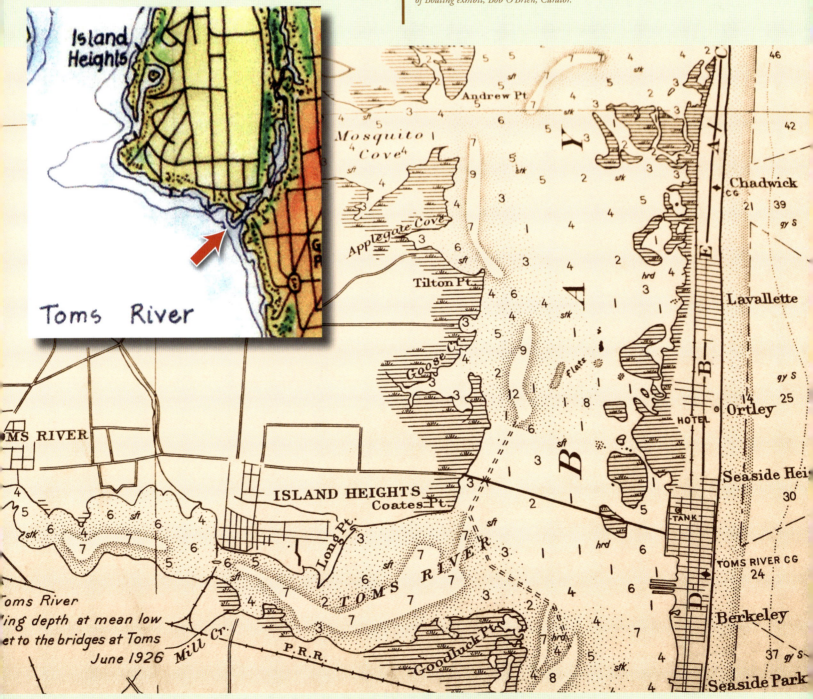

These Algonquian-related tribes of Lenni Lenape trapped with snares, shot with bow and arrow, and fished with lances having razor sharp stone or bone tipped points. They used ingenious fishhooks of bone or shell secured to lines of cord plaited from native fibers. They felled saplings to make weirs to corral fish, suspending nets knotted with the same cord, and held to the bottom by tied sinkers of shaped stone.

The Lenape laboriously chopped or burnt through the trunks of large trees from which they made dugout canoes using fire and scrapers of shell and stone. It is estimated a team of men working constantly could turn out a dugout several yards long in three weeks. These vessels gave them access to rivers, estuaries, and when weather permitted, to the sea-islands. They were the first fishers and mariners on Barnegat Bay, even as it was created during sea-level rise thousands of years ago.

Native Americans often burnt the landscape to drive game during hunts, to clear land for dwellings, or for swidden-style agriculture. Persistent, periodic droughts and uncontrolled lightning strikes are nothing new, so fire has always been a part of Pine Barrens' ecology. There is evidence this was so in 1609, where I will take my readers next.

Henry Hudson's Discovery

You must come back with me now, through the pen of Robert Juet, an Englishman aboard the Dutch sailing vessel *Halve Maan*, sent out to explore the fabled Northwest Passage. *Halve Maan*'s master was Henry Hudson his English birth name, and we know his ship by her English name the *Half Moon*.

This was a different kind of sailing from what any modern seaman has experienced around Barnegat Bay. None of the common appliances that ease our handling of boats had even been conceived yet—items such as roller-bearing blocks, synthetic lines and canvas, light alloy or titanium fittings, and corrosion-resistant cable rigging of stainless steel; not to mention our modern binoculars or electronic aids and certainly no auxiliary engine there at the touch (usually!) of a starter button.

We join *Half Moon*, over 400 years ago now, on the night of September 1–2, 1609. Crewmen near the bows sounded depth with a hand-cast lead first at 21 fathoms (126 feet), then a half hour later at 16 fathoms (96 feet). They were approaching shore, the most hazardous part of any voyage at sea. The wind was at the south and their squaresail yards were each braced (canted) to port, with all sails drawing. This was no catboat; twenty lines were trimmed to position this small ship's half dozen principal sails, a dozen more lines steadied and supported the six yards to which these heavy sails of hand-sewn flax fiber were bent.

Few men today have experienced the profound darkness comparable to a 17th-century ship at sea in the wee-hours on a moonless night. On this night a slim crescent moon had long set in the west.[19] Fire was a constant and real danger aboard wooden ships, and while coals might have been banked in the focs'l sequestered on the little stone cooking hearth that served as her galley, there was only one open flame in a tiny lantern that illuminated the ship's compass.

The helmsman would steer to that light from his position at a whipstaff (a wooden lever attached for mechanical advantage to the ship's massive rudder and tiller). He was located deeper inside the ship under her high poop deck. He could not see the stars or movement of the sea. Only the creak of hemp line in blocks and the groan of ship's timbers as she rolled to the swell let him know they were underway. He steered functionally blind of the surrounding sea and almost certainly illiterate, keeping the

FIGURE 1-17. **A modern replica of Henry Hudson's *Halve (Half Moon)*. She is on a port tack here, heading about as much to windward as she is able, about 50 degrees off the wind.**

© *New Netherland Museum/John Mangrum*

mark for "North by Northwest" on the ship's lubber line. He did this "from twelve until two of the clocke." At each turn of the ship's (half-) hourglass, a peg was inserted on a small traverse board showing what course he'd kept and for how long.

On deck another sailor with a helper would regularly "cast the ship's chip log"—a triangular wooden board fastened by a bridle to a roller on which a long light hemp line was spooled. Thrown in the sea, the board floated vertically, kept so by a small lead weight let into one side. The drag of this wooden chip log in the sea would pull out the log line, through the man's hand, counting where knots had been tied in the line approximately every 28 feet. Meanwhile, his helper held a small minute glass quite like a modern transparent egg timer, with sand running through from the top part of its hourglass shape to the bottom. When the last grains fell he would call out "Mark!" and the sailor's hand would clamp down on the line. The number of knots that had passed through the sailor's hand was the ships speed in knots. Any excess would be roughly measured off by the sailor's arm-span, as an estimate of fathoms, roughly four between each pair of knots. *Halve Maan*'s speed that night, for example, might logically have been called out as "Four knots, two fathoms, Sir." There was no glancing down at the GPS or an LED-illuminated electronic knot-meter reading 4.50 Kts, converted at the touch of a button to 5.18 mph!

They were now some 27 nautical miles off what would become the New Jersey shore, at about 39 deg 20' N, 74 deg 47' W.[20] They continued sailing with decreased soundings "and so Shoalder and Shoalder until it came to twelve fathoms. We saw a great Fire, but could not see the land…"

Native Americans or lightning had ignited a conflagration in the pines. Although the *Half Maan* was five miles off the coast, at 39 deg 43' N and 73 deg 58'W and at least a dozen nautical miles from the inland pine forests, the fire was still visible.

Barnegat is believed to be a contraction of the initial Dutch name *Barende-gat*. Some translate this as "breakers inlet," though modern Dutch dictionaries do not reflect this definition of *barende*. The inlet later appeared on charts as "Burning Hole" and I have always thought Juet's record of the "great fire" was the source of that appellation.[21]

Still, from *Halve Maan*'s deck, they "…could not see the land; then we came to ten fathoms [a prudent depth with a shoaling bottom nearing land which was not visible] whereupon we took our tackes aboord and stood to the Eastward East South-east." They would not chance running upon shoals in the dark. Far more complex than today's fore and aft sailing vessels, they did not tack, but brought the "tackes" [lines controlling the outer yardarms on the port side] inboard and turning most of 180 degrees to port, reversing the position of all their sails to slowly retrace their course seaward *four glasses* or two hours to await sunrise.

In the morning, the masthead lookout saw the suspected land and advised the deck "from the West by North, to the Northwest by North, all like broken islands …" As land emerged over the horizon, the highest points (in this case the dune crests and sections of maritime forest on Long Beach Island) were first seen as pieces of land along the line of view, hovering a bit above the horizon like broken islands. Upon approach, they would slowly merge to reveal the entire shoreline.

Juet continues "then we loosed [eased their sails] in for the shoare and fair by the shoare, we had seven fathoms. . . . From the land we first had sight of [Long Beach Island] until we came to a great Lake of water, as wee could judge it to bee [Barnegat Bay] being drowned Land, which made it to rise like Ilands, which was in length ten Leagues" [thirty miles, they reckoned].

Their perception of the coast here was fleeting, but we know that tide was ebbing strongly through Barnegat Inlet that morning because Juet writes, "The mouth of that Lake hath many shoalds, and the sea breaketh upon them as it is cast out of the mouth of it. And from that Lake or Bay, the Land lyeth North by East [actually about 20 degrees east of magnetic north], and we had a great streame out of the Bay."

Barnegat had thus been discovered by Europeans, and Juet records his impression of the coast: "This is a very good Land to fall in with and a pleasant Land to see."[22] Most of us who love this land and the waters here have to agree with him.

Hudson's discovery was first referenced on a map by Don Alonzo de Velasco in 1611, which shows Juet's inlet as a notch in the Jersey coast. Don Alonzo's map is very sketchy on the Jersey shore, but shows incredibly good detail for the Chesapeake region just south, thanks to the better—actually meticulous—cartography of Captain John Smith just three years before!

Exploration by Onrust

In 1613, Adriaen Block's ship *Tyger* was burned by accident at New Amsterdam (today's New York) and, following friction among his crew, some left aboard other ships. Others, including Block's ship's carpenter, remained, and they built a smaller exploration vessel. Some called her a 'yacht' because the Dutch word was jaght or jaghtskip, and others called her a 'sloop,' either of which could be a hunting or exploring vessel and is supposed to refer to a light maneuverable sailing vessel used for pursuit.[23] Her builders named her *Onrust* (Dutch word for restless). Adriaen Block, following on reports of an earlier exploration by Bartholomew Gosnold in 1603, took this small vessel and cruised the southern New England coast. He discovered and left his name on beautiful Block Island.

We don't know what *Onrust* looked like, but much historical work has gone into analyzing the type of vessel she might have been from cryptic references, contemporary woodcuts, and shipwrecks exhumed during the draining of one of Holland's *polders* or diked regions. Speculation places her between 30 and 50 feet, of modest draft, a characteristic discussed at length for Dutch vessels in *Silent Maid* owner Edwin Schoettle's book *Sailing Craft.*[24]

It might seem courageous or even foolhardy for the *Onrust* to sail through Barnegat Inlet based on Juet's description in 1609. However, if the crew of *Onrust* had coasted down from New York on a morning northerly wind and anchored off the lower end of Island Beach, they could wait for slack tide and perhaps even a brisk southerly and then sail and row their way inside. It is clear from the subsequent Cornelius Hendrickson map (see Figure 1-19) that they spent some time in Barnegat Bay (perhaps several days and nights) and certainly enough time to use wind and tide to cover the length of the estuary. In a boat that beats poorly to windward, it would have taken a couple of days to navigate to the head of the bay and back. Some significant rowing also might have been required, unless a fortuitous northerly wind appeared when they were at the Bay's freshwater head. Tide was not a factor in upper Barnegat Bay because in 1614 there was no connection shown with the ocean at the upper end. (Even today upper Barnegat's astronomical tides are but six inches!)

They sailed down past Manahawkin at least far enough to document its juncture with *EyerHaven* (Egg Harbor). That southerly leg required at least a single turn of tide from ebb to flood, and enough wind to make use of it.

The Bay Is Charted

Cornelius Hendrickson's 1616 map is the first detailed representation we have of Barnegat Bay. It was based wholly on Adrien Block's explorations in *Onrust*. Men coming into this estuary in a sailing or rowed shallop had their work cut out for them. Like similar explorers six years before on the Chesapeake Bay, they likely made notes and perhaps sketches that are now long lost, but later they transmitted these either in verbal or drawn form to mapmakers back on the continent.

Latitude in Hendrickson's time might have been determined with a noon-sight using a Davis backstaff,[25] a rather frail wooden pair of joined quadrants that allowed the angle of the sun above the horizon to be determined with reasonable accuracy. The voyage aboard *Onrust* from New Amsterdam was very likely in the warm months. This meant that the noontime sun was very high in the sky and the angle of elevation was thus somewhat harder to read than at lower latitude or a different time of year.

FIGURE 1-18. The author uses a modern replica Davis backstaff during a trans-Atlantic voyage in 2007.

Larry Baswick photograph

Using tables of declination that mariners had worked out over many decades, the height of the sun above the horizon was known for many latitudes on each date of the year. With the backstaff read multiple times as mid-day and solar noon approached, the height would first increase as noon came near, it leveled off around the exact time of noon, and then readings would decline again into the afternoon.

The navigator recorded and averaged the highest readings to establish a best guess at the sun's maximum elevation. In summer—near the June Solstice—the sun was somewhere around 20 degrees north from the plane of the equator (that's why we have hot summers!). Therefore, the observed noon altitude must be corrected by subtracting this declination to approximate latitude for the chart. In any event, Hendrickson's map is off target, showing the 40th parallel 16 to 17 nautical miles (that is, 16 to 17 minutes of arc) farther north than its actual position.

Inadequate as this seems, they were not doing too badly. On a voyage I took in 2007 using replicas of these instruments, I averaged about 7/10 degree error each day over a 17-day passage—sometimes high, sometimes low, but I was off on average 42 miles of latitude. Such errors are why ships were lost and, in no small measure, contributed to the thousands of shipwrecks on New Jersey's Atlantic coast.

Making notes underway in a small boat must have been troublesome for those charting Barnegat Bay in 1614. Imagine making orderly entries in ink on parchment bound up-bay in one of Barnegat Bay's screaming afternoon summer southerlies with spray coming over while trying to avoid capsizing, which would be a disaster with all one's worldly supplies, fresh water, and victuals aboard!

I think these explorers used a kind of pencil for their field notes and then copied them "fair" in ink once stable and ashore. Where, after all, do you think the term "lead pencil" came from? Actually, a hard form of natural graphite similar to what we use today was discovered in the British Isles in 1564. It made darker, sharper marks than metallic lead and its use spread widely—first as graphite "sticks" wrapped with string, then inserted in a hollowed wood enclosure. These wooden pencils were first mass-produced in Nuremburg, Germany, in 1662.[26]

We are not sure which creeks and smudgy shoals *Onrust's* crew actually visited or drew while on the water there, but some of the major features quickly tempt the modern sailor to assign names to them from today's charts.

FIGURE 1-19. Cornelius Hendrickson's seminal map showing Barnegat Bay was published in 1616 and based wholly on Adrien Block's explorations in *Onrust*. The portion illustrated here is shown from (then un-named) Sandy Hook to Egg Harbor (*EyerHaven* in Dutch).

Ocean County Historical Society, Closed Sea exhibit focusing on Kent Mountford's 2002 book

Barnegat Inlet itself has two principal shoals shown; one directly in the mouth and a flood-tide delta inside the inlet. As the rapid incoming tide scoops sand waves out of deeper channels, its velocity slows inside the wider bay and the sand is deposited in a rough fan shape. The same thing happens during ebb tide, but the sand is swept out into coastwise shoals on the ocean side. This is why waves break at the mouth of Barnegat Inlet in any kind of weather, and why, in 1609, Robert Juet, Henry Hudson's mate and journal keeper wrote: "The sea breaketh upon the shoals as it is cast out of the mouth of it."

Today the U.S. Corps of Engineers keeps redirecting sand accumulations to reduce the hazards to navigation, but in my half century on Barnegat bay I've seen both these shoals appear and reappear in several forms. I have run aground upon them and had my heart in my mouth while exiting the inlet in heavy weather when long swells were breaking across the entire channel as seas telegraphed from an offshore gale mounded up when encountering the shallows.

Well inside Barnegat Inlet, on Hendrickson's chart, shallows smear over the bay bottom all the way across what we call Oyster Creek channel. Even today, it is a shifting labyrinth along which the bottom changes faster than repositioning of the buoys that mark the route.

South of the inlet towards modern Manahawkin and Egg Harbor, the broad shallow flats were there 400 years ago (and are still there today) along with some of the islands –or their progenitors—which we now chart. Anyone with draft greater than a couple of feet needed to rigidly adhere to the few natural channels.

Today a dredged channel angles out and back under what was, in my youth, the old Manahawkin Causeway with its loose-nailed and rattling board decking. It is now the high spanned Manahawkin Bridge. Sailing in those waters, one was—and certainly is—draft constrained.

Prudent seamen look at these differences between coastal ocean and estuary and then look for different kinds of boat to fit the restrictions of draft and shorter choppier wave conditions. Weather, even geology in some sense, determines what the boats will look like. Edwin Schoettle wrote: "… it is obvious that the designs [of boats] were somewhat controlled by the character of the waters and [even] the nationality of the early settlers."[27] Catboats fit this development model pretty well; with a heavy mast very far forward, they are less suitable for plunging into head seas while sailing offshore or for navigating the hazards of rushing tide and breaking inlets. The catboat's shallow draft, wide beam for capacity, and stability in gusty winds—coupled with simple handling—speaks well to negotiating estuaries with tricky channels and thin waters!

On the 1616 map, shoals that can be construed as the modern "Tices Shoal" and other shallows west of the Squan Peninsula (off Modern Lavalette) are shown farther up the Bay. At the head of Barnegat Bay, it is easy to identify the Metedeconk River, which, on the scale of Hendrickson's chart, winds back some 15 miles into then untracked woodlands. Today's Herring Island is clearly shown at the Metedeconk's mouth. A shorter tributary pointing north is either Beaverdam Creek or some interpretation of Herbert's Creek, which was eventually excavated and channelized for the Bay Head-Manasquan Canal during the late 1920s.

Henrickson's map reflects some geographic uncertainty about several creeks farther south towards Barnegat. We can interpret a complex of Green Island and Mosquito Cove (well, Silver Bay) or perhaps we see the branches of modern Toms River. Surely south of there and well opposite Barnegat Inlet we see a Cedar Creek, maybe a Stouts Creek, and both (an unbifurcated!) Forked River and Oyster Creek. We cannot know what *Onrust*'s crew actually drew in their notes or agreed from memory upon what they had seen.

Charting of Barnegat Bay continued over the next two centuries. This was not a prime harbor for shipping when Delaware and New York were so close, but mariners did explore occasionally. John Thornton, about 1682, calls the inlet "Burning Hole" and names "Barnegatt Bay." He also names the Manasquan River in Monmouth County and shows an unnamed Metedeconk, Toms River (its North and South branches), Forked River, and Oyster Creek with those remnant Pleistocene post glacial hills inland thereof. There is the suggestion of a dent in the Island Beach Peninsula slightly south of Toms River, but you might suspect it an intermittent breakthrough from ocean to bay. No inlet was shown at that location in an earlier 1670 map. Thornton's next version of the map in 1689 actually loses much detail and the name Barnegatt Bay, but describes the Island Beach Peninsula as "Low Sandy Land."[28]

BARNEGAT BAY'S WATER QUALITY

Beneath much of Barnegat's watershed (covering 668 square miles [1730 km^2][29]) and under the entire Pine Barrens lies a great subterranean sand box into which rainwater has percolated for many thousands of years. These ancient waters have a mixed fate because some of this recharge—the restoration of water supply by rains from above—has slowly seeped through layers of relatively impermeable silts and clays and formed deeper aquifers; these layers sloping slowly downwards towards the east. While southern New Jersey is of relatively low elevation, the interior portions are still higher than the coast.

As the aquifers accumulated millions of cubic meters of water they flowed downhill toward the coast, still deep underground and confined by the impermeable layers. If a pipe was simply bored into them, the water would spout up above ground. This is called an artesian well. At a few places on the barrier islands, this was discovered in the 19th century in an attempt to drill down for freshwater to supply the

FIGURE 1-20. *(Top)* The artesian fountain in front The Engleside hotel on Long Beach Island.

Woolman and Rose Atlas

(Right) Catboats and other local craft drift into the Engleside's bay shore at day's end.

Photograph given to Kent Mountford by John Engle Taylor, grandson of Robert Barclay Engle, 1970

FIGURE 1-21. *(Left)* A white cedar bog woodland along Rt. 70. *(Right)* Clear grain white cedar planks 14 inches wide shown seasoning at Beaton's Boatyard in Mantoloking.

Kent Mountford photographs

increasing number of resort hotels. Robert Barclay Engle had such an artesian well in front of his hotel, the Engleside on Long Beach Island. The well provided a seemingly inexhaustible fountain. Of course, that source of pure water was thousands of years old. This deep aquifer—an underground reservoir of freshwater far beneath the surface—has since been penetrated by so many wells elsewhere, that its supply of artesian pressure has been exhausted.

Bayard Randolph Kraft reported that one of the island hotels had been built too close to the sea and its artesian water supply was now offshore in "deep water." One local claimed he could still find the site of this artesian spring in the early 20th century by the temperature of the upwelling, fresher water off the coast.[30]

These ancient water reserve aquifers beneath the Pine Barrens were well known by the end of the 19th century, and Philadelphia, not far west of New Jersey, was eager to tap into them to supply growth and development, both industrial and domestic. It was with great and improbable wisdom that the Pine Barrens were preserved from this fate and much of the pinelands kept wild for many decades.

The streams in this part of New Jersey are acidic because they do not have calcareous, or limestone, rocks that dissolve and neutralize the water. The clear water in these streams is often tinted to tea color by *humic acid leachates* from leaf materials (conifer needles of the pine forest and the vegetation in white cedar bogs). Under natural conditions—when uncontaminated—these tributaries and their surrounding soils contribute very little nitrogen from the forest to Barnegat Bay.

Nitrogen, one of the two primary nutrients (fertilizers) necessary for all plant growth, was thus naturally in short supply to the coastal bays. Thus, plant plankton in these streams and rivers was quickly starved for nitrogen, assuring the waters remained clear (despite their tea color) and were essentially pristine. Mariners coming along the coast often sought out the water of these colored streams because of its keeping qualities when put in casks with a tight-driven bung and carried to sea for long periods.

More shallowly beneath the surface of the Pine Barrens lies another water resource— the groundwater—recently soaked into the sands and resident there for at most a few years. These waters relatively quickly trickled among and fed into the labyrinths of shadowy white cedar bogs. They then flowed through the quickly dried piney soils to water the Pine Barrens' many streams—from the Metedeconk to the Mullica River and all the Barnegat Bay tributaries between.

These reserves of water more immediately reach Barnegat Bay as one of its primary sources of freshwater. This together with more immediate stream flow dilutes what would otherwise be a more uniformly salty bay. Some of this, about 12%, seeps directly through and under the Bay's marshy western margins. New Jersey's former state geologist, the late Kemble Widmer, told me about this in the early 1960s, as I first learned about the history of Barnegat Bay. Kem said, "Look at these aerial photographs from the depth of winter, when the bay has been frozen and we've had westerly winds, and you can see the great ice sheet detach from the western shore of the Bay, where warmer groundwaters—they are always in the 50s Fahrenheit—have melted it free." He was sure—with minimal data in those years—that this groundwater input was important.

The lands behind the "Barnegat Coast" were developed more and more heavily until, in the modern watershed, immense amounts of driveway, side-street, mall parking, roof, and highway surfaces (which shed rain immediately) accelerate the flow of water into tributaries and carry with them the contaminants of a surrounding dense, human population largely unaware of the importance of this runoff.

This water now represents about two-thirds of the freshwater entering Barnegat through its tributary streams. For centuries freshwater inflow had posed no untoward consequences other than to reduce its saltiness in proportion to rainfall of the current year. More recently, in the years when highways began crisscrossing the pines from Toms River to New Egypt, from Tuckerton to Waretown, from Point Pleasant to Bricktown, the effects carried by the watery messenger became the dramatic bearer of human-generated pollution.

Salt in Barnegat Bay

There is enough salt in our veins to make us not very far from seawater. This is also true of organisms in Barnegat Bay, but they are always immersed in their watery environment and have relatively little ability to control movement of salt in and out of their bodies. Many critters, therefore, do not move over the entire Bay, but stay where salt is either more or less as they require.

That's particularly true for rooted plants that can't move about. This book will talk about how opening the Bay Head Manasquan Canal changed upper Barnegat from a freshwater lake to a much saltier habitat, with barnacles and boring shipworms to trouble wooden boats where none had been before.

Freshwater from the land, flowing through sandy ground and down tributary rivers around the Bay, also serves to reduce salinity where it entered the main Bay. On the other hand, where inlets have pierced the barrier islands, considerably saltier water flows in twice a day and some of the diluting freshwater flows out to sea. When inlets opened and closed through history, these dynamics changed. This was especially true for Cranberry Inlet, which radically changed Toms River's history, and for the bay complex's southern end where Little Egg Inlet similarly introduces and releases water.

In my several years working as a scientist on Barnegat Bay, I encountered wet and dry periods that also made large differences in salinity. For many decades, salt content has been expressed by scientists as parts per thousand by weight and written abbreviated as "ppt" or shown by the symbol "‰." Seawater is somewhere around 35‰ and near-coastal water around 30‰. Inside Barnegat Bay near the inlets it ranges from 23‰ to 28‰, on a rising tide with water coming into the bay, and from 17‰ to 21‰ near ebb tide when fresher water is leaving the bay. In the upper bay where tributary inputs

FIGURE 1-22. A setiger, the juvenile form of a polychaete worm. Billions of these live in the sediments of Barnegat Bay, and they are food for the finfish we covet. The species change from one end of the bay to the other partly as a result of salinity. Adult "Clam Worms," several inches long, are popular bait for recreational fishermen.

Kent Mountford photomicrograph

still have an influence, despite the Bay Head-Manasquan Canal, salinities might range from 12‰ to 19‰, depending on the year and rainfalls.

Saltwater is also distinctly heavier than freshwater, so the incoming tide slides along the bottom as it enters the bay, with relatively little mixing into fresher layers above. Similarly, lighter fresher water tends to flow out with less mixing than might otherwise occur. Quite a bit of these fresher waters actually are washed back into the bay with the subsequent flood tide and compound the problem since contaminants have not really left the system.[31]

Barnegat Inlet in particular has large sandbars, deposited just inside the bay where swift tidal currents in the inlet channels dissipate and spread out like a fan. This serves as a further barrier to mixing. What this means is that materials entering the bay tend to be trapped there because of reduced mixing. That was biologically useful when the larvae of fish and small bottom-dwelling organisms were kept in the bay to serve as food for foraging predators. However, once mankind began pumping sewage, petroleum, and other chemical pollutants into the rivers and open bay, they tended to stay there too or settle out and become trapped in bay sediments. This resistance to flushing out materials in the bay can be expressed as a turnover time—how long it takes to remove essentially all of what has been dumped in the bay. In a wet January, for example, this can happen in 24 days, but in hot and dry months this can stretch to 74 days—long enough to cause serious pollution problems. For the sailor in today's Barnegat Bay, this can make the water quite turbid and unappealing for swimmers.

Barnegat Bay has been seriously over fertilized by nutrient materials washing off the land and brought down by rainfall. It thus contains too much burgeoning life for its own good. I could see this as a nascent biologist while working in the bay as early as 1964.

Upon moving to the Chesapeake Bay area in 1971, I was astounded by the abundance of unpleasant jellyfish, the stinging sea nettles (*Chrysaora quinquecirrha*). I was, thereafter, amazed that polluted Barnegat Bay had escaped this infestation. My amazement ceased in the 1990s when they suddenly appeared and have, as I feared, prospered. These organisms also, to some extent, favor intermediate salinities, so that presently sea nettles are concentrated in the upper portions of Barnegat Bay and less of a problem in the lower bay nearer Barnegat Inlet.

Adult and potentially reproductive sea nettles sometimes are advected by tides through the Chesapeake and Delaware Canal and occasionally reach as far as Cape May, where I've seen them at least twice. It is possible that the minute resting stages of *Chrysaora* could be carried by currents for additional great distances and, once in favorable conditions, it might only have been a matter of time before they found a home in polluted, over-enriched Barnegat Bay. The species is sometimes reported as far north as southern New England,[32] though Barnegat Bay had until now been spared, save for a single rare observation by Thurlow Nelson over 80 years ago.

No solution for this jellyfish problem has been found in the Chesapeake Bay after a half century of study and legislation; I fear none is likely in Barnegat Bay.

Effect of Nitrogen on the Bay

Streams draining from undisturbed forest lands into Barnegat Bay have about 0.04 to 0.05 milligrams (mg) of nitrogen per liter of water, barely the equivalent of a tiny speck on the tip of a table-knife. When lands are developed, surfaces are paved, and runoff

FIGURE 1-23. **The stinging sea nettle (*Chrysaora quinquecirrha*), a recent maritime plague visited upon Barnegat Bay. Stinging cells extend to the tips of the longest tentacles.**

Kent Mountford photograph

accelerates (with all the effluents people cast upon it), the nitrogen load delivered to Barnegat Bay rises to from 1.1 to over 2 mg, a many-fold factor of increase.

This nitrogen, which was once in short supply and where its unavailability had limited the growth of plant plankton in the past, rapidly began stimulating the growth of algae and causing increasing turbidity and algae blooms in Barnegat Bay. Repeatedly fed new nitrogen, the algae and specific species that had once been unfamiliar occurrences in the bay bloomed like weeds in a manicured lawn. Experiencing one of these massive blooms (of dinoflagellate *Polykrikos*) in the early 1960s in lower Barnegat Bay helped spur my study of plankton marine biology as a career and resulted in my first professional interactions with scientists at the Sandy Hook (NJ) Marine Laboratory.

Following World War II and later the Korean War, a significant exodus started from the warrens of urban North Jersey and New York. People wanted to escape these environs and return to the land, to capture a more rural way of life, and to make their way economically at the same time. Many of these men and women started family chicken farms. In the early 1950s, the human population of Ocean County was 38,000;[35] eventually the chicken population would reach 6,000,000! With no management of the chickens' abundant manure, which lay or was spread on the ground, nitrogen from this source moved into groundwater and inevitably towards the neighboring streams. Some waterborne nitrogen was delivered quickly; other portions were delayed in slow-moving groundwater for decades . . . and may still be arriving to over-fertilize the bay with residual nitrogen input.

Commercial coastal fisheries became a source of feed for chickens and other livestock. The menhaden fishery (at one time a major processing plant was on the Mullica River) extracted fish oils for use in everything from cosmetics to paint. The solid residues—full of protein and minerals—were sold as fish meal for livestock, including chickens. Nutrients harvested from the sea were thus returned to the land and watershed via chicken manure.

Most of the chickens and eggs come from elsewhere today; there would hardly be room, or a neighborly welcome, any more in most parts of New Jersey's crowded coastal counties for large feedlots or industrial brood houses. But humans have replaced chicken pollutant inputs with nutrients coming from fertilized suburban lawns and gardens; running off thousands of roofs, roads, driveways, and parking lots; or falling with rain as the washed-out microscopic particles from internal combustion engines. Nitrogen is the most potent killer of water quality in Barnegat Bay and its streams. In the watershed, 70% of the land is now almost saturated with development.[36]

From its discharging tributary streams, Barnegat Bay proper received in recent years about 172,000 pounds (lb) (78,000 kilograms [kg]) of nitrogen a year; from surface runoff alone comes 57,330 lb (26,000 kg) of this; and Little Egg Harbor receives another estimated 310,905 lb (141, 000 kg). In wet and dry years the total nitrogen load varies widely. For example in 2001, it was estimated at 855,540 lb (388,000 kg) versus 2,079,315 lb. (943,000 kg.) in a particularly wet year[33]

If by some miracle we were to end all these sources of polluted runoff, who knows how long it would take for groundwater and the Bay's tributaries to purge themselves from all the decades of abuse and run clear again.

BARNEGAT BAY'S WEATHER

During the times when Henry Hudson first navigated alongshore and *Onrust* first explored the estuary, the weather patterns that swept over the barrier islands as they

FIGURE 1-24. **A livestock feeding product once produced from harvested coastal migrating schools of the abundant Menhaden or "Moss Bunker" fish** (Brevoortia tyrannus). **Coastal stocks of menhaden have since been widely depleted, and the fish processing plant on Mullica River Island has long been a dramatic ruin.**

Kent Mountford photograph

migrated west were probably the same as those we encounter today. Winter storms roaring up the coastline, generally along a course of southwest to northeast, and hurricanes all have counterclockwise wind circulations that hook northeast winds in against the coast. The waves driving ashore and the force of wind combine to scour the beaches and gnaw away at dune structures. The result is that sand is sucked offshore and surf line advances farther landward. Low barometric (air pressure) readings associated with these storms exacerbate the high tides by literally creating a bulge in the surface of the sea, making high tide higher by virtue of a surge.

There is a phenomenon in the northern hemisphere called the Coriolis effect, where water masses blowing across the surface of the sea are deflected towards the *right* facing downwind. Water moving on the surface of the sea follows this path. Initially, the water is driven to the southwest by northeast winds and is actually deflected some 45 degrees. Thus, it flows directly against the coast outside Barnegat Bay and literally piles up along shore. This is true for the mass of water, but also for objects afloat. That is why unusual amounts of debris accumulate on Barnegat Bay's ocean beaches during Nor'easters at the wrack line, where high tide has reached. Higher water levels also mean that waves break farther on shore and run higher up and sometimes over the beaches.

The erosive effect is redoubled when these storms coincide with high tides, especially with spring tides that occur twice each month when the gravitational forces exerted by sun and moon coincide. Sometimes on the open natural coasts, like Island Beach, the dune line is breached and sheets of wave-driven sand sweep back across the barrier beach. This is called a 'wash-over' and in major storms this sand and water flow inundates the swales or small valleys back of the beach and can cover the bayside marshes. When the forces are powerful enough, a new inlet can be carved.

Kathleen Reiley, who grew up along the coast, wrote a memoir about her youth in the 1880s and recorded her family's precarious life in a little rented beach house at Chadwick, which experienced virtually annual wash-overs from ocean to bay even during summer nor'easters. There were no dunes, nor any shrub growth to begin accumulating sand to build them. Reiley writes that because of later interest in developing this land with saleable lots, there was a conscious program of building a line of shrubs and branches to stem the wash-over events. Slowly, sand did accumulate, stimulated by natural growth of American beach grass and other pioneer dune vegetation, and the lots were parceled off, ready for the coming of the railroad! Development on the barrier islands, first with virtually expendable shacks, was a slippery slope as people with real money made their marks.

The opening of inlets must have happened scores of times in the past thousands of years. Navigable passages like Cranberry Inlet established Toms River as a seaport for about 52 years. In March 1962, the carving of a new inlet at Beach Haven was considered a major disaster during what was then considered a rare storm of 500 years' return frequency. But, just half a century later, during Superstorm Sandy in October 2012, a temporary flowing inlet at Mantoloking swept away many homes that had been in place for over a century.

These disasters were only such because our development practices have stood in the way of natural processes that have operated for millennia. Future major storms will be viewed as increasingly destructive because the density of investment and the cost of construction and repair escalates with every passing year of unwise development and, sorry to say, redevelopment in each storm's wake.

From autumn through spring, the passages of such storms are almost inevitably followed by north to northwest winds bringing in clear and usually cooler weather.

These winds rapidly even out the breaking surf leaving long, regular waves with their crests blown back by the offshore wind. While they last, modern surfboarders ride these with delight. In Barnegat Bay, these winds tend to blow water down and out. Persistent northerlies, which are normally accompanied by a rising barometer, can combine with the semi-monthly spring low tides and strong winds down the bay's axis to create extremely low water levels. At Mantoloking, where the astronomical tide is but six inches, the amplitude during very windy periods can vary as much as a meter (39 inches). Boats at shallow moorings can be left sitting on the bottom for a day or so, and wide sand flats can be exposed along natural west-facing shorelines at Island Beach. The opposite occurs in southerly gales causing temporary flooding of the boatyards and low-lying roads around Bay Head and Mantoloking.

Colder seasons are times when hunters and commercial fishers have traditionally used the bay. From late spring through early autumn and all the lazy summer months in between is the time when recreational and competitive hordes of boaters swarm Barnegat Bay and its tributary rivers. It is then that the unique wind patterns of east coast estuaries, which are favorable to seasonal sailors, come into serious play.

Most significant is the amazingly reliable and welcome sea breeze. The dominant wind flow in summer along this coast is from the southwest. This wind brings hot spells and moves thunderstorms along a general southwest to northeast course. Mornings can be hot along Barnegat Bay in summer with feeble winds for sailors. Any flow from the landward direction can bring biting greenheads or black flies to harass one's ankles or any unprotected parts dangling down in the cockpit.

The land behind Barnegat Bay, all the while, is warming and the air above ground is responding to this heat as well, becoming progressively lighter by expansion. Like a hot air balloon, it begins to rise and the vacuum beneath it must be replaced by something. That is quite regularly a flow of air beginning from the sea, moving tentatively from the east with little ripples or *cat's paws* on the surface of the bay just west of the barrier islands.

As the warm air inland rises, it accelerates like bubbles from the bottom of a cauldron just beginning to boil. It seems that hot sometimes! As these bubbles of air rise, they encounter cooler air a couple of thousand feet above the ground. When hot, humid air cools, water vapor condenses and a line of puffy clouds will begin forming, perhaps a mile inland from the bay's western shore. They may persist or may not, but these uplifting areas continue rising—generally as long as the heating continues. This draws in air by vacuum from the adjacent ocean—an accelerating sea breeze.

The air-mass of wind, initially east, moves across the barrier islands and bay, sometimes quite a significant sailing wind over by Lavallette, or Seaside, or Barnegat Light, but not felt at all mid-bay or on the western shore. This mass, moving across the face of the earth, follows the same deflection from Coriolis effect that Nor'east storm winds do. As a result, the wind clocks from the east around 40 degrees or more until it is southeast to south in direction, blowing directly up the bay by afternoon.

This is one of the most reliable sailing winds I know of. The warming of the land is almost always enough to start the circulation, and the sea surface temperature is almost always cool enough to provide the replacement flow. Decades ago I met a man at some inland U.S. city who reported he'd grown up along Barnegat Bay even more decades before. "Is the wind still so reliable? It used to come in every day 10:30 or 11:00 o'clock. Does it still do that?" Generally yes, I informed him, and here decades later writing this I can say that it still (usually!) does.

Strong summer southwest flows, during what we call a heat spell, can overwhelm the sea breeze effect, literally pushing it offshore and away from the coast. The sailor at sea can sail in a sea breeze sometimes while the beaches only a mile or two west

FIGURE 1-25. **The infamous greenhead fly** *(Tabanus americana)* **alight on the author's hand.** *Inset:* **Profile showing the biting mouth parts.**

Kent Mountford photographs

FIGURE 1-26. Bay Head Yacht Club canoe outing in the summer of 1890. Almost all of approximately 17 sailboats in the background are catboats.

Phillip A. Schoettle collection

may still be sweltering. A land breeze (west to southwest) furthermore, if strong and persistent, will blow warm surface water in the near-shore ocean out to sea. The sea will maintain its approximate level whatever the wind does, however, and to replace the warm water being blown offshore, colder water from the deep coastal ocean will slide in to the beaches and make for very cold swimming. In some years, I have seen surf water temperatures plunge from the 70's F to the upper 50's (20° C to 10° C) virtually overnight. At the same time, heat spells with persistent offshore winds can raise air temperatures in coastal communities to over 100° F (38° C) and people wonder if it's any better here than in Newark or Philadelphia!

Relief eventually comes as a frontal passage, often after a violent squall line containing thunder squalls. The wind, after rain, will shift northwest and is markedly cooler and provides stunning relief after a hot spell. Depending on the strength of a front, the wind will then slowly veer (shift clockwise) within hours or a day or so. It will continue clockwise and sequentially to the north, nor-east, and east before returning to the southerly quadrant and another temperate and delightful sea breeze.

Once transportation to and from the coast had been worked out, the New Jersey coast resorts developed during the latter 19th century due to Barnegat Bay's reliable sea breeze winds. People welcome escape to the shore in modern times; just imagine what Philadelphia and New York were like 125 years ago with stifling Victorian garb; coal and wood cooking stoves that ran 24/7; absolutely no air conditioning; and not even the thought of an electric fan.

Wind patterns and an understanding of them were how and why commercial sail developed on Barnegat Bay, and why catboats, garveys, and sneakboxes dominated the scene. They were the shipping vessels—the economic engines—that supported salt extraction, gill-netting, pound fishing, hook and line harvesting, eelgrass gathering, salt hay cutting, and the moving of wood, iron ore products, fishery and shellfish harvests, agricultural produce, and people. All of it flowed from the availability and utilization of wind and tide forces on Barnegat Bay.

BARNEGAT BAY'S WATERSHED FORESTS

Starting in the 1950s as tremendous waves of development swept over the landscape, wildfires were vigorously suppressed by New Jersey's forest service. Slowly, for the first time in centuries—perhaps thousands of years since the glaciers—the forest composition changed from dominant New Jersey pitch pine (*Pinus rigida*) to oak-dominated hardwoods (*Quercus spp.*). In my adult lifetime—since the 1950s—there have grown large stands of oak, particularly west towards Medford on NJ Route 70, with trees now more than half a century old.

With unintended consequences so often accompanying human interference in relatively stable, self-rejuvenating natural processes, these stands of oak have provided edible corridors for the spread of the gypsy moth (*Lymantria dispar*). (The gypsy month was intentionally, but ignorantly, introduced in an attempt to build an American silk industry.[37]) The caterpillars from gypsy moth infestations repeatedly defoliate trees and especially oaks year after year. Many older trees, thus weakened, die and become roadside and fire hazards.

To walk through one of these forests in late spring, with all the leaves eaten away, bits of chopped vegetation, and specks of caterpillar frass (that's feces) raining down continually is an eerie experience. Sunlight streams down to the forest floor at a season when all should be in deep leafy shade. The caterpillars, thus fed, metamorphose into the moth stage, which enables the whole cycle to be repeated the following spring.

Gypsy moth infestations are cyclic, running from a couple to a few years, but over the run of decades they have spread far and wide along the Appalachian Mountain chain through New Jersey, Pennsylvania, Maryland, and Virginia doing untold millions of dollars in damage to forests, which could have sustained the ecosystem, or at worst, been the source of valuable hardwood construction timber.

Now large, once robust, oak trees, among the Pine Barrens in New Jersey, stand as dead wood, their naked, and progressively falling arms extended far into the air. It is uncertain what the next ecosystem adaptation or disaster might be.

The Pine Barren's 1.1 million acres of native scrub pitch pine forest, in addition to being quite tolerant (resistant) to killing by ground fires that have been their lot for centuries, would have been unaffected by the gypsy moth. Of course, we coastal and maritime enthusiasts believe ourselves insulated from such ecological events because we are now building most of our boats with petroleum-based fiberglass resins, painting them with urethane finishes, and caulking them with synthesized compounds like polysulfides and silicones!

DEVELOPMENT AND ITS IMPACT ON BARNEGAT BAY

This natural system with all its sustainable resources was not to be kept intact. When human settlement and later commercial development began, people were unwilling to have the assets they built be repeatedly wiped out by natural events like storm over-wash and shoreline erosion. The erection of bulkheads and groins to retain the sand, the dredging, and bulkheading of shorelines followed. P.R. Jivoff calculated that by

2006, 40% of the once natural shoreline of the greater Barnegat Bay and Egg Harbor systems had been hardened with engineered structures.[38] In seven years, this was up by another 7%. On the barrier islands, stone groins, jetties, artificial dunes, and beach nourishment from offshore sand deposits has consumed tens of millions of dollars in the last several decades. Hurricane Sandy in October 2012 demonstrated how ineffectual these attempts are when nature takes a serious stab at them.

Recognizing this history, the impermanence, the vulnerability, and yet the regenerative capacity of these habitats, it is important to grasp that in just a few lifetimes billions of dollars of development has overwhelmed these beaches—all bound to someday disappear, condemned by the very geology of this region. We have not heeded this lesson and struggle now trying to hold the line against an advancing Atlantic Ocean, trading up the property values as we go—ever riskier investments as they may be!

CATBOAT TIMES ON BARNEGAT BAY

Back in 1928, Edwin J. Schoettle wrote, "Probably the most interesting study of boats concerns their early history, the origin of many types and the reasons for the existence of each type."[39] He would probably have subscribed to my view that local boat species evolve to meet demands of the waters upon which they sail. Those that are unsuitable are winnowed out or relegated to sideline positions in a working fleet. Schoettle spells this out for his home waters "in [the period] 1890 to 1920 [where] 75% of the boats on Barnegat Bay were catboats . . . these boats were fun to sail, fast in light and heavy winds, the good beam furnished plenty of cabin room for cruising and extremely large cockpits. Catboats were used for over a hundred years in . . . American waters."[40] Schoettle's hundred years is, at this writing 186 years, and catboats are still increasing in number on Barnegat Bay.

Here follows the very complex and comprehensive history of just one of these boats—*Silent Maid*.

FIGURE 1-27. **Toms River Yacht Club catboats #61, #116, #31, and #27, circa 1900.** *Silent Maid* carried number T-82 after Edwin Schoettle joined the yacht club.

Bob O'Brien, New Jersey Museum of Boating

ENDNOTES — CHAPTER 1

1. Edwin J. Schoettle, *Sailing Craft* (New York: MacMillan, 1928), p. 88.

2. Claude M. Epstein, personal communication with Kent Mountford at Periglacial Features of Southern New Jersey Symposium, Richard Stockton College, October 10-11, 2003.

3. Erosion on Island Heights: AliceMay Weber Wright provided co-located photographs from 1930 and 1970, which show long and sometimes collapsed cliff-face stairways on the eroding banks. She described the loss of an entire street, paralleling the Height's western shore, and provided the second image showing stabilization with stable vegetation that was established by 1970

4. Mark Demitroff and Frederick E. Nelson, "The Periglacial Legacy of the New Jersey Pine Barrens, USA" (poster presented at Tough Choices—Land Use under a Changing Climate Conference, Berlin, October 2, 2008).

5. Ralph T. Ward, *Steamboats: A History of the Early Adventure* (Bobbs-Merrill Company, 1973), pp. 53-57.

6. Ward, *Steamboats*, 61-62

7. J.H. Morrison, J.H., *History of American Steam Navigation* (Stephen Daye Press, 1958 [orig 1903]), pp. 28-29.

8. Orrin Pilkey, Duke University, and Matthew L. Stutz, Meredith College. *Sea Technology*, Environmental Monitoring, June 2011, pp. 66-67. Their refereed paper is published in the *Journal of Coastal Research*.

9. Joseph Shisler, personal communication to Kent Mountford, 2010.

10. Discussions on the topic at Atlantic Estuarine Research Society, March 10, 2006.

11. Don Shomette. "Recounting the Revolutionary War Battle of Chestnut Neck, following which the British lost HMS Sloop of War *Zebra* in Little Egg Inlet" (Unpublished manuscript, 2013).

12. Several brief breaks in Barnegat's barrier islands have occurred in storms, but none, including the dramatic opening of an inlet at Mantoloking during Hurricane Sandy in October 2012, were permitted to remain.

13. Pauline S. Miller, *Ocean County: Four Centuries in the Making* (Ocean County Cultural and Heritage Commission, 2000).

14. Documents of the American Revolution: Joshua Huddy Era, Exhibition at Monmouth County Library Headquarters, October 2004 (www.Co.monmouth.nj.us/page.aspx?Id=1800). Reading the considerable archive of original documents relating to Joshua Huddy and his hanging, one finds the story far more complex and far reaching. While he was executed in error, his earlier behavior indicates he was a rough character, but his death ultimately brought the terrible internecine violence in New Jersey's Monmouth County to an end.

15. www.http-//en/wikipedia/wiki/toms_river_new_jersey.

16. Miller, *Ocean County*.

17. Miller, *Ocean County*, 100.

18. Miller, *Ocean County*, 374.

19. Calendar-24.comunited-states/moon/phases/1609

20. Plotted on 1987 Chartkit Region 3, 10th ed., NY to Nantucket, pg 3. Soundings on these offshore charts, as in the 17th century, are in fathoms and, despite a likely 1 meter sea level rise since 1609, the approximate shift from 21 to 16 fathoms can be found with course NNW to Barnegat at this position and the subsequent ones given. Compass variation today is about 14 deg, whereas Juet found "the land to haul the compass 8 degrees" in 1608.

21. Miller, *Ocean County*, p. 6.

22. Robert Juet, *Mr. Hendrick Hudson's Derde Reise Onder Nederlandsche Vlag, Van Amsterdam Naar Nova Zembla, America, En Terug Naar Dartmouth England* (London: Lime House, 1609).

23. Captain William "Chip" Reynolds, Director, New Netherland Museum, Albany, NY. Email to Kent Mountford: "Jaghts ranged in size from, about 10 Tons to about 150 tons . . . (one purported) replica *Onrust* was less a jaght, and more an enlarged sloep . . . with a cabin below decks, (and) but one sprit rigged mast."

24. Gerald T. White, "Yachts of the Netherlands," in *Sailing Craft*, Edwin Schoettle. (New York: MacMillan, 1928), pp. 256-276. White subsequently founded the Westlawn School of Yacht Design, through course materials from him during the 1960s, I learned something more about small craft naval architecture.

25. Captain John Davis, an English navigator, invented the backstaff in 1594. The backstaff was an improved tool. W.T. Reynolds, Captain of the current replica *Half Moon*, says the original ship was known to also carry a simpler navigating tool called a cross-staff.

26. http://pencils.com/blog/pencil-history/

27. Schoettle, *Sailing Craft*, 90.

28. John Thornton (circa 1682) and Thornton and William Fisher (1689), "A Large Mapp of Virginia, Maryland, Pennsylvania East and West New Jersey (Jarsey)" in *Atlas of Historical Maps of Maryland 1608-1908*, E.C. Papenfuse and J.M. Coale III. (Baltimore: Johns Hopkins Press, 2003).

29. Michael Kennish, personal communication to Kent Mountford, 2013. Kennish and colleagues have written over a hundred refereed publications on the Barnegat ecosystem.

30. Bayard Randolph Kraft, *Under Barnegat's Beam* (New York: privately printed, 1960), 71.

31. (George) Guo Qizhong, Norbert Psuty, George Lordi, Scott Glenn, Matthew Mund, and Mary Downes Gastrich, "2004 Hydrographic Study of Barnegat Bay," Division of Science, Research and Technology, New Jersey Department of the Environmental Protection.

32. Howard M Weiss, "Marine Animals of Southern New England and New York," *State Geological Survey of Connecticut, Bulletin 115* (1995), 1.04.

33. www.Soildistrict.org/aboutus/about_our_region. The 38,000 people in the 1940s had by the 1950s become 56,622 and by the present (2014) to 560,000. This population still doubles with summer visitors added.

34. www.Soildistrict.org.

35. C.M. Wieben, Ron Baker, R.S. Nicholson, and M.J. Kennish, "Assessing the Sources and Variability of Nutrient Loads to Barnegat Bay and Little Egg Harbor, New Jersey (paper presented at AERS Spring Meeting, Atlantic City, New Jersey, 2010).

36. Katherine Reiley, "Miss Katherine Reiley's Trip to Chadwick 1881" (manuscript transcribed by Ferdinand Klebold in 2003) in *The Society Schroll*, Ocean County Historical Society, October 2009.

37. U.S. Dept. Agriculture, "The Gypsy Moth in North America" (http://www.fs.fed.us/ne/morgantown/4557/), 2013. The larva of the gypsy moth were introduced by E. Leopold Trouvelot in 1868 or 1869.

38. P.R. Jivoff, quoted at Atlantic Estuarine Research Society Meeting, March 10, 2006.

39. Schoettle, *Sailing Craft*, 87.

40. Edwin J. Schoettle, written reminiscences (circa 1945), shared by Polly Schoettle Miller with Kent Mountford, 2012.

FIGURE 2-1. Edwin Schoettle's catboat *Silent Maid* in 1924.

A publicity photo by Johnson Brothers Boatyard now property of Suzanne Mitchell Davis, with permission

2

Schoettle Times: Before *Silent Maid*

Papyrus was the first paper made about 4400 years ago from the sliced stems of an Egyptian reed. A true paper, prepared by Imperial courtier Ts'al-Lun, was first recorded about 100 AD in China. Papermaking is a process using soaked plant fibers beaten to a pulp, strained out on a fine screen, and peeled off when dry. This technology spread widely. The first paper mill in America was started in Roxboro, Pennsylvania, by German immigrant Wilhelm Rittenhouse in 1690.

In 1832, Charles Fenerty made newsprint, which was the first paper made from wood pulp. Corrugated or pleated paper was patented in 1856 by two Englishmen—Healey and Allen. In 1870, American Robert Gair developed the cardboard box that was made to be folded in assembly. In 1871, New Yorker Albert Jones patented the first cardboard shipping materials.[1]

Paper, well, the business of paper built Schoettle's catboat, the Silent Maid.

Silent Maid's story has its deepest roots, unlikely as this may seem, with decisions made in the politically unstable Germany of early 19th century Europe. From there descended the forceful and innovative Schoettle generation from which *Silent Maid* arose. Unraveling their history requires some background that would have been impossible but for the help of Philip Schoettle, nephew of Edwin Schoettle, who gave me a chart of the family's genealogy. Since given names were repeated from generation to generation (there were, for example, at least four Ferdinands), I surely would have been lost without the complex dendritic chart Phil supplied!

The family name in the original German was spelled "Schöttle," with an umlaut over the "o" approximating the sound of lip-forming both "o" and "e" at the same time. Even the German arm of the family seems to have adopted the use of the "oe" spelling. The American Schoettles pronounce their name as "Schuttle." The earliest date recorded in that genealogy was written in a family Bible by Marie von Schoettle and marks the birth of Wilhelm Schoettle on April 4, 1803.

Wilhelm's future wife, Christine Henne (Schoettle), was born in 1816. This year was remarkable in history because much of the world had unprecedented and destructive weather, which compounded the political unrest. In 1815, the eruption of the immense Pacific *Tambora* volcano had begun darkening earth's atmosphere with a cloud of fine suspended ash, and the loss of sunlight over much of the northern hemisphere throughout 1816 put Europe and America through the "year without a summer." The impact on agriculture was incalculable. Thomas Jefferson, just retired from the U.S. Presidency and back farming at his plantation Monticello, recorded many extreme low temperatures that year.

FIGURE 2-2. **Schoettle family arms.**
Provided by Philip Alden Schoettle, Bay Head

His farms suffered crop failures that deepened the indebtedness that would hound him to his grave.

Frosts in Trenton, New Jersey, were recorded on and after June 6 of that year. There was drought throughout the Eastern U.S. and famine in Ireland, England, France, and elsewhere. Environmental and economic disruptions echoed for decades and had vast impacts on European politics. This may have had a role in the Schoettle family's later dislocations, due to the many German states then contending for power.

The New Jersey Coast, then standing far in the future for Wilhelm Schoettle's descendants, was a social and economic backwater, still imperfectly known. Tanner's 1816 map of New Jersey shows Cranberry Inlet still opening into Barnegat Bay (it had closed in 1812) and though several bay tributaries are on the map, Toms River, where the Schoettles would someday live, was entirely missed.[2] Despite the difficult year, some entrepreneurs anticipated a brighter future, and the first New Jersey seaside hotel for recreational visitors opened at Cape May!

The Schoettle's family seat was in Hohenfels-Esslingen, Würtemburg, a municipality that lies in Hangelsbach Valley. This once-volcanic region is surrounded by three mountains rising about 1900 ft. (580 M). Politically, in the early 19th century, these mountains were part of the Rhineland-Palatinate and later part of Prussia. From a social climate prior to 1848, power and military force was systematically coalesced as "unification of the German Nation State" proceeded.[3]

The Schoettle family records no maritime history in Europe; one man was a *Bäkermeister* (master baker). Bakers were valued crafts people in the early 19th century German States and were compensated at levels above those of common tradespeople. Wilhelm was designated *Professor*, and was remembered as a very strict old-time schoolmaster. He also had strong political ideas that were not in accordance with the contemporary government. He was apparently vocal about his views.

Family tradition records that Wilhelm opposed the rising militarism, which would eventually spin Europe into successive wars. With this warlike philosophy in the ascendency, and when Wilhelm was 36-years-old and a father, the family was politically banned for some years and lived in *Schwartzwaldkreis* (the Black Forest, a partially forested region of many municipalities in the west of Germany).

These were, according to Philip Schoettle, very hard times for the family.[4] Wilhelm's son Ferdinand Eberhardt was born there in 1839, second of seven children. He later recounted that, as a child, he had been tasked with gathering and hauling home the family's firewood. The banishment lasted a few years, said granddaughter Mary, but despite the hardship, Ferdinand managed a good education, to fit him for a schoolmaster's career as well.[5]

These were serious times that engendered strong ideas amongst the *intelligentsia*, too. Frederic Chopin composed a spirited *polonaise* in 1848, the year of revolution in France. His lover and companion, the woman activist George Sand, was so excited by the piece she said it should always thereafter be known as "The Heroic." Most Americans know this piece from its romantic adaptation as the popular song "Till the End of Time."[6] Edwin Schoettle and his wife Sara, supporters of the Philadelphia Orchestra in their time, would know this piece from a later context. Such are echoes of this strife, which filtered down to our century.

Ferdinand Schoettle, rejecting violence and fearing it would spread from troubled France and envelop his life, found his prospects for staying in Germany less and less attractive. He thus resolved to immigrate to the United States, arriving on June 27, 1859, just after his 20th birthday. He settled in Philadelphia as part of a sustained stream of Germans migrating to the new world, which had begun in the latter 18th century and would continue to do so through much of the 19th century.

Accustomed throughout his youth to the modest summer temperatures in central Europe, Schoettle was shocked at the intensity of summer heat in urban Philadelphia.[7] People in those times also had no concept of humidity and its relationship to discomfort. The dress codes of the time were inflexible, for business and polite society, despite the onslaught of summer heat and, of course, there was nothing like an electric fan or air conditioning. Young Schoettle, nonetheless, persevered and made his way in this strange, uncomfortable environment.

FIGURE 2-3. Part of the current German Federal Republic, an inland region where the Schoettle families lived during the early to mid-19th century.

Within the year, in May of 1860, young Ferdinand filed declarations in the Court of Common Pleas to become a U.S. citizen. An eager and creative young man, he entered the paper business in Philadelphia with Mr. Charles Beck.[8] While employed there, he looked carefully at bottlenecks in the manufacturing process. He found a serious one in the cutting of blanks to be formed into boxes, which had been done by hand. His solution was the invention of the shears. Ferdinand's grandson Karl Schoettle describes this innovation as two counter-rotating blades into which thick stacks of paper were fed. The blades acted just like high-speed scissors, cutting the entire stack cleanly.

Grandson Karl indicates that his grandfather patented this device and that it was financially successful. In 1930, Ferdinand's daughter Mary wrote that as a young girl her father gave her "a good sized diamond in a gold pin"[9] for making fair copies of the patent documents.

Ferdinand, thereafter, forged out into business for himself, with the shears carving a pathway for him. He was successful enough that, at his premature death, his wife "would never have to worry about keeping the wolf away from the door." [10] His choice of the paper business was not unprecedented. After all, German immigrant Wilhelm Rittenhouse had been the first paper manufacturer in America! Relations with his original partner Charles Beck apparently remained cordial, and Beck later had a house near the Schoettles on Island Heights. Charles Beck, Jr., would be a shipmate of Ferdinand's son Edwin in 1926.

Ferdinand started manufacturing paper boxes on a small scale in 1860 or (the *Gazetteer* says) 1861. "The superiority of the product, however, speedily developed a growing demand that taxed his facilities to the utmost."[11]

Edwin Schoettle, speaking of his father, said that in the early days of American industrial consolidation, many products, such as knit goods, were produced by individuals working all hours of the day and night in home workshops. In Philadelphia, one public-spirited man offered his barn as a place where women could come together and do their craft in well-lighted common conditions. The single location also served as a marketplace for selling their goods. Ferdinand made all the boxes for these knit goods, which required quickly satisfying the demand for a large number of containers.

Edwin said that a driver would take each day's box production by wagon the six miles up to Chestnut Hill, where the barn/ factory was located and take orders from the producers for the next day's work. He returned with those orders and the people in the box factory would work until they'd completed the units for delivery the next day—regardless of how late they toiled to complete them. Two nascent industries thus fed each other's growth.[12]

With his feet on the ground, circa 1864, Ferdinand married an Irish-American girl named Mary A. Galvan, who was three years his junior. Between 1867 and 1886, they had nine children; that was a lot of work. Surviving to adulthood were five boys and two girls, all born in Pennsylvania.

Most of the broader Schoettle family remained in Europe, but a brother William (Wilhelm) Gottlieb (b. 1846) who had migrated to Chicago resided with Ferdinand at the 1870 census, and later died in Philadelphia.[13]

Philip Schoettle said that generations into the family's American experience, some of the U.S. scions visited the old country and found relatives there stiff and, well . . . Germanic, sitting upright with stiff white celluloid collars![14] Philip, likely the most laid-back of all the Schoettles today, smiles at that experience.

Ferdinand and his family then lived in Germantown, and he commuted by train into the city. While he toiled at making his way to captain part of American industry, sailing as a sport was already developing on Toms River. The Toms River Challenge Cup, inaugurated in 1871, was one of the world's earliest racing trophies and set the scene for the Schoettles and the *Silent Maid* to come.

Ferdinand became a naturalized U.S. citizen in 1872, which seems a long wait, though that's what the history records. Also in that year, the now-successful Schoettle Paper Box Company moved to a larger 20 by 300 foot facility along Branch Street, extending through an entire city block to a four-story building at 11th Street and Race Street. This was the largest factory of its kind in Philadelphia at that time. This district in Philadelphia is now known as Fishtown and lay near Schmidt's Piazza (so named for the famous German beer!)

Edwin J., the fifth child and fourth son of Ferdinand and Mary (who would build *Silent Maid*), was born in 1876. This was the United States' Centennial Year, and his father placed an advertisement in, *Burley's United States Centennial Gazetteer and Guide* to publicize his successful and growing firm. The authors of this *Gazetteer* took it from there. To give perspective, Burley's characterized the American paper box industry at that time as comprised of 234 companies employing 4486 people, 3062 of whom were women. Production of the industry in 1875 (the most recent available year) was valued at $3.9 million. Schoettle's factory was one of only ten paper manufacturing enterprises nationwide powered by steam engines.[15]

In 1884, Schoettle's earlier version manufacturing machines were entering the used market as newer refinements came on line. In 1875, Schoettle's patented shears[16] had been the foundation of his family fortune. The *Printer's Circular & Stationers & Publisher's Gazette* for that year carried five advertisements for "30 inch Schoettle's Patent Straw Board Cutter(s)" at $45 each.[17] Schoettle progress and innovation was swift and efficient.

* * *

In 1880, Mary and Ferdinand lived in Philadelphia at 202 Wister Street with children Mary, William, Ferdinand, Mark, Edwin, and Ralph. A three-story frame house still occupies this residential neighborhood address.[18] Ferdinand had certainly not acclimated to Philadelphia's stifling summer heat and with resources now at his command, it was time to seek relief for himself and the family.

Recent railroad extensions to the Atlantic coast began offering urban residents access to sea breezes and saltwater bathing with just a few hours' travel. The Pennsylvania Railroad (PRR) had built its line from Camden across central New Jersey's Pine Barrens to Beachwood, and then in 1881 across Barnegat Bay to Seaside Park. Many people traveling to the coast for recreation simply stopped on the bay-shore at Barnegat Pier and spent the day fishing or enjoying the cool afternoon bay breezes. Starting about 1915, an adjacent cottage community developed, which would be called Ocean Gate.

Island Heights itself was growing in influence and economic significance and a few years later a wooden trestle on driven pilings was erected to create a rail spur, which crossed Toms River in a northerly direction to serve that community's transportation needs.

This extended direct rail service to Island Heights. Once ashore, there was a half-mile spur of track with a coal and lumber depot at the end. There, a switched "Y" shaped branch allowed cars to be left for loading and unloading. The working cars and engine were still backed up (yes, in reverse) going one way across Toms River. A railroad station was constructed at Island Heights in 1884, and later from this location, a wide boardwalk promenade swept down the breezy south shore of Island Heights.

A traveler, writing for the *New Jersey Courier* in June 1902, describes crossing the Toms River trestle in a railroad passenger coach. The opening portion of the trestle, or draw, was hand-cranked open and shut.

"At Island Heights we cross over the new draw, which winds as slow as a Waterbury watch. [The Waterbury watch was a famously accurate brand of pocket-watch, widely used by railroad men at the time. They ran a long time, thus took a while to wind!] From the bridge can be seen the beautiful panorama of Toms River to the west and to the east, its green and buff shores, blue waters, and gleaming white sails. . . . Island Heights [the] village above shows its best from the river—as picturesque a bit of scenery as one could wish to see."[19]

The laborious and slow swing bridge was apparently unmanned and boats wishing to pass were expected to have their crews open it themselves, and then restore it as they found it.

FIGURE 2-4. Catboats negotiate an inconvenient swing-bridge. This one crossed Barnegat Bay to Seaside in 1881, carrying rail service to the barrier island.

Watercolor (1905) by Dr. S.C. Street, Island Heights. Donation M.Gowdy and L. Page, Ocean County Historical Society

FIGURE 2-5. In 1883, the PRR Bridge causeway (background) crossed Toms River just upstream of Island heights, interfering with free passage for these two reefed-down catboats.

Crosstrees, Schoettle family, with permission

With such relatively swift and convenient transportation available from Philadelphia to the shore, Ferdinand Schoettle found his potential escape from those infernal hot summers. He looked across the Delaware River to New Jersey and determined to bring his family to Island Heights. The settlement there, on what was once called Toms River Island, had been started in 1877 by Rev. Jacob B. Graw, a Methodist minister from New Brunswick, NJ, as a camp meeting site and summer resort. He formed the Island Heights Association and purchased 172 acres of which 10 were made into the campground on which 30 cottages would be erected.

FIGURE 2-6. **One of the tiny camp meeting cottages erected atop Island Heights.**

Kent Mountford photograph

The Reverend John Simpson[20] was Superintendent of the Camp Meeting Association at its founding. You know intimately the face of his grandson H. Ormand Simpson, who became the real life model for that iconic 1942 poster of Uncle Sam pointing right at you, which was created by Ocean County artist Charles R. Chickering.[21]

Considered one of the community's founders, Howard Van Sant built one of the earliest permanent homes there in 1879. He would later write a popular book *Barnegat Pirates*[22] and for a time became Mayor of Island Heights. In the late 19th century, other homes followed, residents being drawn by the ethical and environmental attributes of this high ground almost surrounded by water. Ferdinand Schoettle (or, as Mary Schoettle Mitchell suggests, her *grandmother*[23]) engaged a small rental house for the summer of 1882, using Van Sant as agent. It was on the bluff overlooking water, east of where today's community access pier is located.[24] The cottage had a fine view towards Barnegat Bay and the distant barrier islands, with unbroken access to prevailing and cooling southeast and southwest bay breezes.

The entire Schoettle family, by then including two daughters, three brothers, and Edwin at age 6, arrived on the train, no doubt hot, tired of breathing smoke, and inhaling cinders from the locomotive. Since the rail trestle across Toms River was not completed until 1883, they also had to take a boat across to Island Heights that first day. "Mother," Mary Galvan Schoettle, settled the whole bunch in Van Sant's rental cottage and they began homemaking as evening fell.

FIGURE 2-7. **Mary (Galvan) Schoettle reading a newspaper aboard son Edwin's catboat *Scat*, before 1917. This portrait suggests the aplomb that sent her home in a huff from rustic Island Heights.**

Mary Schoettle Mitchell in the Catboat Association Bulletin, *No. 58, March 1979*

The mosquitoes, it is said, came out (as they always do)[25] and during the night a fierce Barnegat thunder squall swept in from the southwest, its lightning dramatic over Toms River, and the gusts of wind especially frightening atop Island Heights' bluffs.

When daylight came, Mary Schoettle bustled straight to Mr. Van Sant and tried to break the lease. He was unyielding, and she stomped back to Ferdinand announcing in no uncertain terms that she would "not have my daughters stay in such a place."[26] She was on the next train with the girls back to Philadelphia and proper, polite civilization, leaving Ferdinand and the four boys to face these rigors alone. "Thank God," Edwin wrote years later that he had not been dragged back to Philadelphia.

The boys thrived on Toms River, quickly taking to the water. "The summer was replete with many interesting incidents," Edwin Schoettle wrote late in life. "I learned to swim and row and . . . was allowed all kinds of liberties with (my) row boat."[27] Thus young Edwin found one of his life sources of energy and enthusiasm. A later brochure touting the region's recreational virtues said: "One season at Toms

River remodels a man's ideas of sport and recreation, and two seasons makes Tom's (sic) River a habit that lasts as long as life itself."[28] It was exactly that for Edwin J. Schoettle, and it was much the same for his brothers and, to some extent, his sister Alice, who at least also seemed to dabble in boating.

At age seven, Edwin started sailing with his brother Marc in a borrowed 15-foot gunning sneakbox owned by Bill Brown who lived on the South bank of Toms River. The boys' enthusiasm for sailing was quickly apparent. Edwin, being unspecific, later recounted in his book that he'd owned "a half dozen small craft, designed by builders" before *Silent Maid* entered his life.[29]

FIGURE 2-8. An old gunning sneakbox found buried after a storm on Swan Point by Craig Mohr in 1958. It shows a small cockpit, fold-down wooden oarlocks, and iron runners for beaching or hauling the boat over ice. It would have had a "cat" spritsail rig the spars of which could be stored inside the boat and the cockpit covered with a hatch.
Right: The author's sketch plan for this same gunning box.

Kent Mountford photograph

"DEVIL'S COFFIN"
A 12' BARNEGAT BAY SNEAKBOX AFTER CAPT. HAZELTON SEAMAN, 1836

NOTE: MOTOR BOARD, GUN LOCKER ON STBD, IRON RUNNERS FOR ICE. CEDAR W. COPPERFAST. KM.

Meanwhile, Edwin's father's influence in manufacturing was growing in downtown Philadelphia to which Ferdinand commuted from Germantown. The book *Illustrated Philadelphia, Its Wealth and Industries, 1889,* described Ferdinand Schoettle as the "leading, most able and enterprising paper-box-manufacturer in Philadelphia." By then Ferdinand employed about 150 men, using "the finest patented machinery run by steam power . . . [making] every variety of round and square boxes to order for the dry goods trade, the gents furnishings and fancy goods trade, grocery houses, druggists . . . while the lowest cash prices are quoted." Now, how could you beat that combination?

Ferdinand was said to be "possessed of sound judgment, progressive methods and a thorough knowledge of the wants of the best classes of trade." The company's product specialty was "rigid, set-up style boxes" according to Karl Schoettle's account.[30] Hinting at significant personality traits, i.e., control, that had accompanied him from Germany, "Mr. Schoettle gives close personal supervision over every department of his model establishment."[31] These traits he would pass on to his sons. Edwin, Karl Schoettle says, learned the business from his father as a child, but after his father's death, his brother William ran the original company.

Edwin followed in his father's industrial footsteps by starting his own paper box company. One of his contributions to the industry was to perfect boxes that folded along pre-scored lines (like the bakery containers with which I grew up starting in the 1940s). His success was eventually such that he bought the company that had been his father Ferdinand's and refined the manufacturing processes for both product lines. Edwin was later instrumental in mechanizing many formerly mind-dulling, hand-performed operations, and the introduction of steam power to his factory greatly accelerated production. He also had an early role in founding the paper industry's leading publication *Shears*, which not surprisingly began covering techniques he had pioneered!

Edwin said that his father was ". . . a man of determination and temper [and] his hands fell many times heavily on those who did bad work or did not follow his instructions, but those

FIGURE 2-9. Letters patent and one mechanical drawing for variations on a paper box machine filed by Ferdinand Schoettle's estate in May and September 1895.

Schoettle Estate, Karl Schoettle

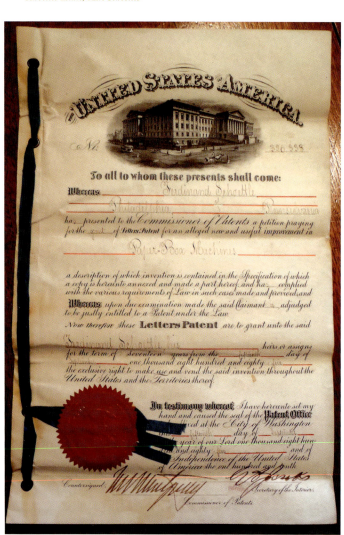

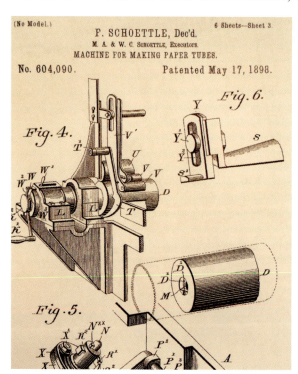

who were efficient cherished his few kind words, respected and liked him.[32] These elements of character seem to have been inherited or adopted by Edwin in the raising of his own sons!

Ferdinand Schoettle died on June 12, 1895, at the relatively young age of 56 when his youngest children, Alice and Arthur, were only two and three years old, respectively. While Mary Galvan Schoettle carried on as matriarch until her death at Philadelphia in 1917 at age 75,[33] there was certainly a vacuum in the family hierarchy. Ferdinand's success in life and business, however, was merited and would continue to benefit the generations that followed.

* * *

In 1896, the brothers (William then about 30, Ferdinand II two years younger, Marc 26, Edwin 23, and Ralph 20) engaged family friend and architect Charles Klauder and built their own communal family cottage on five acres of sloping land above the bluffs at Island Heights. They named their place the Anchorage. It was a modest cottage with a commanding view out toward Toms River and heated by a central fireplace. Upstairs was a single, large room with ten beds lined up to adequately accommodate them and the younger boys.

It was a neat and compact sailor's homeport: above the warming mass of brick fireplace, which must have burnt constantly in autumn weather, a hatch through the sleeping loft floor gave access to a dry locker for storing sails. A shed-roofed porch ranged across the entire front, and in the eaves at each end were doors through which small boat spars and rigging could be slid for winter storage.

While Edwin and Marc were accomplished sailors, their brothers William and Ferdinand II eventually built power boats. Ferdinand II built his steam yacht *Mary* in 1910 (named for his older sister Mary), but apparently no pictures of this yacht remain. Also in 1910, William commissioned the *Alice* (named for their other sister Alice), an unusual steam yacht with a very big stack at Toms River. James Kirk, a shipwright[36] well known

FIGURE 2-10. **The Anchorage shortly after 1910 when 14 years old.**

House: Suzy Mitchell Davis photograph
Sign: Kent Mountford photograph

FIGURE 2-11. **The Anchorage in 2011 then owned by Phil and Marga Reynolds.**

Kent Mountford photograph

FIGURE 2-12. *(Left)* **The east side spar port over Anchorage's porch.** *(Right)* **Inside the spar locker, which had not been opened since 1971, forty years earlier.**

Kent Mountford photographs

The Schoettles and the Philadelphia Society

For Ferdinand Schoettle, fitting into the Philadelphia society and culture was not easy. While some German immigrants had served in the American Revolution, the immigrant Schoettles were culturally somewhat apart from their Pennsylvania neighbors with English roots. The German American community was a large one, however, and they developed well in the United States.

Ferdinand Schoettle had been "educated for a school master's job, he knew figures, bookkeeping and costs, with a well-developed liking for mechanical things, a natural disposition toward order, cleanliness, integrity and a square deal. He was an unusual figure and a striking personality. He was, however, still a shy man who could never overcome his awkwardness or **embarrassment in the society of people of his own intellectual and financial standing.**"[34] (Author's emphasis)

Ferdinand realized that Philadelphia, one of the nation's oldest cities, was more or less ruled by families descended from the founders. There was an annual ball called "The Assemblies," at which daughters coming of age were presented to society. When son Edwin Schoettle was of age with his own family, he refused to join this game. His family would make their own way in this free society. The Schoettles were ultimately in the Social Register and some still are, however, many in the family now find no use for this.[35]

FIGURE 2-13. William C. Schoettle's unusual steam yacht *Alice*, built in 1910 and named after his sister. This painting was done by Captain Niels Christian "Frank" Olsen who ran the yacht for her entire time under Schoettle's ownership. *Alice* is towing a skiff used by Schoettle and his friends while sport fishing. This is called the "Popsy" painting, Frank's nickname in the family.

Image from his daughter Eileen Fancher

to the family, might have been *Alice*'s builder since he was still building other smaller steam yachts in 1913. Only a single photo of the *Alice* exists, Scotch taped and a poor second-generation copy, but the boat interested me and I later found that her skipper had made a painting of her, made available through the courtesy of his daughter Eileen Fancher (see Figure 2-13).

From the first, *Alice* was captained by Niels Christian Olsen, always called "Frank" according to his daughter. When the yacht was replaced with *Alice II*, Frank also skippered that vessel through 1941 when she was decommissioned, possibly because of the beginning of World War II.

FIGURE 2-14. Will Schoettle's Sweisguth-designed, Morton-Johnson-built cruiser *Alice II*, about 1936. Schoettle's yacht was still run by Captain Frank Olsen here at the helm, and whose daughter Eileen Fancher, at this writing (2013), still lived in Island Heights.

Schoettle family photograph, Suzy Mitchell Davis

FIGURE 2-15. Little Alice Schoettle, shown about 1886 at age four[37] and as a striking young lady . . . the face that launched at least two ships! Unwilling to submit to the constraints of Victorian convention, she declined more than one offer of marriage.

Polly Schoettle Miller collection

FIGURE 2-16. **Island Heights 1905. Looking west toward Toms River Yacht Club.**

Fred Wagner, Pennsylvania impressionist. Permission of Roy Pedersen collection. The Davis family have this or a copy in their possession in Philadelphia. (Suzy Mitchell Davis)

William Schoettle, Eileen Fancher recalls, was extremely particular about the state of maintenance of his yachts. No one with improper shoes was allowed aboard, lest the impeccable decks be marred. William was an avid fisherman, but no one was allowed to land a fish on the *Alice*. One or sometimes two smaller boats were always towed during regular weekend fishing expeditions for the actual boating and cleaning of catches. From Memorial Day through Labor Day, these trips were an almost unbroken chain, a routine which William and two loyal gentleman friends followed quite rigorously for many years.[38]

In the late 1800s around Beach Haven on Long Beach Island, Edwin Schoettle was keenly aware that catboat racing was well established. He also knew there was lively competition among the fishing and sporting boats—sometimes 40 or more were locally raced with other contests held farther up-bay vying for the Toms River Cup. Established in 1871, the Toms River Cup is still raced for annually; it is second only to the America's Cup for longevity amongst U.S. racing trophies.

The field of catboats was blown away in 1901 when Philadelphian John P. Crozer (who summered at Beach Haven) commissioned the Herreschoff Boat Building Company to design and build *Merry Thought*. Nathaniel Herreschoff was called the "Wizard of Bristol" and was world renowned for the beauty, success, and innovation of his designs. His catboat *Merry Thought* was 31 feet, 2 inches overall; 26 feet, 0 inches LWL (length on the waterline when properly loaded for sailing); 11 feet, 0 inches beam, and just 27 inches draft.[39] According to Herreschoff,[40] she cost $2125 to build,[41] but others said she totaled out at $5000—more than any Barnegat Bay local could afford. Half her ballast was carried inside the hull as lead shot; John Brady says it was in bags with leather handles and could be moved to weather to hold her down when beating and to adjust trim of the boat while sailing.[42] *Merry Thought* was a very successful boat and shook the Barnegat Bay racing community thoroughly.

As Edwin developed his competitive spirit before 1900, he began watching the racing record of another catboat designed and built in 1896 by the six Crosby brothers' yards at Osterville, Massachusetts. The family built a class of catboat called variously "Crosby Cats" or "Cape Cod Catboats." Of note was the *Scat*, one of a series of design refinements built annually for and owned by Mr. F.M. Randall of Larchmont, New York.

On June 26, 1898, *The New York Times* records the sale of the class champion catboat *Scat* to Gouverneur Morris. His namesake and perhaps forbear (I think it was his great grandfather) may have been Ambassador to France Gouverneur Morris. This famous American diplomat, had a controversial role in the imprisonment and near guillotining of American patriot and author Thomas Paine during the Reign of Terror following France's late 18th century revolution.

Edwin later wrote in his own classic book *Sailing Craft*: "The *Scat* [had racing] success far greater than all the others Mr. Randall had built. . . . At that time when the *Scat* was sailed from port to port she was the cynosure of the eyes of all builders and fishermen. The **lightness of construction** and the stepping of the mast further aft, the existence of shrouds to support the light mast, the self-bailing cockpit and the built in cabin with bulkhead all aroused curiosity and interest."

Edwin's daughter Mary Schoettle Mitchell reported *Scat*'s dimensions as LOA 30 feet, LWL 28 feet, beam 12.0 feet, and draft 30 inches. *Scat*'s main was 900 square feet.[43] Edwin, in his own hand, claims it was 1000 square feet; her boom was after all 36 feet long![44] Her lines drawings do not show the portion of her rudder below waterline, but in a picture of her aground north of Atlantic City, light showing under her counter suggests that *Scat* had a balanced rudder (portions of the blade both fore and aft of the stock or shaft) rather than the simple pintle-and-gudgeon hung "barn door" rudders on most catboats of the time. While shown in Figure 2-21, this feature was nowhere discussed in the documents I recovered.

FIGURE 2-17. Schoettle's *Scat* in 1900, sailing to weather in Barnegat Bay. The round port in the forward face of her cabin trunk is diagnostic in pictures of the 1896 *Scat*.

Schoettle family photo, Suzy Mitchell Davis

Lines Drawings

For centuries wooden ships were built by "rack of eye," expressing the internal (and proprietary!) vision of the builder, or following a set of arbitrary rules set by supposed experts in the field. By the 17th and centuries, it was common for a builder to propose his design using a model carved of wood, or (as in the case of European Admiralty models) built in minute detail down to the last frame, plank, and decorative carving.

As the variety and creativity of boatbuilding—naval, commercial, or recreational—expanded, it was necessary to find a way to accurately describe how the boat would be shaped. This, starting in the 1700s, was accomplished by accurate scale drawings that represented sections through the shape of the hull along three axes: (1) crosswise, where the boat was figuratively sliced like a loaf of bread; (2) lengthwise, along planes or "waterlines" as if you sequentially lowered the boat into the water, and marked where the wet mark reached at each stage, and (3) lengthwise sections as if cut vertically splitting the hull down its center and then similar sections, or slices, were made making outwards towards the boat's point of maximum width.

These longitudinal sections gave an idea about how water would flow along the hull, and thus some indication of speed and efficiency. Once this system was established, persons of experienced eye could take these lines and judge a great deal about how a boat would behave in the water; her speed, stability, sea-keeping abilities, and plain handiness as a working vessel.

Often this "set of lines" was used to build an owner's or builder's model of the boat, and in the lofting, or laying down, of full-size timber pieces on the shipyard floor for the actual structural members to be built. Quite importantly, when a boat was successful—or unsuccessful—the characteristics of the design could be reproduced again and again, or changed.

The lines drawings of *Scat* are shown in Figure 2-21.

FIGURE 2-18. A detailed 19th century builder's model in restoration at the U.S. Naval Academy, Annapolis, MD.
Kent Mountford photograph

FIGURE 2-19. Shipwright John Brady's sawn-apart "waterline" sections and a completed scale model of *Silent Maid* made at Philadelphia Independence Seaport's workshop on the water after the original boat was measured and her set of lines drawn out following her donation to the museum in 2010.
Kent Mountford photograph

Looking closely at the sailplan, the balanced rudder is again possible to infer, especially since the lines drawing show no skeg or deadwood.

H. Manley Crosby, who had a shop in Brooklyn, incorporated such a rudder in his 1903 *Step Lively*, which anticipated many later Class A catboat features. Built for the same Randall as *Scat*, *Step Lively*'s rudder looked like a standard transom hung "barn door" rudder above water, appears to have the same underbody profile that I infer for *Scat*, with a free standing rudder and no skeg.[45]

I emphasized "lightness of construction" because this was to prove a challenge for all the newer racing cats once they were placed under the strain of heavy weather sailing!

FIGURE 2-20. *Scat* coming and going.

Photographs by Edwin Schoettle, provided by Suzy Mitchell Davis

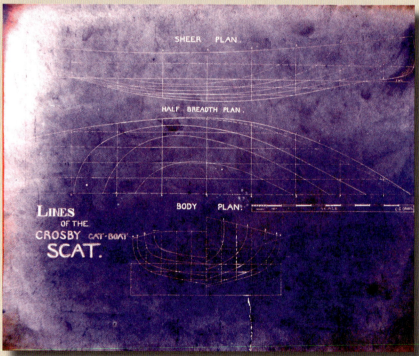

FIGURE 2-21. Blueprints of the lines and sail plan of the Crosby Yard's 1896 catboat *Scat*, brought to Barnegat Bay in 1900 by Edwin J. Schoettle.

Toms River Seaport Society

FIGURE 2-22. Catboat *Vagabond* shown in this detail from a 1903 photo taken at Island Heights. Scaling from the men, she could be over 30 feet.

Beth Truex Johnson collection, also at Ocean County Historical Society

FIGURE 2-23. *Scat* about 1903 with *(L-R)* Edwin, Marc Schoettle, and friend Charles Bilyeu working at her mainsheet traveler.

Schoettle image from Polly Schoettle Miller

It would also catch up with *Scat* after she had been sailed by the Schoettle family for three decades.

Scat piqued the interest of *Rudder* magazine in 1897, and she certainly aroused Edwin's interest, because in 1900 he and family friend and architect Charles Klauder sought to buy her from the then-current owner "a man named Gouverneur Paulding II, who tried to skin us alive when he sold *Scat* to us at $275 with the knowledge there was a lien on it for over $300."[46] The broker negotiated the deal and finally cleared the title.

Significantly, they made the choice to keep her name. Once *Scat* was in Barnegat Bay, Edwin, his brother Marc, Charles Klauder, and brothers Charles and Leonides Beck campaigned her at races up and down the bay and coastwise between Barnegat Inlet and Atlantic City. The Becks were apparently sons of Charles Beck, with whom Ferdinand had gone into business in the 1860s. Charles Beck also had a house in Island Heights next to where the Schoettle sons built their cottage, Anchorage.[47]

In 1900, Amos Lewis of Forked River built the catboat *Bouquet* from a design by A. Cary Smith. Pretty and fast, she had a cabin that could be removed for racing—a common feature in Barnegat charter cats, which contributed to the general opinion that they were wholesome boats fit for both cruising and racing. *Bouquet* began racing with great success and was with her immense open cockpit an impressively big daysailer without her cabin.[48]

Edwin contended that after 1900, both *Scat* and *Bouquet* "influenced the design and construction of all [future] catboats."[49] Still, *Bouquet* was not the only challenger at the turn of the century; boats were being designed by local men like F.O. Bailey, V.D. Bacon, W.P Kirk (who was a member of one of the Toms River builder families elsewhere mentioned), and by outsiders like Charles D. Mower (naval architect and later friend and sailing companion to Edwin). Even the famous Nathaniel Herreschoff, "Wizard of Bristol" (RI) weighed into the fray. The latter had designed *Wanda* for owner Fred Bedford, and she was so fast, she virtually ended catboat racing on Long Island Sound.[50] There was strong competition to build a boat to win the many trophy cups being raced for around Barnegat Bay.

In 1902, a test for *Scat* was posed on Barnegat Bay. Another cat, the *Franroy*, was built to compete for the Sewell Cup at Seaside Park. The *New Jersey Courier* speculated:

"The *Vagabond, Lazyjack,* and *Bouquet* [all] think they can see the Sewell Cup ensconced in their cozy parlors, wreathed in red after the second Saturday in August."[51] Besides *Franroy* there were other boats in the fleet of eight, including the *Vim,* built 1900 (she lost her sail). Edwin, sailing *Scat,* did not win. *Bouquet* took the Sewell Cup, which she had won before.[52]

Edwin and his mates campaigned *Scat* as far south as Atlantic City. On one such cruise in 1903, they ran aground in Grassy Bay,[53] Edwin describing this as about 15 miles north of Atlantic City. Tension on the anchor rode in Figure 2-24 shows they had tried to pull her off at first, but were unsuccessful. The fall of tide, several feet, left *Scat* high and dry, exposing her cut-away forefoot, counter stern, and the rudder with light passing under the grounded boat, supporting my contention about its unusual configuration. They sloppily furled her mainsail, walked around on the dried out flats, took a picture, and let her sit, anchor out, until the tide refloated her.

Short trips for a morning or afternoon sail took *Scat* across Toms River about a mile west of Good Luck Point. The beach was wide and sandy, backed by pine woods with clumps of summer eelgrass drifted ashore from the shallows. With her shoal draft, *Scat* could be nosed ashore, and in light airs her main simply left hoisted, luffing slowly in the breeze.

Edwin speaks for thousands of us who later rued destruction of the bay's pristine shorelines: "This wonderful beach was ruined when it became the waterfront of Ocean Gate [an early developed community] started about 1915." (See this handwritten note in Figure 2-25). Whatever would Edwin think about the waterfront development that

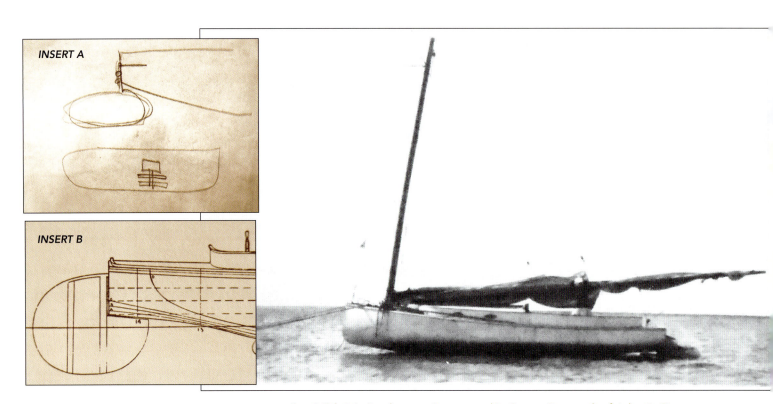

FIGURE 2-24. *Scat I,* Edwin's Crosby cat, sits aground in Grassy Bay north of Atlantic City. Note the light showing under her stern, which could suggest a balanced rudder design. *Inset A:* Sweisguth's sketch of a balanced rudder. *Inset B:* H. Manley Crosby's 1896 balanced catboat rudder on *Step Lively.*

Main photogragh: Schoettle image from Polly Schoettle Miller
Inset A: Toms River Seaport Society
Inset B: Catboat Association[54]

Scat's Decades with the Schoettle Family

Scat remained in the family for at least three decades. Edwin writes in his book *Sailing Craft* (1928) "It is interesting to note that the *Scat*, built in 1896 and now over thirty years old, is at present doing duty racing and pleasure sailing."[55] True enough, but her relatively light construction was exacting an eventual toll on her soundness.

In 1923, Edwin says that *Scat's* stem iron (supporting the mast from strains bending the mast towards the stern) was carried away during a fall race at Mantoloking, and the mast "was broken half through at the deck" (surgically, this was a green-stick fracture, where the fibers of the mast separated, but the mast still stood at an angle). He blames the fitting failure for the break. His crew gingerly sailed Scat home with the mast at a rakish angle. The split was fixed by having an iron collar three-feet-high fashioned to cover the entire break.[56] (Of course, this was before the era of Resorcinol glues[57] or epoxy adhesives.)

In 1925, Edwin's daughter Mary set off from Toms River in *Scat* with brother Ferdinand and family friend Jan Crabbe for the annual Beach Haven Cruise, down-bay a distance of some 19 nautical miles as the crow flies. My guess is that once down Toms River, they were hard on the wind and Scat, being a quarter century old by that time, was getting pretty soft in the bilges. Mary recalls that "we had gone only a few miles when we realized that the cabin floor was full of water. We just managed to get her to a pier . . . and . . . We were quite the heroes of the weekend. Our friends renamed the boat the *Scat Sunk*."[58]

Scat was sold to a Mr. Walker of Walker Electric Co. (later William and Scott) for $875. Edwin's own notes give the date as 1922, but he contradicts this later. Mary Schoettle Mitchell remembered her last sail as 1925. When later sold perhaps two times, however, the boat was taken back to New England from whence she had come.[59]

The *Scat* name was resurrected by the Schoettles almost 20 years later. The lovely and practical Lightning Class, designed by Rod Stephens, was introduced in 1939. Within three years of racing, the class had grown to 750 boats. Edwin bought one of these boats in 1941 and named her *Scat* harking back to his wonderful old catboat, and that was the last *Scat* in the Schoettle fleet!

SCAT-1 on the beach across the Toms River about on a mile west of. Good Luck Point this beautiful beach was ruined when it became the river front of ocean gate – started about 1915

FIGURE 2-25. **Scat** nosed up on a deserted natural shoreline that later became the developed community waterfront of Ocean Gate.

Schoettle image from Polly Schoettle Miller

has since beset poor Barnegat Bay? I shared his frustration many times as most of the last large undeveloped tracts were swallowed during my own youth.

Eventually, in 1907, when wife-to-be Sara entered his life permanently, Edwin bought out Klauder's share in the boat and *Scat* remained his primary catboat for nine years, with Sara his most valued crew.

* * *

For the Schoettle brothers, the communal arrangement at Anchorage worked for a while, but as family circumstances evolved, Marc and Edwin began bumping against each other in such close quarters and changed their personal plans. Marc had been feeling his way into the culture of Bay Head for some years. There's a photo taken by him there about 1888 (when he was just 15) of the Bay Head Lifesaving Station and its crew and inscribed on the back: "Hope these nice men won't have to be called out [to sea]."

By 1902, Marc Schoettle was sailing his own sloop *Dyriad* around and outside Barnegat Bay. He moved to Bay Head in 1915 and built a house facing the sea at Goetz Street and East Bay Avenue, which still stands. This was intended to be a Schoettle family house, to be shared with his mother, four brothers and two sisters.[60] Marc Schoettle soon courted and, in 1920, married Reta Clarkson Metcalfe, daughter of Bay Head's Mayor Robert Henshaw Metcalfe.[61]

Group housing bodes ill for newlywed couples, as his brother Edwin would also soon realize, and Marc bought a different house and two extra lots at 21 Howe Street in Bayhead, where he and Reta began homemaking. The Schoettle family was instrumental in founding Bay Head's Catholic Church, and Edwin's wife Sara subsequently donated one of the stained glass windows.[62]

Edwin met Sara Mullarky, likely at the Convent of the Sacred Heart, which she attended with his sister Alice. He was struck by this pretty little girl (seven years his junior) and reportedly told her "When you get old enough, I'm going to marry you." Good to his word (he was never known to be other than that) he proposed to her, perhaps in 1904 when she was 21, by which time, Edwin was already planning to build his own home at Island Heights. Edwin says of Sara "she was still Sara L. Mullarky at that time," and came to sail with him aboard *Scat* early in the 1907 season. He was truly in love with this young woman and they sailed together many years "with great success and joy . . . Thank God for Sara."[63] They were married

FIGURE 2-26. Marc Schoettle's sloop *Dyriad* entering Barnegat Inlet in 1902.

Philip Schoettle photograph

FIGURE 2-27. *(Left)* Sara Mullarky at her marriage in 1907 to Edwin J. Schoettle and *(right)* likely aboard catboat *Scat* in 1907. This is my favorite picture of her.

Photographs from Crosstrees, Suzy Mitchell Davis

in 1907 and Charles Klauder, the architect, former *Scat* co-owner, and close friend, was Edwin's best man.

Edwin's and Sara's first child was named Edwin; followed by Mary, born 1908; Ferdinand was born in 1911; and finally there was Karl A. born in 1914. Sara had other babies that did not survive. All four offspring reaching adulthood were born in Philadelphia.

Children did not dissuade Sara from sailing everywhere with Edwin on *Scat*.[64] Of course, it was easier when family resources enabled sufficient household help! Edwin's personal notebook recorded arriving with the family at Crosstrees together with four household staff, and all according to his appraisal were doing well![65] Sara must have been pretty far along with one of her pregnancies by then, because she delivered later that summer.

Daughter Mary Schoettle Mitchell recounts that the ladies of Island Heights Yacht Club were nonetheless scandalized when Edwin and Sara packed up the bassinet and took her sailing the same year she was born (1908)! Mary had many happy memories of *Scat*, aboard which she sailed through much of her teen years, until at least 1925.

For Edwin, the communal summer house Anchorage and the Bay Head residence were impractical now that he had a bride. The idea for their Island Heights home, conceived in 1904,[66] was fleshed out starting in 1909 when architect Charles Klauder designed a "cottage" and construction was started on a parcel at the summit of the community's ancient periglacial dune.[67] Clearing the ground for construction left the home site surrounded by naked sandy lumps and Edwin was quick to engage local gardeners setting this to rights with plantings and a lawn. It seems that the dwelling was ready for occupancy in 1910.

The house would be known as Crosstrees, an apparent play on the woodlands around it and the nautical term describing timbers aloft at the mainmast head of a square rigged ship. These support tightened rope shrouds and enable the lofty topmasts of a sailing vessel to stand against storm winds.

FIGURE 2-28. **Crosstrees in October of 1911 (with** [probably] Sara Schoettle standing out front) and *(right)* the home in 1920, looking eastward and up from the bank at the remarkable sash windows. *Inset:* Looking up at the mainmast crosstrees of **Dove**, a replica square rigged barque.

Schoettle family photographs, Suzy Mitchell Davis
Inset: Kent Mountford photograph

A singular feature of the house was the set of immense, counterweighted, downward sliding window sashes that disappeared into slots stretching below the foundation. Edwin particularly wanted Klauder to design these to catch and cross ventilate with every hint of summer breeze.

Since they were built in a time before easily available, large, tempered glass plate, subsequent generations still have to wash the 32 small panes in each. There is also the matter of puttying and painting them, too!

FIGURE 2-29. **Looking south in the great room at Crosstrees, showing architect Charles Klauder's huge downward-opening, 32-pane sashes. What a dramatic room in which successful sailors could relax.**
Kent Mountford photograph

FIGURE 2-30. **Twenty-foot sneakbox** *Arran*, **1907.**
Orton G. Dale, Ocean County Historical Society, with permission[70]

*   *   *

Charles Mower of Bowes and Mower (Philadelphia naval architects and engineers) designed a class of 20-foot sneakboxes for which Edwin negotiated with Barnegat Bay Yacht Racing Association (BBYRA) to establish as a racing fleet for Island Heights Yacht Club. Mower would supervise their construction in Atlantic City at a group rate, per boat of $275, plus $40 for a sail.[68] Mower suggested in his letter to Edwin that folks could join in this group offer at the same price, but he could not guarantee it for any later sign-ons. These swift boats were raced hard with a large crew heaving sandbags from leeward to windward at each tack as additional ballast.

It's not clear how Edwin and Francis Sweisguth found each other to begin what would be a virtually lifetime collaboration, but Sweisguth, working in the office of William Gardner, had made a name for himself in 1910 by drawing the plans and successfully tweaking the design of what became the Star class of sailboats. This fleet grew by leaps and bounds and is still raced internationally well over a century later.[69] Edwin, an avid racer, would certainly have known of Sweisguth's success. There was at least one Star boat in the family which one of the boys sailed.

In 1913, Sweisguth, working from his address "Room 1768 E. 42nd St. in New York," decided to go beyond his Star class and produced his first design for Edwin: the *Mull* (a nickname for Edwin's wife Sara *nee* "Mull"arky). *Mull* was a 20-foot, cat-rigged sneakbox and Schoettle said this "marked the end of all this [moveable ballast and excessive crews]; she was sailed without sand bags and a crew of just three. Ferdinand (III) when he was young sailed the *Mull* as a slavey [mate] under Captain Herbert III" (yes "III") whose father was a Toms River physician. (Herbert would himself become a prominent medical man in Newark, New Jersey.[71]) Ferd received a great deal of attention and bore high expectations to match! One of the nicknames Edwin used for this son was "#3."[72] The strain on the Schoettle sons, levied by their high-powered father's expectations, may show in Figure 2-34!

Mull won the pennant for several years.[73] These big, hard-sailed sneakboxes may have been precursors to the class "E" bilgeboard Scows, which Edwin, together with Frank Thatcher and brothers Mitchell and Edwin Chance, had an important role in bringing to Barnegat Bay[74] in 1924. Grandson Michael Schoettle says that Edwin fronted the money for the first brace of "E"s,[75] and when the boats were delivered, Edwin felt the price was too low for the quality that had been supplied and sent the boat builder a supplement.

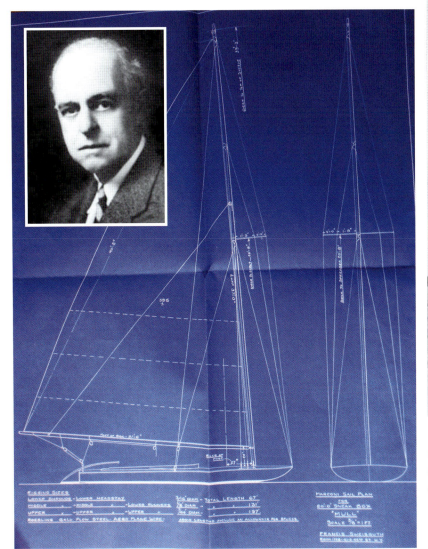

FIGURE 2-31. One of the Jones and La Borde Class E scows brought to Barnegat Bay. This may be the *Sandpiper* shown off Island Heights about 1925.

Toms River Seaport Society

FIGURE 2-32. *Mull*, Edwin's first Sweisguth-designed catboat, spreading 396 square feet in her main. Inset: Francis Sweisguth, naval architect, 1882–1970.

Toms River Seaport Society / Inset: Open source photo

These boats, in their time, were the fastest sailing vessels afloat. The Schoettles eventually owned three of them.[76] From at least 1926, Americans competed in Canada for the Sewanhaka Cup, a prized trophy since its establishment in 1898. Canadian crews dominated the field when racing on their own familiar waters. However, when the Barnegat "E" Scows started racing on their New Jersey home waters, Edwin's sons Edwin Jr, Karl R., and Ferdinand P., along with friends W.D. Horrocks, F. Slade Dale (Skipper), and others began to come into their own. A key element was sailing in Barnegat Bay, where they understood bottom topography, the unusual and sometimes predictable daily wind patterns . . . and they had enthusiastic friendly bystanders!

FIGURE 2-33. Transporting a Class E scow. Edwin Schoettle was one of a group who introduced these boats to Barnegat Bay.

Toms River Seaport Society

FIGURE 2-34. Three Schoettle sons [Ferd (#3), Edwin Jr., and Karl] flank a more matronly Sara at the helm, probably of *Scat II*, which would then have been a fairly new boat. The boys seem a bit dour for such a happy moment!

Photograph from Ferdinand Schoettle IV

FIGURE 2-35. Edwin filed this patent for a machine that would make paper tubes—consider paper towels and toilet tissue today!

Karl Schoettle image

At Seaside Park, Charles E. Lucke reported in the October 1930 *Yachting* magazine "young Ed Schoettle, (was) sailing the fast *Sally* . . ." (Sally was another family nickname for Sara, which her husband sometimes used, so this could have been a Schoettle boat.)

From race to race, the Canadian and U.S. teams switched boats in rotation, so that slight advantages in design, rigging, or how a sail was cut were smoothed out over the whole set of events. Nonetheless, moving boats from Canada to the U.S. was not easy in those times and all of the races were sailed with local boats, with some days ahead of the matches to let the Canadians acclimate.

Despite the home turf advantage, Dale and Ed Jr. were surprised in one race, when, with first and second place in hand for their boats, the predictable wind died away to nothing! All four boats in the contest had to anchor until eventually a zephyr of wind crept in . . . from a different direction carrying the "Jersey Tars" to victory: 42 points to Canada's 37 in eight races.[77] At the end of the race series, the American sailors thus defeated the skilled team of visiting Canucks.[78]

* * *

Edwin did not flag in his business interests despite all this energetic sporting activity. His businesses continued to grow and his technical knowledge was put to work improving manufacturing and filing new patents. In 1913, he and C.A. Garrett filed U.S. patent no 1032781 in July "for a paper box cutter."

Edwin also founded the Precision Manufacturing Company, through which patents were filed for equipment automating the production of other types of set-up type boxes. Grandson Karl says that some of this machinery was still in use as late as 2006. Edwin went on to create (and sponsor) several other paper product companies, sometimes taking these opportunities to assist a particularly promising entrepreneur. Karl also said that when World War I broke out Edwin's company pioneered "the first paperboard packaging for ammunition and automated the process of packing the boxes."[79]

Family members told me the Schoettle Paper Box Company also invented paper packaging that kept bread fresh for several days, allowing much wider product distribution. Few are the American households that did not benefit (and still do!) from that innovation. The same innovation was marketed to the meat products industry—notably hot dogs!—which had previously been hung in long skeins by butchers right out in the air or shipped essentially in open trays. No accounting for the flies, I suppose!

Edwin's primary business was quartered in a new nine-story building on North 11th Street. Designed by his friend and architect Charles Klauder, it was constructed in 1916 by the Turner Concrete Company and was the first pre-cast concrete structure in the city. It stands to this day and still has the family name framed in brick and emblazoned with tile over the entrance.[80]

Edwin was a man of energy and creativity moving on several fronts. Burning the candle at both ends seemed to be one of his characteristics. That trait would catch up to him in a few decades as multiple life pressures increased. Nervous exhaustion was one of the complaints described for men under pressure during this generation.[81]

FIGURE 2-36. Huge rolls of paper stock delivered at Edwin Schoettle's loading dock, where he thoughtfully cautioned draymen to water their horses frequently, providing buckets for the purpose.

Photograph from Karl Schoettle

FIGURE 2-37. Classic Harmonie Hall was razed to make way for the Schoettle Box Company building. Today it would likely be on the Historic Register!

Photograph from Karl Schoettle

FIGURE 2-38. The E.J. Schoettle Co. building at 525-33 N. 11th Street, Philadelphia, as it appeared in 2012.

Lawrence Rust, Broker, Philadelphia, with permission.

Inset: The brick and tile cartouche preserved over the main entrance. In 1957 when the building was for sale, it was advertised as having 148,000 square feet of floor space.[82]

John Wanamaker's Concern about Urban Youth in 1900

Island Heights was changing and growing too. In 1899, John Wanamaker, creator of the iconic American department store, was concerned about the moral development of the "cash" boys and girls employed in his huge Philadelphia and New York stores, whom he called Wanamaker Cadets.[83] So in 1900, he set up a military-style tent camp with a large communal building called The Barracks on the flat eastern portion of Island Heights where (of course) unisex groups of cadets were brought from the Delaware River ferry on a special train with vestibuled cars.

Taken from the depot at Island Heights by wagon, they were cycled for two weeks through what was a disciplined, but surely life-changing, experience for many urban youth.[84] Wanamaker operated the camp until the U.S. Army took up residence there during World War II.

Cranberry Inlet, long gone in Schoettle's time, had opened in 1720, piercing the Island Beach peninsula just opposite the mouth of Toms River. Incoming tidal currents eventually deposited enough sand to form permanently vegetated islands in Barnegat Bay. These remained after Cranberry closed in 1812, but would someday be a stepping-stone for another Barnegat Bay bridge.

The seaside site was later chosen for Toms River Lifesaving Station #13, built on the Duluth (architectural) plan, in 1872. A private house was built nearby two years later, and in 1875 came the Sea Side Park Hotel. These structures were a nucleus around which the two communities; Seaside Park (1898) and Seaside Heights (1913) eventually coalesced.[85] The railroad causeway, crossing Barnegat Bay from Goodluck Point in 1881, accelerated the flow of tourists and commerce, creating development opportunities for these nascent towns.

Pressure for access to the Jersey Shore was increasing and Americans found that automobiles liberated them from dependence on the railroad's fixed schedule. On the barrier Beach, a first road to Bay Head was completed in 1910; the year Edwin Schoettle first occupied Crosstrees at Island Heights.

What later became today's Route 70 extended across the New Jersey Pine Barrens giving access to Toms River's north shore and the Schoettles would soon be driving to Island Heights, their increasing wealth and busy schedules not suited to time constraints and lack of family privacy aboard a crowded train. Edwin, once a railroad user, would someday convert to an opponent of the rail trestle stretching across Toms River which now interfered with a sailor's liberties on the estuary!

Island Heights' businessmen, apparently including Edwin Schoettle, saw the potential for a roadway—I avoid saying *highway*— bridge crossing Barnegat Bay to the seaside. This would complete a loop, as had the railway, and make Bay Head and points north along the coast accessible by car. As private investors, a group of businessmen formed the Island Heights and Seaside Heights Bridge Company, and in 1914 began driving piles for a wooden toll bridge to Pelican Island and beyond. This was not an auspicious time to invest in access to a recreational coastal village. World War I had just broken out and much of the world would be in turmoil and pain for the next half decade. While Edwin was a second-generation American, he still had a German surname and this must have given the family some concern. Who, after all, might win this terrible conflict? German submarines actually sunk three U.S. vessels off the U.S. east coast during 1918, challenging sovereignty of our territorial waters for the first time since the War of 1812. This was an eerie premonition of vastly greater depredations during World War II.

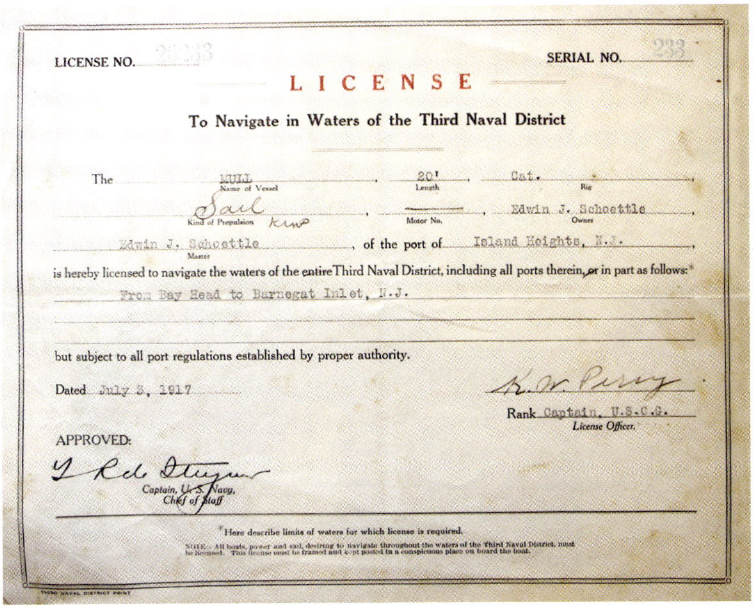

LICENSE NO. 20233 SERIAL NO. 233

LICENSE

To Navigate in Waters of the Third Naval District

The MULL (Name of Vessel), 20' (Length), Cat. (Rig)
Sail (Kind of Propulsion), (Motor No.), Edwin J. Schoettle (Owner)
Edwin J. Schoettle (Master), of the port of Island Heights, N.J.
is hereby licensed to navigate the waters of the entire Third Naval District, including all ports therein, or in part as follows:*
From Bay Head to Barnegat Inlet, N.J.

but subject to all port regulations established by proper authority.

Dated July 3, 1917

Rank Captain, U.S.C.G.
License Officer.

APPROVED:

Captain, U.S. Navy,
Chief of Staff

*Here describe limits of waters for which license is required.

NOTE.—All boats, power and sail, desiring to navigate throughout the waters of the Third Naval District, must be licensed. This license must be framed and kept posted in a conspicuous place on board the boat.

THIRD NAVAL DISTRICT PRINT

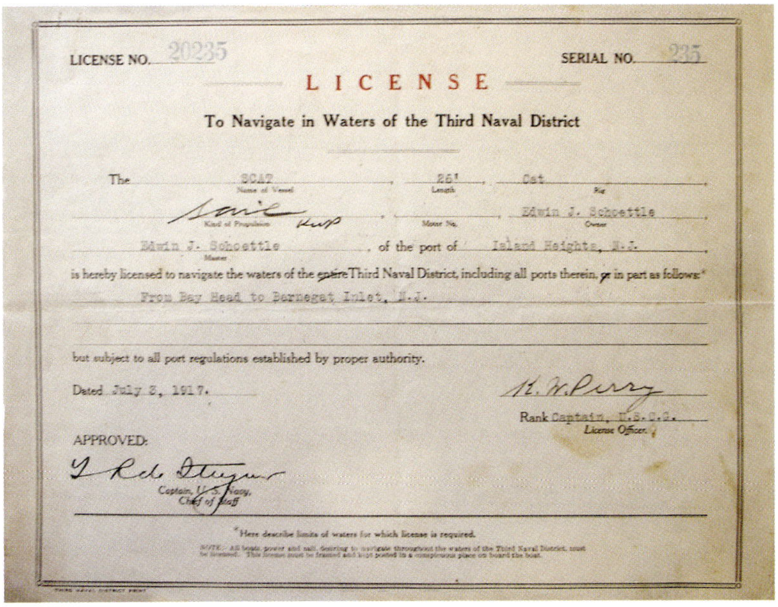

LICENSE NO. 20235 SERIAL NO. 235

LICENSE

To Navigate in Waters of the Third Naval District

The SCAT (Name of Vessel), 25' (Length), Cat (Rig)
Sail (Kind of Propulsion), (Motor No.), Edwin J. Schoettle (Owner)
Edwin J. Schoettle (Master), of the port of Island Heights, N.J.
is hereby licensed to navigate the waters of the entire Third Naval District, including all ports therein, or in part as follows:*
From Bay Head to Barnegat Inlet, N.J.

but subject to all port regulations established by proper authority.

Dated July 3, 1917.

Rank Captain, U.S.C.G.
License Officer.

APPROVED:

Captain, U.S. Navy,
Chief of Staff

*Here describe limits of waters for which license is required.

NOTE.—All boats, power and sail, desiring to navigate throughout the waters of the Third Naval District, must be licensed. This license must be framed and kept posted in a conspicuous place on board the boat.

THIRD NAVAL DISTRICT PRINT

FIGURE 2-39. Schoettle's licenses from the Third U.S. Naval District to sail *Mull* and *Scat* during World War I. A similar permit for Schoettle's first motorboat was also issued in 1917.

Displayed at Crosstrees, Suzy Mitchell Davis

Nonetheless the bridge project went forward; its local momentum was great. Residents who lived on the barrier island before it was finished tell of taking pregnant wives to the mainland in sufficient time to assure that they would go into labor under the hands of a proper physician. That would become moot with automobile access.

The World War was a terrible conflict, but distant America had what it perceived was a certain insulation. In a time before capable air forces and easily launched missiles, Edwin's access to his beloved Barnegat Bay was preserved during the years of conflict, and in fact was officially sanctioned. He obtained licenses to sail *Mull* and *Scat* as well around Barnegat Bay during the summer of 1917.

The Schoettle Children Learn to Sail on *My Pal*

During 1919–20, just after the end of World War I, Edwin teamed up with boat builder Cornelius Irons of Silverton to build a scow called *My Pal*,[86] a stable, simple sailboat to serve as a school for his young sailors, chiefly 7-year-old Karl. But the boat also became, in Edwin's words, "a particular friend to Ferd." *My Pal* was built of white pine in Schoettle's barn at Island Heights, where Irons showed up to participate in the lofting, framing, and planking.[87] Edwin thought this a very successful project. There is here a coincidence in degrees of separation between Edwin and me: Cornelius Irons also built the 1924 Barnegat catboat *Spray*, which my then wife to be and I bought during our engagement in 1970.

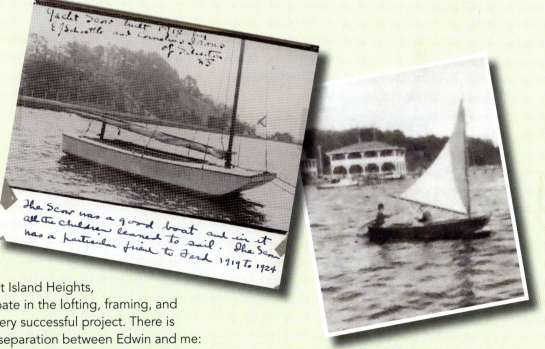

FIGURE 2-40. The cat rigged scow *My Pal* on which the Schoettle children learned to sail.

FIGURE 2-41. **The bridge in which Edwin Schoettle was an apparent investor, shown here in an old postcard owned by the author. The ice-breaking strongbacks ate on the opposite side and not shown.**

The Shinn family built the bridge to Seaside under contract and on the north side, installed reinforced piling ramps or strongbacks rising out of the water and facing up-bay. The bay, then grading to fresh water at Bay Head, froze hard most winters in those years creating huge miles-wide sheets of ice. Tides and strong northwest winds created immense friction forces across miles of solid ice, and when edge melting broke the ice's attachment to upper bay shorelines, wind would begin to drive floes against the pilings that supporting the road portion of the bridge. The ramps would lift and crack the ice sheet as it progressed, saving the structure from destruction. Remnants of these structures were still visible north of the (more modern) Mathis Bridge in the early 21st century.

Completed the year following the driving of its first pilings, the wooden bridge opened December 1, 1915. Until that time, many locals and many visitors, choosing not to use the train, which was not scheduled for *their* convenience, simply sailed across the bay for their business. The bridge, becoming known simply as the *wooden toll bridge* had a fare structure that tells a lot about the needs of the times. Each person crossed for a dime, but a horse and buggy cost a quarter. Livestock, according to historian Pauline Miller, "led or driven" across the bridge were ten cents each.[89] It's unclear whether the investors ever made any money on the tolls, but the state of New Jersey eventually bought the bridge in 1922. At that time tolls, likely quite onerous for users who believed they had a birthright to cross the bay unimpeded, were discontinued.

Pleasure traffic moved from the west to the peninsula as well; where sailing parties might have taken people across the Bay, they could now drive over. A local woman, Joan Fitzpatrick, tells of outings from Beachwood (on Toms River) with a local teacher who packed kids, five at a time, into her car and ferried them across the old rattling wooden bridge. She drove them to what was then the Phipps Estate (now Island Beach State Park) where the children gathered driftwood for a campfire to toast hotdogs. These events, with the sound of the surf behind them, were repeated a couple of times each spring and fall.[90]

The old bridge functioned for many years until government funds financed a replacement bridge with an electrically powered draw. This structure, the Thomas Mathis Bridge, was completed in 1950. It was also built by the Shinns, as would its successor the J. Stanley Tunney Bridge, a second, higher span without a lifting draw, which was commissioned in 1973. All these bridges used those once-flood tide delta islands—principally "Pelican Island"—on the west of the barrier island as stepping stones to cross Barnegat Bay.

FIGURE 2-42. **The Thomas Mathis Bridge (1950), foreground, and the J. Stanley Tunney high bridge (1973), background, shown in 2011 from Pelican Island. Both carry Route 37 across Barnegat Bay to Seaside Heights.**
Kent Mountford photograph

* * *

The Schoettles, at least until after World War I, were living in Chestnut Hill, a northwest Philadelphia suburb. They also owned prime land on the southeast corner of Rittenhouse Square, 237 South 18th Street, the very heart of the city. Grandson Karl in his family history says that Edwin and Sara had a house there and lived in it,[91] but not long after he had *Silent Maid* built in the mid-1920s, Edwin sold this property to John McShain (1898–1989) and upon that site the famous Hotel Barclay was built.[92] It opened in 1929 and was soon Philadelphia's most popular hotel, figuring prominently in the City's social and economic life and even as the setting for an obscure early science fiction movie thriller about freezing time.[93]

A condition of sale was that the Schoettles would receive an apartment on one floor of the Barclay. So, upon completion of the hotel, Edwin and family moved in. There is the suggestion that he may have begun having health problems about that time. He subsequently reigned there as patriarch, inaugurating an annual gathering for the Christmas holidays at which all the young Schoettles were summoned to make public statements before the assembled family about their achievements for the year. Polly Schoettle Miller, Edwin's granddaughter, fondly recalls these events, during which she acted like the fictional child Eloise at New York's Plaza Hotel, running around in outlandish (but to her) stylish garb.

These events were unpleasant memories for some family members because Edwin, like his father before him had high standards, and high expectations. He was gentler with the youngest, and with the girls, who when tongue-tied, would be helped along with saying their piece while sitting on Pop Pop's knee. This presents a conundrum in understanding Edwin Schoettle, the man, who caused the *Silent Maid* to be built. He was a hard-nosed father, demanding the best performance from each of his sons. If they were to be sailors—in which capacity they seemed to thrive on Toms River and Barnegat Bay—they damn well better be *good* sailors.

Given the Victorian standards firmly grounded in Philadelphia at the turn of the 20th century, this is not so much harsh as *expected for real men* at the time. Michael Capuzzo in his book *Close to Shore* writes extensively of this post-Teddy Roosevelt mind set as it was exported from Philadelphia to the Jersey Shore in a time in America where a man in business after 1900 "had to run faster just to catch up." Capuzzo describes Philadelphia physician Eugene Van Sant's "Victorian conviction that home, wife and four children were the sacred harbor in the tempest of the world. . . . [but] upon his children, he turned the stoic disciplined countenance of nineteenth-century manhood."[94] This *countenance* leveled concern at any son that did not match this ideal of manhood. I think, probably like most upper class Philadelphia fathers, this was in Edwin's directed gaze as well, and his strict German heritage did nothing to soften it.

FIGURE 2-43. Karl R. Schoettle in his first boat, built by Cornelius Irons from Silverton, New Jersey. He was a strong oarsman at 5 years of age.

Edwin Schoettle

Edwin wrote on one such growing son: "Karl was such a neat kid, and lived with us for a long time when we were at Island Heights for two winters. He did not go to boarding school at as young an age as the other boys."[95] This would appear to have been 1918–20, a tumultuous time spanning the end of World War I.

Not all of his sons stood up well to the pressure of his expectations and memories of time at the family estate Crosstrees varied from one to another. Grandson Michael, with a quizzical look, conceded that his grandfather had sometimes "been mean" to his less responsive sons. Perhaps he just expressed disappointment, hard for a kid to take, or perhaps there was more severe disapproval. On the other hand he openly delighted with those who excelled. Two grandsons later became Olympic contenders—Michael Beaver Schoettle twice so (once a Gold)[96]—and have left marks on the world sailing scene and Karl, a third, believes he has voyaged more sea miles than either of his siblings.

These were not wallflower boys: Andy (Ferdinand) raced a 5.5-meter yacht with Britton Chance in the 1952 Helsinki Olympics. They brought home a bronze medal. Andy was also a staunch family man, and his kids were tough too. Newt Kirkland says he once wrestled with Andy's son on the floor of their living room in Lawrenceville, NJ. "We even broke some furniture!" Newt laughingly says. He dated Andy's daughter Joanie Schoettle, and though she lived away from home with her brother "her father still gave me a hard time!"[97]

Edwin Schoettle, at the same time, was much gentler on his daughter Mary; most of the girls in the wider family have memories solely of his kindness, but says Suzy Mitchell Davis, "You will have other opinions from the other grandchildren."[98]

Sketching what we know about Edwin Schoettle, the man—and fairly interpreting it—requires jumping about a bit in history, which liberty I now take.

"Yes, my grandfather was very generous," says Michael Schoettle, son of Edwin's Ferdinand, but he goes on to recount that after his father Ferdinand had joined Edwin's paper box company, he had entrepreneurial instincts of his own and came to the boss one day in 1946 or 1947 proposing a set of ideas that would re-organize the company in light of post–World War II economic climate. The next morning Edwin simply fired him. Ferdinand went on to a successful career of his own, but the sting remained. "That should be in your book," says Michael. His brother Edwin also received this strong rebuke when trying to make changes in the *status quo*.

Polly Schoettle Miller, who had particularly warm feelings for Sara, whom the grandchildren called "Ganny," said that such estrangements deeply hurt Edwin, and he suffered from these losses but did not have the softness or flexibility to heal them.[99]

Another grandson, the younger Karl Schoettle who was also eventually in the paper box business, witnessed ample evidence of Edwin's generosity within the industry. Calling on one of his own clients, the company's president looked at Karl carefully and asked: "Are you the son of Edwin Schoettle, the box manufacturer?" This affirmed, the client continued, "Please, let me get my father"—who had to be chauffeured from his nearby home. When he met Karl, with extended hand he said: "Your grandfather and I started this company; he set me up and made it possible for me to buy him out at a reasonable price." He was still grateful and remembered those times, long gone, with affection.

Edwin was sometimes instrumental in helping employees become successful entrepreneurs. In 1926, Edwin hired—for $350 a month—25-year-old Arthur Newth Morris, who had been a printer and part-time Presbyterian minister. Edwin by then had a group of paper box and printing companies that bore his name. While Morris worked for Edwin, he managed several hundred employees and also went on the road, visiting east coast meat packers to market, among other things, Schoettle *hot dog boxes*, which prevented product shrinkage in a time when the filled casings were simply hung by merchants in the open like bunches of bananas. Arthur Morris had potential, and in 1935, Edwin bankrolled him $7000, which together with Morris' own savings enabled him to buy a company of his own. Before long, Edwin realized how valuable Morris had been and within six months tried to hire him back for $25,000 a year. When he declined, Edwin again helped him by selling him one of his own companies! Morris' then-modest enterprise has morphed today—with many acquisitions—into the giant Rock-Tenn Company with sales (in 2002) of $1.44 billion.[100]

Morris' son later remembered: "It was in the middle of the Depression . . . and Edwin Schoettle sat me on his lap and lectured me on the importance of hard work and then gave me a brand new one dollar bill."[101] Morris went on to paint a picture of Edwin as manager of business and of people, quoting Palmer Smith, who owned one of Edwin's factories after his death: "He was considered a fantastic leader, and his employees adored him. . . . He was innovative, and put together mechanical machinery the likes of which I have never seen."[102]

FIGURE 2-44. Edwin J. Schoettle in formal portrait, ca. 1930.

Crosstrees, Suzy Mitchell Davis with permission

* * *

Edwin Schoettle whom his friends called "the Skipper" was, in his later years, also something of a naturalist. In 1941, he, Sam Scoville, Jr., and a botanist friend travelled through the Pine Barrens towards Cape May to watch the annual hawk migration, stopping at Bennett's Bog where Edwin learned to identify native grasses. Later, birdwatching at Cape May Lighthouse they saw a rare parasitic jaeger (or Arctic Skua, *stercorarius parasiticus*) and 26 hawks wheeling in the sky at one time.

The birds, each autumn, collect at the Cape, feeding to build strength and to await a brisk northerly wind to speed them on their southerly migrations over the dangerous open waters ahead. The Schoettle party wandered farther, trading bird identifications in nearby wetlands "if you can't name 'em in three guesses" Scoville challenged, "then you can't associate with bird experts like the Skipper and myself."[103]

Edwin telephoned Scoville again during the autumn of 1941, just before the horror of WW-II descended on America, and proposed another trek through the Pine Barrens, which journey with their botanist friend, the three men commenced. Imagine the Pines almost three-quarters of a century before this writing six hundred square miles of uncharted and forgotten sand roads exploring the ruins of old iron furnaces, of Double Trouble and Bamber Lake. Bogs surrounding Bamber were then what their owner assured Schoettle and his party, a gold mine in wealth from cranberries. In reverie, the three friends came near to giving up their day jobs, "buying a bog apiece and living like kings in the Barrens."[104] In the next few years, Edwin would have reason to remember that day, as he indeed did, or we would not have had this account.

There was also an informal, seashore side to the man, shirtless and in shorts, sweating in the New Jersey summer sun. When Mary Schoettle's intended, James Mitchell, came courting, he found his future father-in-law on the porch, thus attired, and figured him to be one of the gardeners![105]

FIGURE 2-45. Edwin Schoettle, the informal man, munching a snack while seated on *Silent Maid's* cockpit coaming as she sails along northbound in a southwester with the developed barrier island to starboard.

Crosstrees, Suzy Mitchell Davis, with permission

Island Heights Recollections

Initially, even by the 1920s, all the roads on Island Heights were simply packed sand tracks through the mostly pine vegetation. The roads ran east-west and were connected by a few side streets. The narrow lanes had unmarked edges, and trees came right next to the vehicle tracks, which were always sought for shade against the summer sun. An old Island Heights' photograph shows how one family painted white horizonal strips on a a road-edge pine tree hoping to spare its lethal impact from some careless automobile operator.

Recollections,[106] jotted on a single sheet of paper, were left by one of the Schoettle children, possibly intended for some future, more detailed, history. The only clue that an Edwin Schoettle offspring left is the line "Herb [-bert III] sailed the *Mull* 20-foot sneakbox for my father in 1914— after that Tom Horrocks did." Other information gleaned from this document lends insight into the family and the community:

- The Schoettles apparently had a horse and buggy before autos came along, and it was kept at the ready by Van Schoick's stables. Grandfather Ferdinand Schoettle's daughter, the children's beloved Aunt Alice, had a horse there named Rob Roy.

- The Schoettle kids earliest friends included Margery Horter, Cath Adams, Virginia O'Malley, and later Lucille Gutmann (who married a Horrocks). The Schiffer family, Edna, George and an older sister Marguerite were also listed. [Note all these friends were girls, leading me (and Schoettle's granddaughter Suzy Davis) to conclude the writer was Mary Schoettle Mitchell.]

- Dr. Edward III's daughter Julie's maternal grandfather Daniel J. Egan lived across from the Yacht Club in one of the old turreted houses.

- The Schoettles attended St. Joseph's Roman Catholic Church, which was a place for social positioning. The Egans, says the writer, always sat in the front pew on the *right* side, and the Schoettle's sat in the front pew on the *left*! Behind the Schoettles sat the Kelly's who had built a house on the Southeast corner of Summit Street (at its intersection with Maple). Crosstrees was at the very top of the hill: #1 Summit Street.

- Dr. Charles III's family was always closely associated with the Schoettles, the children were Edward, Charles, Herbert (who sailed *Mull* for Schoettle apparently in a memorable match with *Vanitie*) and a daughter Helen who, like the Schoettle's Aunt Alice, never married.

Mary, if she was the writer, recalls the layout of stores on Main Street in Island Heights' center: the Davis drugstore, Bogerts, Stanwoods (next to which there was an Atlantic and Pacific Tea Company store at one time). Then came Vienech's, Ayers, Siddons, the Post Office, a Tea Shop on the corner, and McKeig (after which she writes "Spam hambergs"). Maybe she meant Taylor Pork Roll, a legendary Jersey product!

There was, up to the mid-20th century, a hotel on the corner of Oak and River Avenues near the pavilion or summerhouse that sat on the river's edge. A Maryland colleague's mother went there as a child and remembers being taken down to the waterside to see an organ grinder with his neatly uniformed little trained monkey.[107] There was more than one hotel on Island Heights over the years, but this one, Eileen Fancher (daughter of Frank Olson, captain of a Schoettle family boat *Alice*) suggests was the "Perrineil," which folks thought was so named because it opened every year, closing each fall because there was no central heat. Not so, says Fancher, it was owned and operated by the Perrines (a Barnegat boatbuilding family), who lived nearby.[108]

FIGURE 2-46. **Money Island Road in 1924. Pines surrounded the cottages and sand roads connected them.**

Alicemay Weber-Wright

By 1920, says Mary Schoettle Mitchell, *Scat* was no longer the sensation she had been at first. Edwin began thinking about a new boat, and by 1921, he had commissioned Francis Sweisguth to design a *Scat II*. Sweisguth was at that time working in the design office of William Gardner and Company, designers and brokers at 1 Broadway, New York City. In that year, Sweisguth drew an abstract design as a feeler called just "A 30 foot Catboat."[109]

It is clear from correspondence that Sweisguth is junior to Gardner in this relationship, and the quite famous Gardner visits an unidentified local boatyard more than once in the spring of 1921 without Sweisguth being present; Sweisguth refers deferentially to "Mr. Gardner" more than once as builder's decisions are made on *Scat II*. Sweisguth and Edwin had great respect for Gardner, who was one of America's foremost naval architects. Gardner designed the schooner *Atlantic*, which set the famous record for trans-Atlantic crossing time of 11 days, 16 hours, 22 minutes for the Kaiser's Cup.[110] This achievement stood for almost a century until multi-hulled racing machines broke the mold by sailing boats nothing like those designed in the past.

Scat II was finally commissioned to be built by the Townsend Boatyard on Hooper's Basin in Berkeley, which was just north of Seaside Park on the Barrier Island. The cabin layout below decks made *Scat II* a comfortable cruising boat and would later serve as a model for the *Silent Maid*.

FIGURE 2-47. **Mary Schoettle Mitchell (oil, 1920s).**
Suzy Mitchell Davis, with permission

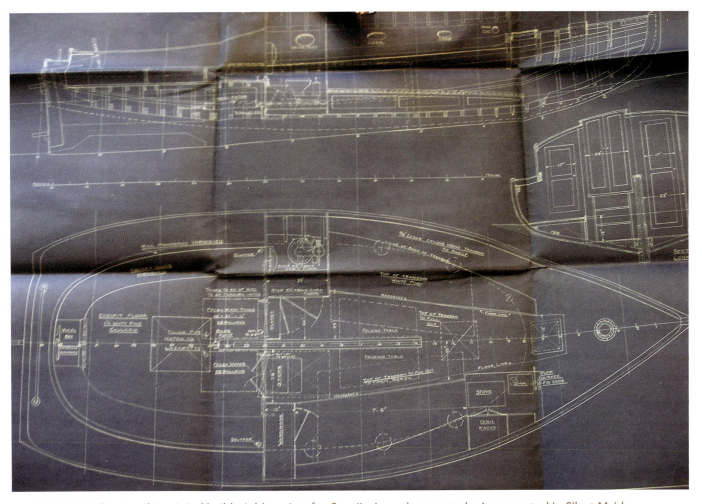

FIGURE 2-48. Sweisguth's original builder's blueprints for *Scat II* mirror elements to be incorporated in *Silent Maid* three years later. Small portlights forward in the cabin trunk echo *Scat*, but were never cut through in *Scat II*.
Toms River Seaport Society

Correspondence from Sweisguth to Edwin in March shows their mutual attention to detail and hints at a growing friendship between them. Letters start out "Dear Mr. Schoettle," and talk about size of blocks for the peak and throat halyards. Sweisguth suggests gin blocks with lighter and stronger metal frames instead of the traditional ash cheeks. He also suggests wire halyards to stop the peak from sagging and spoiling the set of the sail. He suggests keeping the ash shell blocks for the runners (running backstays they would pound on the deck and rails when cast off and wooden blocks did less damage to paint and deck).

Over subsequent years the warmth of the friendship between these men—designer and owner—would grow. Sweisguth signs his letters "Francis," with regards to the family, joy over the successes of his friend's sons. Edwin speaks of "my friend Francis Sweisguth," and writes an encomium to him in his book *Sailing Craft*. Only in Edwin's last year of illness had they lost touch, but he still sent Sweisguth an interested client.[111]

By late May, *Scat II* was launched, her mast stepped, and it was found that the spreaders holding out the main shrouds seemed to swing too far aft, which could interfere with the sail. Sweisguth writes to Edwin that "Mr. Gardner " says the forestay must be set up much tighter, in order to bow the mast forward, and that this will put the spreaders in line with the main shroud chainplates, solving the problem.[112] This may have had a role in the ultimate mast failure some years later. Edwin considered *Scat II* to be slightly over rigged. Her boom was 36 feet long, and he gives her sail area as 1000 square feet.[113]

Edwin invited Sweisguth to come take a look at the boat and arranged for a taxi to meet the designer at the train. However, Sweisguth declined the taxi, stating that he would take no reimbursement for coming to the boat. Upon inspection of *Scat II*, Sweisguth concluded that the bow was riding too high in the waterline.

FIGURE 2-49. *Scat II* ready for launch in Townsend's Boat Yard at Hooper's Basin in the spring of 1921. Two forward circular port lights, shown in the drawings, as in the original *Scat*, were not installed in *Scat II*.

Schoettle family photograph

While *Scat II* had "1500 pounds of outside ballast in the scag [skeg]," Edwin and Sweisguth discussed using some of the original *Scat's* ballast until the new boat could be tried under sail. Sweisguth suggested they should wing out some of the ballast inside the hull, expecting it will be a trick getting the distribution right. Sweisguth's notes indicate that when the ballast was correctly distributed, the boat should float on her marks and result in a waterline length of 27 feet, 3 inches. "This is the way the boat should trim when everything is aboard and in racing trim."[114]

This required some negotiating with the yard, since the original *Scat* had been offered as part of the bargain with her builder. The transaction of transferring *Scat* never occurred.

Sweisguth wrote after a visit to Crosstrees at Island Heights: "I want to thank you for a very pleasant afternoon and evening. I would not have missed it for anything . . . I hope to go down again very soon. Call at the office when you are in the city. Yours sincerely, Francis Sweisguth".

Interactions between Edwin and Sweisguth continued into July 1921 as the mainsail dimensions were adjusted. Design area was 900 square feet, but with changes it was recalculated, and the center of effort changed on the blueprints to 840 square feet.[115]

Edwin apparently sailed *Scat II* in competition just before July 23, 1921, and wrote to Sweisguth advising him that he had won a race that Saturday. That letter does not survive, but Sweisguth's letter of reply does. Sweisguth is elated, and he is already contacting Ratsey and Lapthorn for a new *Scat II* sail on Edwin's behalf, concluding: "I am very glad you won Sat and you do it again this Sat and for the rest of the year. With best wishes, Francis." Sweisguth becomes a bit more familiar in this closure! Mary Schoettle Mitchell writes that *Scat II* went on to be Barnegat Bay Champion in her class that year, racing mostly against the older style cats like *Bouquet, Gem, Me Too,* and *Virginia.*[116]

* * *

FIGURE 2-50. *Scat II* fitting out at Hooper's Basin after launching at Townsend's yard in Berkeley on the barrier island in 1921 showing her huge "barn-door" rudder.

Polly Schoettle Miller

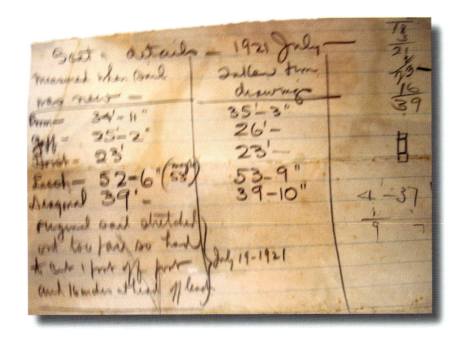

FIGURE 2-51. Schoettle's notes from July 1921 detail of *Scat II*'s sail dimensions. This is Edwin Schoettle's handwriting.

Suzy Mitchell Davis

FIGURE 2-52. Sara Schoettle, Mrs. Horrocks, and Judge Louis McKeenhan aboard *Scat II*.

Schoettle family photograph, Suzy Mitchell Davis

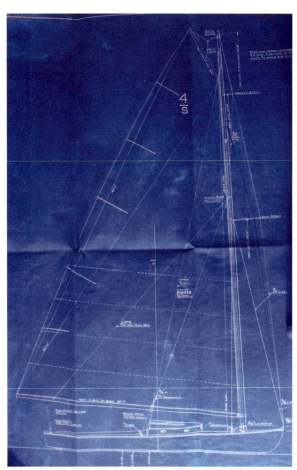

FIGURE 2-53. **Forcem's 1923 sailplan with short Swedish gaff.**

Francis Sweisguth blueprint, Toms River Seaport Society

Edwin Schoettle had many guests sail with him aboard *Scat II*. Among them was a Judge Louis McKeenhan, who became so excited about the sport that he approached naval architect Charles Mower to design a new cruising/racing catboat for the competitions on Barnegat Bay. She was the *Mary Ann*, first of the famous Class A catboats. She won the coveted Toms River Cup in both 1922 and 1923.

A number of competing boats were quickly designed to Charles Mower's designs, including *Spy, Bat*, and *Lotus*. Francis Sweisguth joined the competition with *Tamwock*, which was a very successful boat. *Tamwock* was, as Schoettle reported, unfortunately lost in a fire while hauled out "at the Rote-Vautier Boat Yard" in the spring of 1939. [117]

This fire was a real Island Heights local disaster. When the yard was found burning, the schooner *Mattie E* was on the marine railway and was being scorched by the intense, increasing heat. Britt Applegate, who acted as Island Height's Fire Chief, acted quickly. He took an axe and cut the heavy manila cable holding her so she slid down the ways on her own, launching out into Toms River and thereby saving herself. The local fire chief at that time expressed his concern publicly about there being enough water pressure to service fire hoses at Island Height's hilltops, where some of the more elegant homes, like Crosstrees, had been built.

Applegate also sailed Class A catboats for Edwin Schoettle and was one of the most skilled local sailors. He was later first mate on the schooner *Mistral* owned by the Scofield family, who were yacht club members and friends of the Schoettles. *Mistral* had been built in a yard at South Toms River. [118]

Tamwock's success baited Edwin Schoettle into the game. With *Scat II* no longer the sensation she once had been, Edwin began discussing his own ideas about making a faster catboat. Sweisguth at first wrote to Edwin asking why he didn't simply buy *Tamwock*, which might then have been available. This successful catboat was owned by the Diss family, which was ultimately connected to the Schoettles by marriage. In the end, Sweisguth was pleased to take the offered commission to design a new Class A catboat and incorporate new ideas Edwin put forward. Edwin put together a consortium of three other yachtsmen to spread out the finances and responsibility for the boat's design and construction. They named the boat *Forcem*, sometimes short-handed as "4-som"; either version is a play on the group, or foursome, who joined the venture. [119]

The boat was to be built by John Kirk who had a boatbuilding operation in Toms River Village, across from today's Huddy Park. Her spars were separately commissioned from the Pigeon Hollow Spar Company in Massachusetts, with a 7/8″ mast track carrying the luff and a special slide for the rig's small Swedish gaff. Pigeon-Fraser of Boston, Massachusetts, created extremely light spars; one set was the wing supports of an early airplane that flew in 1916. [120]

Papers with *Forcem* written on them say the mast shipment from East Boston, MA,—a spar 48′ 3″ long cost $49.50; the mast cost just $183. Four-inch, ash-shelled blocks from Merriman totaled $55, or $5.25 each. [121]

Edwin drove hard bargains, and when *Forcem* was completed, he inspected the bills Kirk submitted, declining to pay an addendum of $200 for coamings around the cockpit. Kirk pointed out that Sweisguth's plans showed no coamings, and he had put them on simply to finish the boat. Edwin remained steadfast, refusing to pay. Eventually, Kirk just threw them in as customer goodwill. [122]

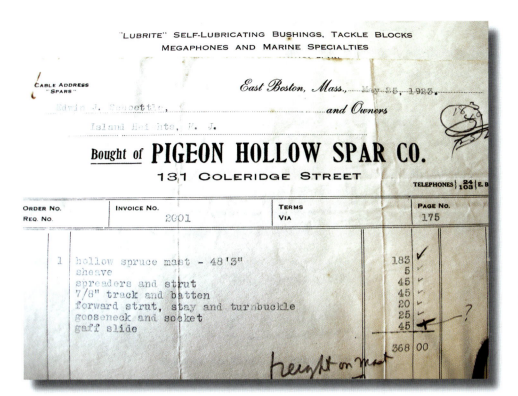

"LUBRITE" SELF-LUBRICATING BUSHINGS, TACKLE BLOCKS
MEGAPHONES AND MARINE SPECIALTIES

CABLE ADDRESS
"SPARS"

East Boston, Mass., May 25, 1923.

Edwin J. Schoettle, ... and Owners

Island Heights, N. J.

Bought of PIGEON HOLLOW SPAR CO.

131 COLERIDGE STREET

TELEPHONES { 24 | 103 | E. B

ORDER NO. REQ. NO.	INVOICE NO. 2001	TERMS VIA	PAGE NO. 175

1	hollow spruce mast - 48'3"		183	✓
	sheave		5	✓
	spreaders and strut		45	✓
	7/8" track and batten		45	✓
	forward strut, stay and turnbuckle		20	✓
	gooseneck and socket		25	✓
	gaff slide		45	✗ ?
			368	00

freight on mast

FIGURE 2-54. The order for *Forcem's* hollow spar, with track and batten plus a slide for her short Swedish gaff. She sailed with this, as did other Class A catboats, only for a short time. Note Pigeon also manufactured megaphones!
Philadelphia Independence Seaport Museum

Sweisguth was thinking ahead of his time in designing *Forcem's* sail, with its small (essentially aircraft technology), light, hollow-built Swedish gaff. Without the massive, surging traditional gaff waving about aloft and lowering *Forcem's* stability, he could get a lot of sail area high up. (Much like the 2012-era "wing" sails that, with modern synthetics, can be built with immense roach along the leach—outer edge of the sail—and still stand in faint airs thus holding their shape.) Sweisguth drew the sail out with five battens and three strong sets of reef points, sending his plan (apparently—see Figure 2-58) to Ratsey and Lapthorn, who were to ship the completed sail as a parcel directly to Edwin at Island Heights. He also had the foot of the sail, that small gaff, and the luff of the sail travelling along mast and boom with slides on tracks, which avoided turbulence and venting around loose fitting mast hoops or lacings.

With Francis Sweisguth's successful design of *Tamwock*, one would have expected his *Forcem* to be a winner as well. As suggested, Edwin Schoettle seemed to have a great deal to say about the design of this boat. He was by then familiar with a wide range of sailing vessels, literally worldwide, and was probably developing a network of sources upon which he would draw for his well-received book *Sailing Craft*, still five years from publication. Sweisguth drew *Forcem's* Swedish gaff sailplan in March of 1923. This seems to be a transition from long, but high-peaked, gaffs in the two Scat designs, and the Marconi or jib-headed mains eventually adopted by the new fleet of Class A catboats.

Perhaps Edwin's inputs, while well informed, did not help Sweisguth with his project because the boat clearly did not meet expectations. As she was being raced in 1923, a letter from Sweisguth deals with changes they might make to improve her performance. There was discussion between them about steering and mast rake. They also contacted Ratsey and Lapthorn about re-cutting the mainsail and at the same time gave consideration to a new mainsail for *Scat II*.

FIGURE 2-55. Schoettle and Sweisguth's Class A catboat version *Forcem* with her Ratsey main. The boom is 27'0" and the sail was originally cut 26'6", but Sweisguth later suggested it be recut to improve handling, as seemingly shown here.
Suzy Mitchell Davis

Scat II After the Schoettles

When Edwin Schoettle sold *Scat II* it was with the condition that her new owner would change the boat's name. Edwin was planning to name his next boat Scat III and thought it would be confusing to have a *Scat II* and *Scat III* literally competing with each other on Barnegat Bay. This covenant was not completely honored by the new owner according to Mary Schoettle Mitchell. It seems the owner changed the name slightly to *Scatt II*. Edwin in his own handwritten records states that *Scatt II* remained in the bay, being "sold to Daniel Bates of Philadelphia who sailed it successfully for years," and he shows no discomfort at another *Scat* or *Scatt* being in Barnegat Bay. Schoettle continues: "Later, in 1935, *Scatt II* became the property of [the] McInery[s] of Mantoloking who wrecked it completely."[126] However, *Scatt II* was not wrecked completely as recorded by Edwin Schoettle . . . she was to have a long life to follow. By 1951, *Scatt II* was in the hands of Jimmy "Red" Kellogg, a New York City financier, who rescued and owned numerous boats that he considered valuable to the bay's history. (His son Peter describes this fluid assemblage of boats as "quite a fleet.")

By the time "Red" Kellogg owned *Scatt II*, a motor had been installed, which was largely rusted out and only occasionally ran. This had clearly not been a Schoettle addition. None of the Schoettle sailboats (his family is unanimous on this) ever had a motor. Edwin Schoettle did write about *Splinter*, a 20-footer built by Faunce of Toms River: "The first and only motor boat we owned up to 1941. Sara and Edwin Schoettle made a voyage from Island Heights to… (text destroyed)… to Atlantic City in this boat 1 day each way—1925."[127] He wrote that *Splinter* was built in 1920, but his memory seems faulty here, because three years before, like *Mull* and *Scat*, he had her licensed by the U.S. Navy in 1917 during the First World War.

Kellogg sold *Scatt II* to young Clinton Trowbridge in 1951 out of Johnson's Boatyard in Bay Head, where she had been languishing out of water on blocks. *Scatt II*'s story thereafter is interestingly told in

FIGURE 2-56. *Scatt II* awaiting sale at Johnson's Boatyard in Bay Head where Trowbridge found her languishing in 1951.
Copyright Clinton Trowbridge

Trowbridge's own book, *The Boat That Wouldn't Sink*, published in 2000.

Trowbridge had been visiting his wife's family in Mantoloking, and they heard about *Scatt II* from "Red" Kellogg.[128] Kellogg told the Trowbridges that he'd had an offer of $900 over the phone that morning. Luckily, Trowbridge and his wife were there in person with their $600 in life savings, and Kellogg sold the boat to them.

Scatt II sank immediately upon launching, but was patched up enough to leak only moderately. When the Trowbridges purchased the boat, she had three clean breaks in her keel, a patchwork of lead sheathing had been nailed over undetermined flaws, and it was claimed she had been rammed head-on into a bridge piling during a blow.[129] There was, he reported, a six-foot splice in the mainmast, around which the following story hovered: it had been broken off along the New Jersey coast "when the *Mauritania* went down" (more probably the passenger liner *Morro Castle*), which caught fire during a Nor'easter and went ashore, still burning, at Asbury Park on September 8, 1934).[130] Many commercial and pleasure craft, and purportedly *Scatt II* had gone out braving the rough water trying to rescue people during the disaster that claimed 137 lives. The story given Clint Trowbridge was that this was when her mast was broken. The fate of *Scatt II*'s mast is given clearly by Edwin Schoettle as a failure during a sailing race, after which his crew sailed home with the rig all askew. A repair was made by fitting an iron sleeve over the broken area. There is no record of the heroic *Morro Castle* mission, romantic as the tale Trowbridge recounts might be!

Having never sailed anything larger than 19 feet, Trowbridge found everything about the boat twice as large and complex as expected. Sailing her to Maine, they owned her for 26 years, had remarkable adventures, and near death escapes, in addition to experience running a charter business.

In 1976, when *Scatt II* was 55-years-old, she appeared for sale in the *Catboat Association Bulletin* #50. While she was probably built for a couple of thousand dollars, the asking price was $7800![131] This reflects much the same hubris *Silent Maid*'s owner would show at the end of that classic boat's sailing life!

FIGURE 2-57. *Scatt II* under sail in the 1950s. She was really old here and her main is considerably shortened from the original.
Copyright Clinton Trowbridge, photo by Phil Kundhardt

In an undated letter to Charles J. Beck (one of the investors in *Forcem*), Edwin discussed their lack of success with their boat: "Let's not race with a 'hacked up' outfit as circumstances hold us into this year. Let us save up for a year and then get a replacement boat next year." Still discussing Francis Sweisguth as designer of choice he goes on: "I definitely feel we . . . ought to go after the thing right or else not aspire . . . " I believe this is the first hint that the boat ultimately called *Silent Maid* would be built.

Schoettle family lore indicated that *Forcem* was scuttled: sunk outright off the end of the Schoettle pier on the west side of Island Heights. Presumably she was carried down by her ballast. If the legend were indeed fact, her remains would still be out there on the bottom with anything above the surface of Toms River's muddy bottom reduced by shipworms to honeycombed remnants!

Edwin Schoettle's own hand, however, indicates that *Forcem* (he writes this both as *Four Some* and *4 Some*) "was sold after one year of sailing."[123] He also records the cost of *Forcem* as $1626.98 (Figure 2-58), and John Kirk, her builder claimed he lost $505 on the building of her. All Edwin received for his investment was $1000 on the resale![124]

The Schoettles were still sailing *Scat II* while the *Forcem* venture was in progress. Sara Schoettle wrote on the back of an old *Scat II* photograph that she and Edwin were ultimately disappointed in *Scat II's* performance, and did not keep her very long. This is surprising since *Scat II* sailed for the Schoettles at least four years. However, several elements, such as the double-block aloft and three-part tackle for the throat halyard, had proven themselves and would be retained in the future.[125]

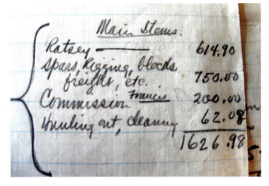

FIGURE 2-58. A handwritten list of some of the expenses fitting out *Forcem*. It seems Sweisguth's commission for her design was $200.

Toms River Seaport Society

FIGURE 2-59. *Scat II* in 1921. Sweisguth's first large Schoettle catboat, annotated in Schoettle's hand.

Polly Schoettle Miller

A Tale of Two Bridges

The *Silent Maid*'s easily accessible home waters were eventually circumscribed by three bridges, two of them railroad trestles: the one connecting the rail spur to Ocean Gate and crossing Toms River; the rail bridge to Seaside Heights; and the vehicular traffic causeway to Seaside Park in use by 1918. Rail service had come to this region with an eye to stimulating tourism or excursion traffic, but had really been sustained by the commercial freights connected with the shipbuilding and charcoaling industries.[132]

Edwin Schoettle had a strong connection with these three Toms River area bridges. The railroad causeway across Barnegat Bay was first owned by the Toms River and Barnegat Railroad Company. It had been in place since July 4, 1881 and, with track laid to Bay Head in 1882, this completed a loop with railroad service to the rest of that coastline, northern New Jersey, and New York City. As early as 1871, another rail line had crossed the state to Tuckerton, and H.C. Woolman (author of a famous regional atlas) told his audience that "doubtless the time is not far off when the entire New Jersey shore, from Sandy Hook to Tuckerton, a distance of about 90 miles, will be thickly studded with hotels and cottages."[133] He was right beyond his wildest economic fantasies; much to the detriment of the natural ecosystem, which was the original amenity to attract people. Would that he'd been at least partly wrong!

The railroad brought development to Ocean Gate, where my mother's extended family had a small cottage. My mother spent part of a summer there about 1919. The trestle left the shoreline for Seaside Park at what became known as Barnegat Pier and this, like Ocean Gate, became a stop and destination for fishing, picnicking, and enjoying the reliable sea breeze. The trestle, of course, came ashore in Seaside Heights, about where 14th Street is today. By 1900 it is said that Seaside's principal export was seafood, and the equivalent imports were coal and lumber.

Engineers are sometimes not distinguished for their forethought, and they had not properly reckoned the power of wind and tide of the ice of frozen Barnegat Bay. In the winter of 1913, a floe driven against the causeway created enough pressure to destroy 600 feet of the bridge and end train service until repairs could be made.

In 1883, the Pennsylvania Railroad constructed an 1800-foot rail bridge across Toms River upstream of Island Heights, which terminated at Pine Beach. A station at Island Heights was added in 1884 half a mile from the line's coal and lumber depot, and a "Y" or spur of track was installed that allowed cars to be sidelined. Trains backed over Toms River to reach Island Heights.[134] There were comments by 1902 that the layout was not efficient because the engines had to maneuver to get their water tanks filled. Water, boiled off as steam during operation, had to be regularly replenished.

Trains to this stop brought the Schoettles to their Island Heights properties, just a quarter mile from Crosstrees. From the sailor's perspective, despite a small manually operated horizontal swing opening, this trestle irritatingly blocked half the river from convenient boat transit. Travelers across the bridge in 1902 described the operating of the "new" swinging draw as being as slow as winding a Waltham watch.

Runyon Colie, speaking from personal experience of the similar Mantoloking Bridge across upper Barnegat Bay, described how sailors would often volunteer to help, or in a keeper's absence, have to manually open the bridge themselves so they could pass. One climbed up to the operator's position and turning a geared key, which would slowly wind the balanced swing bridge open, then closed after the boats were through. He indicated the key had two positions,[135] with different gearing, depending on the strength or impatience of the person doing the winding.

If you were approaching any of these bridges downwind in a stiff breeze, this presented a problem of handling the boat, heaving against the abutments, and dealing with the bridge at the same time.

In winter, duck hunters from Toms River headed south towards Island Beach on shooting expeditions sometimes avoided using the draw at all, simply coming up against the causeway near one end and horsing their sneakbox up and over the bridge deck, to re-launch on the other side, then sailing away.[136]

By the mid-1920s, passenger traffic was dwindling on this portion of the railway. "By 1930," said Schoettle dock-boy Jack Lafleur, "train travel locally was almost over. The railroad asked to stop service, and its request was granted [in 1931]."

FIGURE 2-60. The **1884 wooden pile swing bridge over upper Barnegat Bay at Mantoloking.** These early bay bridges all operated on similar, simple hand-powered mechanical principles.

Bay Head, Mantoloking and Lovelandtown Museum

In 1934, the bridge was dismantled and all the pilings were pulled. According to the family, Edwin Schoettle felt great satisfaction when all that trestle work had been removed and one could sail unimpeded the entire length of Toms River for the first time in 51 years. Lafleur later reported that the removal of this blockage on the river was considered one of Edwin's best achievements, as he was one of the prominent advocates for ending rail service to Island Heights at the time.[137]

Suzanne Mitchell-Davis said that at the end of all this reshuffling at Island Heights, the Schoettles somehow acquired ownership of the waterfront parcel where the rail causeway had left shore. This turned out to be a valuable piece of property once a very different Island Heights began to develop.

The vehicle bridge crossing Barnegat Bay to Seaside Heights had been anticipated by real estate promoters who were offering 40-foot oceanfront lots to the public for $100. Wouldn't you like to still own a couple dozen of these today? Summer train excursions began to these properties in 1909. In 1913 Seaside Heights was incorporated, which was the same year Christian Hiering started the Barnegat Power and Cold Storage Company producing both electricity and ice!

Two years later a bridge project was begun by the Island Heights and Seaside Heights Bridge Company.[138] Its route chose to leave the mainland near Coates Point and crossed today's West Point Island before joining the barrier island. The natural channel ran close to the middle of Barnegat Bay here, and the opening to pass transiting boats was placed here. This was not a swing bridge, but a true drawbridge, which lifted on cables. It was hinged at the eastern end, not unlike those we associate with medieval castles.

Learning from the railroad's experience, stand-off pilings were set with angled ice breakers on the north side of the bridge. This was usually upwind to the prevailing winter gales so that these structures would crack and dissipate energy from heavy ice sheets, which drifted southwards during winter on northwest or northeast blows. Though not shown in Horrock's drawing, a number of these strongbacks could still be seen—still working—throughout my youth and as late as the early 21st century poking up above the water and extending from the west shore to the north of both the 1950 Thomas A. Mathis Bridge and the "old" drawbridge span.

Jack Lafleur claims that the Island Heights and Seaside Heights Bridge Company actually involved Edwin Schoettle and other associates. (I've been unable to prove this.) He says the syndicate later sold the bridge to the State. The bridge cost $153,477.90 to construct. The completed structure opened for traffic on December 1, 1915, as a toll bridge; one supposes to recoup those costs. A horse and buggy and its driver cost $.25, plus a dime for each passenger. A car and driver was $.40, but passengers cost $.15. While children under 5 were free, animals, like cattle or pigs, still cost a dime, demonstrating that, like today, the bulk of people are mostly thought of as cattle and pigs!

The rail bridge across to Seaside Heights continued active through the World War II years. There is a picture of a steam engine pulling a short freight train in 1944, but operations ceased on December 1, 1946, when in the wee hours of the morning a fire destroyed 300 feet of the trestle. The Federal Trade Commission authorized discontinuance of service, and a bus service across the automobile span was inaugurated instead. Most of the trestle was removed, leaving two long stub piers on either side of the bay; the so-called Barnegat Pier and another at 14th Street in Seaside Heights.

That was the first year I took a boat ride on Barnegat Bay as a kid. Had we been able to get through the obdurate Mantoloking Bridge, I might have seen that trestle, but by the time we sailed *Silent Maid* down the bay I thought it had always been an open venue such as we found! All the tracks from Seaside to Bay Head were pulled up by 1949, and through Mantoloking and south Bay Head that right-of-way, subsequently grown up in wild brush and thicket vegetation, was slowly devoured by the upscale houses that have since been built on Barnegat Lane and Rt. 35 South!

Another bridge, the Manahawkin Causeway, crossed Barnegat Bay from the mainland to Long Beach Island.[139] It was first built on driven pilings to carry the Pennsylvania Railroad in 1886, but it was ultimately decked with cross planking nailed on. It took only a short time for the jostling of automobile and truck traffic to shake loose the nails and make the trip over a noisy, unsettling, and clattering experience.

There's an interesting ecological sidelight to this old wooden bridge. Herring gulls (*Larus argentatus smithsonianus*) were not so abundant as in modern times. They would aggregate, according to Witmer Stone, on sandy points, and these clever gulls found that dropping shellfish from high altitude on hard surfaces would open them for consumption. In his book *Bird Studies at Old Cape May*, Stone includes a photograph taken by R.F. Engle (hotelier on Long Beach Island) before 1937 of the Manahawkin Causeway peppered with thousands of smashed clamshells![140]

The causeway was ultimately replaced by a high bridge, with no draw, which is in service today.

FIGURE 2-61. **The Seaside drawbridge. Henry Horrock's fanciful 1932 interpretation, with lines of irritated drivers backed up in both directions.** *Alicemay Weber-Wright*

FIGURE 2-62. By the mid-1920s, Schoettle had constructed three "barns" around Crosstrees, north and west of the main house. The longest was a capacious spar shed (long enough ultimately for *Silent Maid*'s enormous mainmast!).

Inset: Enlargement of photo showing Sara Schoettle, the three boys, and Schoettle's dog Whiskers.

Suzy Mitchell Davis

The failure of *Forcem* set the scene for *Silent Maid* to come a year later. Sweisguth and Edwin Schoettle would have discussions maturing plans for a new cruising catboat. Sweisguth had designed a dud, but Edwin trusted him yet again for what would become his favorite and most famous boat.

The die was cast and Sweisguth writes "I would like very much to see the bay again and if I can get away for a few days will try to make a run down there—Remember me to Mrs. Schoettle."

The Schoettle family's "physical plant" was thus in place as Edwin and Sweisguth began their complex march towards construction of the *Silent Maid*.

Morton Johnson, of Bay Head, now enters as a new, key player and merits more extensive development in this history.

ENDNOTES — CHAPTER 2

1. http://inventors.about.com/od/pstartinventions/a/papermaking.htm

2. H.S. Tanner, 1816. (Map of) New Jersey, Lucas Fielding, Jr., Publ. Philip Nicklin, Philadelphia.

3. Wikipedia (http://wikipedia.org/wiki/Hohenfels-Essingen).

4. Philip Schoettle, personal interview with Kent Mountford at Manasquan and Bay Head, New Jersey, plus subsequent correspondence, September 2009.

5. Edwin Schoettle, 1936, *op. cit.*

6. The song "Till the End of Time" was made popular by performer Perry Como in the 1960s. The tune is almost note for note from Chopin's Polinaise opus 53 in A flat major.

7. Mary Schoettle, account of her father Ferdinand Erhardt Schoettle, preserved by Philip Schoettle, 1930.

8. Eileen Fancher, 2013, corresponding with Suzy Davis and Kent Mountford. She said the family had a 3-story Victorian house next to the Schoettle boy's "Anchorage" on Island Heights, mostly visited by two older ladies they called "the Misses Beck," but in 1926 one of Edwin Schoettle's crewmates to Bermuda was a strapping Charles "Becky" Beck, Jr., likely a son of his father Ferdinand's early business partner.

9. Mary Schoettle, account of her father.

10. Ibid.

11. Sylvester W. Burley and C.H. Kidder, editors, *Burley's United States Centennial Gazetteer and Guide* (Philadelphia: S.W. Burley, 1876).

12. Edwin Schoettle. Speech at Drake Hotel, Chicago, January 21, 1936. Manuscript found in an old desk belonging to him.

13. Karl R. Schoettle, "EJS," unpublished family document detailing Edwin Schoettle's history, September, 2006.

14. Philip Schoettle, 2009.

15. Burley and Kidder, *Burley's United States Centennial Gazetteer and Guide.*

16. Philip Schoettle (2009) and Suzy Mitchell Davis (2010), personal communications with Kent Mountford emphasizing that the shears were Ferdinand's invention. Philip describes their operation as two rotating (circular) shear blades that continuously cut like scissors. I have been unable to locate this U.S. patent searching "shears" or "Schoettle."

17. *Printer's Circular & Stationers & Publisher's Gazette*, Vol. 1884. "Strawboard" for the paper packaging market, as its name implies, was made of chipped hay or wheat straw fiber, pressed with a binder and sizing. This is similar to how heavier "chip," "flake," or "particle" boards are made for the construction industry today.

18. www.Google.com/maps?rlz=1T4SNNT_enUS368387&q=202+E+Wister+Street+Phil

19. *New Jersey Courier*, June 26, 1902. Microfilm archives, Ocean County Library, Toms River, New Jersey. The "original" drawbridge through the trestle had apparently been replaced. The time reference is to the Waterbury "long wind" watch, which has an unusually long spiral mainspring and takes a long time to wind.

20. Eileen Fancher, correspondence correcting my original information, not Howard Simpson, 2013.

21. Ocean County Historical Society, *Along the Toms River: Images of America* (Dover, NH: Arcadia Publishing, 1996).

22. Howard Van Sant, *Barnegat Pirates,* Issue 104 of Neely's Popular Library. (F. Tennyson Neely, 1897).

23. *Catboat Association Bulletin*, No. 58 (March 1979), p. 11 (provided to the author by Mary Schoettle Mitchell). An article in the bulletin referred to Edwin Schoettle at Island Heights: "His mother took a house there but she didn't like the mosquitoes, which at that time were famous. She hauled her two daughters back to Germantown, Pennsylvania."

24. Karl Schoettle, "EJS."

25. Suzy Mitchell Davis, 2010.

26. *Catboat Association Bulletin,* No. 58, p. 13.

27. Edwin J. Schoettle, written reminiscences (circa 1945), shared by Polly Schoettle Miller with Kent Mountford, 2012.

28. National Park Service: Resorts and Recreation. http://www.nps.gov/history/online_books/nj/chapt2a.htm

29. *Catboat Association Bulletin,* No. 58, p. 12.

30. Karl Schoettle, a history written for family consumption, September 2006.

31. http://freepages.geneology.rootsweb.ancestry.com/-blberg/gl/p1223.htm

32. Schoettle, speech at Drake Hotel.

33. Phillip Schoettle, genealogy provided to Kent Mountford, 2009.

34. Mary Schoettle. Before her death in 1933 at age 66, daughter of Ferdinand Erhardt Schoettle wrote an unusually candid history of his life and personality. Source of text: Philip A. Schoettle, Bay Head, NJ.

35. Suzy Mitchell Davis, personal communication with Kent Mountford, 2012.

36. Ocean County Historical Society, *Along the Toms River*. James (or John P.) Kirk or his father William P. Kirk, who advertised building "all classes of sailing and steam yachts."

37. Edwin Schoettle, written reminiscences.

38. Eileen Fancher, personal correspondence with Kent Mountford, July 30, 2013.

39. *Guide to the Haffenreffer-Herreschoff Collection*, Hull # 428 (Bristol, RI: Massachusetts Institute of Technology).

40. Herreschoff is not pronounced as most people think, based on its apparently German phonetics. The Newport (RI) Herreschoff Museum's curator instructed me that it is properly spoken *"Hair's Off,"* a form rarely heard elsewhere!

41. John Leather, *The Gaff Rig Handbook* (Woodenboat Books, 2001 edition).

42. John Brady, "Jersey Cats" in *Wooden Boat Builder* (2010), 7- 8. www.woodenboatbuilder.com/pages/jerseycats.html

43. *Catboat Association Bulletin,* No. 58, p. 12.

44. Edwin Schoettle, written reminiscences.

45. John M. Leavens, *The Catboat Book*, (International Marine Publishing Company, 1973).

46. Edwin Schoettle, written reminiscences.

47. Eileen Fancher, personal correspondence to Suzy Davis and Kent Mountford about the Beck House, July 29, 2013.

48. Ocean County Historical Society, *Along the Toms River. Bouquet* is pictured gaff main raised and cockpit visible in this Arcadia volume.

49. Edwin J. Schoettle, *Sailing Craft* (New York: MacMillan, 1928).

50. Ibid., p 100.

51. *New Jersey Courier*, Toms River, July 3 through August 14, 1902.

52. Ibid.

53. United States Coast Pilot, 1983. Grassy Bay, ICW mile 60.3 is a shoal area mostly bare at low water (as "Scat" discovered!)

54. Leavens, *The Catboat Book*, p. 18.

55. Schoettle, *Sailing Craft*, p. 100.

56. Edwin Schoettle, written reminiscences, p. 5.

57. Resourcinol glue was a British invention (c. 1943), first successfully used building Mosquito fighter aircraft of laminated plywood.

58. *Catboat Association Bulletin*, No. 58, p. 12

59. Edwin Schoettle, written reminiscences, p. 1.

60. Philip Schoettle, writing to Kent Mountford, June 2013.

61. Philip Schoettle, 2009.

62. Philip Schoettle, sent Kent Mountford commemorative materials on the Church's centennial, June 2013.

63. Edwin Schoettle, written reminiscences, p. 1.

64. Karl Schoettle, a history written for family consumption.

65. Suzy Mitchell Davis, showed Schoettle's daybook for Crosstrees to Kent Mountford, 2011.

66. *New Jersey Courier*, December 28, 1934. From "Our Early Files: 30 years ago (1904)" "…Ed Schoettle was planning to build his home at Island Heights."

67. Suzy Mitchell Davis, correspondence with Kent Mountford, 2011. She uncovered notes suggesting that construction had started in 1909.

68. Charles Mower, letter to Edward Schoettle, December 18, 1913.

69. Star Class History (http://www.starclass.org/about.shtml)

70. Sam Merricks, *F. Slade Dale: The Life of His Choice* (Ocean County Historical Society, 1998).

71. Edwin Schoettle, written reminiscences, p. 4.

72. Annotated photograph provided by Polly Schoettle Miller to Kent Mountford, 2012. Ferdinand died in Bermuda March 16, 1968, at King Edward Hospital, while serving as U.S. military officer, leaving five children.

73. Karl Schoettle, a history.

74. Ibid.

75. Michael Schoettle, interview with Kent Mountford, Bay Head Yacht Club, at Ferdinand's memorial service, June 18, 2011.

76. Karl Schoettle, a history.

77. Charles E. Lucke, "Barnegat Bay Crews Win International Series with Canada," in *Yachting Magazine*, October 1930, pp. 76-78 and 112.

78. Ibid. Three Schoettle sons and Slade Dale were up front in these competitions.

79. Karl Schoettle, a history.

80. *Ibid*.

81. Michael Capuzzo, *Close to Shore* (New York: Broadway Books, 2001).

82. William J. McCarter, *Realtors*, Philadelphia, advertisement for Schoettle Building sale, 1957.

83. www.islandheightsboro.com/history1.htm

84. Ibid.

85. Pauline S. Miller, *Ocean County, Four Centuries in the Making* (Ocean County Cultural & Heritage Commission, Toms River, 2000).

86. Schoettle (one of Edwin's sons, date unknown) hand written recollections found at Crosstrees, 2011.

87. Edwin Schoettle, written reminiscences, p. 6

88. Edwin Schoettle, written reminiscences, p. 4.

89. Miller, *Ocean County,* p. 510.

90. Joan Fitzpatrick, "Growing up in Beachwood, Part 2," in *The Society Scroll*, Ocean County Historical Society. August 2013, p.4.

91. Karl Schoettle, a history. ". . . lived in Chestnut Hill, then apparently in Philadelphia on Rittenhouse square. Their property was sold to John McShain, who built the Barclay Hotel on this site."

92. http://en.wikipedia.org/wiki/Barclay_Hotel

93. Science fiction: I speculate this film may have provided the initial connection between Edwin Schoettle and L. Ron Hubbard. Hubbard founded the discipline of "Scientology," but starting about 1932-33, he was best known as a writer of pulp fiction novels, and after the mid-1930s, he was involved in many movies on similar subjects. http://en.wiki/L._Ron_Hubbard.

94. Capuzzo, *Close to Shore*.

95. Edwin Schoettle, written reminiscences, p. 3.

96. William Schoettle, wrote to Kent Mountford on November 8, 2009: "Edwin Schoettle was my great-grandfather, Ferdinand Schoettle O.B.E. my grandfather, and Michael Beaver Schoettle is my father. . . . My father and uncle have kept up the leadership in sailing, . . . My father is a two-time Olympian and one-time Gold medalist and Uncle Andy came in 4th in the

Olympics. My father has also done a lot to promote the sport, like Edwin. He was team leader of the U.S. Team in 1992 when the U.S. team . . . was the most successful team of any sport at the Olympics that year and helped found a training center in Long Beach (CA).

97. Newt Kirkland, interviewed at Philadelphia Independence Seaport Museum on August 10, 2010, where he was at work restoring the original *Silent Maid*.

98. Suzy Mitchell Davis, 2010.

99. Polly Schoettle Miller, personal communication with Kent Mountford, 2012.

100. www.fundinguniverse.com/company-histories/Rock-Tenn-Company.

101. Robin Levine, 1999. "A Boxboard Containers International Special Report," Supplement, 20th Century Leaders of the Box and Carton Industry, Edwin J. Schoettle, 1999, p. 39.

102. Ibid.

103. Samuel Scoville, Jr., "Hawk Day,", April 11,1942, p. 576.

104. Samuel Scoville, Jr., "Land Forgotten," *The Sunday School Times*, July 18, 1942, pp. 298-299.

105. Davis, 2010.

106. (Probably) Mary (Schoettle) Mitchell, undated, handwritten manuscript sheet found at Crosstrees in 2011.

107. Anonymous, a Toms River resident recalled this in an interview, but chooses not to be identified, 2011.

108. Eileen Fancher, correspondence to Suzy Davis and Kent Mountford, July 29, 2013.

109. Francis Sweisguth, drawing preserved at Toms River Seaport Society, 1920.

110. Francis Sweisguth in *Sailing Craft*, p. 299.

111. Edwin J Schoettle, letter to Judson Smith in February 1947 suggesting how to find Schoettle through *Rudder* magazine. Schoettle dies at Christmas that year.

112. Sweisguth to Schoettle on William Gardner's stationery, June 6, 1921.

113. Edwin Schoettle, written reminiscences, p. 5.

114. Sweisguth to Schoettle pencil notes, Toms River Seaport Society, 1921.

115. Francis Sweisguth, several blueprint sheets, Toms River Seaport Society, 1921.

116. *Catboat Association Bulletin*, No. 58, p. 12

117. Edwin Schoettle, written reminiscences, p. 8.

118. Riley "Snapper" Applegate, recounted during interview with Kent Mountford, 2010. His nickname is "Snapper" because folks felt he was argumentative!

119. *Catboat Association Bulletin*, No. 58, p. 14.

120. Photograph in the Schoettle papers thus annotated. Philadelphia Independence Seaport Museum, copied in February 2011,

121. Ibid.

122. Thomas Beaton, interview with Morton Johnson Bell in Philadelphia January 18, 2012. Notes appended from reviewing these with Tom Beaton the following day.

123. Edwin Schoettle, written reminiscences, p. 8.

124. Notes taken at Philadelphia Independence Seaport in research and discussions with John Brady, January 8, 2010.

125. Francis Sweisguth, likening the designs of *Scat II* and *Scat III* (*Silent Maid*), Toms River Seaport Society, c 1923.

126. Edwin Schoettle, written reminiscences, p. 5.

127. Polly Schoettle Miller, 2012 (in: N.L. Stebbins. 1889. *Yacht Portraits of the leading American Yachts*. Boston Photoengravure Co, Boston). A note slipped in this volume reads: "Surprise, Many of the boats owned by Edwin J. Schoettle are illustrated with photographs pasted on the rear pages of this book" and thereto appended are about 20 pages of photographs with detailed handwritten notes by Edwin Schoettle. A true treasure trove for this writer. This reference, p 3.

128. "Red" Kellogg was James C. Kellogg heading the "syndicate" J.C. Kellogg and Sons, created to save old, worthy boats. (See Kellogg Chapter)

129. Clinton Trowbridge, *The Boat that Wouldn't Sink* (Port Jefferson, NY: Vineyard Press, 2000).

130. www.http://e,.wikipedia.org/wiki/SS_Morro_Castle (1930)

131. *Catboat Association Bulletin*, No. 58, p. 14.

132. National Park Service, 2005. "Resorts and Recreation, Chapter II" http://www.nps.gov/history/online_books/nj1/

133. H. C. Woolman. 1871. quoted in Chapter 2 of National Park Service document: http://www.nps.gov/history/online_books/nj1

134. Ocean County Historical Society, *Along the Toms River*, p. 73.

135. Runyon Colie, interview with Kent Mountford at his home in Mantoloking, 2005.

136. Lifting sneakbox over Seaside railroad causeway was recounted to the author by contemporary Applegates.

137. Edwin Schoettle, (probably) *New Jersey Courier*, excerpt of article written by Schoettle himself (date uncertain).

138. History of Seaside Heights, NJ, Business Improvement District http://www.seasideheightstourisn.com/history.htm

139. http://twp.Stafford.NJ.us/town-square/history-of-stafford-township, 2012. The first bridge to Long Beach Island was to carry the Pennsylvania RR, which travelled to Barnegat Light until 1923-26. The bridge washed away in 1935. The first automobile causeway was built in 1914-15. NJ Route 72 was built to Manahawkin in 1930.

140. Witmer Stone, *Bird Studies at Old Cape May*, Vol II, Plate 49 (Dover Publications, Inc.: 1965 edition). The photo was by R.F. Engle (proprietor of the Engleside, elsewhere discussed). It originally appeared in *Bird Lore*. Engle took photos in the early 20th century, including a wonderful scene with catboats and other small craft.

FIGURE 3-1. Commodore Edward Crabbe's 60-foot schooner *Shellback* launching at Morton Johnson's Bay Head, New Jersey, boatyard, ca. 1928.

Beth Truex Bell photograph

Shellback under full sail.

Dan Crabbe with permission

3

Morton Johnson, Boatbuilder

The upper extremity of Barnegat Bay was a near-fresh backwater at the time of first European settlement. It was to become a center of commercial and recreational boatbuilding by the early 20th century. Stable and bustling as a shore community by then, it is where the *Silent Maid* would eventually be born.

This northern end of Barnegat Bay was fed by several small streams draining from pine woods and deciduous forested uplands. Its watershed was adjacent to, but separate from, the Manasquan River. The Manasquan was the next estuary up the coast and discharged directly into the Atlantic Ocean.

In the distant past, inlets piercing upper Barnegat Bay periodically opened or closed as coastal storms dictated. These inlets were closed during the early settlement period. To the west of Barnegat Bay lay the broad nearly freshwater, but faintly tidal, Metedeconk River navigable in small sailboats for about four miles inland. Beyond that, the narrow, incised Pine Barrens portion of the river could be explored much farther in a light canoe. Native Americans, who first peopled the area, travelled seasonally to and from the coast along its course. They also stopped at the tidal head of the Metedeconk River for its deposits of colored clays, which they used for ornamental purposes and perhaps for pottery making. Tendrils of the river reached into today's Turkey Swamp wildlife area, over 17 miles inland, and today cross Route I-195, a major shore traffic artery, far into New Jersey's hinterlands.

In a time before land disturbance, the surrounding sandy soils provided a vast surface and groundwater reservoir to maintain conditions of very low salinity in upper Barnegat Bay. This environment sequestered habitat for underwater tidal freshwater meadows, which provided an incredible food supply for migratory waterfowl every autumn and winter. The birds flew southward then returned northward along what would be called the "Atlantic Flyway." Teeming flocks in seeming limitless supply were there in abundance simply for the shooting. Thus developed a need for small boats to take advantage of this resource—either for dinner, sport, or market.

The tributary streams were fertile habitat, too. Even at the end of the 1940s, the habitat was enough to make Susan Hemmer, then a 14-year-old girl, wax lyrical:

> I used to take my little 12' runabout way up into the Beaver Dam Creek— there was a spring way up there, ice cold and water the color of tea—and wild orchids— and I'd pick teaberry leaves and chew them. [There were] so many turtles, too. And down around the bridge in August when the snapper blues would run, a light spinning rod and a few spearing for bait—it was so lovely! I'd scoop up soft shell crabs and sell them to the neighbor lady down the street for 35 cents each. It was a wonderful place to be a kid.[1]

She found the old schooner *Emma C. Berry*, then sunk pretty low and moored along Beaver Dam Creek. "I'd pack my P.B. and J's [peanut butter and jelly] and off we'd go—*Emma C.*, me, and my fertile imagination. What a trio! . . . I remember the awesome beauty of the wood on the *Emma C.*—it was heavy, solid, important looking. I remember the wooden blocks [pulleys] for *Emma*'s schooner rigging."

Susan would not recognize her former haunts today, occupied as they are by tens of thousands of people. "It hurts my heart to see how the shorelines have been devastated in the name of 'improvement'…"[2]

Several people took up land at the head of the Bay in the middle 1680s, receiving grants of surveyed parcels from the Proprietors, who were acting on behalf of the King of England. John Hance took up his land in 1685. It fronted on the ocean and ran west spanning both sides of a small cove or cut and included the mouth of the tributary called Herbert Creek. Herbert Creek drained fertile, wooded land north to where the Manasquan River drainage began. This creek mouth would become the Bay Head terminus of the Manasquan Point to Pleasant Canal 243 years later, an engineering effort that forever changed the ecology of the habitat that John Hance knew.

Another settler, whose ancestors would come to the head of this Bay, was Francis Chadwick and his son John who emigrated from Oxford, England, in 1680. The Chadwicks would ultimately be intertwined by marriage into the wider family tree of Morton Johnson, boatbuilder. Settling near the Shrewsberry, the Chadwicks were the third Caucasian family living there among the Native Americans. John had one known son of the same name who was born in March of 1713. Starting at age 25, John, Jr., had 11 children by Ann Martha Jackson. He lived until age 70 when, during the American Revolution, he was ". . . killed by Tories [British sympathizers] in New York Bay April 18, 1783."[3]

By the middle of the 19th century, the Chadwick family had spread along the north Jersey shore. Much of the land surrounding the head of the bay was owned by Elijah Chadwick. Family records claim Elijah died in 1837. A generation was skipped, but another Elijah R. Chadwick was born in 1837. In 1877, this Elijah and his brother William P. sold 45 acres of dunes, grass, and sand to three Princeton, New Jersey, bankers—Edward Howe, William Harris, and David Mount, who had resort development visions in their heads.[4] The wider Chadwick family owned more sandy land south along the Barnegat peninsula near what was later called the Chadwick Fishery. They farmed the sandy, well-drained soils there and also took in seasonal guests.

David Mount and his compatriots thus founded one of Barnegat's most prestigious communities, the ultimate wealth of which was critical to aggressive yacht racing on the bay and in spurring a vibrant recreational boatbuilding industry. The family name is still carried by Mount Street, Bay Head. His grandson Tom, who lived nearly 100 years, was a popular and central figure in catboat sailing—and in a later chapter here—during the 20th century.

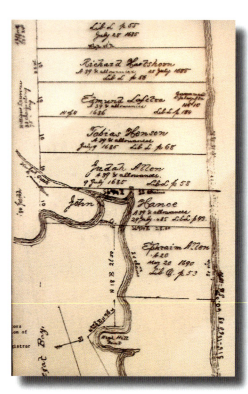

FIGURE 3-2. John Hance's lot at the head of Barnegat Bay, 1685.

Bay Head Historical Society

In 1878, Benjamin Hance owned his forbearer's parcel of land and established a boatyard at Bay Head.[5] Hance had (at least) two employees—William Johnson and his son Morton, the latter born in 1864, just as the American Civil War was ending. Morton was apprenticed to his father and honed his boatbuilding skills by working on beach skiffs and the rugged surf boats that serviced offshore pound nets.

In 1880, Morton Johnson, at age sixteen, bought, or assumed ownership of, Hance's boatyard. The firm would eventually become Morton Johnson and Company.[7] In the latter part of the 19th century, at the head of this then-freshwater estuary, they built mostly rowboats, canoes, and small cat-rigged sailboats. Drawing on local practice and the bay's commercial fleet, Morton's boatbuilding skills expanded, and he focused on building catboats for a long time.

Morton's first boat, as he told it (more probably the *first large* catboat he built), was the *Victoria*, built *ca.* 1893. *Victoria* had an active career as a catboat. Later she suffered the indignity of being reduced to a lumbering motorboat.

Her owners (at one point the Loveland family) sailed her down to Atlantic City in 1908 and during an overnight stop, crewperson Emma Johnson laundered her female companion's impossibly bulky petticoats, perhaps to be fresh for the next public appearance: "on the boardwalk at Atlantic City, Life will be peaches and cream."[10] Maggie Loveland peeled potatoes in the companionway as there was no refrigeration or convenient, pre-prepared foods for cruising sailors in those days. They were even sailing with an infant aboard. Imagine that on a hot, windless August afternoon when the hungry greenhead flies were coming off the marshes. No matter, it will cool down after sunset, just as the mosquitoes are coming out.

There is some uncertainty about the statement that *Victoria* was the first boat Morton built because Johnson family records list that he had built (maybe under Hance's or his father's supervision) an earlier catboat called the *Kitty* in 1875. *Kitty* was rebuilt by another local shipwright who installed new frames and planks. *Kitty* still existed in 1960 when the Truex family, who had worked for Johnson, finally lost track of her.[11]

FIGURE 3-3. *(Left)* The Morton Johnson–built catboat *Victoria* sailed the Lovelands to Atlantic City in 1908. *(Right)* Details of this trip and the ladies preparing dinner.

New Jersey Museum of Boating, Bob O'Brien, with permission,

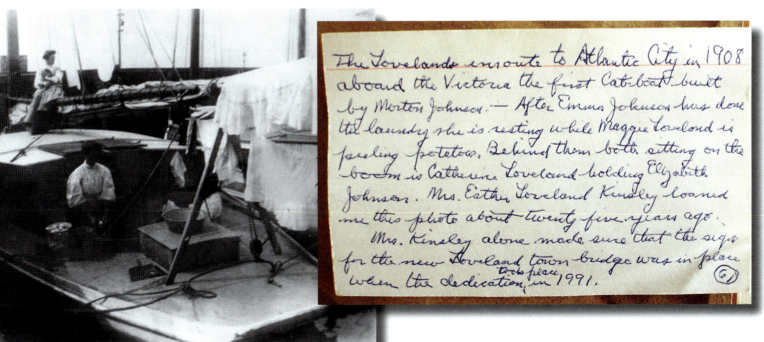

The Origins of the Barnegat Bay Catboats

The Barnegat Bay catboat tradition seems to date back before the Civil War. In 1855, Captain Samuel Birdsall of Waretown was said to have introduced the first one to the bay, sailing her down from New York, where the catboat was already a successful transplant from New England. The 20-foot *Lounge*, as she was named, was apparently intended as a pleasure boat with a curved stern, unstayed mast (set well forward), and a single gaff sail—pretty much the design for subsequent catboats. Joseph K. Ridgeway, a local bayman, recalled this introduction of catboats to Barnegat Bay when he was interviewed in 1912. He also remembered Benjamin Seaman on West Creek building the second catboat *Little Frank*, which was 18 feet long in her keel. Seaman went on to build a third catboat of 20 feet, according to Ridgeway "for a racing boat."[7]

In writing his own history of catboats, *Silent Maid*'s first owner, Edwin Schoettle, felt that catboats, strictly speaking, dated back farther still on Barnegat Bay. He notes Captain Hazelton Seaman's creation in 1836 of the indigenous sneakbox (many of which were fitted with a single-sailed spritsail rig), which you might call a catboat.

The catboat went on to evolve into a type widely used by fishermen and skippers taking out sports for pleasure on Barnegat Bay. The mast was well forward of a spacious cockpit that was comfortable and capacious, and the single gaff sail could be managed by a single hand. In a sudden blow, it was easily scandalized to take pressure

FIGURE 3-4. Gaff head catboats depicted with fishing lines being trolled through Barnegat Inlet in 1874. The boats have underslung rudders and broad wineglass transoms.
Rose's Atlas of the New Jersey shore from www.NOAA.gov

off the too-large sail by dropping the peak of the gaff in a "Bahamian reef." My uncles always said "aboard a catboat in trouble, just shoot the man at the helm;" their premise being that without fighting the tiller or wheel, she would just round up into the wind, essentially stop, or heave to, and flog her sail until tended to.

continued on page 82

FIGURE 3-5. Much-acclaimed regional artist Gerard Rutgers Hardenbergh lived much of the time on his houseboat/studio, which was moored in Scow Ditch next to Hance's boat shop. *(Left)* His watercolor of Hance's boat shed (note that all the boats shown are catboats). *(Right)* A photograph of Hardenbergh's houseboat/studio, flying the American flag just as a light nor'east morning wind begins. It will clock 'round to south later.

Bay Head, Mantoloking, Lovelandtown Historical Society

FIGURE 3-6. *(Left)* Nine catboats queued up at Island Heights in the 1880s. *(Right)* Catboat sterns, showing the overhung, raked and 'wineglass' transoms, and an Ocean Gate Yacht Club burgee.

Alicemay Weber-Wright

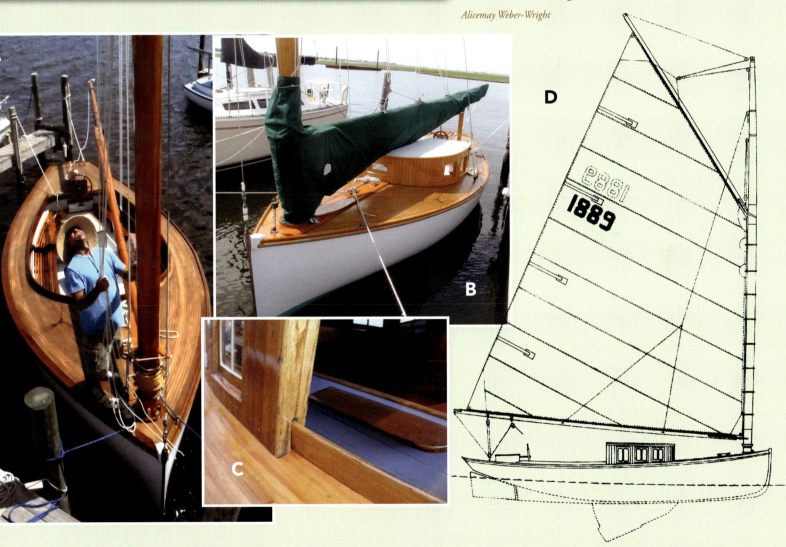

FIGURE 3-7. *(A) Myth* without her cabin. *(B) Myth* with flat-topped cabin in place. *(C)* The join of portable cabin slipped over cockpit coamings. A small drop-leaf table is rigged on each side of the centerboard trunk. *(D) Myth* with her 1889 sailplan as a rebuilt version, constructed in 1939 by Morton Johnson.

Kent Mountford photographs

The Origins of the Barnegat Bay Catboats *(continued from page 80)*

What evolved as pretty standard on Barnegat Bay was a centerboard hull broad of beam, plumb stem, mast unstayed, and fairly low freeboard with an overhung, or counter, stern, wineglass transom, and an underslung rudder.[8] Picture after picture shows catboats of this ilk tied up to the piers of summer resorts competing for afternoon sailing parties or sports to take out shooting. Many have sit-on-top summer cabins for sunshine-averse ladies of the time. These would be lifted off and left ashore when the boats were used for fishing at other seasons.

Catboat captains would inevitably race each other, if only to demonstrate which boat was the best pick in order to get new customers. The same competition was keen when trying to get fresh-caught fish to the railroad station for icing and shipment or to their prime hotel kitchen buyers. This seems all bucolic and collegial from our perspective 130 years later, but at the time success meant more food on the family table, money for boat maintenance or replacement, and I'll bet things could get pretty intense.

Sailboat racing, however, was also a lot of fun, and many summer residents (the Schoettles among them) hired or partnered with local baymen as their captains, sailing local catboats against each other for sport and trophy. Schoettle had Herbert III on his sneakbox *Mull*, Captain Hook on the *Scat* or *Silent Maid*, and later Britt Applegate on his Class A catboat.[9]

FIGURE 3-8. Morton Johnson aboard his self-proclaimed first catboat *Victoria*, built in 1893. Thirty-five years later, when they were both much older, he would buy *Victoria* back as a memento of his formative years. By that time she had been rigged down to a powerboat, fitted with a big deckhouse with a dead flat coach roof, which was the style at the time.

Beth Truex Bell, from William Truex

From 1888 to 1890, Johnson designed and built *Myth*. *Myth*, with largely the same configuration, has been rebuilt and reproduced a couple of times and still sails on Barnegat Bay today (see Figure 3-7). In 1900, Johnson designed and built *Vim*[12] for Manasquan Pavilion owner Forman Bailey. In her first years, *Vim* raced respectably and once beat the *Silent Maid*.[13] She also was a Mantoloking harbor-mate of *Silent Maid* for decades. The beautiful *Vim*, completely restored to her 1900 racing trim by Bill De Rouville's Boat Shop in Beachwood on the Toms River, was re-launched in May of 2014 by her owner Henry Colie.

Most of Johnson's early career was building boats in fresh water. It was not until about 1928 to 1931, when the Point Pleasant to Manasquan Canal first opened, that saline waters lapped at his shores. Also, (once Cranberry Inlet closed in 1812) there was no connection to the Atlantic north of Barnegat Inlet until 1931. Nonetheless, during the early decades of the 20th century, Johnson made a name for himself turning out some superb catboats.

The stable and successful personal life of Morton Johnson bears some attention. He married in the early 1890s and sired nine children, of whom one, Alex, died young. His eldest son Hubert, born about 1892, was a sailor by age 14. In 1906, Hubert successfully raced *Arran* (see Figure 2-20), a 20-foot sneakbox built by his father. In *Arran*'s first two years, this boat (named after an island in the Scottish Firth of Clyde) was recorded as the "winningest boat" in the history of the Barnegat Bay Yacht Racing Association.[14] This established Morton Johnson as capable of delivering boats that could win races.

As adults, Morton's sons each had roles in the boat business. Hubert and Paul joined the company, then their sisters Edna (who married Johnson employee Tracey Truex) and Elsie, who married Floyd Ayers. Ayers was probably a self-educated, but later licensed, engineer and became known as Morton Johnson's naval architect. Part of the wider success of the Morton Johnson Company was the continuity of these trained and committed offspring, their spouses, and a wide spectrum of other near relatives, carrying his business through the next generation!

Johnson was always open to new business and, in fact, was fishing to build a catboat for one of Schoettle's brothers, Ralph. At the end of August 1922, Johnson wrote Ralph to say the hull alone, finished and in the water, would cost him $2000.

FIGURE 3-9. *Vim*, built by Morton Johnson in 1900, is here being launched by owner Henry Colie after complete restoration at De Rouville's Boatyard in Beachwood on the Toms River, May 2014.

Kent Mountford photograph

FIGURE 3-10. An unidentified Morton Johnson catboat takes shape at Bay Head in the early 1900s.

Photo by F.S.D., clipping, files of Beth Truex Bell

Johnson concludes: "Trusting I may be favored with the order and assuring I will give you a Job you will be proud of. Yours Very Truly." I've found no evidence Ralph Schoettle proceeded with the project.

The important Class A catboat phenomenon began in 1922 when Federal Judge Charles Louis McKeenan (1876–1925), summering at Toms River, commissioned New York naval architect Charles Mower to design a catboat that he hoped would win him the Toms River Challenge Cup. She would be 28 feet overall, 22 on the waterline, 11 feet, 8 inches beam, and a skinny 30 inches draft, board up. The design for the new boat also would incorporate the latest innovations of hull design and sail aerodynamics that modern yacht design had to offer. Unlike most gaff-rigged contemporary cats, she would ultimately hoist a 605-square-foot Marconi mainsail and her lofty 45-foot mast would be stiffened and supported by wire-cable shrouds and forestays.

Morton Johnson was chosen as builder of McKeenan's boat, and the project was kept more or less under wraps. Constructed throughout the cold months and spring of 1922, the *Mary Ann* was launched on July 1. Just two days later she "showed a clean pair of heels"[16] to all the traditional catboats then in the fleet and walked away with the 1922 Toms River Challenge Cup. The fleet was in shock, and with *Mary Ann*'s singular victory, most traditional catboats were knocked out of the competition. During the subsequent winter, four new similar boats were built for the 1923 racing season. That was the year that Edwin Schoettle had James Kirk built *Forcem* (*Foursome*, *4-Some*, and *Four Some*, as it is variously reported!) from Francis Sweisguth's design. F.P. Larkin of Seaside Park had Sweisguth draw a completely new design for his catboat entry called *Tamwock*. Edward Crabbe of Toms River had Mower design his *Bat*, and she was built by Morton Johnson. A fourth catboat, *Helen,* was also built that winter.

In 1923, all these competitors originally sailed with short six-foot, so-called Swedish gaffs, against *Mary Ann*'s Marconi sail. *Mary Ann* beat the lot of them. *Helen* and the Kirk-built *Forcem* were slow enough that they never raced again.

During 1924, Morton Johnson was commissioned to build the *Spy* from *Mary Ann*'s plans for Frank Thatcher of Seaside Park. The Swedish gaffs were all discarded for the races in 1924. The new class, now considered Class A catboats, all raced with Marconi mainsails and have done so ever since.[17]

Class A catboats were built with single timber white oak keels and many sailed for 60 years prior to a rebuilding and replacement fervor late in the 20th century. This rejuvenated catboat racing on Barnegat Bay, because, with an essential 'one-design', the playing field was leveled, and the true contest could be among sailors and crews of varying skills. Of course, this was not quite true; within the parameters of boat measurement rules, skilled designers and sailmakers could still make the difference for men of means with the resources and interest to experiment. *Forcem* and the later very successful *Tamwock*, were examples of this wide spread of failure and success in performance!

This flurry of activity showed that Morton Johnson's was a very busy yard in 1923 and 1924. Tom Beaton, reflecting upon that generation says that in 1925 his grandfather David Beaton[18] had come to America from Scotland's Gourock on the Firth of Clyde, emigrating at age 38 to find work as a boatbuilder. He came to Bay Head and applied to Hubert Johnson, then in business with his own yard. Hubert Johnson was fully staffed at the time and serving the area as a marine engineer, eventually focusing on building and servicing powerboats in a time of escalating gasoline engine use. His lapstrake sea skiffs came to define the genre. Hubert sent the newcomer Beaton across the little bridge separating the two yards to his father's place, and Morton Johnson immediately hired the new Scotsman. Dave Beaton worked out so well that Hubert later said his biggest mistake had been not hiring Dave himself!

Dave Beaton thought highly of and liked Morton Johnson a great deal. Dave, on marrying, built his own home (on a parcel bought from the Hance family) working nights by kerosene lantern after a long day at the yard. One evening Morton came by to see how Dave was doing, bringing with him an apple and some lunch.[19]

Morton Johnson seems to have been genuinely liked by the rest of his employees, as well. In his prime, he was a strong man and his son Paul was as well. "The [Johnson] boys would put a shoulder under [a very heavy] boat and just nudge it where it had to go" said Tom Beaton, reflecting his family's memories of working with them.[20]

That said, Tom Beaton quotes Morton's son, Paul Johnson, who ran the yard after his father's death as saying: "My father was building a lot of boats and bid them cheaply [to get the business] in those years . . . while they were good boats and the [hull] cross sections taken from the offset tables were good, there was not a lot of lofting and laying down [the lines]."

The builders would set up molds, only as many as necessary, using the table of offsets and let the ribbands take their natural curves. This saved a lot of time, which was always at a premium in a busy boatyard. I interpret the comments to say the wood, in a sense, did the fairing for them.

Johnson, like the Herreschoffs, liked to make half models and once he was pleased, built the boat from that three-dimensional representation. Paul Johnson later told the Beatons, it was hard to make money from Sparkman-Stephens designs, because they were very fussy about all the steps and came down to make sure the workmen were adhering strictly to the plans.[21]

It's not easy to fully convert an accomplished boatbuilder to more rigorous adherence to the plans of a naval architect so some variation may have crept in. Johnson nonetheless had a particular eye for hulls. He once was striking in the waterline and boot top of a brand new sailboat soon to be launched and his own naval architect Floyd Ayers challenged him, "You haven't done any calculations, how can you know where she's going to float?" "I **don't** know," Johnson replied, but when she was launched, she was on her marks. Such is the skill, oft derided, of "building by rack of eye."[22]

Commodore Edward Crabbe[23] of Toms River had two schooners built by Morton Johnson over the years, *Windjammer* and *Shellback* (see Figure 3-1). These were serious,

FIGURE 3-11. Morton Johnson with some of his many builder's half models.

Beth Truex Bell family archive

FIGURE 3-12. (Left) Painting of Floyd Ayers, Morton Johnson's naval architect (artist's name illegible). Ayers was also an artist, a waterfowl carver, and played both violin and organ. One of the boats built at Morton Johnson's yard, not coincidentally, was for the owner of the Magnus Organ Company.[15]
(Right) Floyd and Elsie (Johnson) Ayers in 1992.

Images from Morton Johnson Bell

graceful sailing yachts. *Windjammer*, a shoal draft centerboarder, was a contender in the 1926 New London (CT) to Bermuda race, with Crabbe skippering and both Edwin Schoettle and designer, Charles Mower, among the crew. Crabbe may have named his schooners after Chatterton's popular book of adventure-tales *Windjammers and Shellbacks*, London 1926.[24]

According to Lachlan Beaton, told to his son Tom, one of these schooners as delivered was somewhat longer[25] than her plans had shown. When this was called to Morton Johnson's attention, he responded, "That's OK, I won't charge you any more for the difference."[26]

In 1925, Johnson would build another boat from one of the two blueprint sets of *Mary Ann*.[27] She was a slightly deeper midsectioned version called *Lotus* constructed for J.P. Truitt, Jr., of Island Heights. Edwin Schoettle would later buy *Lotus* for his own family to sail in the competition among members of the Class A catboat fleet. Prior to that, however, he had in mind a more ambitious project. To improve upon his less than stellar effort with *Scat II*, there would be a *Scat III*.

On January 5, 1923, Francis Sweisguth sent Schoettle preliminary plans for a new catboat (which would ultimately become *Silent Maid*) for his consideration on which ". . . the lines . . . look very good. The freeboard at bow, the beam, headroom and stability of this boat are more than *Scat I*."[28] Sweisguth seemed to be trying to get the best of *Scat II* incorporated in a boat that could make use of the unsuccessful *Forcem*'s rig. Sweisguth wrote Schoettle again on January 16 asking if he liked the plans and enumerated the virtues of her lines and the ability to "swing [a sail of] 698 sq. ft. easily."[29] This, however, was not the winning design that would later emerge from his drawing board.

Schoettle had definite ideas about catboats in general and was a strong advocate for the species. He also had high regard for Sweisguth's ability. He stated that "to design a fast, well-balanced catboat of any size that will handle well under all conditions of wind and sea is an accomplishment much more difficult than the average yachtsman or amateur designer can appreciate."[30]

Sweisguth sent him blueprints of a hull, mast, sail, and rigging plan on May 24, 1923. We don't know what boat they have on paper, but designer and owner turned in their discussions to rigging details. Schoettle adopted successful tackle details and sheeting from *Scat II* and thought about making use of some old *Scat* blocks and at least one from *Forcem*. Thirty-five blocks were on the list. Sometime in 1923, owner and designer planned to meet the following Saturday morning. Sweisguth would phone Schoettle when he arrived at Toms River, and then be picked up.

Schoettle's new catboat might ultimately have been intended to be the largest cat ever built, but in 1902 C.C. Hanley had already built the 33-foot, 4-inch *Thordis*, viewed by some as his masterpiece. However, it is likely that either Sweisguth or Schoettle were aware that this Buzzards Bay (MA) boat was sailing about.[31] Schoettle's new catboat would be 33 feet, 5 inches when finally measured!

There were a number of other cat-rigged boats that exceeded both in size. One, which came through Barnegat Bay around 1959, was a retrofit from some other rig. She was 45 feet long, to my eye ungainly, and owned by a then popular New York news anchor. We rendezvoused with this huge boat, but the news anchor and his family were not very friendly or interested in us! Today, on the Chesapeake's Eastern Shore, Iris Clarke sails and charters her great-grandfather's 41-foot *Selina II*, built on Long Island Sound in 1926.[32] Maybe for a short time *Silent Maid* could have been the largest true catboat afloat, as was warranted to us at the time my family acquired her . . . maybe not!

From *Scat III* to *Silent Maid*

Sweisguth created a pencil sketch for Schoettle showing how various designs for the stern and moveable ballast would play out in waterline length, which they both realized would affect speed in the finished vessel. On this single sheet of paper, Sweisguth headed the notes with the name *Scat III*, but a pencil notation was made next to the name correcting it to *Silent Maid*—the very first appearance of her final name.

Wayne Blake of the Catboat Association told me that plans for the new catboat appeared in *Rudder Magazine*, showing only her Marconi rig, and that the boat was named *Scat III* at that time.

Schoettle's reason for this shift in name, according to his daughter Mary (Schoettle) Mitchell, was that *Scat II*'s new owner failed to satisfactorily honor his agreement to change the boat's name after purchase. He simply added an extra "t" making her *Scatt II* and let it go at that. The names, spoken in future race discussions would thus sound the same, engendering confusion. Mitchell said this angered her father, but Schoettle later showed no residual consternation over this in his own writings.

Silent Maid was apparently not Schoettle's first choice as an alternative. Wayne Blake said that once *Scat III* was crossed off, Schoettle intended to name the new boat *Sally Constant*. Wayne was puzzled by this, but I immediately understood this was using one of Sara's nicknames, and constant surely reflected Edwin's appraisal of her devoted partnership in their life together.[39]

Schoettle's choice of the new name Silent Maid will likely remain an enigma, but there are several routes I followed trying to understand it. Renaissance playwright Ben Jonson first produced Epicoene or "The Silent Woman" using the Blackfriar Children, a company of boy actors in 1609. The story focuses on the search for a truly quiet female partner by the principal character. With this premise humorously

resolved, the play was the first legally performed in England after the Restoration of Charles II to the throne. Samuel Pepys, the famous diarist, attended a London performance of this work in 1660.[40] Schoettle might possibly have known of this work; or...

Richard Strauss later rewrote Epicoene as an opera Die schweigsame Frau, or "Silent Woman," the overture of which is a delightful score, easily evoking a sprightly sailing vessel. Unfortunately, near as I can determine, it was first publicly performed in Dresden during the summer of 1935, a little late to inspire Edwin Schoettle!

FIGURE 3-13. Sign outside the public house "Silent Woman Inn," Dorset, England, a recent version of an old idea used elsewhere in the past.

In England there is at least one pub in Dorset called the "Silent Woman Inn" outside which the sign for which depicts a decapitated, buxom, but fully dressed, maiden. Similarly, there was a "Silent Woman" restaurant in Waterville, Maine (from which one could still buy plates in 2011 with a similar logo).

Had Schoettle any reservations about his wife, this might have been a tongue-in-cheek dig, but he apparently was continually delighted with her, and she was often his sole sailing partner aboard the new yacht.

Lastly, the Marc Shoettle family home in Bay Head had a domestic employee who, because of her limited ability with English, was very quiet and was called the "Silent Maid."

With no probable resolution, the enigma remains—started with the two words "Silent Maid" penciled and underscored on a sheet of paper all those years ago.

Sweisguth at one point discussed bronze-shelled blocks rather than the wood cheeked and varnished ones. But later said he'd ordered the list from Merriman. Those wood-shelled blocks were the original durable ones rigging *Silent Maid*, and which I varnished more than once, while my family owned her.

The wire bridles Sweisguth designed for this prospective boat spread bending loads along the length of the gaff, and also allowed the point of force application to shift optimally along the wire as hoist and peaking of the gaff progressed. These bridles would be with *Silent Maid* to the end of her sailing days along with the 631 feet of running rigging which Sweisguth estimated![33] Schoettle elsewhere writes that (either estimate or actual) the cost of "spars, rigging, blocks, freight, etc. $750.00."[34]

Sweisguth wrote again on July 24, 1923, first congratulating Schoettle on his win racing presumably *Forcem*, by the wording, the previous day. "You always sail for all the boat is worth and deserve to win the other races too.[35]"

Schoettle seemed to have been eyeing Morton Johnson as builder for a new boat, whatever that might be. Johnson replied in a typed letter regarding a visit from Schoettle, and on October 3, 1923, proposed either a new catboat (hull only) of 27 feet for $1350 or a duplicate of *Scatt* (sic. *Scat II*) for $2350, if Schoettle gave him the old *Scat* (*Scat II*) as part of the deal. The *new* catboat issue was still unsettled.

Writing in 1927–28, Edwin Schoettle harked back to the price of new catboats in the 1890s when ". . . the average price for a 30-foot catboat, completely rigged, was about $1000 to $2000."[36] Despite costs being significantly higher in 1923 and despite his comfortable personal financial condition, Edwin was still looking for those old-time prices!

Johnson offered a catboat contract for "both or either of them as soon as I hear from you." The letter is signed this time FOR Morton Johnson by S.W. Van Note. It is a measure of the technology of the times when Johnson's stationary "Morton Johnson Boat Builder and Designer" listed the phone number as "Bell Phone: Point Pleasant 79." There was no ten-digit dialing in those days.

Schoettle, ever the sharp dealer, annotated the letter in his hand "Changed to $2000.00 if I provide toilet, wash stand, sink, water tank, ballast." A more ambitious project than a copy of *Scat II* was afoot.

On October 9, 1923, Sweisguth, handwritten to Schoettle, was pleased *Scat II* was to be sold, and said that on the previous Saturday, he had been in Bay Head, talking to Johnson who he "hopes will build the new boat." Sweisguth stated for the record, "We want the new boat to be a monument to us all." How prescient.

Schoettle, again writing in praise of his designer friend Sweisguth, said he "is so thorough and painstaking in his work that it would be almost impossible for him to design a poor boat." Hmmm, the issue of *Forcem*'s failure seems to have been lost here! "…it is nevertheless to his [Sweisguth's] credit to say that, as a token of his versatility, to do large and small craft equally well is an accomplishment he has reason to be proud of; and it is to this part of his work that I wish particularly to pay tribute.[37]"

Schoettle went on to say that *Scat II* (also a Sweisguth design) with her wide squared off transom, lots of buoyancy aft, and relatively fine bows tended to go by the bows when pressed rail-under. Sweisguth sought to correct this by giving the new boat more overhang and a transom that tucked up some out of the water.

On his drawings, this would lengthen her some 2 feet, 4 inches,[38] and Sweisguth asked Johnson how much that lengthening would cost Schoettle. This is reflected in a December 1923 letter from the latter: "You spoke 3 feet (for) $150," but Sweisguth says only again "Can you do boat for $2000 price?" Schoettle, always the sharp, tight-fisted businessman was behind the scenes tightening the screws!

This lengthening at the stern would give the boat even more waterline length—and thus speed—when heeled, and the curve in her buttocks (vertical longitudinal sections showing shape of the hull) would become long and flat—resulting in still more speed.

Schoettle's letter continues, "You may draw up your regular form of contract and send it to me for my signature," stating that correspondence should be sent to him in Philadelphia until Christmas, then to Island Heights where, presumably, he would be living and thus closer to inspect the project as it moved ahead. "Give me plenty of notice of when you will begin the work, as Francis and I wish to be there when you start and go over with you the lines on the [lofting] floor, etc."

On December 28, 1923, Edwin Schoettle and Morton Johnson enter into a formal contract and payment schedule. The agreed price for this new boat was to be "twenty-five hundred dollars." This seemed pretty clear to me; and that's not $2000.

The simple contract between Johnson and Schoettle was agreed upon and became a living document through which we can follow the course of the construction of the boat using Johnson's proposed payment schedule.

Schoettle immediately started pushing Johnson to change things: "The two thousand dollar price was figured on a square stern boat (like *Scat II*). You said if we extended the stern three feet you would have to add $150.00 to the price. We have only extended the stern two feet. Can you make the price Two Thousand Dollars to cover this boat just as she is designed?"

Change orders are common occurrences in almost all agreements today, but here it seemed the owner and builder started out in two different directions. Look at the construction plan; there is a lot of extra wood and detailed work in those last couple of feet. I'll bet Johnson had to think hard about that request! The two of them don't seem to be directly discussing it in the surviving papers.

At signing, Schoettle paid Johnson, likely in person, the first installment of $250. The contract page also is annotated by notes on accessory expenses Schoettle logged, with which he estimates the total cost

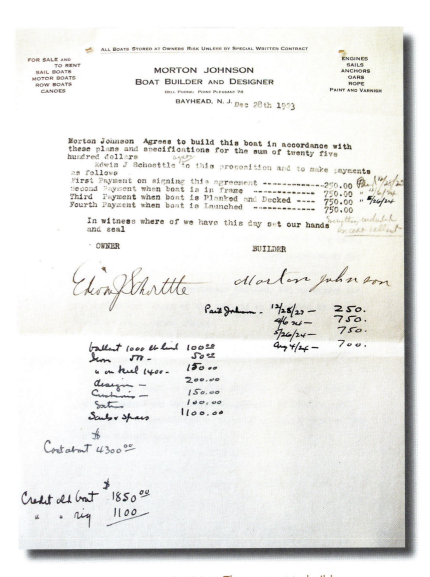

FIGURE 3-14. The contract to build *Silent Maid* showing Schoettle's payment schedule, accessory costs, and other assumptions.

Toms River Seaport Society Archive

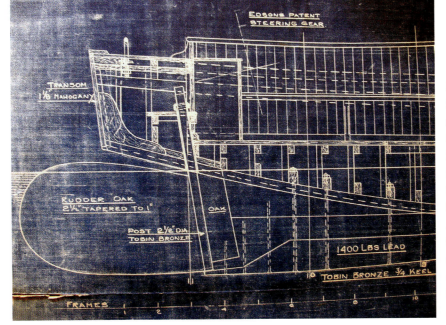

FIGURE 3-15. *Silent Maid*'s construction plan around the stern. This sheet was, I believe, modified and reprinted for reproduction in Schoettle's book *Sailing Craft* (1928) because it incorporates reference to the *Maid*'s racing wins in 1925 and 1926. It also suggests that *Silent Maid* had originally been designed at 34-feet length. Did adjusting this to the final 33' 5" happen during Schoettle's negotiation with Morton Johnson? He originally wanted $150 more for the full lengthening as Sweisguth envisioned. The book twice prints *Silent Maid*'s length as 34 feet, consistent with the blueprint, but at odds with Schoettle's printed text!

Francis Sweisguth papers, Toms River Seaport Society archives

The Schoettles Love of Music

The Schoettles, as elsewhere described, apparently were serious music lovers, regularly attending symphony concerts in Philadelphia. One might suspect this was just perfunctory social-circle participation, but they also dedicated an entire room to music at Crosstrees. It is not unlikely that the couple paid attention to new trends in music even as they were creating their new sailing yacht.

Putting the beginning of 1924 into context, it was literally the start of a new era in American music. In February 1924, Paul Whiteman's orchestra, with Ferdie (actually Ferde) Grofe as his arranger,[42] held a concert in New York City's Aeolian Hall called "An Experiment in Modern Music." The program introduced a jazz version of Sir William Walton's "Pomp and Circumstance," to the original of which I'll wager most of my readers marched during at least one graduation ceremony! Also on the agenda was Grofe's orchestration of George Gershwin's "Rhapsody in Blue," arguably the first symphonic adaptation of jazz themes, and one of my personal favorites.

These contributions would alter the tone of American music thereafter; *Silent Maid* would do the same for catboat sailing!

of *Silent Maid* will be $4300. You couldn't VARNISH *Silent Maid* for that money here in the 21st century . . . let alone barely fit her with a proper dinghy![41]

I was surprised to see Schoettle making the assumption of an $1850 credit for the "old boat," presumably *Scatt II*, and some assumptions about the value of her rig. Her actual later sale to private hands was never recorded as a dollar amount.

The original blueprints of Sweisguth's plans have only been partly preserved. Instructive reductions of these drawings were published by Edwin Schoettle in his book *Sailing Craft* so readers can inspect them at small scale. Sweisguth's original lines were carefully drawn with plenty of sections, waterlines, and buttocks to define what Sweisguth wanted to achieve in the shape of this hull. There are four diagonals that appear to assure the lines were properly faired and, if lofted correctly, would create a hull accurately representing the designer's vision. Six offsets on the boat's barn door rudder give ample instruction to the builder for reproducing its profile.

John Brady, shipwright at the Philadelphia Independence Seaport, where *Silent Maid* was transported for restoration (and construction of her replica from 2007 to 2009) was surprised to find her oak keel timber had a serious flaw (an area of compromised strength). "I don't know why Johnson used this piece of wood," Brady mused.[43]

 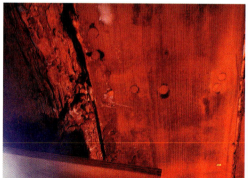

FIGURE 3-16. *(Left)* Crack in *Silent Maid*'s deadwood, adjacent to the ballast cutout and just below a defect in the original keel timber. At right, in the left photo, the original lead keel has been replaced for museum exhibition with a wooden replica. *(Right)* A large thwartships crack in the *Maid*'s keel looking forward, starboard side, ahead of centerboard trunk.

Kent Mountford photographs at Philadelphia Independence Seaport, January 2011

Placement of the defect was just above where almost half the depth of her deadwood was cut away to make an aperture for the lead ballast keel. This meant less wood—less structural strength—in an area where the hull could have used more support.

Also, it was also clearly in conflict with Sweisguth's specifications, in which:

> . . . best of material and workmanship to be used in the construction. Timber to be well seasoned and **free from defects**. The owner or designer shall at all times have the power to reject and [any] defective workmanship or material and this defective workmanship or material to be replaced by the builder without extra charge. . . . Scantlings: Keel, White oak, sided to 10 inches tapered from aft of centerboard trunk to 3 inches at transom.

Sweisguth thought his boilerplate contract couldn't have been clearer. How could that keel ever have gotten by?

This area of weakness also would be where *Silent Maid's* engine (offset to port) would be bedded in her in later years; more weight and torque in an unfortunate place. This was not significant in the years when she was new, resilient, and a pure sailing vessel, but became of more importance by the 1950s when she was three decades old and subject to some unexpected shocks.

The keel timber in question must have been well in place when Schoettle's next payment came due. The vessel was, as specified, "in frame" and $750 was paid to Johnson on April 6, 1924. Schoettle (or less likely Sweisguth) typing an undated letter states that: "The following frames forward of the transom . . . Port side . . . #2, 6, 22; Starboard . . . #10, 20, 28 are badly checked and should be replaced or a frame set in alongside to reinforce them. I know that if left as they are they will break sometime in the future. I have had this happen in another boat and do not want to have the same experience over again."

Johnson suggested in conversation that the boat's planking was too light and Schoettle gave him permission to increase the thickness. Schoettle said the garboards and sheer strake "could be 1- 1/8" and of yellow pine" then corrected himself: "The sheer strake could be made of mahogany as the topsides are to be varnished." While minor, this seems to be yet another change in plans Schoettle has introduced. "The keel, stem, and framing of the *Scat III* look good." But he corrected several inadequate fastenings, requiring "through bolts to shelf, plank, and frames. Screwing them to the deck beams alone is not sufficient. . . . I wish you the best of luck with the planking and hope to see you again in a few weeks. Yours very Truly (unsigned)."[44]

In an unusual move, not specified by the plans, Johnson elected to mortise in the heel of each frame to the keel. "It was just one of the things he did, I guess," commented John Brady, of the Philadelphia Independence Seaport.

Johnson chose to fasten her planking with galvanized nails and did not choose screws, which would have given greater holding power. He chose bronze for the keel bolts. I'm sure Schoettle would have preferred bronze screws in the planking, but Johnson was within the original specifications doing what he did.

This is counter, however, to a specific preference stated in the April 20, 1924, Schoettle (Sweisguth?) letter: "In regard to plank fasteners I prefer brass screws or copper rivets, I do not think nails will hold. Please see that the frames are well oiled [against checking]."

The choice Johnson made was one widely used in small-boat building, and some builders claimed that it resulted in a tighter structure because corrosion expanded the fastenings into the wood fibers, locking them more tightly. This firmly held opinion was typified by a letter from Chesapeake shipwright M.M. Davis to yacht designer John G. Hanna in 1928. He says in part:

> Galvanized fastenings will last almost for a generation . . . my grandfather built in 1872 a schooner about 80 feet long in which the fastenings were all galvanized. We had the occasion about two years ago [that would have been 1926] to haul this boat . . . and the fastenings were as good as the day the boat was built . . . galvanized fastenings . . . will last twice as long as any wood that can be obtained for either planking or ceiling. . . . Why spend considerable money for copper fastenings. In my judgment it would be much better to use this money in other parts of the boat where it would serve a much better purpose.[45]

Galvanized might last "almost a generation," but *Silent Maid* would have to sail from 1924 until 2005—81 years or well past two and half, 30-year generations! Schoettle and Sweisguth's preference was ignored and the die was cast for iron sickness [46] problems in the ascendency by the time my family owned *Silent Maid* starting in 1953. This was at the end of her fastening's first generation (driven 1923, assessed in 1953). Galvanized iron corrodes slowly but inexorably in wet wood, once the hot-dipped zinc coating erodes or cracks the iron inside corrodes (rusts) combines with oxygen from water or air and the chemical oxide is bulkier than pure iron. It thus tightens the fastenings within the wood and is for a while stronger.

Whenever metals are mixed in a structure where they will be immersed in salt water, the salt solution connects them electrolytically. This creates a battery with weak, continual current flow where one metal, the 'less noble' on the table of elements (iron or steel for example versus copper or bronze), will corrode away over time. It is only a matter of time before the weaker metal fails structurally.

A few of *Silent Maid*'s ancient construction blueprints are preserved at the Toms River Seaport Society. Among them are a few from other predecessor or speculation boats. Sweisguth labels one sheet dated from November 1913 as a "35 foot Catboat," so he had thought about big cats before! In 1920, he designed a 30-foot catboat, which might have been a *Scat II* version.

It is interesting that in Schoettle's book *Sailing Craft*, *Silent Maid* is twice labeled on the figures as "34 feet," while her actual on-deck length was 33 feet, 5 inches (see Figure 3-17). Schoettle's text gives her overall length at 33 feet, and in my father's copy of *Sailing Craft*, the pencil lines drawn on the page as he tried to reconcile this discrepancy are still there. The photo-reduction on MacMillan's printed page is only 3¾ inches long and accurate scaling is difficult. However, Schoettle much later wrote an interested admirer that the *Sailing Craft* figures could be photo-enlarged from the text ten-fold without significant distortion,[47] good enough for the study plan this man sought.

Penciled notes by Schoettle for *Scat III* annotated for *Silent Maid* give her overall length, including stem band, as 33 feet, 5 inches, and a "short waterline of 28 feet, 8 inches, and long waterline 29 feet, 3/8 inches." I can't help but wonder if that exact length was intentional. She was just an inch longer than C.C. Hanley's 33 feet, 4 inches *Thordis*, built in 1902 to sail on Buzzards Bay, Massachusetts.[48] When we bought the *Maid*, we were told, on special authority (the Broker!) that she was the largest "true catboat"—whatever that meant! Schoettle also includes a note "sail 784" but the BBYRA measuring committee gets a total of 816.18 square feet. These apparently were numbers decided before the boat's name change. At a later time, Schoettle adds ballast information in ink on this page (which is consistent with the BBYRA measurer H.B. Scammell's

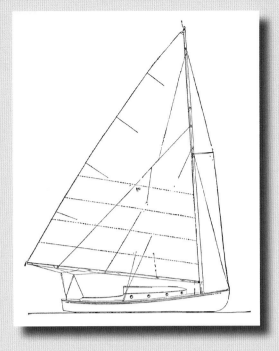

SAIL PLAN OF SILENT MAID — GAFF-SAIL

SAIL PLAN OF SILENT MAID — MARCONI RIG

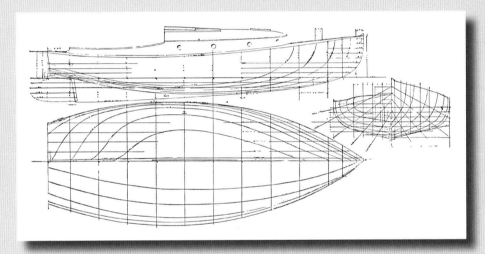

THIRTY-FOUR-FOOT CATBOAT, SILENT MAID — LINES

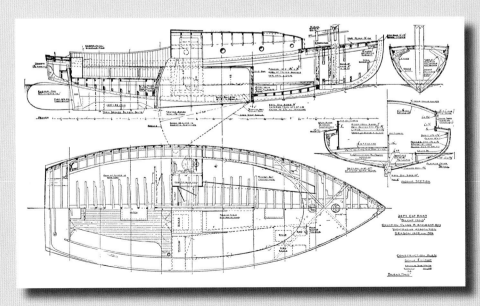

FIGURE 3-17. Sweisguth's design drawings of *Silent Maid* and captions for each as printed in Schoettle's *Sailing Craft.*

THIRTY-FOUR-FOOT CATBOAT, SILENT MAID — CONSTRUCTION PLAN

data for 1926). Her *total* ballast, fixed and moveable, would be 2900 pounds, distributed as follows:

1924 Ballast, *Silent Maid*

7 Bags 50 lb (lead shot)	350
20 bricks of 25 lb (lead)	500
4 Pieces of lead	150
5 Pigs of lead	500

For a total moveable ballast of 1,500 pounds

An innovation in the new catboat was also to be a large cast outside ballast keel of 1400 pounds. This was let into the deadwood as shown in Figure 3-16 , at an especially vulnerable place in the *Silent Maid*'s structure. This monolithic ballast was cast at the yard, per Sweisguth's specifications. Schoettle got a price for lead (which was 10 cents a pound in 1923), and the process was likely as described below. A note in the Toms River Seaport files also documents that he purchased 400 pounds of lead from the estate of a deceased Barnegat sailor of his acquaintance for a bargain two cents a pound.

A wood mold was made and sand was piled around it to carry heat away to avoid it burning. The inside surfaces were faced with asbestos mixed in plaster of Paris. Dowels were set up exactly where the keel bolts (Tobin bronze, in this case) were to be passed through. A vat heated by wood fires or kerosene burners held the melting lead. Chunks of new lead were thrown in cold, and all slowly became an amorphous fluid.

When the lead was ready to be run into the mold, care had to be taken that the tap and whatever flume was used to guide the pour were preheated so they would not cool and plug the flow. Lead contacting the faces of the mold cooled fastest, as the heat was carried away by the sand piled around it, but because the wood molds charred, these surfaces still usually needed finishing. Irregularities were chipped or planed away by chisel, thus setting the final shape that would remain throughout the vessel's life.[49]

The *Maid*'s gaff rig could spread 950 square feet as designed. With her spar far forward, the twisting forces would be immense as the sail pried mast against its partners and the weight of the boat. These forces plus the weight of several crew perched on the opposite rail to weather twisted the hull, with a lever arm of over six feet. (The lever arm around center of buoyancy is about half *Silent Maid*'s beam.) Sweisguth, anticipating this, incorporated two long, diagonal, rail-to-rail bronze straps affixed under the deck, crossing just behind the mast partners. Each would carry the strain as tension along a greater portion of the hull and, on the side away from the wind, spread the compressive forces as well.

At one time *Silent Maid* might have been planned with a set of jaws on her boom, as well as her gaff. Jaws are a simple wooden "Y" shaped yoke that rides against the mast as a pivot allowing the boom to swing side to side in sailing. My old 1924 cat *Spray*, built by Cornelius Irons, had jaws on both the gaff and the boom: cheap and simple. Sweisguth, however, sends Schoettle a drawing in which he shows that a gooseneck fitting can give ten more degrees boom angle, winging out on a dead run. This fitting of galvanized iron as originally installed on *Silent Maid* is a mechanical pivoting mechanism and gives a small advantage racers would seek. *Silent Maid* has, thereafter, always had a gooseneck boom fitting.

Specific paperwork does not survive, but since Edwin had patronized Pigeon Spar Company with fabricating *Forcem*'s mast at an earlier time, it is possible that the *Maid*'s spars were built off site by the same company. This firm, which was also noted for

FIGURE 3-18. The heaviness of *Silent Maid*'s mast partners revealed during her refit in the 1980s.

Marie Darling photograph

FIGURE 3-19. Sweisguth's undated sketch to Schoettle demonstrating the downwind advantage of a boom gooseneck over wooden boom jaws, as were used aboard *Silent Maid*.

Toms River Seaport Society

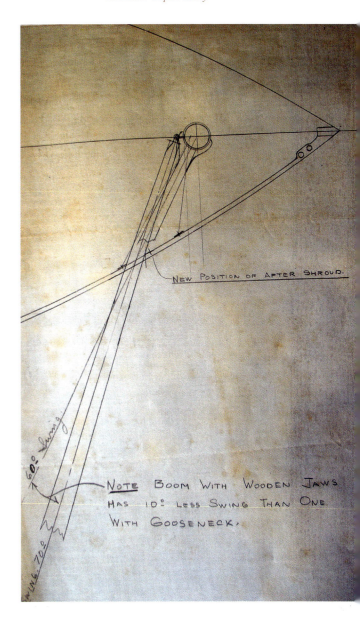

NEW POSITION OF AFTER SHROUD.

NOTE BOOM WITH WOODEN JAWS HAS 10° LESS SWING THAN ONE WITH GOOSENECK.

fabricating framing spars for early wooden aircraft, supplied many then state-of-the-art constructions over the following decades, including those for John G. Alden's 1931 schooner *High Tide*, built in Maryland for J. Rulon Miller. The five spars in *High Tide*'s rig cost $1600.[50] No cost for *Silent Maid*'s impressive mast has been preserved.

There was a rumor extant around Barnegat Bay that a Marconi rig mast for *Silent Maid* had been built, but when Sally Schneider and her friends searched for it in the mid-1960s, the story was that it had been "burned in a barn fire."[51] This could have been the Island Heights boatyard fire that destroyed the A-Cat *Tamwock*, or perhaps there was some confusion around the eventual torching of the Schoettle's spar shed (or barn) at Crosstrees. The latter, it was said, had been built to accommodate *Silent Maid*'s enormous (gaff rig) mainmast, which at the end of the day was not much different in length from a Class A catboat's. Family members suggested offhand that Edwin's generosity with boat parts may have found the spar donated to some other boat.

Wherever the spars were built, there were a number of charges from Morton Johnson for working on the mast, wire splicing, the mast hoops, and rigging among submitted bills, and I believe she sailed her entire working life with whatever original stick was stepped in her that year.

Schoettle's third installment on *Silent Maid* was due when she was planked and decked. This check was given to Johnson on May 20, 1924.

Silent Maid's interior layout was envisioned to be the same as that employed in *Scat II* with a head aft on the port side and two extra-long berths/settees, which could accommodate two reasonably short people head-to-tail for sleeping. They would also serve as seats when food was served on two mahogany drop leaves mounted to each side of the centerboard trunk. The galley was to go forward on the starboard side, in what I'd consider the most inconvenient and hot portion of the cabin.

Schoettle seemed satisfied with this. (I suppose it was to be poor Sara who would be cooking —literally and figuratively—bent with low headroom, over the hissing burners of their Primus stove!) *Scatt II* stored nearby at Johnson's boatyard was to serve as a model for the layout.

The final payment, another $750, was to be made when the boat was launched. Here some difficulties began for Schoettle, because as summer and the sailing season approached, he had expected to have *Silent Maid* in commission by June 1 based on his correspondence with Johnson. No way would this happen; there were too many loose ends. He wrote Johnson upon receiving a punch-list of jobs at the end of July that detailed a lot of work on spars and rigging, varnish, copper paint (then just $1 a quart!), interior carpentry, hinges, cabin screens, steering gear, etc. occurring between June 19 and July 28.

Sweisguth's specifications called for *Silent Maid* to have one prime coat and three coats of white. The bottom planks were to be painted with approved green. However, it was decided by Schoettle, earlier in the game, that the topsides would be finished bright in varnish. Morton's crew must have done exemplary woodwork in planking, which would show off well with vanish. Varnish does a poor job of hiding defects, so Schoettle seems to have had confidence when he decided to have the *Maid*'s hull finished bright. There was also the usual brightwork on cabin trunk, trim, cockpit seats, and sole.

Standard for the time was a thinned coat to penetrate into the wood's open grain, followed by perhaps eight coats, between each of which the entirety was sanded with increasingly fine grit paper. Morton Johnson Bell's grandfather Tracey ("Trace") Truex (who had married Morton's sister) worked at the yard during those years, as indeed had the next two generations of Trace's family, who later worked for "Uncle Paul," Morton's son. Trace was an accomplished finish painter as distinguished from the guy told to slap on a coat of primer. He and all the yard birds worked six days a week.

The finish jobs were a specialty, and it is likely that Trace Truex lay on those first gleaming signature coats of varnish that defined *Silent Maid* during her halcyon years.

Notable was *Silent Maid*'s holly inlaid mahogany steering wheel, a fixture that has survived the vessel's entire 90 years. Its cost was never specified, but a few years later in 1935 William H. Whiting Company in Baltimore sold them for $66.60.[52] Apparently this wheel, obtained elsewhere, had not been shipped until August 17, and Schoettle was charged $2.94 for *expressage* on that accelerated delivery, though Johnson later credits him for much in dispute. Johnson considered many small items like this wheel issue to be extras, and he sent Schoettle a bill for $849.31.

Schoettle—press of business no doubt— took his good time to evaluate this bill and, complying with the contract, makes his agreed final payment of $700 on August 4, 1924. He then handwrote Johnson (in an undated letter): "Your charges for extras seem high and some of the items should have been included in boat contract." He went on to list several issues suggesting there were things, such as the cracked frames and moving the end-log on the

FIGURE 3-21. Mark Orr is mirrored in his varnish work on the replica *Silent Maid*'s topsides at Beaton's Boatyard in April 2012.

Kent Mountford photograph

centerboard trunk, which had been done incorrectly and had to be fixed. Schoettle asked him to ". . . write me how much to take off the bill; send me a complete corrected [word missing] as the old bill and balance brought forward do not agree in bills I have here."

Schoettle seems to have taken possession of *Silent Maid* just before (or by) the first of August, but there is no record of any launch celebration. Schoettle was particular about sails, especially when a boat had only one sail. He stated the sail's quality was of utmost importance in a boat's performance. By November 1923, Schoettle had obtained a quote of $614.90 for a sail from Ratsey and Lapthorn, but it is not clear whether they actually made the first sail.[53] She certainly sailed with *something* laced to her spars and hoops through the rest of 1924 and into 1925.

In August 1925, *Silent Maid*'s next mainsail was cut and sewn in 10-ounce duck by George R. Burrows on South Street, New York City. The order specifying the dimensions for her sail is preserved—an impressive 51 feet, 10 inches on the roach, clew to the peak of her gaff! That year Burrows featured a picture of *Silent Maid* in its advertisements and touted her successful racing.

Arguing over the payment of outstanding bills, Johnson and Schoettle went back and forth again and again over the next several months. Johnson sent Schoettle a bill in October 1924 including 16 hours for "[building hatch] screens and varnishing [them]" for $16.50; the labor varnishing was $1 an hour, and this same rate appears in several places. The varnish itself was billed at $1.25 for a pint and a half. Varnishing today (a 2013 datum!) at the only Barnegat Bay yards worth their salt runs $100 an hour. The screens were apparently mahogany framed ones for the hatches and companionway doors, because those for the six circular bronze port-lights were separately billed at $11.

SILENT MAID

DESIGNER
Francis Sweisguth, N.A.
Ford & Payne

OWNER
Edwin J. Schoettle, Esq.
Philadelphia

1925 CHAMPION

Barnegat Bay Class B Catboats

GEO. R. BURROWS, Inc.,
2 South St.,   New York City

Cable "Burrosails", N. Y.
Telephones Bowling Green 9062 and 9063

Johnson billed again on October 31, 1924, for a residual $221.89 for the lettering on the *Maid's* transom. Morton Johnson Bell recalls that this work was "contracted out," to a local who was expert in handling that delicate task. "He would come in at the end of the day, when there was no dust flying and little wind around the yard."[54] He would do his job in the quiet and while the light was still good, outlining the letters, applying the sizing, daintily pouncing in the incredibly thin gold leaves, supplied as a little book, the pages of which would just cover a square foot. If there were no bubbles or errors and the lettering was perfect, he would burnish with a tool to the finished wood surface, and it would be ready to be sealed under preserving coats of varnish. A September 20, 1924, invoice from Johnson to Schoettle included "4½ books (gold leaf) $4.95." In the ridiculously inflated gold market of 2014, this could cost $229.00.[55]

Johnson sent yet another bill on November 25 for the same $221.89, but apparently things were still comfortable enough between them that he added for the winter 1924–1925 "storage for *Silent Maid* 33 ft @ $1.50, $49.50."

One of the outstanding issues submerged in the joy of signing the contract was that Schoettle believed Johnson had agreed to store *Scat II*, so that some good features and interior layout could be copied from her. Also, apparently in the interim, *Scat II* had been sold by Schoettle himself, and he understood that "the boat would be stored without charge to me or Bates [Daniel Bates of Philadelphia, her next owner] . . . and you would get the work in spring [fitting the boat out]."[56]

Johnson wrote back to Schoettle denying that he had agreed to store *Scat II* gratis; only if he had bought her from Schoettle for his own account. He seems to have typed this letter himself using a manual typewriter (there were no others, of course!) but with an old two-toned ribbon that made the "o"s into solid black dots, and which had a shift key that allowed him to highlight the much overdue date of the bill with red ink. He states his case plainly: "…in fact I think when all extrys [sic] are paid for that you have far the better of me, as you have a boat you could not duplicate extras and all for a lot more money than you paid for her, and am sure were given all your contract called for and more."

Schoettle made still more and final corrections to the account, deducting the storage Johnson had added for *Scat II*, the pesky expressage shipping charge for the *Maid's* steering wheel, and the marine toilet Schoettle had provided per the original agreement. He reckoned an amount he felt just and also paid the *Maid's* storage for winter, sending Johnson a check for $154.52 on December 1.

The deal is finally done and *Silent Maid's* career has begun!

Figure 3-22. (Top) The Burrows sail advertisement after *Silent Maid* won the Bay Class B championship. *(Bottom)* The 1925 Johnson Brothers Boatworks' original photo from which the ad was crafted. Edwin Schoettle and his hired Captain Hook are aboard.
Schoettle family, with permission

Morton Johnson's After Morton Johnson

The juxtaposition, in Bay Head, of three boatyards all bearing some variation of the Johnson name was always confusing to me as a young man. Nobody bothered to explain that Hubert Johnson had been Morton's eldest son and his engineering skills put him in position to focus his business on the powerboat side of recreational boating. My own first little cabin sailboat was brokered out of Hubert's yard for a big $750, but I never saw the owners or managers, only the helpful friendly yard birds. Johnson Brothers Boatworks, directly adjacent, was run by two Johnson brothers, Zachariah and Abraham, unrelated to Morton's family. For some reason, these were the people who had one of the classic photographs of *Silent Maid* taken (Figure 3-22) and it has since always been credited to "Johnson Bros." It appears also in Schoettle's *Sailing Craft* on page 97.

The third facility, Morton Johnson's yard, went on to build a lot more than catboats and some very elegant yachts emerging from his yard over the following decade. Having built the schooner *Windjammer* for Commodore Edward Crabbe of Toms River, they built Crabbe a second schooner *Shellback*.

The efficiency of some of the yard's craftspeople was demonstrated during construction of their largest schooner *Osprey* in 1932. Dave Beaton was set to work caulking one side and two men the other. Beaton worked five seams at once, pounding in lengths of cotton with a caulking mallet. He finished the entire side of her hull before the other two, who then wanted him to come over and work with them. He replied simply "No" and went on about his business.[57] Beaton was, for the time, well compensated and happy with the money Morton paid him, which could have been $0.80 an hour. He was good enough that Johnson let him put in as many hours as he wanted; so he could have earned a Depression wage of $48 a week, when my own father, a tool and die maker, was struggling with a new wife to bring home $15 weekly.

The yard seemingly weathered the great depression. In fact, Morton Johnson, Inc.'s, largest yacht—the schooner *Osprey* built for Mr. Carmen Runyon[58]—was launched July 1, 1933. This might well have been the last boat that they launched while Morton was still at the helm. He died in 1933 at age 69.[59]

In his later years, Morton Johnson received a lot of deserved attention as people looked back on his long career, and the many fine boats he and his workers built. As he got older, he looked to escape some of the bustle of the active yard and carved out an area in the big shed of the yacht yard—a space on a mezzanine, overlooking the main floor. Here, at his own speed and to his own standards, he built the kind of small boats he had started with a half century before.[60]

continued on next page

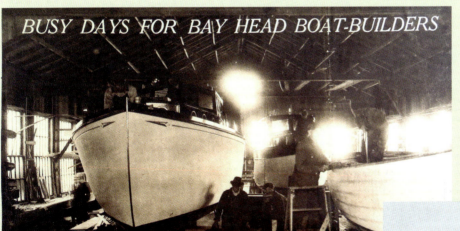

FIGURE 3-23. Inside Morton Johnson's shed in May of 1928 showing a $20,000 cabin cruiser at left.

Photo from unknown newspaper by H.C. Dorer. Beth Truex Bell family archive, with permission

FIGURE 3-24. Morton Johnson boatyard flooded in 1933, with a member of the Bell family demonstrating the depth achieved.

Beth Truex Bell family photograph

Morton Johnson's After Morton Johnson *(continued)*

Also in 1933, a strong set of gales flooded the boatyard. This was not unprecedented because the Bay served like a funnel during prolonged southerly wind events. These events could be exacerbated by additional water coming through on a flooding tide from the Point Pleasant-Bay Head canal, which only became a regular occurrence when the periodically closed Manasquan Inlet was stabilized in 1931.

On his passing in 1933, Morton Johnson's yard was run by his son Paul Johnson. Paul paid attention to the business and it prospered. Young men who worked in the yard, should they slack off during work hours, got the standard caution, "Look out! Paul's coming; keep busy." Presumably, while Paul Johnson was supervisor, the yard built *Alice II* for Will Schoettle, Edwin Schoettle's brother about 1936. In 1937 an accidental fire raged in the yard, destroying the main construction shed, but the facilities were rebuilt as necessary and business resumed.

While many men from the Jersey shore enlisted or were (later) drafted into military service during World War II, this conflict and the desperate rush (as with Liberty Ships at Baltimore) to provide transport for men and materiel provided an immense boost for the Johnson facility. Enough able men remained around Bay Head to build the lifeboats that would save thousands of lives when ships went down. Dave Beaton supervised this work; he considering that the greatest contribution he could make to the war was saving lives.[61]

At one point the company was lauded, and its staff assembled for a photo to celebrate the 1000th boat completed. Beaton considered this one of the true high points in his working life.

During the 1950s, under Paul Johnson, the boatyard was back in the business of building pleasure boats again. Each summer, many extended family members were employed as seasonal workers. Tracey Truex was still painting boats with a steady hand and his attractive daughter Beth was in school at Manasquan. She went on to New Jersey College for Women (later Douglass College of Rutgers University). She left after a year to attend her ailing mother, but ended up marrying one of the Manasquan High teachers, who also worked every summer at Morton Johnson, Inc. When he grew to working age, their son Morton Johnson Bell was reminded each spring to "write Uncle Paul and ask if he'd like you to come back and work at the yard again this summer." Morton Bell smilingly said that he always did and in summers he worked six days a week making $80![62]

The company was fully functioning with many of the old hands plying their trades around sheds still awash with skiffs, relics of hardware, and rigging from the 1920s when the Silent Maid came into our family life in 1953. The first winter we owned her she was stored under cover in a shed only yards from where her keel had been laid a generation before and next to an impeccable Herreschoff Rozinante.

Tom Beaton thinks that the Morton Johnson family, two generations out, "ran out of sons" interested in following the business. In the 21st century, liberated daughters from the same creative gene pool might have been just as interested in boatbuilding and women might well have run a still better business! For whatever reasons, the yard closed in 1969, and this prime maritime business property is largely a high-end condominium development today.[63]

FIGURE 3-25. The schooner *Osprey*, one of Morton Johnson, Inc.'s, largest yachts. She appears to be over 80 feet on deck. *(Beth Truex Bell)* **(Right)** *Osprey* rigged. *(Axel Carlson photo given to Kent Mountford by Morton Johnson Bell)*

HULL SPECIFICATION

--FOR--

BUILDING

a

CABIN CAT BOAT.

--oOo--

GENERALLY:
The Yacht is to be built in the best possible manner from the lines and drawings supplied by the architect.

The best materials are to be used in the construction. The wood to be well seasoned and dried and the boat built under cover.

SCANTLINGS.

KEEL:
White oak plank 8" wide by 1-7/8" thick tapered to stem at forward end and to 6" at after end.

STEM:
White oak, sided 3-1/2" moulded and scarphed as shown.

SKEG:
Y.P.
Oak - moulded as shown on plan. Sided 5" at top against keel amidships and at center board slot, tapered to 4" at bottom. To be tapered to siding of rudder post aft and to 2" by 1" at extreme forward end. To be bolted to keel and floors with through bolts.

TRANSOM:
Mahogany 1" thick. Secured to keel with oak knee as shown.

RUDDER:
To be of Oak, 2" at forward end, tapered to 5/8" at after end. Rudder blade to be fastened to stock with 3/8 Tobin bronze bolts, and to be edge fastened with 1/4" Tobin bronze rod.

STERN POST:
Oak.

CHAPTER 3
APPENDIX:
Specifications
for Building
Silent Maid
(CONTINUED)

TILLER: To be of locust or oak.

FRAME SPACING: To be 10" center to center.

FRAMES: White oak bent to shape, moulded 1-3/8" sided 1-1/4". Extra frames at chain and runner plates.

FLOORS: Oak - on frames forward and aft of the center board trunk to be (steam bent 1-3/8" x 1-1/4".) At center board trunk to be same siding as frames and moulded as shown.

MAST STEP: Mast to be stepped on stem - Center board trunk logs to run forward to form mast step.

CENTERBOARD TRUNK: End posts to be of oak 2-7/8" x 1-3/4". Bottom trunk logs 1-1/2 thick moulded as shown and to form back-bone. Upper plank to be 3/4" cedar. Cover to be 3/4" mahogany.

CENTERBOARD: Mahogany - 1-1/4" thick, to be well bolted with galv. rod. Edges of board on bottom and back to be sharpened to 1/4". Board to be weighted with lead. Bottom of board to have bronze shoe.

DECK BEAMS: Oak 2" x 1-1/4". Large beams 2" x 2" at mast, ends of cabin, cockpit and hatches as shown.

KNEES: Hanging knees the same thickness as frames where shown. Lodge knees to be placed at mast and at heavy frames.

SHELF: Yellow pine 2-1/4" x 1-1/4".

CLAMP: Yellow pine 5-1/2" x 1" tapered to 4" at ends.

BILGE CLAMP: Yellow or Oregon Pine 1-5/8" x 3".

DECK BRACES: Oak and Spruce as shown on plan.

CHAPTER 3
APPENDIX:
Specifications
for Building
Silent Maid
(CONTINUED)

PLANKING: To be of white cedar. To finish a scant 3/4".

DECK: To be of cedar 5/8" thick. Plank to be narrow, underside to be varnished to prevent warping. Deck to be covered with 6 oz. canvas.

RAIL: To be of Mahogany 1" x 1" at bow tapered to 1" x 3/4" at stern. Mahogany board 3/4" thick at stern.

COCKPIT: As shown on plan. Coaming mahogany 3/4" thick. Fore and aft carlings and braces of oak and spruce. Cockpit floor 5/8" x 3" cedar slats. Beams oak 1-3/4" x 7/8" with braces as shown.

CABIN TRUNK: Sides, Mahogany 3/4"- Roof 1/2" cedar, canvas covered. Roof beams Oak 1-3/4" x 1" spaced 12". Companion slides, door and steps mahogany. Cabin floor pine 5/8" thick with hatches for access to bilge. Cabin floor beams 1-5/8" x 1" Oak. Transoms or seats on each side. To have fixed and swing posts as shown. Mahogany grab rail as shown to be fitted.

BOOM CROTCH: Oak- with socket at after end of cockpit.

HULL METAL WORK.

RUDDER POST: Bronze - 2" Diam. Tobin Bronze /Shafting ____ 1.9" outside diam. with casting at head to take tiller casting. A brass tube or pipe to run from keel to cockpit floor secured with casting at keel and at deck.- Or Stuffing Box

TILLER FILLINGS: Bronze tiller jaw to tiller and bronze cap on rudder post. Tiller to hinge.

DECK STRAPS: Two sets of straps at both mast holes bronze 1-1/2" x 1/16".

CHAPTER 3
APPENDIX:
Specifications
for Building
Silent Maid
(CONTINUED)

CHAIN PLATES: Two sets of chain plates of Tobin bronze, for both rigs, with 2" x 1/16" strap under mast.

RUNNER PLATES: Two sets to be 1-1/2" x 1/8" x 18" bronze.

DIAGONAL STRAPS: 1-1/2 x 1/16 Bronze. At Chain and runner plates connecting the plates at deck with keel.

STEM CASTING: Bronze - with two eyes - one for head stay and another at water line for bobstay.

FASTENINGS: Size and form of fastenings to be submitted for approval. Fastenings in planking to be wood plugged.

DECK METAL & IRON WORK: Deck to be provided with bronze chocks at bow, main boom traveller, cleats, halyard leads and eye pads. Half round brass at end of stem and at halyard leads on deck.

SPAR METAL & IRON WORK: Mast to have bronze gooseneck, spreader sockets, shroud cleats, eye pads for blocks, bronze sheave cleats etc. and 1" bronze track.
Boom to have bronze end band and 3/4" Track withouthaul, toping lift cleats, etc.
Gaff- bronze end band and sliding gooseneck.

TURNBUCKLES: Five of bronze- Merriman's patent.

PAINTING.

TOPSIDES: One priming and four coats of white.
Bottom three of approved green.

COCKPIT: Floor painted, seats, stanchions, coaming, end of center-board varnished.

HOUSE: After end sides moulding and companionway varnished, roof painted.
Rail, spars, tiller, etc. varnished.

CHAPTER 3
APPENDIX:
Specifications
for Building
Silent Maid
(CONTINUED)

-5-

RIGGING.

WIRE: Standing and running wire to be galvanized plough steel of 225,000 lbs. tensile strength.
Halyards wire with manila tails spliced in.

HALYARDS & SHEETS: Of best quality Plymouth manila.

BLOCKS:

Topping lifts	2 Cleat Blocks.
Mainsail halyards	2 Sheave.
" "	2 Whip block.
Main Sheet	3-1/2" Ash Blocks.
Runners	2 - #2 Gin Double.
"	4 #2 " Single (2 beckets)
Halyard leaders	4 #2 Leaders.

Winch 1 Marine Mfg. Co. Rail Capstan.

Blocks to be of bronze - polished.

SPARS:

Mast 49' - 0" - 6-1/2 greatest diam.-Spruce Hollow.	
Boom 28' - 6" - 5" " " Spruce Hollow.	
Gaff 14' - 0" - 4" " " Hollow of special design.	

1. Susan Hemmer, email to Kent Mountford, 2009.

2. Susan Hemmer, email to Kent Mountford, October 10, 2010.

3. Suzanne Bell Patton, in handwritten Johnson Family papers at Philadelphia Independence Seaport Museum Philadelphia, undated.

4. Sara Amy Leach, "Historic American Buildings Survey; Barnegat Peninsula Communities" (Washington, D.C.: National Park Service, 1991), 2.

5. Leach, "Historical American Buildings Survey."

6. Schoettle Collection 56, papers archived with the Morton Johnson collection at Philadelphia Independence Seaport Museum, Philadelphia, undated.

7. Beth Truex Bell, uncollated typed sheets archived with Morton Johnson papers at Philadelphia Independence Seaport Museum, viewed and imaged in 2011.

8. Ibid.

9. Riley Applegate's conversation about the Schoettles with Kent Mountford, 2010. Also with Roy Wilkins, September 2009.

10. The boardwalk at Atlantic City, with temporary planks, was first laid out in 1875. The song, lyrics by Gordon Mack and music by Myrow Josef, was from a 1946 20th Century Fox film "Three Little Girls in Blue."

11. Morton Johnson Bell, interview with Kent Mountford at Philadelphia Independence Seaport Museum, 2012.

12. Ibid.

13. Evelyn Ogden showed Kent Mountford the BBYRA record of this race in the 1920s, 2012.

14. Schoettle Collection 56.

15. Morton Johnson Bell, to Kent Mountford quoting his sister Suzanne Patton, 2012. Floyd was born on August 19, 1896, died on July 13, 1992. Elsie was born on February 23, 1895,and lived to age 100 in 1995.

16. Edwin Schoettle, undated personal notes from Polly Schoettle Miller.

17. Beth Truex Bell, 8 (7.)

18. Tom Beaton, 2012. David Beaton, born on September 10, 1886, emigrated to the United States in 1924, having worked for the Adams Boatyard in Gourock, Scotland. He died in 1976 at the age of 90.

19. Tom Beaton, subsequent discussion on Morton Johnson, September 11, 2012, around Dave Beaton's birthday.

20. Tom Beaton, conversation over previous notes, September 1, 2012.

21. Ibid.

22. Floyd Ayers, as told to Tom Beaton many years ago, thence to Kent Mountford, September 2012.

23. Barnegat Bay Sailing Hall of Fame, http://bbshof.org/members/EdwardCrabbe.shtml, accessed 2010.

24. E. Keble Chatterton, *Windjammers and Shellback: Strange True Stories of the Sea* (T.F. Unwin, Ltd., 1926). (This was later reissued at least twice in North America.

25. Tom Beaton recalls this difference as two feet. Commodore Crabbe's descendant, Dan Crabbe, thought this possible but, frankly, doesn't know. Related to Kent Mountford verbally in 2013.

26. Beaton, 2012.

27. *Mary Ann* and *Spy* were true sister ships, but *Lotus* was subtly different and deeper. Sweisguth and Mower discussed mast rake and shortening the boom to correct her weather helm.

28. Francis Sweisguth to Edwin Schoettle, January 5, 1923.

29. Francis Sweisguth to Edwin Schoettle, January 16, 1923.

30. Edwin Schoettle, *Sailing Craft* (New York: Macmillan Company, 1928), 106.

31. John M. Leavens, *The Catboat Book* (International Marine Publishing Company, 1973), 135.

32. www.sailselina.com/about-selina-II.htm

33. Francis Sweisguth, probably 1923, undated list with notes.

34. Edwin Schoettle, probably 1923, undated list with notes.

35. Francis Sweisguth, letter to Schoettle July 24, 1923.

36. Schoettle, *Sailing Craft*, 101.

37. Schoettle, *Sailing Craft,* 106.

38. Schoettle, *Sailing Craft*, 108.

39. Wayne Blake, discussion with Kent Mountford at the Catboat Association's 52nd Annual Meeting, Mystic, CT, February 1-2, 2014. Noted in Log *Nimble,* 2014, page 7.

40. Ben Jonson, cited in http://en.wikipedia.org/wiki/Epic%C5%93ne,_or_The_silent_woman

41. *Silent Maid*'s 2011 Beaton-built dinghy *Maid Service* cost $4000.

42. Ferde Grofe also wrote the popular and evocative "Grand Canyon Suite"

43. John Brady, discussion with Kent Mountford at launching May 19, 2012, and previously in Philadelphia.

44. Francis Sweisguth? Undated, unsigned letter to Morton Johnson.

45. Geoffrey M. Footner, *The Last Generation* (Solomons, MD: Calvert Marine Museum, 1991), 61-62.

46. As corrosion proceeds, however, there is less iron and more corrosion product intruding into and degrading the wood fibers. Eventually the dwindling iron shafts of the nails break. They have no strength now to hold the planking in place, and the wood around the broken fasteners is too soft to hold a new one driven in place. Such failures occurred twice during the Mountford family's ownership of *Silent Maid*.

47. Edwin J. Schoettle, letter to Judson Smith, February 1947.

48. Leavens, *The Catboat Book*, 135.

49. Footner, *The Last Generation*. Ruby Dixon worked on casting a keel at the M.M. Davis Shipyard in Solomons, MD, and was interviewed by Footner.

50. Footner, *The Last Generation,* 87.

51. Marie Darling, interview with Kent Mountford , 2011.

52. William H. Whiting Company catalog, Pratt and Gay Streets, Baltimore, MD (1935), 70.

53. Edwin J. Schoettle, notes on "major items" of expense for *Silent Maid*, probably 1923.

54. Morton Johnson Bell, miscellaneous family papers.

55. 23K gold leaf booklets at $50.90 (www.Amazon.com/goldleafbooklet).

56. Edwin J. Schoettle, letter to Morton Johnson (undated 1924) and bills sent between them July-December 1924. Toms River Seaport Society.

57. Beaton, 2012.

58. Henry Colie, email to Kent Mountford, May 5, 2014, identifying Carmen Runyon's *Osprey III* in the photograph.

59. Morton Johnson Bell to Kent Mountford, October 8, 2012.

60. Thomas Beaton, discussion with Kent Mountford about Morton Johnson, September 1, 2012.

61. Beaton, 2012.

62. Morton Johnson Bell, 2012.

63. William Schoettle, Item 56, The Schoettle Collection (now at the Bay Head, Mantoloking and Lovelandtown Historical Museum) 1969.

FIGURE 4-1. *Silent Maid* sailing off Island Heights in 1925. She already has two patches in her mainsail despite its five sets of reef points, which would have allowed more conservative sailing! The main is marked "S," not yet showing Schoettle's TRYC racing number "T-82." Captain John Hook is likely at the helm and Schoettle the passenger.

Crosstrees photograph, Suzy Mitchell Davis

4

Edwin Schoettle and His *Silent Maid*

*S*ilent Maid's sailing life began with her final delivery into Edwin Schoettle's hands, possibly about the first of August 1924. Edwin's final dealings with Morton Johnson did not leave an especially favorable taste in the mouths of the principals, but the new boat was functioning and finally under Edwin's command as a living vessel. Edwin left no flowing letters or journal entries to share with us about her commissioning or his enthusiasm as he learned about his new yacht. He was still on speaking terms with Mort Johnson, because before the construction yard bills were finally settled, he was already arranging for her winter storage at the boatyard in Bay Head.

At Toms River on June 27, 1924, Barnegat Bay Yacht Racing Association (BBYRA) published Barnegat Bay Yacht Racing Rules and set the dates for competition. A copy of these on yellowed newsprint was among Edwin's papers, preserved for 88 years.

New rules were set for Class B catboats, almost as if the *Silent Maid* was being anticipated. Any catboat over 20 feet was free to come forth in competition. In order to handicap faster boats so they could fairly compete with slower ones, the committee applied the artificial concept of racing length, which was to be determined by taking one-quarter of the overall length, plus one-quarter of the waterline length, plus one-half the sail area in square feet. (This should have been *square root* of sail area, no doubt a misunderstanding by some typesetter at the newspaper!) I, the non-racer, get the principle, but what I gathered from this printed rule makes no sense. Rules published in booklet format the next year by BBYRA made more sense and will be discussed later when Edwin has formal measurements done of *Silent Maid*.

FIGURE 4-2. **Edwin, Jr. (L) at 14 and Ferd III (R) age 12 handle** *Silent Maid* **coming home from a four-day cruise to Beach Haven during** *Silent Maid*'s **first summer in 1924. They tow Ferd's favorite boat** *My Pal*, **which he no doubt sailed while his parents socialized ashore.**

Schoettle family photograph from Polly Schoettle Miller

FIGURE 4-3. **An aerial view of** *Silent Maid* **running away from the fleet south of Goodluck Point.**

Vignette from a photo in Bill DeRouville's Boat Shop, Bayville, NJ, in 2011, with permission

Edwin writes in his book *Sailing Craft* that *Silent Maid* ". . . although rigged with a gaff sail . . . gives the 28 foot Marconi rigged Class A catboats, nearly eight minutes (480 seconds) handicap in a ten mile race." Edwin said *Silent Maid* could run away from the fleet across the wind or off the wind, but could not make up this handicap on a triangular course, including a windward leg. In the old days, Tom Beaton told me, races were sailed from navigation buoy to buoy, where wind on each day became a variable in the equation, the course not being structured to include all points of sailing by resetting dedicated race buoys.[2] Operating under this scheme, the 1924 racing season progressed to its conclusion.

Reconstruction of details of *Silent Maid*'s racing records has not been possible, but some of the dynamics and the end-of-year standings for five key years were preserved by diligent folks at BBYRA.

Silent Maid's shakedown and fine-tuning must have gone reasonably well because she was racing as a Class B catboat by summer's end—and summers on Barnegat Bay then pretty much ended on Labor Day. Though details of all the races have been lost, it was not an auspicious start for Edwin's hard-fought investment in the *Maid*. The trophy was won by *Spider* skippered by a man named Snyder. *Silent Maid* was last in a fleet of ten boats, with 2 points versus 23 for the winner! She was, in fact, beaten by Bates sailing Edwin's old boat *Scat II*.

From some point during the summer there is a family photograph showing Edwin, Jr., and Ferd III aboard the *Maid* returning from what is likely the boat's first cruise (see Figure 4-2). The date is pretty firmly locked in by Edwin's annotation in which he states that Ferd III, born in 1911, was 12 years old in the photograph.

I recall when I was Ferdinand's age, my *own* boat was always more important to me than my dad's wonderful *Silent Maid*, and I always wanted to tow her wherever the *Maid* went! Ferd was clearly of the same mindset because despite the brand new *Silent Maid*, he towed his scow *My Pal* all the way to Beach Haven. I can imagine Edwin grumbling a bit at this because he must have wanted his beautiful catboat to exhibit her very best sailing form on a first cruise like this. Son Edwin, age 14 in the photo, having been born in 1909, is seen sweeping up any trace of debris from the cockpit—crumbs from sandwiches or sand from improperly cleaned shoes.

Silent Maid's true working life, however, probably begins the following spring in 1925 when Edwin understands her, and she begins to advance in the Class B catboat fleet.

Evelyn Ogden has recovered one race record early in the 1925 season in which she proudly points to an early victory of *Vim* (the catboat she owned many years later) over Edwin Schoettle's *Silent Maid*. Remaining records do reflect, however, that by the end of the season *Silent Maid* was Barnegat Bay Champion, giving Burrows' sail loft the right to front this achievement in their advertising literature.

One of the contenders in the 1925 series was *Me Too*, a catboat built for Manasquan skipper F.O. Bailey. Bailey was an avid catboat racer and several times in the past had gone back to Morton Johnson with a new boat design, sure that his luck would be different the next year.

Edwin's initial racing season began his run of 17 good years sailing the *Maid*—years before the Second World War began to devour his life. It is ironic, but he left very little in the way of records that would lead us through those years—very little of his impressions, joys, or disappointments. We must draw on other sources, grasp at straws, and infer from the snippets others have left us to fill out this story.

One thing is clear from all sources: Edwin loved *Silent Maid*, and he was deeply invested in her, since with his friend Francis Sweisguth, he had collaborated in creating a series of four boats. *Silent Maid* was the agreed culmination of their work. Edwin's nephew Philip Schoettle rhetorically asks: "Was the genius of Edwin J. Schoettle creating a boat that beat all comers . . . [was] the *Silent Maid* merely a vehicle to show off . . . [his] . . . sailing skills . . . could anyone win with the *Silent Maid?*"[3]

FIGURE 4-4. Edwin Schoettle sits on the lee cockpit coaming and Captain John Hook, his hired gun, with a generous sunhat, is at the helm.

Vignette of 1925 photograph, Suzy Mitchell Davis, Crosstrees

I would say it took both the boat and the people, which did not necessarily mean just Edwin, to make a successful racing season. Captain Bailey was a contender again in the 1926 racing season, but *Silent Maid* swept the field and became Class B catboat champion a second time. The achievement was repeated in 1927. Captain Bailey was in that competition for yet another year, apparently still aboard *Me Too*. In 1928, however, maybe Edwin's luck changed and there was Bailey sailing *Me Too* taking the Class B Catboat Championship.[4] Edwin's run of three years as champion was still pretty impressive and enough to turn *Silent Maid* into a classic.

Bailey was Class B catboat champion again in 1929. Among spotty records found in a newspaper by some careful BBYRA sleuth, Edwin's old boat *Scat II* took the championship in 1930 and 1931 with different owners. However, this is where available records from BBYRA fade away, along with them our chances of hearing about *Silent Maid*'s racing record again.[5]

Edwin sailed, apparently quite often with Sara, down Barnegat Bay on overnight trips. One hopes these times together were at least touched with romance, since they were by all accounts sincerely devoted to each other.

To the surprise of many observers, Edwin and Sara could handle the boat quite handily by themselves. Edwin was forward hauling the two gaff halyards—throat and peak—together or separately as he nursed the gaff aloft with the jaws just behind the peak. Sara would have been aft in the cockpit tailing them, and belaying to the appropriate cleats, mounted on the aft face of the cabin trunk. Aboard the *Maid*, with no engine in those decades, this operation must have been done from anchor or tied off at

FIGURE 4-5. Rare look at a luncheon below decks on the Frank Du Pont Marston family's catboat from Robbins Cove on Toms River. Katherine Marston (1856–1941), Frank's wife, is at left. While deaf, Kathryn was an avid catboat sailor, and in the winter she was an avid ice skater. With their sandwiches, these ladies are drinking beer from a distinctive bottle type, vintage about 1910.

Beth Truex Johnson and Ocean County Historical Society

FIGURE 4-6. **Edwin and Sara Schoettle aboard *Silent Maid*, circa 1925. They sail while the boat is still fairly new. I suspect this was taken, sun high, on a spring day, as a light sea-fog dulls the horizon astern. This picture, from the Schoettle home Crosstrees, inspired a drawing in his later book *Sailing Craft* (see Figure 4-18).**

Mrs. Lewis Kleinhans photograph, (courtesy of Suzy Mitchell Davis), the back of which is annotated in Sara's hand regarding Harry Parker's use of it for the drawing he did for the book.

FIGURE 4-7. **An early version Primus brand, 2-burner pressurized kerosene, or paraffin, stove like *Silent Maid*'s. Lighting it required priming with alcohol. Small galvanized iron rods could be inserted in the brackets (arrows) on each rail to stabilize pots when the boat was underway.**

Kent Mountford photograph

a piling so the *Maid* would lay head to wind long enough for this to be done in a seamanlike manner. This would then leave enough time to let the boat yaw back and forth, till her head was where they wanted it and they could make her pay off on whichever tack they wished. Edwin and Sara's daughter Margaret Schoettle Mitchell wrote that while her mother might not have been the greatest sailor herself, with her devotion to Edwin, she was an absolutely "perfect First Mate."[6]

A couple sailing alone was no mean accomplishment for a vessel of the *Maid*'s size and immense sail area. Whatever people observed under ordinary conditions, the achievement was quite significant when making sail in a serious blow. Being anchored probably cut the couple some slack, but then came the problem of breaking out the *Maid*'s big fisherman anchor![7] This anchor, still aboard when my family owned the *Maid* decades later, was a 40-inch, 35-pound kedge with folding stock. It was hard enough for us to handle, but was still, according to specifications of the time, pretty light for a boat *of Silent Maid*'s size and windage. Tables in the 1930s recommended a 90-pound anchor for a 33-foot auxiliary cruiser.[8] That, in fairness, would have been a bear to break out on a vessel with no windlass. So for a lunch hook, I'll stand with Edwin's choice given the options in his era.

"Down the bay," as is often casually referred to, could have meant many things, but on Barnegat south of Goodluck Point and the tricky bridge passage, there opens the whole lower estuary to cruiser and sailor. Places to shelter at anchor are not abundant, but under usual summer afternoon wind conditions there are some islands and low marshy prominences behind which, or creeks within which, a cruising couple could lie quietly and privately at anchor overnight.

The *Maid*'s galley, in her original configuration, was forward on the starboard side, deep in that cavernous cabin with just the skylight hatch to ventilate below decks. The stove, as drawn in Sweisguth's plans, was seemingly set into or on top of the galley counter, so it does not seem to have been a coal/wood fired "Shipmate" style.

The early 20th century modern alternative, a Primus stove, was probably Schoettle's choice. It is most likely that the stove he and Sara used—a two-burner, countertop model—and this was still aboard when we owned the *Maid* 30 years later, so I became intimately familiar with it.

Primus is simply the Latin word for *first* and was adopted as a brand name by its inventor, a factory mechanic named Franz Wilhelm Lindqvist in 1892. Reliable kerosene (then called paraffin) stoves like this went with Roald Amundsen to the South Pole, with Fridtjof Nansen in his expedition, and on Richard Byrd's successful try to reach the North Pole.[9] The

FIGURE 4-8. **Detail of Goodluck Point at the Mouth of Toms River in 1924, showing the Pennsylvania Railroad trestle crossing to the Island Beach Peninsula. The draw was very near the Western shore of Barnegat Bay because the natural channel ran close inshore there.**

U.S. Coast and Geodetic Survey Chart, 1924, Paul Smith

Primus was indeed reliable and well known. In the *Maid*'s case, it did yeoman service in the galley for almost half a century.

The Primus, I was surprised to learn, was not without hazard, and I reminisce with some concern about Sara deep inside that cabin, with her ample hairdo, full skirt, and a loose blouse, bending over that stove to get something out of the double-door cabinet above it.

In the (Austral) summer of 1920, a bunch of guys anchored to make tea in Arkle's Bay, Aukland, New Zealand. With both Primus burners "in full blast, without any warning, it suddenly exploded. A sheet of flame shot up over 20 feet high, and enveloped both the cockpit and cabin. There were six persons on board. Mr. Glass . . . nearest the stove . . . threw it overboard. . . . Several were . . . burnt about the arms, legs and body."[10] One couldn't have thrown *Silent Maid*'s stove overboard that easily. The user was simply trapped too far inside the cabin.

It is unclear what Sara would prepare on such jaunts, but likely household staff had made up some more easily heated meals to carry them over lunches, Saturday night, and at least a breakfast.

Mantoloking resident and world-class sailor Runyon Colie recalls that his father took their catboat down to Barnegat Inlet on a regular basis. Aside from the so-called winter anchorage, there were some pretty good, sheltered refuges among the labyrinthine channels winding through the Sedge and Clam Islands, and towards the sea. Inlets like Barnegat, with dramatic tidal flows, develop two deltas of sandy deposits, one offshore and one inside the bay. Those inside, laced with deep, clear water rushing in from the sea have bottoms of clean white sand. Copper paints in the 1920s were only modestly effective in forestalling marine growth, and if you were racing a boat, it was best to be sure her bottom was clean. These paints, while soft, were not intentionally ablative in the modern sense (that is designed to wear away the surface layers while sailing), but with a light brushing as you stood alongside in shallow water with a brisk flowing tide to keep visibility clear, you could do a pretty good job clearing off soft fouling organisms. The Colies used these pleasant conditions down by Barnegat Inlet to clean growth from their boat bottoms.

Edwin had the *Maid* down there an unknown number of times, but it's highly likely he and his crews used the same convenient spots to clean her wide bottom as well. This could well have been an annual ritual in mid- or late summer.

FIGURE 4-9. The original gas-fired kitchen stove at Crosstrees, circa 1909, where *Silent Maid* provisions must have been prepared. It is here showing off fourth generation Schoettle descendants: Nathaniel Cummins and Sara and Caroline Davis in September 2010.

Kent Mountford photograph

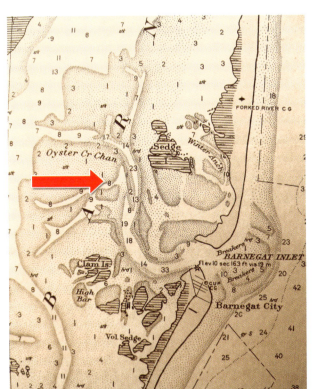

FIGURE 4-10. Channels laced the flood-tide delta inside Barnegat Inlet on this 1924 chart. Depths were in feet at low-tide. Some skippers sailed their boats down here for a mid-season bottom scrubbing.

U.S. Coast and Geodetic Survey Chart, 1924, Paul Smith

FIGURE 4-11. *Silent Maid* nosed up on a sandbar, somewhere down Barnegat Bay. A deepwater channel clearly runs right alongshore here! *Inset:* That might be some development on part of Long Beach Island, at the horizon with groins built to forestall erosion along Barnegat Inlet.

Crosstrees photograph, Suzy Mitchell Davis

* * *

In August 1925, Edwin Schoettle ordered a new mainsail for *Silent Maid* from George R. Burrows, Inc., located at 2 South Street (along the east River) in New York City. It was made of 10 ounce duck; this time not Egyptian cotton. The sail was 22' 8" on the hoist, 25' 4" along the gaff, 34' 6" along the boom and (ignoring roach) an impressive 51'10" along the leech. Perpendicular to the edge of the sail along a line drawn to the gooseneck, the measurement, in Edwin's very faint handwriting, appears to be 20¾'. The boom was set with some angle of steeve, to clear those in the cockpit, and thus the sail's diagonal was to measure 38' 8". These dimensions in Edwin's drawing on Burrows order form describe two triangles, joined at the hypotenuse. I was able to use these measures to calculate the designed area of this sail at 863.9 square feet.[11] We can thus say with some certainty that this was her racing sail area, at least with that piece of canvas.[12] This area is something less than the anecdotal "950 square feet" claimed when we purchased the *Maid* in 1953.

Writing a decade later, Howard Chapelle states that, in measurement, roach and the curvature of other parts of the sail should be ignored. The designer, says Chapelle,

FIGURE 4-12. This lovely sloop raises sail from anchorage behind some of the low sandy islands inside Barnegat Inlet. There's a catboat just peeking in at the left in this undated picture.

Schoettle family photograph, Suzy Mitchell Davis

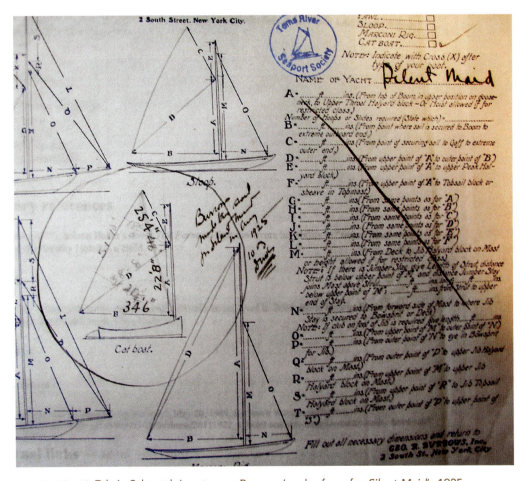

FIGURE 4-13. Edwin Schoettle's notes on Burrows' order form for *Silent Maid*'s 1925 mainsail of about 900 square feet. (Measured without roach it is 864 square feet; measured with estimated roach it is 898 square feet.)

Detail from archived form, Toms River Seaport Society, with permission

should always draw in some roach, leaving its actual construction to the sail maker who will make judgments based on the cut and stretch of the chosen canvas.[13]

Roach, in sails with their cloths cut horizontally, can usually stand with a width about 1/3 the batten length.[14] In 1924–25, *Silent Maid's* mid-leech battens appear to be about 48" in length. Thus, one could create a roach that technically would add enough area to bring the sail to almost 900 square feet. Sweisguth's drawing, as published by Edwin in his 1928 book, however, shows his version of the mainsail with even less roach.[15]

On August 20, 1926, Edwin had *Silent Maid* officially measured by the Barnegat Bay Yacht Racing Association. Measurement was done in accordance with Rule I as done for Class B catboats.

$$\frac{\left[\dfrac{\text{Length Overall} + \text{Length Waterline} + \sqrt{\text{Sail Area}}}{2}\right]}{2} = \text{Racing Length}$$

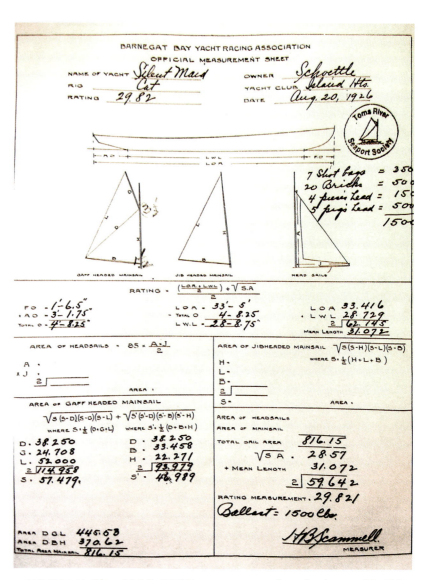

FIGURE 4-14. *Silent Maid's* BBYRA measurement form for August 20, 1926.
Toms River Seaport Society, with permission

H.B. Scammell was the official measurer. This is as good a set of statistics as we can find for her as a finished and working yacht. The measurements were made with 1500 pounds of ballast aboard, mostly pigs and bars of lead, but of which 350 pounds were in 7 shot bags, including 20 brick-size pieces of lead.

This weight put her down in the water to where her waterline length was 28' 8¾", and LOA at the extreme was 33' 5". By the BBYRA formula her measured length for competition (LOA + LWL /2) was 31.072. Based on actual measurement of her sail attachment points, the calculated sail area was smaller than that indicated by the Burrows measurements above, just 816.15 square feet. As shown in Figure 4-14, her rated length came out to 29.821 feet.

In *Sailing Craft*, Edwin claimed that in the standard ten-mile course the *Maid* was assessed an eight-minute handicap against the rest of the catboat fleet. She had to sail that off to win races.

SCHOETTLE'S 1926 BERMUDA TRIP

In 1926, Edwin Schoettle undertook an unusual adventure, which reveals as much about him as a shipmate as we are ever likely to learn. Cranberry grower Edward Crabbe, who was at one point Commodore of the Toms River Yacht Club, was sailing his big schooner *Windjammer* with some success and was inspired to try her in the New London, Connecticut, to Hamilton, Bermuda, race—a classic international yachting contest.

Edwin had become good friends with Crabbe and his son "Mac" (McEwen) and was thus invited to join a crew of seven men to make this voyage. Crabbe sailed, or had *Windjammer* sailed, from Barnegat Bay to New London and there did final fitting out for the coming race, taking on his store of provisions—fresh, canned . . . and bottled! Edwin took the train, arriving in plenty of time to take part in final provisioning.

These gentlemen had all been at least social consumers of alcohol since youth, but since 1919 the United States had been under the Volstead Act, better known today as the National Prohibition Act, which made the sale of intoxicating liquors illegal and set penalties for producing them. It was not *illegal* to drink and the well-to-do had mostly

FIGURE 4-15. **Edwin Schoettle is second from the right aboard** *Windjammer* **on June 20, before departing on the 1926 Bermuda Race. Crew** *(L to R):* **J. Fletcher Street, cook; Ed Crabbe, navigator; Bruce Miller, navigator; Ed Crabbe Sr., skipper; Beck Crabbe, naval architect Charles Mower, navigator; Edwin Schoettle, and Charles "Becky" Beck.**

Photo Morris Rosenfeld, NY, Toms River Seaport Society with permission

laid aside large stocks so that their lifestyle was less impacted. For folks not so well off, the result was a *dry* country and the vast and popular proliferation of illegal trafficking. There were an estimated 30,000 to 100,000 speakeasies in New York City alone.[16]

My family home in Warren Township, New Jersey, had been a speakeasy long before we owned it. In my bedroom, the inside closet doorjamb had been spring-loaded to conceal little shelves, just a bottle high. Our neighbor Henry Gauthier told me his father had done some painting for the former owners and in the thick dust on one of those long unopened shelves was the imprint of a handgun.[17] The Volstead Act took effect at midnight January 17, 1920, and it was significant that *within the hour*, prohibition's criminal history was kick-started when six armed men robbed a train taking $100,000 in "medicinal whiskey"—and bootleg liquor[18] was born! As the law was being debated, there was a fight in Congress, spurred by physicians, who said that elected officials had no business telling a doctor what was an appropriate amount of medicinal whiskey that could be prescribed to a needy patient. Medicinal whiskey won out!

Before leaving the States, Edwin and Crabbe had prescriptions written for medicinal whiskey, which would sail from New London and whatever remained or was replaced whilst in Bermuda would come home with *Windjammer* to prohibition America. These important ship's stores were duly signed aboard by an American Port Surgeon!

Edwin made another purchase before sailing. Having visited antiques dealer James Davidson on Howard Street, he succumbed to temptation and bought a curly maple chest-on-chest or high boy and had it shipped back to Island Heights to augment their "modest collection at Crosstrees."[19] This antique is still in the family.

Commodore Edward Crabbe was the skipper on this voyage to Bermuda. He owned in succession two Morton Johnson-built schooners—the 60-foot *Shellback* and the slightly shorter *Windjammer,* aboard which these mariners sailed to and from Bermuda. During this adventure (apparently the only ocean-sailing voyage he wrote about) Edwin kept a log. Entirely handwritten, this log was later bound and illustrated with many photographs taken on the trip. It gives us a deep, largely unguarded look into many aspects of this man's personality. As a yachtsman among peers, Edwin Schoettle was a loyal and appreciative friend—and a stalwart man on watch in bad weather.

This was also one of many opportunities for Edwin to interact with some of the most famous yachts and yachtsmen in the world, part of the knowledge store that would go into his later anthology *Sailing Craft.* The Bermuda log is full of insights into his experiences at sea, showing good humor, and a sense of enjoyment in the face of unpleasant conditions.

"These ten hours were the best of our entire trip. The ocean was terribly rough and gave the yacht a terrible pounding. The bright moonlight made night like day. As the bow of the boat would pound down on a high sea, dividing the waters the spray would go out in every direction for many feet… It was a night to give any one a thrill."[20]

Bad weather was replaced sometimes by frustrating calms during which they imagined the rest of the fleet still had rollicking winds! He and his shipmates were then overjoyed about the fresh winds that returned. He writes: "We had been on the

FIGURE 4-16. The Crabbe family's 56-foot, 9-inch, Morton Johnson schooner *Windjammer* carried Edwin Schoettle and shipmates to Bermuda and back during June and July of 1926.

Crabbe family photograph, Dan Crabbe

Starboard tack for over 60 hours and had sailed in it more than 300 miles. This should be especially interesting to Barnegat sailors that are usually enthused by tacks that last for two hours and take them about eight miles." How true! And in Barnegat, one might want to be sure his vessel didn't run out of water before the end of such a long tack!

They subsequently encountered four days of gale with no other ship sighted and were constantly soaked by spray. Edwin found himself sitting in the cockpit half filled with green water like a bathtub sloshing around his soaked boots, and the ship being thoroughly "wet on deck and below." This suggested to him "the rigors of Cape Horn" and, referring to himself and shipmates, he mused about the "Captains of industry brought down to the creaking Fo'c'sl." He kept to himself some darker thoughts, but recorded in his log "the real dangers which could befall them" in such weather. There was no ship-to-shore radio here, no cell or satellite phones, no GPS, no EPIRB, and only two frail rowing skiffs aboard for all hands in the event of foundering.

During heavy weather, proper meals were impossible for their dedicated cook Hatcher Street: "Seabirds enjoyed Cook's failed rice pudding. He retreated to the products of Messrs. Heinz and Campbell, and the products of hens from Toms River New Jersey." During provisioning, they had provided the ship with jars of a delightful "strawberry jelly (cooked in the sun on a tin roofed house in Toms River)" which was now "mixed with shattered glass on the linoleum of *Windjammer*'s galley."

He waxed nostalgic about the value he placed on his shipmates, some of whom he had known for 30 years: "The sailing game and the men one selects to sail with him are the same as the story of life itself. Good friends with brains make life a pleasure." Edwin shows this deep loyalty to men he fairly considered his equals. In this he behaves differently, separating from his strict posture as a parent of sons for whom he had the highest expectations, and on whom he enforced the toughest standards, applied to prepare them for lives as successful as his own had thus far been.

Windjammer was by no means at the tail of the pack, but did not do very well in this fleet of sixteen vessels, finishing seventh on corrected time. The Barnegat crew were, after all, up against the likes of John Alden's *Malabar VII* (three of Alden's wonderfully designed boats were in this race) the *Jolie Brise*, which had sailed the Atlantic to join this competition, and another famous yacht, Robert N. Bavier's *Dragoon*, which won the race.

Once arriving in Bermuda, Edwin found there was mail waiting for him, which had been sped more rapidly by steamer from New York: "I was handed a wonderful letter from Sara. It was one of her best and was like a visit from home. I took an extra half hour after midnight to answer it in time to catch the early morning (return) steamer to New York." Sailing *Windjammer* he might well have beat his loving letter home, but the vignette shows how much he valued his wife of 19 years. He closed his logbook musing "God bless Sally and her children." Suzy Mitchell Davis tells me Sara idolized him in return. They were to have 21 more years together, the last few sadly finding him ill and in declining health.

Windjammer's trip back to America lacked the pressure of the outbound race, but by then, the crewmembers were all anxious for home. On the completely dark night of July 2, Edwin writes "The spray from the bow of the boat and the wake of the ship in the water was a mass of phosphorescence. Great globes of light would float away on the water and snake-like masses of light would trail out beyond us in the rear. [Even in the dark] birds were hovering about [and] several small flying fish came aboard the boat."[21]

"We sighted during the day whales, porpoises, sharks, flying fish, sea-gulls, petrels and many other evidences of marine life. . . . We passed very close by some fishing boats (and with a good northeast wind and rough seas) a four master under full sail."[22] The petrels sighted would be Wilson's Petrel, *Oceanites oceanicus*, southern hemisphere birds, which spend the Austral winter off our coasts, May–September.[23]

Mindful of the abundant medicinal alcohol they had aboard, Edwin and the rest of the crew expected they might be boarded by the U.S. Coast Guard or Revenue Service and be searched for liquor when they came on soundings off New Jersey. Unlike today's Coast Guard, proscribed with serious and thorough Homeland Security duties, they were cordially greeted offshore by a cutter coming alongside with an officer in a crisp, spotless uniform. When the cutter returned to Barnegat, the Coast Guard officer thoughtfully communicated with Island Heights to inform the family that *Windjammer* was headed home. They made landfall off Seaside Park on July 4, 1926, just eight miles north from Barnegat Inlet. At first light, 0400 hrs, with the sun soon to be behind them, they simply sailed in on the making tide, as vessels had done from foreign ports since the early 1600s.

In his log, Edwin wrote that, for him, ". . . our entrance to Barnegat Bay had some historical interest because we were the first boat that had for some years cleared from a foreign port [in]to Barnegat, [and he speculated] the last sailboat that would affect such a clearance."[24]

They negotiated Oyster Creek Channel, then rounded Sea Dog Shoals (a name lost on modern charts), where they were met by *Alice*, Edwin's brother William C. Schoettle's yacht, then sailed up Barnegat Bay and into Toms River. As they passed Island Heights, gaps in the trees enabled an eager Edwin to see the flowering yuccas[25] at Crosstrees.

On July 5, having debarked *Windjammer* at Toms River to a joyous celebration with the Crabbe's and his own family, Edwin was off "in a few hours and sailing *Silent Maid* to an old-time victory as if nothing unusual had happened to us." I would have done the same, blending the joy of my own vessel, under my own hand, with the adventure at sea just completed.

His log, now in a loose-leaf binder and a circulation copy neatly bound in hardcover, is still passed around affectionately within the Schoettle and Crabbe families after 86 years. It is a delight to read and I closed its covers *liking* this man, who still had a difficult side to him.

EDWIN SCHOETTLE'S *SAILING CRAFT*

Edwin had another project, one that must have consumed prodigious amounts of time—writing what was arguably the first compendium for lay readers on small and moderate size pleasure yachts covering the United States, as well as a number of nations abroad. Following his voyage with Crabbe on the Bermuda trip, Edwin seems to have begun this serious writing project. While there were many accounts of voyages in the sailing literature, in the 1920s nobody had seen fit to summarize what was happening with the multitude of sailing craft used for pleasure around the globe.

He had made significant contacts during his Bermuda time and expanding these, he conceived an anthology or compendium of articles about different kinds of pleasure boats. He had also travelled in Great Britain and to Europe with his sailor's eye cast about for yachts. He mentions visiting Zeebrugge, Antwerp, and Bruges in Belgium, and also the south of France. In Italy there was Genoa and Naples and he writes in third-person his memory of "…sitting on a bench near the Doges' Palace at Venice, dreaming

FIGURE 4-17. Edwin's brother, Will, aboard his yacht *Alice* met *Windjammer* inside Barnegat Inlet on the schooner's return from Bermuda.

Crosstrees photograph, Suzy Michell Davis

about the long ago [and] to be suddenly awakened, when he hears the swash of water and sees an up-to-date 6-metre boat flash by."[26]

Edwin fleshed out his project by writing a large stack of letters to knowledgeable sailors in the United States, Canada, the Netherlands, Great Britain, and South Africa. These letters are all archived at the Toms River Seaport Society in New Jersey. He approached at least 68 potential contributors, waiting for sometimes significantly delayed replies. While many of his closer circle of friends, like Sweisguth and Mower, clearly understood the project and volunteered to participate, not all jumped at the chance. One chap even wanted to be paid; something Edwin was not willing to do. Little did declining contributors suspect how far and for how many decades their words would have spread!

Gerald Taylor White (who later founded Westlawn School of Yacht Design) wrote one of the widest ranging contributions. He summarized pleasure-boating activity in far-flung corners of the globe, including the Baltic States, France, the Mediterranean, Caribbean, South America, pre WW-II Japan, Papeete (French Polynesia) and, Hawaii (not then a U.S. state).

In his own chapters, Edwin spoke intimately and at length about catboats, their role in Barnegat history, and about his experiences owning, sailing, and creating them with Sweisguth.

Edwin's tome *Sailing Craft* ran to a hefty 786 pages and was first published in 1928 by MacMillan Company. The book billed as "Edited by Edwin J. Schoettle" and subtitled "mostly descriptive of smaller pleasure sail boats of the day." This work was quite unusual for an industrialist with sailing as an avocation. Pen and ink drawings by Harry Parker were placed throughout the book, including the one where Edwin dedicated the book to his first mate Sara M. Schoettle. Parker's rendering was based on a photo taken of the couple aboard *Silent Maid* on Barnegat Bay (Figure 4-6).

During World War II while Edwin and Supreme Court Justice Owen Roberts were advising President Roosevelt, the President said that he had heard Edwin had written a book on sailing and he would be interested in a copy. Edwin provided one gratis—who wouldn't!—but he hoped for some small acknowledgement from FDR, and angled with Owen Roberts to see if this could be arranged. Unfortunately, the little note from FDR never came.[27]

Sailing Craft was reprinted seven times: 1934, 1937, 1942, 1943, 1945, 1946 (the year before Schoettle died) and (thus far!) finally in 1949. Copies owned are treasured and, of course, are still traded on the worldwide web.

* * *

As part of her social agenda after 1924, the *Silent Maid* seems to have continued annual pilgrimages down to Harvey Cedars, a long day's sail, or perhaps two, but with a welcoming yacht club and its amenities at the end of the passage. There might well have been more folks on these trips than could sleep aboard. The family reports that having ten people around the cockpit was not unusual—and the *Maid* has carried many more! This was not the destination for Edwin and Sara off on a weekend alone, but it was a tradition carried on by the family for years. The Schoettle's daughter, Margaret, recalls trying to sail her father's then-aging boat (the original) *Scat* down there about 1925 to join the festivities. As elsewhere recounted, they were stopped by uncontrolled leaks, but thought the whole thing a great adventure.

Dedicated to my first mate
SARA M. SCHOETTLE

FIGURE 4-18. Edwin and Sara Schoettle on *Silent Maid* in a slightly idealized drawing that accompanied Edwin's dedication of his book *Sailing Craft* to his wife. Drawing was based on photograph shown in Figure 4-6.

Drawing: MacMillan Company

Crosstrees was always homeport for the Schoettle fleet, and a fleet it definitely became. A road runs around Island Height's perimeter between the Schoettle pier and the high bank where Crosstrees perches with its commanding view. The story is told about a man leading some visitors along that road pointing out the sights. "That's the dock," he said, pointing out the Schoettle's family pier, gesturing to Crosstrees, "the yacht club is up there on the cliff."[28]

We might think that statement humorously uninformed, but in July 1929 a columnist for the local paper wrote: "Edwin J. Schoettle and his boys have the largest fleet of racing craft than any one family in this section can boast, it is claimed here. They have the *Lotus, Silent Maid, Sandpiper*, and *Spray*, besides other boats not racing."[29]

Apparently *Silent Maid* was sometimes moved to a mooring, likely for some activity at the yacht club or for service at the Stokes or Vautier local boatyards. Then-local resident "Jimmy" Glenn, a girl who grew up on Island Heights, says the *Maid* was sometimes moored off among the Class A catboats *Spy, Bat,* and *Mary Ann* in the "cove behind Long Point." When the Schoettles were away, and struck by *Silent Maid*'s beauty, young Jimmy swam out to her, got her feet atop the big barn-door rudder (which protruded a little from under the transom) and climbed into the cockpit. She remembers how large it was compared to other boats, and in those days it was just one big expanse of unblemished narrow planking, with no engine box to disrupt the expanse of gleaming varnish.

Jimmy was daughter of Janet (Letchworth) Glenn who had a treadle sewing machine on the Island. Janet did sewing on demand for all the cotton sails around.[30] Island Heights then had a tiny school, with grades 3, 4, and 5 in one room and grades 6, 7 and 8 in another! Jimmy was in third grade there with Jimmy Sindell, who developed the later state-of-the-art Jet-14 racing daysailer and whose company Siddons and Sindell made a mark in the marine trades.

Jimmy Glenn also said that after swimming in the salty water of Toms River, she and her friends used to go up to the sluiceway at the Crabbe family's cranberry bogs and rinse themselves in the cool cedar colored water. Water from these bogs and from the region's many white cedar swamps is acidic. Some studies show it has having a pH of 4.3,[31] compared to pure neutral water that has a pH of 7.0 and coastal sea water with a pH of 8.5—a big difference! This acidity, some say, is wonderful for washing one's hair—even without shampoo—because it removes the dulling calcium deposits that rob hair of its shine. Even today a bit of vinegar rinse is sometimes used by hair care experts.[32]

There was another side to this deep colored cedar water shared with me by Alicemay Weber-Wright, lifelong resident and historian for the Toms River Yacht Club. She warned that you could *not wear a white bathing suit* in this water, or it would never be white again.

＊　＊　＊

Karl Schoettle, Edwin's grandson, said that Edwin and a close friend, economist Roger Babson (think Babson College, for which Schoettle's colleague Charles Klauder

FIGURE 4-19. *Silent Maid* shown leaving Beach Haven in September 1929 with seven aboard. That wind better freshen if they're to make Toms River! Edwin at the helm; he and Sara both wave so-long to the photographer

Crosstrees photograph, Suzy Mitchell Davis

prepared architectural plans) both anticipated and prepared themselves for the Great Depression. This was prudent, but also courageous given the frenetic bubble of growing wealth that was forming during the 1920s.

Silent Maid was just in her fifth season when the great 1929 Wall Street crash descended on the American economy. It is tempting to say that the immediate Schoettle family was unaffected. After all, his businesses were very valuable to the nation, regardless of whether revenues declined, and Edwin made sure his personal finances were pretty well insulated by that time. The wider family, however, was deeply affected.

Karl cites just one example of Edwin's care and generosity. "My mother often told me how her family lost everything in the stock market crash of 1929 and they, along with many others, would have been homeless had Edwin not taken care of them."[36] Karl Schoettle's uncle on his mother's side was Albert Diss, who owned the famous Class A catboat *Tamwock* and his parents before him owned another famous catboat, the *Virginia*. The Diss family was very well off before the Depression, with apartments in New York and Paris. The reversals devastated their finances and they stood to lose their primary home, as well as their financial security. Edwin Schoettle bought their house outright and gave the title back to them, saving the day and giving them a whole new start.

Roger Babson's Ten Commandments of Investing

Roger W. Babson, a tenth generation Massachusetts's resident, meticulously searched his own ancestors, their histories and personalities. Assuming he had inherited their best traits, he strove to make his life useful. He was an entrepreneur and an exceedingly prominent business theorist in the first half of the 20th century. Born in 1875, dying in 1967, he founded three colleges, most durable of which bore his name, and was most noted for predicting the 1929 stock market crash.

His prescience in this, plus his friendship with Schoettle, allowed both men to be prepared for economic adversity. In a speech on September 5, 1929, Babson said, "Sooner or later a crash is coming, and it may be terrific."[33] Later the same day, the market on Wall Street was said to have plunged a significant three percent, an incident subsequently dubbed the "Babson Break." The catastrophic tumble into the Great Depression followed.

Babson and his economic pronouncements thus gained extraordinary credibility, especially to New Deal advocates like President Roosevelt. Babson's much-publicized "Ten Commandments" of investing bear attention to this very day. With less popular acclaim, Babson actually filed the earliest patents on the concept of a parking meter. Others brought the idea to market, but millions worldwide might revile poor Babson, if this were widely known![34]

Babson's "Ten Commandments"[35]

1. Keep speculation and investments separate
2. Don't be fooled by a name
3. Be wary of new promotions
4. Give due consideration to market ability
5. Don't buy without proper facts
6. Safeguard purchases through diversification
7. Don't try to diversify by buying different securities of the same company
8. Small companies should be carefully scrutinized
9. Buy adequate security, not super abundance
10. Choose your dealer and buy outright (i.e., don't buy on margin)

Karl, writing in September 2006, recalled another anecdote. In about 1996, Karl had made a business call at the Newman Paperboard Company in Philadelphia. "When the receptionist saw the spelling of my name, she called the company president. When he determined that I was a descendant of Edwin J. Schoettle, he called his elderly father, the company founder, at home and then sent a driver to bring him to the office. The elder Mr. Newman spent an hour telling me how Edwin had saved their company and perhaps most of the paperboard and packaging industry in the mid-Atlantic region during the Depression. During the early 1930s, Edwin provided guidance to suppliers and competitors in addition to his own companies [on] every aspect of management, especially how to provide for employees.[37]"

Edwin, by this time in the early 1930s, seems to have lost contact with Francis Sweisguth, their active business of creating boats together being over. Sweisguth was, after all a *YACHT* designer, and the opportunity for bringing beautiful boats to life was slim indeed during the Great Depression.

In my younger years, about 1961, I worked at a boat show in Asbury Park, New Jersey, trying to sell small sailboats when I was between jobs myself. Among our exhibit's walk-through visitors was a man named Frederick Geiger, whom much later I found had a reputation as a naval architect from Philadelphia. He said at that time he was from Staten Island. Somehow we got on the subject of *Silent Maid*, which my family then owned and the conversation transitioned to Francis Sweisguth, whom Geiger had known for a long time. He discussed how hard the depression years had been on Sweisguth: "Poor Francis, sitting in his dusty office . . . he was so glad to have anyone come to get a set of plans; he'd practically give you two sets." Sweisguth would be alive most of a decade after that conversation.

Sweisguth had been a partner at the New York design firm Ford, Payne and Sweisguth. In 1933, he designed the 18-foot Interlake (a one-design). As the Depression eased in 1937, he did the 24-foot "Great South Bay One-Design," but appears to have been inactive thereafter until 1969, when he produced the 22-foot Americat, trying to compete with the popular Marshall catboats.[38] This was apparently his last design, as he died in 1970. Pretty, if not the fastest of boats, Americats are still on the market and sailing, many over three-decades old.[39]

Sweisguth, dying at age 88, had lived long past my own years growing up with the *Silent Maid*. I had pretensions to become a naval architect myself and I regret not having the wisdom to seek him out and meet the man whose work 40 years before had shaped so much of my own life.

*   *   *

In the spring of 1938, Edwin hired an 18-year-old John H. "Jack" LaFleur as his dock boy. It was a decent match because Jack returned the following year as well. Jack was a friend of Eileen Fancher, daughter of Will Schoettle's captain on his yacht *Alice*. Ms. Fancher at this writing, still lives in Island Heights. When this book research began, she put me in touch with Jack to probe his many memories. Though he had passed his 93rd birthday, many things remained perfectly clear, and he wrote to me about the *Maid* as though it had been just last summer.

LaFleur was born in 1920, moving to Island Heights, where other family members lived, when he was five. He thus pretty much grew up as a local. When he went to work for Edwin Schoettle, his job was taking care of what were then five family boats. Principal, of course, was *Silent Maid,* but, as LaFleur remembers, there were two Class A catboats (*Lotus* and *Spy*), an E Scow that he believed belonged to Edwin's son Karl, and an "open cockpit mahogany sailboat about twenty feet in length that Mr. Schoettle had purchased somewhere. He didn't like the boat and one day it disappeared." In contemporary photos, Ferd Schoettle's scow *My Pal* appears, and I'm wondering if, as Edwin's sons migrated on to higher performance boats, he just felt the scow had seen all the use that she was going to get.

LaFleur described the routine on most summer mornings at the Schoettle dock, with all the boats nodding there in the sunshine, their lines slack before the regular afternoon southerlies blew in. "The sails were canvas then and to prevent mildew, the sail on the *Silent Maid* had to be opened and partly raised each morning to dry." One did not casually unbend a sail of that size and complexity, with the hoops lashed on with marline and a long lacing pennant wound the entire length of boom and gaff. That was a seasonal operation.

On the other hand, for Marconi headed boats, said LaFleur: "We had a sail loft and kept the . . . sails inside." This, he described, was in the white building (one of Schoettle's three "barns") where the "sails were in canvas bags and hung from the rafters. There were two [wooden] slats under the bags to support the weight of the sails."[40]

LaFleur kept the boats cleaned, likely running a mop or wrung out cloth over decks and brightwork to clear off beaded dew. He sanded and painted where necessary . . . or when instructed by someone intent on keeping him busy. He did some work at the Anchorage as well, up atop the west-facing bank some distance from Crosstrees, but still overlooking Toms River.

FIGURE 4-20. The Schoettle pier viewed from Crosstrees. *Silent Maid* is the farthest boat out and a Class A catboat, painted white, lies inboard of her.

Crosstrees photograph, Suzy Mitchell Davis

FIGURE 4-21. **View from the Schoettle pier looking up towards Crosstrees, past two unidentified Class A catboats and Ferd's scow** *My Pal* **farthest in.**

Schoettle family photograph

LaFleur never sailed the Class A catboats, recalling "I think that Ferd sailed one of them." (Ferdinand Schoettle, then age 26, was the eldest of Edwin's three sons.) "I don't know who sailed the other." But LaFleur did sail aboard *Silent Maid*: "While I worked at Crosstrees, I always sailed when the *Maid* was taken out." He might have been tired and windblown at the end of such summer afternoons, but when the *Maid* returned to her slip, his work still stretched ahead: "The boat had to be cleaned that same day," he stated emphatically, remembering that discipline from a full 70 years ago!

Philadelphia yachtsman Robert Barrie, who visited Barnegat Bay in the first few years of the 20th century, wrote of the surprisingly low cost of being a yacht club member there. He said that initiation was a mere $10, and annual dues were just $5! Barrie said services of a 'boy' could be obtained for the four-month sailing season for an additional $5, for which the boat was kept clean and brought to the landing when so instructed by the owner![41] Those days are certainly long departed, but just as certainly lamented! LaFleur says he was paid $10 a week for six days worked, and in the second year he got a raise to $12!

LaFleur spoke very well of the Schoettle family. "They were always very nice to me," he recalled, but indicated they were from a different social stratum and did not really socialize with him. He spent a good bit of time with them, however. "On Saturdays we followed the boat races. The family came on Sundays. Usually Mrs. Schoettle came, Mrs. Mitchell [Schoettle's daughter], and sometimes her husband Jim. Friends often came also."

By the time Jack LaFleur came to work for the Schoettles, Edwin Schoettle himself was no longer a racer, but followed racing on the bay closely. Aboard some of his boats, he hired local bay captains, like John Hook and, for the *Lotus,* Britt "Britty" Applegate often sailed for him. LaFleur recalled "Mr. Schoettle always sailed the *Silent Maid.*" [42]

*   *   *

Edwin, proud of his big catboat, had many guests and some I spoke to had memories of contrasting the *Maid* with lesser, or at least older, vessels. One of the bay's strong, early catboat competitors was *Bouquet,* which had been built in 1902. She was a grand boat with an immense sail and eventually owned by Riley Applegate. One of Applegate's crewmembers was George Whittle[43] and he told me that by the time he sailed *Bouquet,* "She was so soft, she was covered with tar and canvas [and] when she tacked the whole bow shifted and re-aligned." About this time Whittle had a chance to sail aboard *Silent Maid* while she was berthed at Island Heights, and he remembers being impressed about the handling and grace of Edwin's class-act yacht.

Some children brought aboard were less than enthralled by *Silent Maid*. One grandchild, who was ten or eleven when Edwin died in 1947, says that when he was four, they took him sailing and on orders he was confined to the cabin so he'd be out of the way. He was scared to death when *Silent Maid* began inexplicably heeling over; he did not have pleasant memories of the experience.

Another racing participant on *Silent Maid* was Mantoloking resident Cornelius "Corny" Boocock. He recalled an experience aboard when the *Maid* heeled, and with her varnished cockpit deck slick from spray, he slid helplessly to leeward and "barked" the flesh off his shin under a hard-framed mahogany cockpit seat.[44]

Despite owning *Silent Maid*, Edwin really loved the Class A catboats. *Lotus* had been built by Morton Johnson in 1924, the same year he finished *Silent Maid*. *Lotus* was owned first by the Truitt family in Island Heights. Edwin praised the Class A catboats as: "The wonderful class of boats designed by Chas. Mower in 1921 . . . deck 28', WL 21, mast 45 feet above deck, sail hoist 41 feet, boom 28 feet long."[45] After his disappointment with *Forcem*, he eventually joined the fray again by buying *Lotus* for his family and especially for his boys to race.

As Jack LaFleur recalled regarding Edwin Schoettle: "He only sailed the *Silent Maid* for pleasure. His sons sailed the racing cats." Still LaFleur maintained that Edwin was not pleased with *Lotus*, since she seemed only to take second-place positions. Schoettle apparently tried changing sails to solve the problem.

Considering Edwin's generosity on the one hand, it is interesting how tight a bargain he could drive. Letters archived at the Philadelphia Independence Seaport Museum show Edwin, in July 1931, shopping for a new mainsail for *Lotus* and corresponding with Ratsey and Lapthorn at City Island, New York. Ratsey and Lapthorn gave him a

FIGURE 4-22. *Lotus* leading other boats in a race at Mantoloking in 1941. Notes in Schoettle's handwriting are all over this and are transcribed for easier reading.

Polly Schoettle Miller

Transcribed text:

"…in 1928 (*Lotus*) was one of eight boats all one class. Seven with the original 2, *Four Some* [Schoettle's unsuccessful A Cat] and to the other *Tamwock*—the *Four Some* was built for E.J. Schoettle by James Kirk at Toms River sold after one year of sailing.

The *Tamwock* was the fastest of the fleet. It was burned in the fire at Rotes [actually Stokes] and Vautier boatyard(s) in the spring of 1939."

To right of photo:

"The boat in the lead is the *Lotus* when sailed by Ferd, Edwin (Schoettle) and a crew of four. Picture taken at the start of a race at Mantoloking in 1941. *Lotus* in 1941 with only 2 races to be sailed was even with the Boat for first place in the season, but the *Lotus* lost the last two races."

FIGURE 4-23. A traditional Barnegat catboat hauled out at Stokes boatyard, the southernmost of two boatyards at Island Heights in 1937.

Original watercolor Richard Albright, courtesy Alicemay Weber-Wright

price of $385 for a new Class A sail. If you have ordered a sail recently you know how long it takes for delivery; my most recent mainsail was months in coming. The company said it could make the sail in a week, but they'd appreciate having ten days! Ratsey sent Edwin a swatch of the proposed cloth; a fine imported Egyptian cotton, which was stamped with the company's name. That swatch is at the Philadelphia Independence Seaport Museum for the handling today!

Edwin also wrote to George R. Burrows in New York City, who had made *Silent Maid*'s second sail. This company said the desired mainsail would be ready in 10 days, but provided him a better price of $332 for a (finer, thus smoother) cloth "A," a sample of which was enclosed with their estimate. Angling to get the job, Burrows said with cotton cloth "B" of lesser grade—for which there is also a swatch preserved with the correspondence—they could make the sail for a still lower price of $286. Schoettle went with Burrows, but said that he wanted the "A" cloth for the "B" price. With no further correspondence, we assume Burrows knuckled under too!

In light of today's suppliers, remember that these turnaround times included getting the finished product bagged and on a train for Island Heights, so that the particular skipper, unhappy with a sail's performance one week, might conceivably have a new sail bent on for the following Saturday's race! In a time of national economic depression, it was clear that having enough money to do this *paid* in more ways than one. It was also a boost for the craftspeople employed and for the economy in general.

Edwin's sometime sailing companion, naval architect Charles D. Mower of City Island, New York, wrote to him on August 29, 1929, musing that only trivial changes separated *Lotus* from the earlier *Mary Ann*, but *Lotus*' sail plan showed her mast raking 3' 9" from the vertical. Mower suggested rigging her mast plumb to move the center of effort forward, which would correct some of her heavy weather-helm. Presumably,

applying less helm might cause less drag and make her faster. Mower here is aware that hauling hard on the helm to hold a boat off the wind can turn one's rudder into more of a brake than steering device! He also said Edwin could shorten the foot of the main along her boom by 12 to 18 inches, for the same reason.

Edwin shared this viewpoint when writing to his naval architect, Francis Sweisguth, who disagreed, fearing the vertical mast with a Marconi rig delivered more down-thrust than a gaff rig. It was not clear to me if he meant the down-thrust of rig weight, or transmitted forced to the mast step.

It is not clear either of them considered a viewpoint put forward in 1936 by Howard I. Chapelle, who said that Marconi (he uses *jib headed*) catboats, in general, have an inherent flaw; that as the sail is reefed, the center of effort for the remaining sail area moves forward and unbalances the boat. A potential way to avoid this, Chapelle muses, would be to rake the mast sharply aft,[46] in the manner of Chesapeake workboats, quite as *Lotus'* original sail plan shows.

Sweisguth, in his letter, said that since the *Tamwock* had won the Toms River Challenge Cup in the 1928 championship, he wondered why Edwin had not bought her? "She is faster although not as comfortable," wrote Sweisguth. Regardless of his words with Sweisguth, when Edwin ordered a new main for *Lotus*, he had it cut for her mast to be vertical. Also he followed the suggestion of shortening *Lotus'* boom and thus the foot of the sail, moving the center of effort forward.

Tamwock was, however, already in the family, since she was owned by Albert Diss, a Schoettle relative. She was also destined, though none knew it at the time, to be ill-fated, and was lost in a fire at the Stokes and Vautier boatyards in Island Heights during the spring of 1939. This was a dramatic fire, during which a pretty schooner was on the ways fitting out. Apparently she was held by rope, not steel cable, and a savvy bystander

FIGURE 4-25. The Class A catboat fleet racing, Island Heights, 1939.

Philadelphia Independence Seaport Museum

took an axe and cut her restraints, allowing her to slide down the ways and out adrift into Toms River, saving her from *Tamwock*'s unfortunate end.

Many decades later, *Tamwock* was reincarnated when the Class A catboats *Wasp* and *Tamwock II* were built from her original lines drawings.[47]

It was likely in this time period that Edwin built the three barns, which were to be storage and marshalling sites for his wide ranging on-water pursuits. They stood to the north of Crosstrees, two small and one large, the latter of which also served as a spar shed.

In their heydays, these structures must have been interesting, active sites—full of hardware and sailing gear that was forever in flux from one boat, one project to another. Suzy Davis (Mary Schoettle Mitchell's daughter) recalls most clearly the bagged sails hanging from the rafters where they would be safe from nesting and chewing mice during the winter. Speaking of winter, Suzy and her cousin Sally (Schoettle) Randolph remember that there was at least one ice-boat hanging from the rafters, ready for Toms River's once truly cold winters,

The shop and spar sheds became something of a community resource for Edwin's friends—racing and sailing companions. One source claimed there may have been as many as 20 spars in there at one time. If a Class A catboat broke her mast during a race,

FIGURE 4-26. Schoettle's favorite group photo of the Class A catboats— *Mary Ann*, *Spy*, *Lotus*, and *Bat*. His notes beneath are transcribed here.

Polly Schoettle Miller

Transcribed text:

"Edwin J. Schoettle was glad to get this photo in 1941 showing all the remaining boats still in commission of a wonderful class of boats designed by Chas. Mower in 192-[obscured] Deck 28' WL 21—mast 45 feet above deck sail hoist 41 feet Boom 28 feet long Lotus boom was cut to 26 feet in 1936. It is obvious in 1941 that this class of boats will not be continued in use after the owners of these boats give up sailing them." [*To the delight of present sailors, Schoettle's prediction fell short!*]

"In 1890 to 1920—75% of the boats in Barnegat Bay were catboats. Despite the fact that these boats are fun to sail, fast in light and heavy winds. The good beam furnished plenty of cabin room for cruising and extremely large cockpits. Catboats were used for over a hundred years up to 1920? in all American waters. In 1850 the catboat was taken to England and sailed for years at South Hampton where it [was a] sensation [illegible]. The English called it a Uni boat" [*actually 'Una'*].

the men could usually go up and *borrow* one from the Schoettle's barn. It was rumored that Edwin had built and kept a spare Class A catboat mast there for just that purpose.

If *Silent Maid* ever actually had a Marconi rig—mast boom and shrouds—it was likely kept here. An additional rumor was that the building's length had been made to accommodate *Silent Maid*'s taller Marconi spar. No one, incidentally, has ever found that spar, and one legend was that it had been destroyed in the fire at the Stokes and Vautier boatyards.[48] More likely, family sources hint, its approximate 54-foot length was cut down six feet and made into a Class A catboat mast. *Forcem*'s mainsail had a similar second life on other Class A catboats.

*   *   *

Railroads had opened much of the New Jersey Shore and vacationing on the coast became fashionable and accessible. People from Philadelphia went to resorts on Long Beach Island and farther south to Cape May. Many from Princeton and northern New Jersey coalesced around communities from Manasquan, Point Pleasant, and Bay Head—the top of Barnegat Bay—or at resorts farther north along the coast from Sea Girt up to Atlantic Highlands.

Until the automobile age was well established, the Schoettles travelled by rail across New Jersey to Toms River, where along the south bank, the tracks went to Ocean Gate and thence over Barnegat Bay to the still relatively undeveloped Seaside Park and Seaside Heights. A spur crossed Toms River and went directly to Island Heights, just down the steep bank from Schoettle's home Crosstrees. Family members say it was just a quarter mile to the house, and this was convenient when individual modes of transportation were limited. In 1915, however, while World War I was still raging, Edwin Schoettle appears to have had a strong role in bringing the automobile bridge across to the two Seaside communities on the Barrier Island.

This was eventually in direct competition with the railroad. For his part, Schoettle probably found he really enjoyed the drive with his family across to the coast from Philadelphia. I must admit, that locals recall him *being* driven by a chauffeur![49] The family could travel on its own schedule, independent of railroad timetables. Edwin decompressed from the week's stresses while speeding (as well as the roads allowed!) through the long green expanse of Pine Barrens. Sara, their children, and guests who travelled with him did not have to contend with sometimes hot, crowded passenger cars, with coal smoke or cinders blowing through open windows, or perhaps annoying passengers during the railroad journey.

In the late 1930s, Edwin became an advocate for ending rail service to Island Heights. It had always been something of a backwater, quite literally, since trains *backed* across the Toms River trestle! There also may have been a small separate engine used for getting cars over to Island Heights. This long timber trestle also cut Toms River completely in half, and required virtually every boat—power and sail—to debark crew, climb onto the untended bridge, and wind open the draw by hand; manually guide the boat through and then (supposedly) close the draw properly. This process irritated railroad passengers as well, since the train, going either way, had to stop and either manually close the swinging drawbridge, or make

FIGURE 4-27. Island Heights street plan showing Long Point on the southeast corner and the Pennsylvania Railroad spur where it entered the village.

U.S. Coast and Geodetic Survey chart 1924. Paul Smith

sure the last sailor had done so, before they could proceed, a process described by ticket holders as lengthy.

Sailboat people mounted a campaign to remove the entire causeway, a decision that polarized the community between locals, and what was perceived as a self-interested, wealthier resort community. Many locals thought that they depended on rail service to come and go. Edwin analyzed the actual ticket sales and showed that they were in decline, and that burgeoning bus service around the navigable head of Toms River could easily provide the connectivity people sought.

Not quite bristling, he did take care to point out that folks of means brought a great deal of economic opportunity with them, and he stated that sailboat—and especially catboat—racing was widely covered in the print media of the day. Large crowds came to follow the action, bringing with them patronage to local businesses.[50] His claim was amply demonstrated in lengthy newspaper write-ups, which are preserved on microfiche to this day.[51]

Jack LaFleur, who worked for Edwin at this time said of Schoettle: "His greatest joy was removal of the railroad bridge across Toms River [because] its removal opened the entire river to unobstructed sailing."[52]

If this hints at elitism by Edwin Schoettle, there is a mitigating anecdote from the history of Island Heights Yacht Club. He and his friends grew to know and treat local sailing skipper Brit "Britty" Applegate as an equal and wanted him to join the Island Heights Yacht Club (IHYC). Edwin had originally hired Applegate as a summer chauffeur, but found him an excellent helmsman on his boats! Mike Frankovich describes him as the first "hired gun" in the Class A catboat fleet. The Barnegat Bay Yacht Racing Association eventually decreed that one had to be a member to sail in its races. In its by-laws, however, IHYC originally had a clause that if you lived locally the whole year, you could not be a member. Some of the IHYC Committee blackballed Applegate and didn't want to change the rule. Edwin and his compatriots literally had to threaten to resign before the old guard knuckled under.[53]

FIGURE 4-28. *Lotus* sails away from the Schoettle pier with her shortened boom. Photographed from Crosstrees' west garden by James Mitchell, Jr., in 1939 with a Toms River Yacht Club race in the background.

Photograph from Polly Schoettle Miller

I don't have the full story here, but Edwin made his primary yacht club affiliation with Toms River Yacht Club, hence *Silent Maid*'s permanent "T-82" sail number, which Schoettle adopted from *Scat II*. This event with Applegate might be at the root of that change, but Edwin's children were still IHYC members throughout their youths.

*　*　*

There was still relatively little development over on the barrier islands in those days, and, should they have ghosted through the railroad draw on the west side of the bay near Goodluck Point, they could then beat up against the wider part of Island Beach (today's State Park) close to where the old Reed family hotel had entertained guests for many years.

There was a creditable sand beach here, likely close to where Cranberry Inlet may have penetrated the strand back before 1812. In some places, the *Maid* could nose

FIGURE 4-29. *Silent Maid* before the wind, Edwin Jr., with Whiskers, Ferd to right of the unidentified helmsman with Sara next to him and Karl the little guy farthest to port. The man in the sweater next to Sara may be Edwin's friend Mac Crabbe.

Suzy Mitchell Davis photograph

up onto the shore and still be afloat. The tide in her early years (before 1931) was of extremely small amplitude in upper Barnegat Bay because of its distance from the Inlet, and the absence of all but modest stream flow entering from tributaries. In light weather, she could lie thus for a long time and not be stranded on the ebbing tide. Wind forces on Barnegat Bay, especially strong seasonal northerlies and the regular summer southerlies, caused water level changes in the bay—three feet or more—which far exceeded the lunar tidal amplitudes, but these were unpredictable, not usual, events.

These low salinity conditions also made for more modest marine fouling, the growth of sessile, or fixed organisms, on pilings and the bottoms of boats. Sailors in the past eventually discovered that even a light slime layer of unwanted growth could slow down a boat significantly, and that a heavy infestation of algae or barnacles would have disastrous effects in competition sailing. This was far less a problem in very fresh waters and increased in magnitude as salinity of the water became higher.

FIGURE 4-30. *Silent Maid* on a jaunt in 1925 with ten aboard, plus Whiskers, the Schoettles's dog. The *Maid* lies absolutely beam-to against the sandy shore and though MacCrabbe has boots on, everybody and presumably the photographer (likely Edwin Schoettle) has gotten ashore with dry feet on this afternoon.

Crewmembers:"Mac" (McEwen) Crabbe (a solid Schoettle friend), the dog Whiskers, Ferd Schoettle, Edwin Schoettle, Jr., Dick Kleinhans, Henry Horrocks, Karl Schoettle, Sara (Mrs. Edwin G.) Schoettle, Mary Schoettle (later Mitchell), Bud Bronson (a Bay Head friend), and Lew Kleinhans.

Crosstrees photograph, Suzy Mitchell Davis

When the Point Pleasant Bay Head Canal was opened in 1928, and Manasquan Inlet stabilized after 1930–31, the intrusion of high salinity ocean water at every tide into upper Barnegat Bay meant that marine fouling organisms became a problem where it had never been a serious issue.

Higher salinity near Goodluck Point at the Mouth of Toms River meant that the "shipworm," commonly and sometimes inaccurately called "teredo," began honeycombing railroad trestle pilings once thought immune because they were in a low-salinity environment. According to Dr. Ken Able, in his research on Rutgers University marine studies in the region, the shipworm in Barnegat Bay was first noted by Professor Julius Nelson in 1914, when their damage to railroad trestle pilings at Manahawkin was discovered. The upper bay was spared this infestation until the 1920s when higher salinity water became routine. Julius' son Thurlow Nelson, a Rutgers professor, found some of these destructive shellfish were *Teredo navalis*, the European pileworm. Not worms at all, they are actually marine boring mollusks related to clams and oysters and, in this case, were very destructive to marine construction. There are also native related species (*Bankia gouldi* and *Bankia fimbriatula*), which can do just as much damage![54]

Predictably, when good biologists are not constructively involved in coastal engineering decisions, the same mistakes can be made repeatedly.

Rutgers, again, was only partly consulted when the Oyster Creek Nuclear Generating Station was commissioned in 1975. It cooled its reactor water by using huge pumps to suck saltwater up once-freshwater Forked River. After heating by passage through the power plant's steam condensing systems, the water was pumped out and down formerly freshwater Oyster Creek and into Barnegat Bay. The result was perfect, virtually year-round habitat for the shipworm *Bankia*, and eventually they bored out most of the docks and wooden structures in the creek.[55] The power company first replaced, then eventually removed all the wooden structures on this once popular boating and fishing tributary, which is now a dedicated discharge canal for the power plant.

FIGURE 4-31. An eight-inch piling totally honeycombed by over six dozen shipworm borings. While no visible outside surface damage appears, the structural integrity is totally destroyed.

Kent Mountford photographs

In the 1940s, it is my suspicion that this damage to the railroad trestle from ship-worms (the remediation of which would have been extremely expensive) played a role in the railroad's decision to abandon service to the barrier beach. A fire in 1946 that damaged a section on the western end of the span was the straw that broke the camel's back. Repairs to the span were never made, trains never crossed again, and the rail service loop along the Island Beach Peninsula, which had made its development possible, was discontinued. The pilings were subsequently all pulled, with the exception of two shorter piers which were left standing on the east shore at Barnegat Pier and the west shore of the barrier island, and the bay was open to unobstructed navigation again as it had been until the 1880s.

∗   ∗   ∗

I've always thought of the Schoettle family trips frequently forging far down the bay, but many of the *Maid*'s sails were simply day trips, likely started after a good sailing breeze had sprung up. Jack LaFleur said that during the years he sailed with the family, the trips were usually confined to Toms River and the bay between the automobile bridge to Seaside and the Pennsylvania Railroad bridge crossing below Goodluck Point to the barrier beach.

This was good recreational sailing when there was a party aboard; the southerlies made for a lot of beam reach sailing on big *Silent Maid* and she loved this point of sailing. She could still show her windward ability pointing up in the afternoon's stiffening wind and spray towards the railroad bridge, likely quite a sight for day-trippers enjoying themselves at Barnegat Pier. The *Maid* could then fall off and run down towards the northern vehicle bridge span to Seaside before coming about or jibing to head back to Toms River. From my time aboard, I can still hear the distinctive clicking of her (albeit primitive) roller-bearing wood-cheeked Merriman blocks as the sheet ran out. The *Maid* would reach back up towards Island Heights and home.

As the afternoon wore on and the sun sank lower towards the Pine Barrens, this leg would often be at decreasing speed, as the lee of the Ocean Gate shoreline took muscle out of the already easing southerly winds. *Silent Maid* then relied on her momentum and broad sail area to ghost on up Toms River. I'll bet the young men aboard sat on the wung-out boom as I often did, watching the wake coming out from under her wide transom, and little bubbles hissing as they burst, clearly audible in reflected sound to those on the boom!

This was lazy sailing, but the *Maid* had no engine and with no propeller drag she was good at ghosting along, taking her miles upriver. The trip was never very long in a really good sailboat—just enough sun and wind for gentlemen and lady guests who were not hardcore sailors.

The *Maid* was not always confined to the bay east of Toms River. Even without an auxiliary, it was routine for good sailors to gain some speed, then luff up and let momentum carry their yachts through the railroad drawbridge. The draw was manned and opened by an attendant, thus easing the problems of passage. The draw opening was far west along the span, close to Goodluck Point, where (the 1924 charts show) a deeper channel was located. This enabled full draft with centerboards down and thus much less side-slipping or leeway while passing the narrow spot. Once through the draw, the entire lower Barnegat Bay stretches wide over the horizon southward to the slender raised finger of Barnegat Light.

Mosquito Cove and Seaweed Point

Henry Horrocks, pictured in Figure 4-30, was very active in Barnegat's yachting community and also a clever cartoonist. He did a fanciful map (Figure 4-33) of the bay with accurate depictions of shallows, where everyone worth their salt had run aground. He also depicted familiar and favored locations like Mosquito Cove, emphasizing its namesake insect. Many of the yachts of the time were depicted under sail, power, or at anchor, and the automobile bridge to Seaside was shown with an improbably long queue of unhappy motorists in their period flivvers, backed up at the draw, and awaiting the passing train of sailboats on their way to the races.

Horrocks had things correct, like those mosquitoes in Mosquito Cove. Decades later during the post-Korean War second-housing boom, developers wasted no time having this name changed to the more market-friendly "Silver Bay" and got the U.S. Board of Geographic Names to sign on so these changes were subsequently printed on Coast and Geodetic Survey, and later NOAA navigation charts.

The Seaweed Point of my youth was known for the windrows of grass that piled up on its southward facing, and thus, windward shoreline. This land exposure was an historic accumulation point for tons of plant debris from the huge beds of widgeon grass (*Ruppia maritima*) off Lavalette, so called for the Widgeon or baldpate duck (*Mareca Americana*), which fed on them each autumn. The beds lie west of the barrier island and the vegetative parts of these plants were naturally shed each summer by the perennial Ruppia rhizome or root stock. Large rafts of these still-floating grasses moved downwind and up bay, adding tremendous amounts of organic material to the underlying marsh and accumulating enough sediment to make parts of this peninsula 'fast land.'

This plant material was and is part of the broad energy flow in Barnegat's ecosystem, and similar deposits washed up on the Island Beach Peninsula and on shorelines north to Mantoloking. The result for bay swimmers is shown in the Figure 7-59 of Captain Bill Evans, showing off a bay-grass drape just a few yards from the moored Silent Maid.

Seaweed Point was a name equally unfortunate for selling real estate, so the adjacent development was amended to "Seawood Harbor." Both places are largely wall-to-wall houses today.

Sanitizing these place names did nothing to impede the reasons for which they were originally labeled, and mosquitoes still plague those who are anchored in Mosquito Cove enjoying a calm sunset, and the windrows of Widgeon grass still pile up on Seaweed Point. Today the mats of vegetation generate complaints to municipal government about the odor of decomposition and a perceived public health hazard. Perhaps the original developers of both places should be exposed to these natural phenomena, punitively and unprotected, at sunset mosquito hour and during widgeon grass decomposition season!

Silent Maid was enough of a feature around the bay that she was given a cartouche of her own on the fanciful Horrocks map (see Figure 4-34). Good humored and exactly on the mark.

FIGURE 4-32. Detail from Horrocks' map showing *Silent Maid* with her Toms River YC racing number and sailing well south of the railroad bridge with a load of folks aboard. Keeping watch on the bow is likely the Schoettle's dog Whiskers. Notice the *Maid* is headed for a depth of 2-15/16th feet, where drawing three feet plus the weight of her crew, she will undoubtedly run gently aground. This copy of the map, property of Alicemay Weber-Wright, was hand water-colored, but too faded for a successful full-scale reproduction (see Figure 4-33).

FIGURE 4.33. Henry Horrock's fanciful and delightful 1932 Barnegat map depicted with all its many boating and cultural community intimations. Notice that the train on the Barnegat Bay PRR causeway is headed directly for the draw which is wide open, with a cabin cruiser just passing through!

Alicemay Weber-Wright collection

Edwin Schoettle and His *Silent Maid* | 137

Photos show the *Maid* nosed up to a steep sandbar (Figure 4-11). I'm betting this was down near Winter Anchorage, where a back channel wound out to Barnegat Inlet, and fast, reversible tidal flow scoured deep white sand-bottomed cuts in the bottom.

The Winter Anchorage was just that for seasonal duck hunters. They would tow little houseboats or barges with shacks atop (even an old cabin cruiser) across from the western shore or down from Toms River as lodging during the waterfowl flyway passages. The men would thus enjoy fellowship, a warming bottle, and hunt the winter flocks feeding on Barnegat's productive eelgrass beds and abundant benthic species. This food supply was immense; the scores of burrowing worm and tiny crustacean species, the small juveniles of recently set clams and scallops. The birds needed the energy from this food after long flights, and the hunters were there to take their share of the fattening migrants.

Runyon Colie, when seven years old (in 1924), remembers his father sailing their catboat down near the inlet to have her bottom scrubbed.[56] (I'm sure the *Maid* did too, given the limited effectiveness of copper paints in the 1920s! What, after all, could one expect from a gallon of "Baltimore Red Copper" at $4.50?[57]) But aside from a bottom scrub, the swimming was great, the ocean breezes cooling, and the wild strand, dunes, and beckoning surf of Island Beach were even more inviting 80 years ago than they are today.

Edwin Schoettle must have valued this time with his wife and family greatly. It was a wonderful relief after running his many businesses, which continued to grow. He had a real sense for this part of American industry that his father had helped found and was considered a major force in paper products manufacture.

Brother William C. Schoettle was also an active boater alongside Edwin for decades. He fished regularly for relaxation. Eileen Fancher's father Frank Olsen skippered William Schoettle's successive yachts *Alice I* and *Alice II*, and his fishing expeditions were an important life passage. He fished with one or both of two good friends, "Mr. Wilder and Mr. Gimmy," and during the tenure of both boats those trips were regular events between Memorial and Labor Day from about 1909 until *Alice II*'s last year, 1941. Eileen Fancher muses: "William Schoettle must have really loved his weekend fishing trips to have kept such a faithful schedule all through those (42) years."[58]

*   *   *

Jack LaFleur worked for the Schoettles over two summers, but by the time he was 20, he was ready for a real job. At season's end, Edwin got him a place in one of his paper box companies. Jack was now making $40 a week. When World War II broke out, Jack LaFleur enlisted, and so did some of the Schoettle family, serving in this conflict with no assurance how it would turn out for the United States and its Allied powers.

All eyes in North America were riveted on the peril to which England was submitted by the Nazi *Blitzkrieg*. The Schoettles must have thought deeply about their German ancestry. There was, after all, still a strong segment of the family in Europe. Ferdinand Schoettle and his parents may have rejected militarism at the time he emigrated, but we are not privy to the struggle that may have gone on in their hearts and minds leaving their Fatherland after many generations.

Edwin became one of many policy advisors to President Franklin Delano Roosevelt. As the United States actively entered the war, most of Edwin's working hours, his family recalls, were spent around the Philadelphia Navy Yard. In this heady assignment as a policy advisor, he was sometimes teamed with Supreme Court Justice Owen Josephus Roberts,[59] and Roger Ward Babson (mentioned earlier in this chapter) with whom he had long friendships.

FIGURE 4-34. **Supreme Court Justice Owen J. Roberts, a Schoettle friend and fellow advisor for FDR during World War II.**

Wikipedia cph.3b11988.jpg

One must have wondered how expatriates like this second-generation German family might fare in the Nazi and Axis powers prevailed by war's end. It must not have been lost on Edwin and his brothers that their father, in the 19th century, had *fled* Europe in opposition to this very sort of militaristic expansionism. The implications of a Nazi victory, essentially worldwide, must have been chilling. The wider Schoettle family's story during these difficult years has not been well documented. However, it seemed that the women drew together and spent much of the time in Bay Head, occupying a couple of houses, including Edwin's brother Marc's home. The church in Bay Head seems to have been very important to the family, with Sara donating one of its stained glass windows.[60]

In pursuit of prevailing in this massive conflict, the Allied powers met at Casablanca, Morocco, on the northwest African coast in January 1943: Churchill, Roosevelt, Gen. George C. Marshall, his British counterpart Gen. Sir Alan Brooke, Generals Eisenhower, "Monty" Montgomery, and Patton gathered to devise a five-pronged strategy that would enable defeat of the Axis powers in Europe and Asia.

Historian Paul Kennedy says it concisely that having strategized they went home, leaving the implementation to others. Kennedy claims it was this middle level of implementers, or problem solvers, who really were the real heroes of World War II.[61] They produced materiel, transported goods, expedited, invented, and made it possible for the foot soldiers to advance and conquer their enemies the hardest way—in field combat.

One of the tools in that fighting was the M-1 Garand Rifle, official U.S. infantry weapon since 1936, which replaced the slow, hand-operated, bolt action 1903 Springfield from the turn of the century. The Garand was a semi-automatic weapon, firing eight rounds from a pre-loaded metal clip as quickly as one could (hopefully) aim and pull the trigger. As each round was fired, the recoil and pressure from the exploding powder, threw back the bolt, ejected the spent brass casing. A spring then drove the bolt forward, stripping off the next round from the clip and chambering it, ready for the trigger to be pulled.

When the eighth round had been fired, the expendable clip would fly out with a loudly audible ping signifying that the weapon was out of bullets. To continue laying down fire, one had to reload, put in a new clip, which was pre-loaded with eight rounds of ball ammunition. "Ball" was a holdover from pre-Civil War times; the bullets on the ends of those cartridges were not balls. They were produced with a point, metal jacketed and with an internal core of lead to maximize momentum and impact.

Those groups of eight rounds, each in its clip, were carried by each soldier in a chain of several sewn pockets of light cotton fabric called a bandolier. The clips could be transferred to their personal ammo belts of heavy canvas and a couple of bandoliers could be slung over their shoulders thus making more ammunition available on patrol or in combat. Being able grab and insert a full replacement clip quickly could mean the difference between life and death, a successful assault or a defeat.

The rounds in each of those clips, while being thrown about, fallen upon, plunged in sand or mud during maneuvers, were stabilized and kept in alignment by a simple cardboard sleeve slipped over them after manufacture. The Schoettle Paper Box Company and its partners manufactured millions of those sleeves. Who knows how many hundreds of millions of rounds were thus made available in an emergency; how many lives were saved just by these scraps of cardboard? The importance of this part of Schoettle's business cannot be minimized for a company still coming out of depression.

Edwin Schoettle was also a member of a stabilizing board for the wider paper industries. There was a lot of competition for war materiel manufacturing contracts, and it would have been easy to assure that all this business was shunted to a few fortunate members of a cartel. Edwin's influence, while very strong, seems to have been directed

FIGURE 4-35. **Modern replica M-1 Garand clips (here with blank cartridges having no bullets) with cardboard sleeves.**

www.ServiceofSupply.com courtesy of Bryan Dibble

rather to assuring that the work was fairly apportioned among companies; thus some companies that were struggling were kept in business and people in a difficult time kept their jobs. Men whose businesses were saved in this manner never forgot Schoettle's even-handed role during the War.

Frankly, it is not known how much *Silent Maid* was sailed during the war years, but it appears that Edwin was only able to get to Island Heights on Sundays; the pressure of business being so intense. I've no idea how he managed fuel for travelling to the Shore during this time when gas rationing and the rigid use of cards limited purchases. Whatever joy he might have experienced sailing fuel-independent *Silent Maid*, the war took a serious toll on Edwin's health. He said at one point that while the orders were coming in at a great rate from home and abroad, the cost or availability of materials and the difficulty of finding suitable labor in a market where most men were overseas and at war made it very difficult to run at a profit. Businesses do *not* do well when running at a loss.

When hostilities finally ended, to everyone's joy, America experienced an immense economic shock. Edwin struggled to regain balance in his businesses during the difficult retooling that followed peace in 1945.

Jack LaFleur, the Schoettle dock boy, returned from service and touched base with his mentor, who again offered him a position with his company. LaFleur declined this time, being ready for different horizons and more than $40 a week, thank you! He worked, thereafter, in the Midwest, never following the water again. He lives at this writing in 2014, in York, Pennsylvania, comfortably retired and travelling whenever and as much as he can.

During this tumultuous, post-war period, Schoettle had serious disagreements with two of his sons—now returned from service—over how their industry was to re-adjust. Edwin had built and run these businesses and simply could not bear sudden interference on the course he wanted to follow. It was deeply upsetting for the two eldest sons, Ferdinand and Edwin, Jr. The resulting estrangement could never be fully resolved in their father's lifetime, something Edwin's wife Sara recognized and suffered along with him. Some feel that this very painful time brought on his first heart attack and left his health severely compromised.[62]

By this time Edwin and Sara had moved from Chestnut Hill to downtown Philadelphia. They then resided at 1830 Manning Street in the city, about two blocks from the historic Barclay Hotel, which around 1940 had been purchased by Schoettle family acquaintance John McShain, known both from Philadelphia and at Bay Head.

McShain was first and foremost a contractor. He helped renovate the White House during President Harry S. Truman's administration. He also built the Pentagon, the Jefferson Memorial and, while he was a resident at the Barclay, his company constructed the Philadelphia International Airport.[63]

When Edwin had his first coronary, treatment at the time prescribed rest and almost total abstinence from exercise. Stairs of any sort became medically unsuitable, let alone loping around the deck and hauling halyards on a 33-foot catboat. From our perspective in the 21st century, ALL of those activities would be progressively encouraged and might well have restored Edwin to reasonable health. Such is long hindsight.

The Schoettles, perhaps encouraged by McShain (who lived at the Barclay some 30 years until his retirement in 1978), took residence on the entire tenth floor of the Barclay, where an elevator made stairs unnecessary. The annual Schoettle Christmas luncheon was where, with the throng assembled "around the table . . . it was a huge table,"[64] each child recounted his or her achievements for "Pop Pop" (as they called Edwin) to

Grandchildren Discover Treasures in Crosstrees' Sheds

Suzy Mitchell Davis, Edwin's granddaughter, remembers that she and cousin Sally (Schoettle) Randolph, had grudging permission from the adults to play around the outbuildings at Crosstrees—that was not really for little girls to do. "Ganny wasn't comfortable with the little girls playing around them."[67] It was for their male cousin, Edwin's grandson Karl then 11 or 12 years old, to get a key or bolt cutter and open Edwin's small shop building, a veritable family time capsule. The summer of 1947 had not found Edwin Schoettle in good health, and when he passed away, like most people, he had left many things still unfinished, hoping to get back to them when his health improved.

Upon opening the shop, Karl walked into a frozen moment in Edwin Schoettle's life.[68] Had Karl read about British Lord Carnarvon's expedition opening fabled King Tut's tomb, he might have related to how archaeologist Howard Carter felt when, holding a torch, he first peered into the tomb, which had been sealed for 3,000 years. When Carter was asked if he saw anything, he famously responded, "Yes! Wonderful things!"[69] Suzy Mitchell Davis says: "I'm sure Karl had an eerie experience there. It was a fairly daunting space!!"[70]

The drama might not have been as intense as the King Tut experience, but Karl walked in on a bit of the past. There was a desk on the left, and the calendar on the wall was from 1947. Covered with dust, boating magazines were stacked on a bench; there was a Sears and Roebuck catalog. To the right was a workbench with tools left where they had been last used. Rigging and hardware hung on the walls, and sails were still suspended from hooks. Suzy remembered mostly the huge coils of manila lines, sheets, halyards, and anchor rode, which were hung up and away from rodents.[71]

Suzy and Sally, as recalled previously, were sure there had been one, maybe two, iceboats hanging from the rafters. There were decades when Barnegat Bay had real winters and hard ice locked in the tributaries. Ice was sometimes thick enough that cars could be driven from Island Heights across Toms River to Beachwood on the south

FIGURE 4-36. An iceboat on Toms River, at Island Heights in 1905. It could have been one of the Schoettle family's, but the image is unattributed.
Ocean County Historical Society

shore.[72] Winters then seem to have been much deeper and more persistent, and the ice on Toms River, and many other Jersey Coast tributaries, was hard enough to allow sporting with these remarkably fast sailing machines.

In my young adulthood, I saw Barnegat Bay frozen many times, and sometimes hard enough for such exciting ventures,[73] but it has now been many a year since more than temporary freezes have bridged all Barnegat's tributaries. Tell me there is no global warming, but after living three quarters of a century, I'm certain things are very different today.

The three sheds, without Edwin and his focus on boats and the Bay, "fell into disrepair by the late 1970s and met their demise in a fire that was set by kids sometime in the early 1980s."[74] How many remaining treasures were thus lost by such thoughtless vandalism?

FIGURE 4-37 Sara and Edwin in Atlantic City and in Boca Raton, Florida, on earlier trips for recreation.

Schoettle family photographs, Polly Schoettle Miller

interpret or admire. After each presentation, "Ganny" (Sara) would give each little presenter a big hug. These events were held downstairs at the Barclay, and ably organized by Caesar, the hotel's headwaiter.[65]

Polly Schoettle Miller relished these events, identifying with the fictional Eloise and her pranks at New York's Plaza Hotel: "One Christmas luncheon (my cousin) Joanie and I got nightgowns . . . from Aunt Peggy and Uncle Karl; we immediately stripped down and put them on and ran around everywhere. . . . They had pleated necklines (and waists which at 4 and seven years old) we didn't have. We went down to the Christmas luncheon in our nightgowns and no one said a word."[66]

*   *   *

Edwin Schoettle apparently had a second heart attack, and this must have given him long brooding periods as he looked to the future. He did not give up, however, and was still thinking about his *Silent Maid*. In July 1947, he received a letter from that long-time admirer of the *Maid*, Judson Smith, then living in Montgomery County, Pennsylvania, and who, unknown to Schoettle, had watched his boat's career for years. Schoettle was at that point in residence at Seaview Country Club in Absecon, New Jersey, and in his words: "recuperating from a severe attack of coronary thrombosis. For that reason I have not used the boat for three years. She is stored under cover at Arthur Stoke's boatyard at Island Heights New Jersey…all rigging [spars?], etc. are in perfect shape."[75]

Making the assumption that Edwin meant three years before the present, this suggests that he had last sailed the *Maid* in 1944. Sadly, with his health already compromised, it would turn out to have been his last sail aboard this much beloved yacht.

Jud Smith enters our history of the boat sincerely interested in *Silent Maid*. He has a side story of his own that will unfold chapter by chapter hereafter, but this time he asks how he might get a set of plans for *Silent Maid*. Edwin replied that the drawings he had published in *Sailing Craft* could be enlarged about ten times without compromising their utility—at least as "study plans."

Assuming Jud Smith was interested in building another replica catboat, Edwin told him that *Silent Maid* had cost him "probably $3500" 19 years ago. (Writing In 1947, he must have meant 23 years ago, in 1924, though after leaving Morton Johnson's boatyard the *Maid* must have had significant subsequent investments.) Edwin further explained to Jud Smith, "[Today's] cost no doubt double or treble that amount."

With respect to securing the full-scale plans, Edwin did not have designer Francis Sweisguth's current address, but suggested the New York phone directory or perhaps writing *The Rudder* magazine. Edwin closed cordially, clearly having enjoyed the chat about his favorite boat.[76] Smith promptly wrote to *The Rudder* and was told he could get a full set of builder's plans directly from Sweisguth whose address provided was then in New Rochelle, New York.[77]

Judson Smith took his brother Fred to Island Heights, and they went aboard the *Maid* where she lay in storage under cover at Stoke's Boatyard. They loved her. Fred, as a lifelong sailor and sometime live-aboard, thought the cabin a miracle. They must have stood in that spacious cockpit and imagined what a sight she would be with sunlit sails half covering the sky above, and the waters of Barnegat Bay rushing along either side and off astern.

Though the sails and spars were stored there and in perfect order, according to Edwin,[78] Jud and Fred never saw her rigged and in the water, watched her sail, or got aboard while she was afloat. Judson still harbored the thought that ownership might someday be in the cards.

I know this tale first because the letter survives and because more than 40 years later my wife's aunt married Judson's brother Fred Smith, and he recounted it from memory. I thought then and still do about what would have happened if Judson had bought the *Maid* and she had never come into my life. How that would have changed my own navigation through the following seven decades would not have been for the better; an interesting matter for speculation, but assuredly I would not be writing this book.

Edwin and Sara Schoettle tried to salvage what they could of his final time, but I'm sure Edwin deeply felt the loss of sailing, time on the water, and the feeling of *Silent Maid*'s deck beneath his feet. With damage from his coronary and frustrated with his increasing lack of control, he suffered what family members describe as a nervous exhaustion.[79]

Today there are certainly better and more workable medications to manage such ailments, which help both patient and family better cope. The Schoettles did the best they could in the mid-1940s. Rest and keeping stress away was then believed the proper route. The family recalls that when outside of Philadelphia, Edwin and Sara spent a lot of time at Seaview, their choice for pleasant convalescence as Edwin sought to turn the corner towards wellness again.

Edwin Schoettle died in a Philadelphia hospital on Christmas Eve in 1947. Born in 1876, he was just 71 years old at his death. There would be no family review that Christmas, which the whole family seems to have considered a true loss.

Sincerely grief stricken at the loss of her life partner, Sara never went into the sail loft or barns again, actually having one of them padlocked. She lived a quarter century beyond Edwin, retaining her wit and faculties and transmitted the stories to her children and grandchildren. Polly Schoettle Miller recalls: "Staying with Ganny was wonderful. . . . She was pure Irish and full of love and tons of stories, . . . which is probably why Pop Pop Edwin loved her so much."[00] She passed away in 1972 at the respectable, well-lived age of 91.

I will always lament that throughout my family's ownership of *Silent Maid* and for eight years afterward, Sara Schoettle was sitting there atop all her history and I never had the sense to look her up and visit. What a boon to this book her reminiscences might have been!

FIGURE 4-38. Sara Schoettle sailing in "Gibson Girl" mode in 1910 and in 1949, two years after losing Edwin.

Photos: Polly Schoettle Miller and Suzy Mitchell Davis

Schoettle's Later *Scat*s

At Edwin's passing, the Schoettles still had one *Scat* under the family flag. In 1941, Edwin had, while still sailing *Silent Maid*, purchased one of the delightful Lightning daysailers. Designed by Rod Stephens, the fleet by then totaled over 750 boats. Named *Scat III*, this Lightning served many years until destroyed in a fire. Her loss could well have been in the vandal-set fire, which destroyed the Schoettle's three sheds full of sailing equipment and historic artifacts. A friend subsequently wrote the family, saying "I heard your Lightning burned . . . you have to get a Marshall.[81]"

Nobody in the family at that time, presumably the late 1960s, knew what a Marshall was and had to be instructed about Brett Marshall's wonderful (then new) fiberglass catboats with Dacron® sails, nylon lines, and almost maintenance-free aluminum spars. As it happened, one was for sale in not too distant Egg Harbor and, of course, the Schoettles bought her promptly and generations of great -and great-great grandchildren have cut their teeth on still another catboat named *Scat*.

FIGURE 4-39. The Schoettle's last *Scat* during Edwin's lifetime was a Lightning, designed by Rod Stephens and introduced in 1939. In 1941, as the class reached popularity—over 750 boats—Schoettle bought his boat and named her *Scat III* (inset image).

Polly Schoettle Miller

FIGURE 4-40. *Scat*, the Schoettle descendant's Marshall catboat, sailing with Crosstrees in the background.

Original painting, Crosstrees, Suzy Mitchell Davis

1. Scott Anderson, *Lawrence in Arabia: War, Deceit, Imperial Folly and the Making of the Modern Middle East.* (New York: Doubleday, 2013.) Quoted by Ephriam Karsh, *The Wall Street Journal*, August 10, 2013.

2. Tom Beaton, discussion on racing, September 11, 2012.

3. Philip A. Schoettle, letter to Kent Mountford, September 12, 2009.

4. "Championship Race Results Archive, 1914-1929," BBYRA, accessed 2012, http://www.bbyra.org/results1920.shtml.

5. Ibid.

6. *The Catboat Association Bulletin*, Number 58, March 1979. "Scat, Scat II, and Silent Maid, pp. 11-17.

7. The *Maid*'s kedge in the Mountford family's time was large and had a folding stock for stowage. It is likely this was *Silent Maid*'s original working anchor. A relatively large 22 lb. Danforth (post WW II) had been added, and this was the hook to which we most often rode, 1953–1964.

8. William H. Whiting Company catalog, Pratt and Gay Streets, Baltimore, MD (1935), p. 3.

9. Primus stove. Later versions went up Mt. Everest with Edmund Hillary and Tenzing Norgay. Primus technology was patented in Sweden but the term 'primus' is now generic. http://.en.wikipedia. org/wiki/.Primus_stove

10. *Ashburton (Australia) Guardian* (per Press Association), "Primus Stove Bursts: Two Men Injured," November 30, 1920, p. 5.

11. Howard I. Chapelle, *Yacht Designing and Planning* (New York: W.W. Norton & Company, Inc., 1936). Calculated using the method on page 96, Figure 2.

12. Edwin Schoettle, dimensions entered in his hand on Burrows order form, clearly labeled *Silent Maid,* 1925.

13. Howard I. Chapelle, *Yacht Designing and Planning* (W.W. Norton, 1936).

14. Jeremy Howard Williams, *Sails* (Adlard Coles Ltd, 1967), 85.

15. Francis Sweisguth, 1926, in Schoettle, *Sailing Craft* (New York: MacMillan, 1928), 100.

16. Wikipedia, "Prohibition in the United States," http://en.wikipedia.org/wiki/Prohibition_in_the_United_States

17. Henry Gauthier, personal communication to Kent Mountford when they were kids on Stirling Road, Warren Township, NJ, circa 1953.

18. "Prohibition in the United States."

19. Edwin Schoettle, "Bermuda Logbook," 1926.

20. Schoettle, "Bermuda Logbook," June 23.

21. Schoettle, "Bermuda Logbook," July 2.

22. Schoettle, "Bermuda Logbook," July 3 and 4. The petrels sighted would be Wilson's Petrel or Mother Cary's Chickens, *Oceanites oceanicus,* southern hemisphere birds, which spend the Austral winter off our coasts, May-September.

23. Richard H. Pough, *Audubon Waterbird Guide* (New York: Doubleday, 1951), 21,

24. Schoettle, "Bermuda Logbook," July 5.

25. *Yucca filamentosa* is called "Spanish Bayonet" for its sharp leaf-tips. A member of the Liliaceae, it grew from New Jersey southward, and by 1950, it had spread still farther north. From June to September, this plant sends up tall spikes with many showy cream-colored blossoms. As Schoettle noted, they are visible a long way off.

26. Edwin Schoettle, *Sailing Craft* (New York: MacMillan, 1928), Editor's Note.

27. Edwin Schoettle, personal notes exchanged with Justice Owen Roberts, circa 1943.

28. Andy (Ferdinand) Schoettle, phone and mail interview with Kent Mountford, July 16, 2010.

29. *New Jersey Courier*, "Local News" column, masthead dated July 19, 1929, page number not on clipping.

30. Jimmy Glenn, interviewed at Chestertown, MD, aboard the replica *Silent Maid*, October 30, 2009.

31. Boyle and Kuser, "Study on New Jersey Cedar Swamp pH," 1994.

32. Nancy Mountford, described to Kent Mountford in conversation, 2013.

33. John Kenneth Galbraith, *The Great Crash, 1929* (Houghton Mifflin Harcourt, 1997), p.84.

34. Ken Fisher, *100 Minds That Made the Market* (Wiley, 2007), pp. 129–132.

35. Babson's "Ten Commandments" of investing (http://en.wikipedia.org/wiki/Roger_Babson)

36. Karl Schoettle, in written document "EJS for Family Consumption," 2006.

37. Schoettle, "EJS for Family Consumption."

38. Sweisguth designs by year at http://sailboatdata.com/view_designer.asp?designer_id=135

39. The Catboat Association website (www.catboats.org), accessed on March 23, 2013.

40. Jack LaFleur to Kent Mountford, October 5, 2010

41. Robert Barrie and George Barrie, 1909. Cruises Mainly in the Chesapeake. Poor Man's Paradise, p 269; Barnegat Bay about 1906.

42. Jack LaFleur to Kent Mountford, January 11, 2010.

43. George Whittle, met and interviewed through Marie Darling at Beaton's Boatyard, June 28, 2004.

44. Cornelius Boocock, recounted to Kent Mountford at Rutgers University, New Brunswick, where he was Dean of Men. 1960.

45. Edwin J. Schoettle, written reminiscences (circa 1945), shared by Polly Schoettle Miller with Kent Mountford, 2012

46. Chapelle, *Yacht Designing and Planning, p.* 240.

47. Russell Manheimer, verbal communication to Kent Mountford, June 20, 2013.

48. Edwin Schoettle, direct quote from Schoettle's handwritten A-Cat photo legend, year missing.

49. Eileen Fancher, correspondence to Suzy Davis and Kent Mountford, July 2013.

50. Edwin Schoettle, a *New Jersey Courier* opinion piece preserved in his papers, year missing.

51. *New Jersey Courier* (decades of this paper are archived on microfilm at the Toms River Public Library).

52. Jack LaFleur, written correspondence to Kent Mountford, January 4, 2010.

53. Michael Frankovich, "Tamwock," in *A Cats: A Century of Tradition*, Gary Jobson and Roy Wilkins (Nomad Press, 2006), 39.

54. Thurlow Nelson, "Destruction by the European Pileworm *Teredo navalis* in Barnegat Bay, NJ." Circular 246 New Jersey Agricultural Research Station, New Brunswick, NJ, 1922, pp. 3–15.

55. *Bankia* and *Teredo* do not *eat* the wood, they bore. They enter the surface of an unprotected wood surface as larvae, they grow, and, using their two small clam-like shells, abrade the wood by drilling tunnels as long as a yard, lining them with a nacreous shell-like material. Their worm-like bodies grow to fill the hollowed space. They *feed* through two minute holes in the surface of the wood, drawing in water to get oxygen, and filtering out the microscopic plankton food it contains. They expel (exhale) their wastes through the tiny adjacent second hole. The holes are nearly invisible and all the damage occurs internally. Thus, the damage is often undetected with disastrous results. These two genera of shipworms and related marine borers cause billions of dollars in damage worldwide. In the past, they were the cause of countless ships sinking in port or foundering in storms because of the structural weakening they caused.

56. Henry Colie, quoting his father Runyon in Kent Mountford's Log *Nimble*, May 14, 2011.

57. William H. Whiting Company catalog, Ibid.

58. Eileen Fancher, correspondence to Kent Mountford, July 30, 2013.

59. Owen J. Roberts was, during WW II, the only Republican on the Supreme Court, and one of just three to vote against Roosevelt's now controversial Japanese Internment Policy. (www.Wikipedia.com accessed in 2013).

60. Philip A. Schoettle, materials sent Kent Mountford from Bay Head's June centennial celebration, 2013.

61. Paul Kennedy, *Engineers of Victory* (New York: Random House, 2013).

62. Polly Schoettle Miller, writing to Kent Mountford, August 10, 2013.

63. "John McShain: Developer Who Built Pentagon," *Los Angeles Times*. September 20, 1989. (http://articles.latimes.com/1989-09-20/news/mn-3_1_john-mcshain-built)

64. Edwin Schoettle, written reminiscences

65. Edwin Schoettle, written reminiscences.

66. Polly Schoettle Miller, writing to Kent Mountford, August 19, 2012.

67. Suzy Mitchell Davis, personal communication to Kent Mountford, 2012. She also recalls that the sheds were not so completely inaccessible, but that the "little girls, were discouraged from playing around them."

68. Karl Schoettle, recounted to family members and others, 2012.

69. http://history1900s.about.com/od/1920s/a/kingtut.htm

70. Suzy Mitchell Davis, interview notes edited from Kent Mountford, 2010.

71. Suzy Mitchell Davis, joint recollections blended here from Suzy's correspondence to Sally Randolph and Kent Mountford, June 2010.

72. Ocean County Historical Society. *Along the Toms River* (Arcadia, 1996).

73. Bay freezes: Kent Mountford Logbook R/V *Beröe*, Entry 109, January 17, 1970. (*Beröe cucumis* is a *Ctenophore*, a group of jellyfish-like organisms found each autumn in Barnegat Bay and was the name of my research vessel while at Rutgers University.) The ice on the east side of Barnegat Bay off the A-7 "Fly Road" on Island Beach State Park was 10 inches thick, while the author was doing scientific research there.

74. Suzy Mitchell Davis, email to Kent Mountford, June 2, 2010.

75. Edwin Schoettle, handwritten letter to Judson Smith, July 11, 1947.

76. Ibid.

77. Boris Lauer-Leonardi, editor, *The Rudder*, July 19, 1947, to Judson Smith.

78. Schoettle letter to Judson Smith, *op. cit.*

79. Suzy Mitchell Davis, interview notes edited from Kent Mountford, 2010 and 2012.

80. Edwin Schoettle, written reminiscences.

81. *Catboat Association Bulletin*, "Scat, Scat II, and Silent Maid."

FIGURE 5-1. Blake Chandlee, at helm, leaves for an autumn boat ride with 14 (maybe 15!) aboard *Silent Maid*.
The guy on deck abaft the cockpit has just taken a dip in Barnegat Bay. The Metedeconk River is in the background.
("Watercolored" version of original photo, which is inset at the top right.)

Partial identifications (left to right from identifiable faces): Fred Grauer, wife Frances, Shirley Grange, Jack Grange, (unknown woman), Craigie Cullen, Blake Chandlee at helm, unknown swimmer, and Edward E. Cullen. (Identifications by Alan and Jody Fitts, 2013.)
Four persons are obscured enough to prevent identification.

Undated Chandlee family photo via Jody Fitts

5

Blake Chandlee's Time

*I*n 1948, Judson Smith (a recurring player in *Silent Maid*'s history) was still exploring the potential of buying *Silent Maid*. Unaware that Edwin Schoettle had died, he
wrote him again, and this letter was passed on to Edwin's son, Karl, then Vice President
and General Manager of the Edwin J. Schoettle Company.

Karl, after some delay, wrote back to Jud on March 23, 1948, informing him of
Edwin's death and noting what a disappointment his loss had been to the family on
Christmas Eve of 1947. He informed Jud that Schoettle's estate had put *Silent Maid* up
for sale and was asking $5000 for her.

For Jud Smith, $5000 was a large amount of cash in a still recovering post-World
War II America. He felt he could scrape together $2000 and wrote back to Karl almost
immediately tendering that amount. He waited a little over a month before Karl again
responded on April 30. He apologized for keeping Smith on tenterhooks, apparently
because he was considering another offer for $3500. Karl was determined to turn down
both offers, although he admitted ". . . there is not much activity in the boat-selling
business at the present time."

Chastened, Jud Smith made no counter offer, but he did not lose interest in the
Silent Maid. He was apparently saving his nickels, because in December 1951, he again
wrote to Karl Schoettle inquiring for what price the *Maid* might now be had.

Silent Maid, Karl told him, had been sold and was in the hands of Blakeley Chandlee,
scion of Schoettle family acquaintances from Philadelphia and Bay Head. The Schoettle
era of this distinguished yacht had ended and the Chandlee's time had begun.

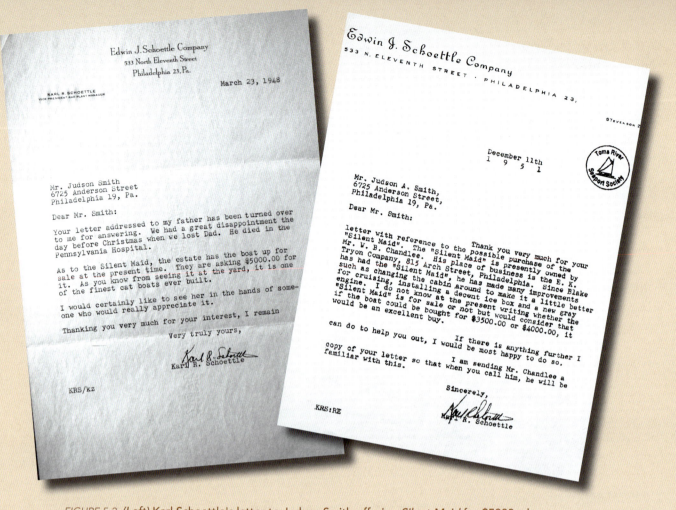

FIGURE 5-2. *(Left)* Karl Schoettle's letter to Judson Smith offering *Silent Maid* for $5000, about $1400 more than she had cost to build 24 years earlier. *(Right)* Schoettle's final letter to Judson Smith, informing him *Silent Maid* had been sold out of the Schoettle family.

Toms River Seaport Society archive

CHANDLEE FAMILY HISTORY

Blakeley (Blake) Chandlee was the descendent of a family of clockmakers, designers of magnetic compasses, and—much later—entrepreneurs in the sporting goods business. The Chandlees' long family history was well documented by E.E. Chandlee, Blake's father, in the 1943 book *Six Quaker Clockmakers*. This labor of love helped greatly in crafting parts of the story to follow.

Benjamin Chandlee, Sr. (1685–ca. 1745) was the first to bring his clockmaking skills to America, arriving at the Port of Philadelphia in 1702. Known in family history as "the Emigrant," he came from Ireland at age 17 and was to become the first in the series of family clockmakers. Abel Cottey (1655–1711) probably built the first clock actually constructed in America, and he apprenticed Benjamin Chandlee, who in his majority came to specialize in tall-case clocks (what we call grandfather's clocks today). These clocks, like the Quakers who built them, were good, solid mechanical appliances, and a number of Chandlee originals survive today. Benjamin must have been more than satisfactory to Master Craftsman Cottey, because young Ben married his daughter.[1]

Tall case clocks were built thus so the weights inside, which powered the escapement (the "tick-tock" we associate with the seconds of our lives!), could descend slowly for seven or eight days under power of gravity without being re-wound to the top again. This slow application of force kept the pendulum swinging and it was the pendulum, its length exactly correct, which enabled the accurate keeping of time.

These clocks, while in use, were not portable –and could not be kept running on a ship, for example- but once in a stable place they ran accurately decade after decade with little maintenance. Virtually the only wear was in the bearings carrying steel axles upon which the brass gears turned, and on the teeth of the gears themselves. I know this because my wife and I own a Montross tall case clock of 1813 from Scotland, which ticked somewhere on this planet while the War of 1812-1815 raged around the site of our home in Maryland.[2]

Benjamin took up land and settled at Nottingham, then part of Baltimore County in Maryland. It was here that Goldsmith Chandlee, Benjamin's oldest son, was born in August 1751. Goldsmith, on attaining his majority, moved south starting a brass foundry in Winchester, Virginia. He not only made clocks, but also made surveying instruments, notably accurate magnetic compasses, which are considered remarkable works of art today. Over a dozen are known to have been preserved to the present day. One compass was made for Lawrence Washington, George Washington's nephew.[3] Another compass, reputed to have been used by the President himself in surveying his own lands, was sold as part of a group of items and papers in 2012 for $167,000.[4]

Generations later, Blakeley's father, Edward Earle Chandlee (known informally as Ned), attended Princeton for a year with the Class of 1908, but left university to enter business. He put his passion for the outdoors to use by building a career that included wholesale sporting equipment. He eventually was made President of Edward K. Tryon Company, an old Philadelphia firm, originally located on Market Street in 1906, but later headquartered at 817 Arch Street.

At the time, this firm was America's largest wholesaler and dealt in hardware, sporting goods, and toys. Sporting equipment was one of the company's hottest lines. One measure of this, in firearms-fixated America, was a single order that Tryon placed on the books of Parker Brothers (gun manufacturers), which ran 12 sheets of legal sized paper![5] The Parkers made exquisite pieces, and in 2013 a now-antique Parker Brothers 16-gauge Damascus shotgun with "honest wear" was being offered for $3695.[6] A light, 20-gauge at the same time was being offered at over $8900 and an Edward K. Tryon catalog, their hundredth anniversary catalog, was selling for $300 in 2011.[7]

Tryon marketed at least a dozen trademarked sports equipment brands, five of which were fishing reels, lures, hooks, lines and rods. Ned Chandlee thus had access to the widest selection of the best products. In his position as executive with "all the rights and privileges appertaining thereto," he used access to all these resources with great alacrity.

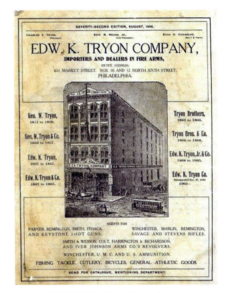

FIGURE 5-3. Ned Chandlee's employer, the Edward K. Tryon Company, was an old Philadelphia firm, which imported, marketed, and wholesaled a wide range of recreational merchandise from bullets to bicycles.

www.picturetrail.com/sfx/album/20080158

FIGURE 5-4. (Left) Goldsmith Chandlee, instrument and clockmaker in the 18th century, made a compass similar to this owned by George Washington's nephew Lawrence. This compass is a Chandlee family artifact.

Image: Jody Chandlee Fitts

(Right) The face of an exquisite 18th century curly-maple tall-case clock made by Goldsmith Chandlee during his Winchester, Virginia, period.

Chandlee family photograph

FIGURE 5-5. **Young E.E. Chandlee Jr.,** Ned's youngest son, on a Jersey Shore beach about 1926 with his cousin "Weedie" Hoy and Miss Hunter, their Scottish nurse. They are sitting on the rail of a pound-net fishing boat. These big skiffs, part of local commercial fishing tradition, were launched daily through the surf and tended pound nets rigged to long tree-trunk stakes driven into the sea floor off the barrier beach. Many fish species migrating along the coast became trapped by the pound net's unique design and these catches were landed in the pound boats directly through the surf. Many local families living nearby bought supper wrapped in a piece of newspaper, directly from the fish boxes of these boats.

Jody and Alan Fitts photograph.

THE CHANDLEES ON BARNEGAT BAY

Ned's grandson Bill Chandlee said the family came to the coast and were among the earliest "out of town" settlers in Mantoloking on upper Barnegat Bay. They built their first cottage on Newman Place in 1909 "when there was virtually nothing on the beaches.[8]" The Chandlees were among many Philadelphian families who eventually came to summer here.

While not sailors themselves, the Chandlee family paid attention to the eager competition among catboat sailors on the bay. Special attention went to the Bay Head catboat *Romp*, owned by Henry Buxton, which won the coveted Sewell Cup at Seaside Heights at least 3 times—1914, 1915, and 1916, which victory resulted in a mention in *The Rudder* magazine. The Chandlee children thus grew up knowing that there was a certain cachet attached to yacht racing.

That first Mantoloking generation of Chandlees were also avid waterfowl hunters, launching their own small boats out through the surf to shoot sea ducks, a group of several species that are winter visitors along the coast. One of these species, the oldsquaw, dives to the bottom, feeding on small clams and crustaceans, and their chortling calls made some distance offshore can be heard from the beach especially later in winter. While "tough and fishy,"[9] and thus not a coveted diet item, they have nonetheless been heavily hunted just for sport.

Ned followed the water enthusiastically, but not as a sailor. He was a dedicated fisherman and raised his son W. Blakeley (Blake) Chandlee, born in 1909, to be an active participant in this endeavor. Blake honored this valuable relationship with his father.[10]

Surf fisherman would occasionally snag some large—unusually big—fish; a giant stingray or the odd shark, but most were unaware of large, truly pelagic (ocean wandering) species that migrated along our coasts offshore.

Jersey Shore's offshore tuna fishing was reputed to have started at Sea Isle City, New Jersey, shortly after 1911. Lodovico and Rosina Monichetti, who were experienced with fishing large tuna at the isle of Ischia off Naples in Italy, were immigrants at Ellis Island in that year. Buying a parcel of marginal land for $500, they employed their lessons from the Mediterranean on the Atlantic coastal ocean.[11]

One of the earliest inklings that these big fish were out there was when a large tuna became entangled in a pound fisherman's rig and was brought ashore as a curiosity, but a destructive one, considering the damage to the man's nets.[12] By 1933, catches of remarkably large fish were reported with a 'season' beginning in August. One tuna taken off Ambrose LightShip by Francis Low's boat weighed 705 lb. One can't help but mention the sharks that were caught as well, notably a great white (*Charcarodon leucas*) caught by Captain Low and brought in to Hoffman's (Brielle) Anchorage around 1939.[13]

This was a remarkable time when populations, including the great billfish, swordfish, white and blue marlin, which had never been fished in these waters, were suddenly subject to predation by man.

The industry working out of Brielle in the earlier years was stymied by the opening of the Point Pleasant-Manasquan Canal in the late 1920s. The result of this flow diversion was that Manasquan River Inlet closed repeatedly, and would have closed permanently but for massive efforts to open and stabilize the channel.

FIGURE 5-6. **Oldsquaw** (*Clangula hyemalis*) decoys by contemporary Bay Head carver Artie Birdsall. *Inset:* A summer Arctic breeder, this oldsquaw, wounded by hunters, makes a rare visit ashore in February 2009.

Kent Mountford photograph

This gave reliable access to the ocean from little Brielle and prior to WWII, as many as 225–250 boats sailed out of this village and the Point Pleasant side of the River. Most were clustered in 6 or 7 'marinas' (a new word in the Jersey Coast lexicon) but there were at least 14 sites where boats tied up.[14]

This big-game fishery was literally enabled by development of the gasoline engine (first with re-purposed automobile motors) and a class of charter fishing boats capable of travelling safely far offshore, with enough fuel remaining to chase their quarry and still get home again. When Ned Chandlee pursued this new sport, his grandson reports that they might stay out chasing fish for a week.

Once offshore in the days before ship to shore radios, charter boats would sometimes release a carrier pigeon to send news ashore of a particularly spectacular catch. One could at one time, rent two pigeons in a small cage with note capsules for their legs for a dollar, on the proviso that, if not used, the pigeons be released near shore so they would be used to flying over the water to reach home.[15] A note sent by pigeon just might result in a news article or a photographer being at the dock when these giants were hoisted up, weighed and measured. In August 1937, for example, a pigeon from offshore alighted on its perch at the Manasquan River Marlin and Tuna Camp to report Mrs. Eugenie Marron's 309 lb fish. Some days well over a dozen big tuna, some reaching 400 pounds, would be hauled up at a single marina, stunning records for rod and reel, at the time; ultimately devastating for the populations of these large, slow-growing pelagic species.

FIGURE 5-7. **A college-aged Blakeley and his father Edward E. Chandlee, at the family summer residence on Newman Place in Mantoloking. Blake and his father enjoyed fishing together, including surf fishing from the ocean beach and going to sea on expeditions.**

Jody and Alan Fitts photograph

FIGURE 5-8.

(Top) **At left a giant tuna brought into Brielle, NJ, at Feuerbach's. In joking contrast Joan Duer Chandlee, Ned Junior's wife, and Bill Blakeley displayed their tiny trophy in 1944.**

Left image: Eloise Wright photograph
Right image: Chandlee family photograph

(Bottom) **Feuerbach and Hansen, Inc., shown in one of this Brielle, NJ, sport fishing center's ownership configurations, was located upstream of the old PRR railroad drawbridge and close to where the current Route 35 Manasquan Bridge crosses the River.**

Postcard owned by Robert Jahn, with permission

FIGURE 5-9. *(Top)* An unidentified friend and E.E. Chandlee, Sr., look on from their fighting chairs as son Blakeley holds their reliable messenger pigeon Homer for a photo opportunity.

(Bottom) Standing by their charter boat's mast atop the cabin and between raised outriggers E.E. Chandlee releases his pigeon, while Blake steadies himself against the rolling boat. Homer flew straight back to Mantoloking with news of the day's events.

Bill Chandlee photographs

Ned Chandlee kept a pigeon house atop the Mantoloking house and would take a few caged birds with him on these expeditions, releasing one each morning to send the day's doings back to shore. Pigeons were the VHF radios and cell phones of the day. They might not have needed that always-missing battery charger, but they did need to be fed regularly.

When Blake Chandlee was a kid he found, under a local family's porch in Bay Head, a neglected and unwanted Dave Beaton Duckboat. It was hull number 7 in a racing class now certainly in the hundreds. Learning to sail in his own boat burgeoned into a lifelong passion for sailing—different from his dad's passion and unique among his siblings.

In adulthood, Blakeley Chandlee became a strapping, good-looking man, whom his niece Jody (E.E. Junior's daughter) compared to Hollywood actor Robert Mitchum.[16] Blakeley married Frances Jopson, who was five years' his junior, and they ultimately had three sons—another E.E. (Ned), William, and Evan Goldsmith Chandlee. Evan and a daughter, Susie, sadly, both died in young adulthood.[17]

Blake and his siblings were eventually given joint ownership of the old family home on Newman Place. Such arrangements are hard to manage (as the Schoettle brothers found at Anchorage on Island Heights) and Blake bought out his siblings' interests taking the home as his own. The senior Chandlees built themselves a new house across the street, thus closer to the ocean.[18]

Blake, who had been a field manufacturer's representative for six or seven years, was well grounded in wholesaling and succeeded his father as President of Tryon Company running it for its owners and founders. As a chief executive, he too had some freedom to pursue his personal interests. He still struggled with heart problems, ones which modern care could probably have managed or corrected. Son William Chandlee says that his father had a dozen cardiac episodes —"heart attacks" they said—before he was thirty. As was often the case in those years, Blakeley continued to smoke and consumed his share of alcohol the rest of his life.[19] These habits must have exacerbated his health problems, but he nonetheless got away with it for some years and continued as an active sportsman and a competitive manager in the business world. The challenge for him was irresistible.

Like Edwin Schoettle, when World War II broke out, Blakeley was deeply concerned. The terrible and often preventable loss of servicemen in war-plane crashes, ship-sinkings, and being cast away in wild places troubled him greatly. At his urging, Tryon developed and packaged a four-inch-square, pocket- sized survival kit containing fish hooks, line, tape, some nutrition, a magnifying glass for fire starting and a small mirror that had a sighting hole and cross-hairs for signaling rescuers. Millions of kits were made along these lines and adapted for land, air, and sea use, then distributed to servicemen, pilots and seafarers. Along the Jersey Shore, every kid who knew Blake Chandlee had one of these little kits.[20]

As a kid, I never met Blake Chandlee, though we summered hardly seven miles from each other, but I knew about these kits. I never had access to one of the originals, but I made my own—in my case with strike-anywhere matches dipped in melted candle wax—and without fail I carried it to school every day, lest I be somehow stranded or cast adrift. Over six decades later, I *still* carry a source of ignition, a tiny flashlight, and a belt-holstered multi-tool (except where forbidden on airlines . . . the very time I would be most likely to need it). Of course, with my own life centered around and on the water there is now my submersible, military-spec, cell-phone.

THE CHANDLEES AND *SILENT MAID*

The Chandlee family knew the Schoettles in Philadelphia, traveling in circles that placed both in the Social Register. Blake was interested in sailing from his childhood boat discovery and youthful time at the Bay Head Yacht Club. When Edwin Schoettle passed away in December 1947, 39-year-old Blakeley certainly heard about *Silent Maid's* availability through the grapevine. Edwin's estate tried to market the *Maid* and her racing record at an asking price of $5000, but as Karl Schoettle wrote at the time, the market for selling boats was not particularly good. One can infer that the offer for $3500 Karl spoke of in an April 30, 1948, correspondence with Judson Smith (mentioned earlier in this chapter) might have been Blakeley Chandlee's bid, and it certainly exceeded the competing offer of $2000 from Jud. Perhaps the Schoettles simply thought Blakeley would make a good and caring owner of *Silent Maid* and they let her go at the offered price.

Silent Maid had been laid up at Stoke's Boatyard in Island Heights, but stored under cover with all her running gear in good order. It was relatively straightforward for Blake to have her launched and–once her very dry planks had swollen and the leaks stopped—get her up the Bay to his neighborhood.

There's a very early picture of *Silent Maid* after Blake's purchase, under tow and before her mast was stepped. The spars, in fact, are strapped aboard on the coach roof and she is leaving a dock. I think this is her departure from Island Heights, based on the still relatively sparse development on Toms River's south shore in the distance. Her topsides are still bright finished with that demanding varnish on hull and transom, which has the gold-leaf letters of her name in place. Her new port of hail, Bay Head, has not yet appeared. She was distinctly under tow since, after all, she was still without an engine, as Edwin Schoettle had sailed her for two full decades.

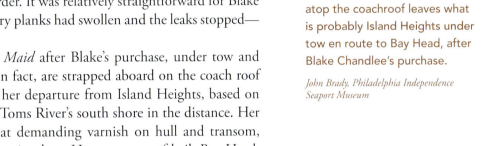

FIGURE 5-10. *Silent Maid* still with bright-finished topsides and transom, and with her spars tied atop the coachroof leaves what is probably Island Heights under tow en route to Bay Head, after Blake Chandlee's purchase.

John Brady, Philadelphia Independence Seaport Museum

FIGURE 5-11. *Silent Maid* in her slip at the Bay Head Yacht Club about 1949, now with white topsides. She has a sailcover, since Schoettle's dock boy was no longer there to hoist and dry the sail each morning. That same white canvas duck sailcover, in much tattered condition was still aboard when my family bought the *Silent Maid* five years later. *(Right)* Hailing port has been painted on the transom.

Chandlee family photograph, John Brady Philadelphia Independence Seaport Museum

The Chandlees were members of the Bay Head Yacht Club, and this was where the *Silent Maid* was kept during their ownership. Blake's son Bill Chandlee says it instantly ". . . third slip on Dock E, harbor side" after sixty years. And, in an email to Peter Kellogg, in 2008, he added "next to Mrs. Booth's boat."[21] This was a great environment at the time for young kids on boats. The big cabin on the *Silent Maid* was babysitter for Bill when he was little: "a fishing rod, box of bait and a net!" It was the same for a number of kids on the dock, who spent time on their parents' boats, all watching out for any problems another kid might have.[22] These kids, without 'helicopter parenting,' were thus taught independence and responsibility within the framework (confines if you will) of the Bay Head Yacht Club, which gave them a proper start in life.

SILENT MAID HAS SOME CHANGES MADE

It seems that within a year, Blake decided that maintaining the *Maid*'s varnished hull was simply too much work and expense. Probably at Morton Johnson's Boatyard, she was wooded (that is, all the varnish was removed with gasoline torches and scrapers). We Mountfords discovered signs of this method, as slight scorches on the wooden planking, when we bought the boat in 1953. She was painted white, and this, to my eye actually made her appear a bigger boat. *Silent Maid*'s mahogany transom was also painted white and her hailing port, Bay Head, was added beneath the simple black lettered name.

Some sources said that Blake and Frances reduced the size of *Silent Maid*'s sail, not being able to imagine how Edwin and Sara had been able to handle such an immense rig by themselves, but comparing the fully stretched sails, boom, gaff and hoist on photos from 1925 and 1953 (when my family bought her) I can detect no difference. I can, however, understand how the Chandlees would be in awe of this immense rig.

In 1949, the *Maid* did not yet have an auxiliary engine, but she was now kept in Bay Head, not at Island Heights where the Schoettle's pier was a convenient place from which to set sail in anything but a strong westerly wind.

Southerly quadrant winds dominate during much of Barnegat's sailing season, and that meant everywhere except the Metedeconk River was to windward from the Bay Head Yacht Club. This location, as the *Silent Maid*'s homeport, was in a small harbor and to get south, she would have to beat through very close quarters along the barrier island shores of Bay Head and Mantoloking or around Herring Island at the mouth of the Metedeconk only to arrive at the Mantoloking Drawbridge.

Not far past this bridge was Swan Point, another narrow spot, before the Bay finally widened. It was thus quite an exercise, and took a fair amount of time to get far enough south in Barnegat Bay to do any serious sailing. This also meant that any time the boat was moved with sail lowered or when rigged down, a tow had to be arranged from a powerboat.

It was clear why this led to installation of *Silent Maid*'s auxiliary engine, but even with three very competent boatyards around Bay Head, this project proved not as simple as one might suppose.

When *Silent Maid* was built at Morton Johnson's, she had some inherent structural difficulties that affected trying to install an engine. First, a large scarph (lengthy joint with overlap for strength) was in her keel just abaft the centerboard trunk, and second, her deadwood was too narrow (athwartships) to support the long drilling path necessary for a propeller shaft. This path required that a shallow angle would be necessary to reach an aperture in deadwood or rudder for the propeller. This location would have given good water flow around the rudder, and thus acceptable steerage, but there was simply not the available heavy wood to permit its drilling. There was also the lead ballast let into the keel, which further constrained any boring through the deadwood, where the shaft would have to pass.

As a result, the engine was installed offset from the centerline on the port side, with the propeller shaft-way drilled through a small wooden skeg installed for the purpose. The stuffing box was inside the hull where the spiral flax packing (which prevented the spinning shaft from leaking water into the hull) could be accessed for adjustment. The shaft was not aligned with her centerline, but along with the engine, it was set at a slight angle, with the hope of counteracting the tendency for the boat to continually try turning towards one side. This was not entirely successful.

Forever after, this configuration meant that *Silent Maid* steered more easily to starboard than to port and backed very poorly in any direction when in reverse. It was also almost impossible to go astern turning to starboard, at least until enough speed was attained to let her huge rudder bite the water and make a difference.

In addition, *Silent Maid* would now have a large, flat-topped engine box in the cockpit, not the wide, unbroken dance floor with which she'd originally been launched. This engine box cover was a lovely piece of wood, incidentally, and would be put to good use by guests as a seat and cocktail table.

It seems that the original engine installed was a four-cylinder Graymarine Sea Scout, which developed 25 horsepower at 2000 rpm, adequate only for a plodding 3–4 knots

FIGURE 5-12. An old Graymarine Sea Scout. This motor was donated for the installation shown about 2000 and has run another 13 years at this writing. *Insets:* The Gray instrument panel and the Zenith updraft carburetor with flame arrestor at left in this picture.

Kent Mountford photographs, Calvert Marine Museum, Solomons, MD

FIGURE 5-13. Blake Chandlee *(left)* aboard *Silent Maid* has here cajoled his father, Edward E. (Ned) Chandlee, *(right)* to take the helm. Ned's unenthusiastic expression says "I'd rather be deep-sea fishing, thank you!" Judging by a high bank along the shoreline astern, I think this photo was taken in what was then called Mosquito Cove, a sail perhaps nine nautical miles south of Bay Head, and the wind is about northwest.

Chandlee family photograph, Philadelphia Independence Seaport Museum

while powering under the best of conditions. This engine was, nonetheless, one of Gray-marine's most durable workhorses, manufactured with few changes for over a dozen years, bracketing the period of World War II.

The Gray Sea Scouts were not wholly without problems. They had a rotary distributor and cap subject to condensation problems. The Zenith carburetor had a tendency to drip raw gasoline out of the flame arrestor when over-choked while trying to start the motor.[23] There *was* a bilge blower that was religiously used. This made for some dodgy beginnings in unpleasant or intemperate weather.

However, this little engine permitted the *Silent Maid* to negotiate the narrows between the barrier beach and Herring Island down through the Mantoloking Bridge and past Swan Point, where decent long tacks could be made sailing to windward down Barnegat Bay. She was, after all, designed to be a sailing vessel, though a little less so while continually dragging those propeller blades through the water.

Besides installing the engine, Blake Chandlee made some other changes aboard *Silent Maid* including the move of her galley from up forward on the starboard side to a position just inside the main companionway hatch. This made a lot of sense, and the layout had space for the porcelain sink, an elegant little bronze hand-pump, and a small counter for handing out food items and drinks to the cockpit. This was where most people ate while aboard anyway.

Mahogany racks for a set of dishes and traditional white ceramic coffee mugs were fastened to the cabin side next to an opening bronze portlight. A reasonable ice-box with cork insulation (all that was available at the time) was installed below the counter. This box, front-opening, had some significant disadvantages. If you swung out the door while on a starboard tack under sail, any significant angle of heel exposed you to the risk of everything inside sliding off the smooth wire shelves and cascading onto the cabin sole. Clearly, this was a hazard for jars, glasses and bottles, which might be lurking behind and leaning against, the door. The lever-type latch was pretty traditional for iceboxes at the time, bright nickel-plated brass, but requiring care to be sure the handle was properly engaged with the latch and brought down securely, or it might open spontaneously during a gust.

'Ice-box' meant exactly that, of course, and for food to be safely chilled, you put in a 25-pound block of ice. Having made the investment of a quarter for this resource, you found that about 10% of it had melted by the time you got it from the supplier to the boat, and when installed, the ice took up about half the available storage volume. It melted quickly and continuously while you were aboard and the drip tray at the bottom of the unit had to be emptied frequently, first lest it overflow, and second so it would be empty enough that it would not spill when the boat heeled, putting all the melt water to leeward. You learned quickly enough to manage these things without making a chore of them.

FAMILY OUTINGS ON *SILENT MAID*

Blake's father condescended to sail with him sometimes, but as an offshore, saltwater fisherman, the senior Chandlee was happier on powerboats. Blake's son Bill, as a kid from age eight to eleven years old, still remembers family cruises aboard *Silent Maid*. They sailed down Bay in the mornings and usually waited until afternoons, when the southerlies came in, to head back north. They had favorite spots, Bill remembers, and Blake could be heard instructing the helmsman "to go inshore in line with that tree" or to point for a prominent sand dune, likely at those few sites along the Island Beach Peninsula where there was still enough water for the big catboat's 32-inch draft—board up, of course. They would nose her in until she touched, then people would slip over the

FIGURE 5-14. The west-facing Barnegat Bay shoreline of Island Beach, with its narrow sand beaches backed by thickets of vegetation and maritime forests of cedars and hardwood have drawn boaters and hunters for centuries: not least the *Silent Maid* and her several skippers over eight decades.

Kent Mountford photograph, 2008

FIGURE 5-15. **From right, Blake Chandlee, owner, his brother Edward E. Chandlee Jr., and Blake's son Bill at age 8, with the Bay Head Yacht Club tee shirt, probably on the Metedeconk River.**

Chandlee family photograph, Philadelphia Independence Seaport Museum

FIGURE 5-16. **"Trophy tuna flag."**

Collection of Roy Pedersen, with permission, Kent Mountford photograph

sides and wade the short distance ashore. The drill required was then to make sure the *Maid* was pushed back out far enough so the Bay's modest, but falling tides, wouldn't strand her. Cooking for their outings was done on a little fire set on the small sandy beaches, which are still found along the peninsula's west-facing shoreline.

Blake Chandlee certainly enjoyed *Silent Maid,* but having been at sea, out of sight of land, with his father on their fishing expeditions, I think he was still enamored with the lure of real blue water and the mystery of those endless ocean swells. Tuna boats, like those Ned Chandlee sailed on proudly displayed small "trophy tuna flags" when re-entering Manasquan Inlet. If they had no catch, that is, they were "skunked," many flew a small red flag bearing the subject animal. One of those was aboard the *Maid* when we bought her!

Silent Maid was a stepping-stone for Blake; not his ultimate choice for a sailing yacht. There were wider horizons than Barnegat Bay. These yearnings were shared among friends and family and, as the word spread, they set the scene for the future sale of *Silent Maid.*

I think Blake also knew that there was a clock ticking inside his own body. His son Bill quips (with incomplete accuracy!) "Chandlee men don't live past 76." [24] The reality was that his father had a dozen cardiac events before he was 30. His work with Tryon was also a source of continuing stress, culminating while he and his family were on vacation in Europe. When they returned, Blake found that the owners had sold their interests to a takeover company, Banner Industries, which at the same time acquired another old Tryon competitor, the Supplee-Biddle Company.[25] Banner merged the two companies, milked them for their assets and liquidated the remainders.[26] Since his family was financially comfortable, Blake accommodated to this, was perhaps relieved to escape wider industrial unpleasantness, and simply went on with his life—making use of what years fate permitted him.

FIGURE 5-17. *Silent Maid* sports a complement of fifteen visitors in this image. This is not a sailing trip, because the sailcovers are still on. A few guests are sitting, or rest their feet, atop the *Maid's* mahogany engine box, so the date is probably about 1950.

Chandlee family photograph, Philadelphia Independence Seaport Museum.

FIGURE 5-18. Susie Chandlee, Blake's daughter, aged 14, at the helm of *Silent Maid* in 1952, shortly before her dad sold the boat to James Kellogg.

Bill Chandlee photograph

Blake and Frannie Chandlee were good friends with James and Betty Kellogg at the BHYC. During their time at the shore, in fact, the two women were considered the best of friends.[27] Jim Kellogg was always interested in saving boats that were part of Barnegat Bay's yachting history. With his sons, Kellogg had formed a syndicate, Kellogg and Sons, which they used in acquiring and rescuing boats they deemed of value.

With this social network in place, when it seemed that *Silent Maid* would be sold, the word was quick to spread and Jimmy Kellogg was there with his syndicate to allay any concern about the fate of this famous old yacht and to start the next chapter in her history. We're unsure what the price was but perhaps Blake gave him a good deal, somewhere in that quoted range of $3500 to $4000.

Following the sale of *Silent Maid*, Blake Chandlee bought a sloop with six-foot draft, which gave her very limited navigating room in shallow Barnegat Bay. She was a New Bedford 35 and he named her *Suban*, an acronym for his children's names—Susie, Billy, and Ann Heath Chandlee. He was a competitive guy and during his *Suban* years Blake raced on his own boat and aboard other friends' yachts, similar in size to *Suban*, sailing to Bermuda and on the Southern (racing) Circuit.

Suban had her own adventures. Blake's daughter Susie (now deceased) and her brand new husband, Alan Fitts took this big keel sloop out sailing and ran her aground, quite easy to accomplish in the confines of upper Barnegat Bay. Embarrassed by their predicament, they saw Edwin's son Karl Schoettle coming in his own boat and he towed them off with good humor . . . then said to the couple "THIS is your wedding present!" and the event became an inter-family joke with none of those involved ever letting the others forget.[28]

Suban left Barnegat Bay and spent a good part of her 15-year stint with Blake in the Chesapeake Bay, on Maryland's Sassafras River from where her racing and cruising career was pursued. Blake Chandlee had owned the *Silent Maid* from 1948 to 1952,[29] and *Suban* was his final cruising sailboat. He passed away in 1985 at age 76 from that heart ailment, which had dogged him most of his adult life. He transmitted an interest in the water to his son, Bill, who, with wife Nancy and two sons, ran his classic Cuttyhunk bass boat in the waters off Cape May, New Jersey, until the kids were grown.

ENDNOTES — CHAPTER 5

1. Jody Chandlee Fitts, an email clarifying for me the relation of Abel Cottey and Benjamin Chandlee, 2013.

2. Kent Mountford, *Past as Prologue* column, "It took a long time to develop accurate portable timepieces," *Chesapeake Bay Journal*, October 2009, pp 12-13.

3. Brass Compass, Goldsmith Chandlee, www.surveyhistory.org/goldsmith_chandlee1.htm

4. Heritage Auctions, Dallas Texas. This compass was passed down through the family of Bushrod Washington; George having had no direct heirs.

5. Album: vintage Sports Dealers: www.picturetrail.com/sfs/album/view/20080158

6. Guns International, http://www.gunsinternational.com/Parker-Shotguns.cfm?cat_id=649

7. William Chandlee, interview with Kent Mountford, January 24, 2011.

8. Ibid.

9. Richard Pough, *Audubon Water Bird Guide* (Doubleday, 1951), p. 102.

10. Chandlee, 2011.

11. Richard Degener, *Cape May County Press*, 2013. www.pressofatlanticcity.com/news/press/cape_may/sea-isle-city-tries-to-protect-a-legacy-in-historic-fish-alley. The Monichetti's grandson celebrated 100 years in the business in 2011. Unfortunately the large game fish populations, now severely stressed despite relatively recent "catch-and-release" policies, have been declining since the 1970s, unable to sustain themselves against worldwide fishing pressure. Catch and release, furthermore does not assure the survival of a fish which has just been fought to exhaustion.

12. Union Landing Historical Society, *The History of Brielle: Union Landing Revisited* (Valente Publishing Company, 1989), p. 54.

13. Ibid., p. 67.

14. Ibid., p. 55.

15. Ibid, p. 56.

16. Jody Chandlee Fitts. Jody made this comparison with Mitchum (1917–1997) during an interview together with Alan Fitts at Mantoloking, January 2011.

17. Jody Chandlee Fitts, emails to Kent Mountford, October 2013. Evan died at age 30 and Susie at 32.

18. William Chandlee, emails to Kent Mountford, August and September, 2013.

19. Chandlee, 2011. Pencil notes of telephone interview with Kent Mountford.

20. Chandlee, 2013.

21. William Chandlee, email to Peter R. Kellogg about the *Silent Maid* reincarnation in Philadelphia, 2008.

22. Chandlee, 2011.

23. Graymarine Sea Scout. www.oldmarineengines.com/discus/message/34321/2867.html

24. Chandlee, 2011, claimed this during this interview, but his brother E.E. Chandlee, Jr., fortunately lived well beyond that target age.

25. William Chandlee, email to Kent Mountford, October 2013, explaining termination of Tyron and Supplee-Biddle.

26. Chandlee, 2011, and another interview with Kent Mountford on September 15, 2013.

27. Chandlee, 2013.

28. Fitts, 2011.

29. William Chandlee, the ownership years of *Silent Maid* were estimated at 1948-1952; his mother's memory was uncertain, as reported in his email to Peter R. Kellogg, on March 13, 2008.

FIGURE 6-1. *(Left)* Jimmy Kellogg, with wife Betty, sails *White Whale* on Barnegat Bay. *(Right)* Jimmy and Betty (and probably their son Rusty) leaving Edgartown on Martha's Vineyard, towing the Dyer dinghy *Whale Tail* with her new 3-HP Johnson outboard and all her code flags "dressing ship," the last flag is (per tradition) hanging below the bowsprit.

M.W. "Rusty" Kellogg photos, ca. 1957

6

Jimmy Kellogg Catches *Silent Maid*

James Crane (Jimmy) Kellogg III was born in New York City in May of 1915 to James Crane Kellogg, Jr., and Ettie Davidson Cissel. The family lived in Elizabeth, part of Union County, New Jersey. Their home was substantial, valued in the 1920 Census at $35,000, and they had two servants in residence, both Irish immigrant women. The Census also listed the senior Kellogg as having no occupation;[1] apparently there was no box to check on the form to report that the family ran a "detergent bluing company,"[2] which was experiencing hard times at the advent of the Great Depression. Jimmy was the first Kellogg to attend the respected Pingry School in Elizabeth, and he finished his secondary education at the Berkshire School in Massachusetts in 1933. He went on to attend Williams College, but left without completing his degree. Jimmy was bright, and he secured a job (drawing on some family connections) as an odd-lot broker with the firm Carlisle-Mellick & Co. Financier Al Rubin later described the young man this way, "Jimmy Kellogg was one of the finest professional short players I've seen in my life."[3]

In 1936, Jimmy was able to put together $125,000, and at the age of 21 became the youngest man ever to buy a seat on the New York Stock Exchange.[4] The next year, he entered his life-long marriage to Elizabeth "Betty" Rankin Irwin, granddaughter of John C. Rankin, a man of long association with Pingry School.

Jimmy's and Betty's first son James Crane Kellogg IV was born in July 1939, and a second son, Peter Rittenhouse, was born in 1942. (Peter would be the one to follow his father's lead in the financial world.) A third son, Richard Irwin, was born in 1944. Finally, Morris Woodruff (who would be called "Rusty"[5]) was born in 1947. These boys would each come into their own at the family's then-summer home at 666 East Avenue, Bay Head.

FIGURE 6-2. **The four Kellogg sons—Jim, Peter, Dick, and Rusty about 1949 on the front steps of the family summer place at 666 East Avenue, Bay Head.**

M.W. "Rusty" Kellogg photograph

Their dad Jimmy was a smart trader and investor; he went where the action was and used " . . . his natural geniality to his advantage in doing business."[6] In 1941, Jimmy joined the firm Spear-Leeds, a specialty brokerage house, when the company was just in its tenth year and looking for fresh talent.

Specialty brokerages were integral to the stock trading system since the New York Exchange was founded in 1792. These firms manage the sale of stocks on the exchange floor[7]—the busy scene we see in occasional TV clips when things are most hectic. They earn commissions when things go up and when things go down! In 10 years, Harold Spear and Larry Leeds made Jimmy Kellogg a 'named partner.' Six years later Jimmy, by then known as a "Golden Boy"[8] on Wall Street, became Managing Partner. Jimmy Kellogg, some sources said, "…made a million and lost it more than in once," [9] but he surely prospered in this business. The company was ultimately known as Spear, Leeds & Kellogg, LP.

Jimmy was congenial and known for always being ready to help out other exchange members. Being part of this old boy network meant that when some members retired from the exchange, Jimmy was often there to pick up their portfolios. This meant both growth and diversification for his company.

Jimmy became a Commissioner of the Port Authority of New York and New Jersey in 1955 and, using his extensive administrative talent, served as an unpaid Chief Executive while the Authority was in its formative stages.[10] As such, he played a substantial role in the construction of the World Trade Center,[11] which, long after Jimmy had passed away, would become a regrettable victim—along with thousands of blameless people—during the 9/11 terrorist attacks.

Downtown Manhattan has always been a hub of commercial activity, and when the World Trade Center was conceived, it was clear that a lot of the traditional businesses that lined the areas narrow streets, would be displaced or in any event would have to change. There was a "radio row" where, by 1960, early transistor radios were being sold at discount: "TWELVE transistor AM radios, public service band, in a free leather case with ear-phone for private listening, shoulder strap and free batteries, only $22."

I bought one of these for myself while in New York City on my first job interview, and using it on our boats in Barnegat Bay, I first really understood classical music —Claude Debussy's *la Mer*—while standing on the bow one night, with moonlight cascading across wind ruffled water.

There was also Maiden Lane, where gold, silver and gems were traded, and Chambers Street where many ship chandleries marketed marine goods to the mariner's trade, and —at first incidentally—to the burgeoning post-Korean War pleasure boating industry. All these cultural icons had to shift around due to the World Trade Center.

While Jimmy Kellogg's career was eminently successful, he also had another side— his love of Barnegat Bay and boats. The Kelloggs were residents in Bay Head during the years when many of the classic old yachts—including *Silent Maid* were still around and showing up in races and at yacht club functions. The Kelloggs had acquired a cedar-shingled frame house at 666 East Avenue in Bay Head and at one point—the Bay Head of an earlier era!—they kept chickens in the small yard adjacent. The family became integrated into the community, which developed around people of academic and business note. Joe Biden, at this writing Vice President of the United States, was counted as a resident many years ago.

The Kellogg home on East Avenue was party to an interesting period in 1949–50 when a man named L. Ron Hubbard rented it from the family in the off-season and

FIGURE 6-3. **The Kellogg's much-modified "Boat House" in 2011.**

used the solitude of a shore house to write and publish his book *Dianetics: The Modern Science of Mental Health.* Then during the summer months, Hubbard rented the Kellogg's home in Elizabeth, New Jersey. While there, he set up the Hubbard Dianetics Research Foundation. [12] Dianetics evolved into the philosophical system of Scientology, and then morphed into a religion. In 2004, the now-Church of Scientology claimed to have eight million adherents worldwide, though an independent survey indicated that "by 2009, 25,000 Americans identified [themselves] as Scientologists."[13]

Lafayette Ronald Hubbard (1911–1986)

L. Ron Hubbard was the son of a U.S. Naval officer who had to relocate his family many times. Young Hubbard, recognizing that he was having trouble adjusting in life, travelled widely exploring several Eastern philosophies, which he found lacking. He briefly attended George Washington University in Washington, D.C. (1931–32). His adventures out in the real world, real or amplified, included chartering a four-masted schooner to explore the Caribbean and an ill-fated Alaskan expedition aboard his own ketch *Mistress*. In the 1930s, he wrote prolifically and later was successful " . . . at a penny a word"[14], as a writer of science fiction and many other genres in pulp fiction literature. He also wrote the scripts for several fairly wel-known movies.

He claimed an epiphany during anesthesia (with nitrous oxide) for a dental procedure, and six days later wrote the detailed manuscript *Excalibur*, which he believed revealed the secrets of success in life and manifested itself in his later works.

He was a commissioned naval officer (Lieutenant, Jr. Grade) in World War II, briefly commanding two vessels but, while enthusiastic and a good navigator, was removed by his senior officers as "incapable of command," notably after shelling an island in Mexican waters, which he believed was a legitimate gunnery target.[15]

It seems Hubbard got to the Kellogg house in Bay Head and then moved to their Elizabeth home through

FIGURE 6-4. L. Ron Hubbard in front of the Kellogg's former house at 666 East Avenue, Bay Head, which he rented in 1949–1950 while writing his defining work *Dianetics: The Modern Science of Mental Health.*

Courtesy of Ben Kracauer, Curator, Bay Head, Mantoloking and Lovelandtown Museum

the offices of his editor and supporter John W. Campbell, who was interested in psychic powers.[16] Hubbard certainly must have had great charisma and could have told and embellished some fascinating tales. I probably would have rented to him as well, after he'd filled me with his enthusiasm. As a trained scientist and historian, I'd know better now.

In the early 1950s, Jimmy commissioned Morton Johnson's 'house' naval architect Floyd Ayers to design a boat for him.[17] Betty, Jimmy's wife, had been on Nantucket and seen the boat she wanted (my guess is that this was a Friendship Sloop), but she definitely required full-standing headroom. Ayers drew a 30-foot full-bodied "Nantucket" cutter of traditional profile, and Betty got her requested headroom. Jimmy chose David Beaton and Sons, boat builders, in Mantoloking to construct her. She was to be called *White Whale* (see Figure 6-1).

Thacher Brown, a childhood friend of Jimmy's sons Rusty and Peter, said, "I first met the Kelloggs in 1953 or 1954 when we went to 666 [East Avenue] before going down to Beaton's to see *White Whale* being built." *White Whale*, Brown recalls, was, aside from headroom, built around a large cockpit, with capacity for many guests and a big ice chest—with a commensurate capacity for their refreshment. A view of her appeared on the cover of *Rudder* magazine while she was being set up. *Lloyd's Register* gives her commissioning year as 1955.

Dave Beaton's son Lachlan (nicknamed "Lally" —pronounced "Lolly") some years later brought home the April 1956 copy of *Rudder* magazine, which was left lying around. As *his* young son Tom Beaton (born 1956) was "glancing at the cover he remarked to his family what a messy shop it was. After a moment or two he realized it was *his* father's shop"[18] recorded by artist Allen Beechel years earlier.

In Beechel's illustration, ship's carpenter Nealy Campbell was planing the bevel on a plank during *White Whale*'s construction. Tommy says that years earlier Nealy had lost a thumb when he accidentally knocked into a shop machine and Lally, trying to get his daughter to stop thumb sucking, told her that if she didn't stop, it would fall off. When she met Nealy, she had been primed by Lally and was eager to see if the threat to his sister was real. Nealy said, "yes, that's true, I used to suck my thumb."[19]

When I was a kid at Beaton's Boatyard in Mantoloking, *White Whale* was one of the more interesting boats that I watched coming and going. She had a traditional gaff rig with fiddled topmast that would enable her to carry a gaff-topsail,[20] a bowsprit, clipper bow, and a rather fat hull with a broad transom stern. As a kid, this was the first boat I had seen in the flesh with ratlines running aloft and a real topmast. Wow, I thought,

FIGURE 6-5. Jimmy Kellogg's boat *White Whale* being planked at Beaton's. Nealy Campbell planes a plank in this Allen Beechel scratchboard art from the cover of *Rudder* magazine's "Fitting Out Issue" in April 1956.

Inset: Beechel sketched *White Whale*'s lines on their rumpled blueprint in one corner of his print.

Calvert Marine Museum Archives, Solomons, Maryland

this was irresistible to a young monkey like me: I wanted to go aloft aboard her in the worst way![21]

Jimmy Kellogg's affection for boats propelled him to do something constructive to preserve them. His son Peter says, "My father would buy all kinds of old boats and sell them off. He [once] sold a sneakbox for $5 and when people went to see it, they thought it had been abandoned and walked away! Maybe he sold that one ten times until one day someone took it, to his surprise. He once sold a boat to Thacher Brown, I think . . . for five cents!"[22] Actually, the boat, a 28-foot catboat named *Pastime,* was sold to Thacher's father John A. Brown and it *was* for a nickel![23] Thacher commenting to me, with the perspective of what his father had gotten into, "I'm not sure he didn't overpay!"[24]

Jimmy Kellogg eventually formalized his boat preservation advocacy into a syndicate called J. C. Kellogg and Sons, Inc., which his son Peter Kellogg says still exists today.

FIGURE 6-6.

(Top) John B. Brown's brother Harry S. (Bud) Brown looks with some trepidation at *Pastime*, a circa 1900 Morton Johnson catboat that Jimmy Kellogg sold to John for a nickel in 1949 or 1950.

(Bottom) Nickel boat or not, Brown got *Pastime* in the water, floating, and rigged with her sail on at Bay Head Yacht Club.

Thacher Brown photographs

FIGURE 6-7. **And here's** *Pastime* **under sail with young owner John Brown at the helm. Nancy and Bill Hamilton also occupy the comfortable cockpit, typical of old 19th century catboats rigged for taking 'sports' and their ladies summer sailing in the Victorian era. Brown even rigged a pipe for his fishing pole, so they could troll with** *Pastime's* **outboard.** *Inset:* **A circa 1940 Outboard Marine Zephyr pushing with 5.4 horsepower!**

Thatcher Brown photograph

The OMC Zephyrs

The Zephyr outboard motors were marketed starting about 1939 by Outboard Marine, an arm of the old Evinrude Company. The Zephyrs were unique in having the cast iron bored for tiny pistons and cylinders, an inch and a half in diameter. Four horizontal cylinders were packed into the motor head, versus most outboards of the period that had one or two. This made the Zephyrs exceptionally quiet and smooth running. The motor pictured on *Pastime* is likely a pre-World War II model built about 1940.

Some Zephyrs were built for the U.S. Navy during World War II, notably to power lifeboats. However, unlike outboards provided under contract to the U.S. Army that were painted olive drab, the Navy models retained their silvery finish and manufacturer's logo. They were durable and, despite their modest 5.4 HP output, they remained popular into the 1990s with some specialized motorboat racers, who modified and sought to get maximum speed out of them.

Many would still be running today were it not for a simple diaphragm serving the pump that fed fuel to the carburetor. When these membranes split, older Zephyrs were useless and replacement parts were unavailable. An elderly Maryland aficionado later tooled up and re-manufactured these parts, but when he died, relatives threw them out in the dumpster[25] unfamiliar with the critical link they played to a whole class of small motors.

FIGURE 6-8. **A full view of a similar rope-start Zephyr, dating from post-World War II. This one has a blue fuel tank and sports the Evinrude logo. Later models had a rewind starter bolted on top.**

Kent Mountford photograph, collection of Ken Kaumeyer

The Kellogg's most well-known home in Bay Head fronted on Barnegat Bay, off Barnegat Lane, and was originally on the west side of the old railroad tracks! It was directly on the narrow North-South Intercoastal Waterway channel behind the barrier beach; it had views out towards sunset and the Metedeconk River.

For decades this home has been known simply as the "Boat House." Jody Fitts recalls that, by the 1950s, the Boat House was a Bay Head icon, noted for well-attended, good parties. She was a teen at the time and friends with Rusty, Jimmy Kellogg's youngest son; she looks back on these times with fond memories.

Jody recalls evening sails with the Kellogg brothers and their friends, Thacher and Andy Brown, on the Metedeconk River. The brothers were responsible and serious sailors, and their parents trusted them with the family boats at an early age. Jody says these "were good teen fun times,"[26] enjoying the cool night wind and calm waters of the sheltered river with friends.

FIGURE 6-9. Jimmy Kellogg's residence, the Boat House, at Bay Head, shown here in 1941. There is a little too much weight in the stern of that skiff!

Henry Bristol photograph, courtesy Bay Head, Mantoloking, Lovelandtown Museum

Jimmy Kellogg sailed the *White Whale* to New England one summer. They were under sail off Nonquitt on the north shore of Buzzards Bay, near New Bedford, then across Vineyard Sound to Edgartown on Martha's Vineyard. Jimmy's son Rusty recalled, "Dad had just purchased the Johnson 3-HP outboard [and put it on their dinghy]

Whale Tail and I was so excited, driving it all around the harbor each night." His brother Peter replied: ". . . brings back great memories!"[27]

There was also another story Tom Beaton recalls about something being wrong with the ballast, and the boat laying over on her ear, but still floating.[28] Rusty Kellogg remembers the story this way:

> Like most whale tales, there is a grain of truth. . . . While my parents were away, friends took *White Whale* for a sail on Barnegat Bay on a windy day—and a strong puff knocked her down. . . . The spreader touched the water to leeward, the cockpit cushions washed overboard, but after a few seconds she righted herself and there was a *lot* of water below.
>
> When Dad heard the story and consulted with Floyd Ayers, the naval architect at Morton Johnson, who designed the boat, they concluded that the boat must've taken on water below (maybe an open head seacock) and no one on deck was paying attention . . . so the excess water caused the boat to be rolled and that's why there was so much to be pumped out. Dad also added lead pigs in the bilge just to be safe. From this event came a little ditty:
>
> > There is a legend 'bout a gaff rigged whale,
> > A happy crew took her out for a sail,
> > They tipped her over, and OH! Did they bail!
> > Hey, Jimmy – Is the *White Whale* for sale?[29]

Jimmy let two young men—Alan C. Fitts and Bill Cannon—live aboard *White Whale* for the whole summer. Alan was working as a lifeguard in Bay Head, and this was not a bad berth for a young man close to finishing college and unsure of where a career would take him. Alan also tended bar for the Kelloggs during their summer parties, and with two seats on the New York Stock Exchange in the family, these affairs must have seen some pretty significant people come through the door. One of them ended up offering Alan a job, which led to a long career—more than half a century—in the world of finance. He was also dating the Chandlees' teenage daughter Susie and would ultimately marry her![30, 31, 32]

* * *

Jimmy Kellogg bought *Silent Maid* from his friend Blake Chandlee in 1952, when the lure of blue water sailing led Blake to acquire his keel sloop *Suban*. It was a natural sequence—the Chandlees had been social friends of the Schoettles in Bay Head during the late 1940s, and they were almost the first to know when son Karl, acting for Edwin's estate, put *Silent Maid* up for sale.

Jimmy probably acquired *Silent Maid* late in the sailing season of 1952 or early 1953. How much he used or enjoyed her is not recorded, but Timo White, a Kellogg family friend and sailing companion of son Peter's, says, "The Kellogg family would put up overnight guests aboard *Silent Maid*. There was some sort of oven in which, one Thanksgiving, they cooked a turkey."[33] Thus the *Maid* seems to have continued her social life under the management of Jimmy Kellogg.

Peter Kellogg tells the story of his father traveling to South Africa and, always interested in boats, he was poking around some waterfront and met an old wooden boat builder. There, half a world away from Barnegat Bay, Jimmy raised the subject of catboats, and the old fellow said, "when I was in the United States, I worked on the largest of the catboats." Kellogg said: "I'll bet my catboat is bigger" to which the South African replied, expecting to end the discussion immediately: "I worked building the *Silent Maid*." "Well," Kellogg replied, "that's my boat!"

FIGURE 6-10. **The Class A catboat** *Lotus* in a later incarnation at Beaton's Boatyard in Mantoloking. There are other pictures of her under way in the Schoettle chapter of this book.

Kent Mountford photograph

FIGURE 6-11. **Cross-bracing straps of bronze were not enough after decades of racing to keep the Class A catboat** *Lotus* **dry. This old work was revealed when** *Lotus* **was finally rebuilt at David Beaton and Sons in 2005.**

Kent Mountford photograph

Peter Kellogg was eleven when his father acquired *Silent Maid*, so his childhood memories of this grand sailing vessel were few. However, Peter has many memories of sailing another catboat. When Peter was seventeen, he and David McShane bought the Class A catboat *Lotus*. Interestingly, the *Lotus* had a very interesting connection with the first owner of *Silent Maid*—it was the same boat Edwin Schoettle had purchased for his sons to race several decades earlier.

Lotus, by Peter's time, was a very old boat and almost anything would open her seams and require herculean bailing. This was despite Charles Mower's best efforts to design her well and despite bronze cross bracing that Morton Johnson had installed when she was built.

Peter's brother-in-law Newt Kirkland recalls two teenagers trying to caulk her: "They were covered head to toe with splotches of black Thiokol™"—then the solution of choice.[34] Thiokol is a thick black paste; some versions require mixing in an accelerator to start the cure. It is usually dispensed from a caulking gun or applied with a putty knife. Messy to work with, it adhered well to wood fibers, cured to a resilient rubber-like material reminiscent of automobile tires, which actually had some permanent elasticity when old wooden planks flexed and twisted. My uncle Chick Leeds was Special Assistant to the General Manager of Thiokol Chemical Corp., at their Reaction Motors Division in Denville, New Jersey. He reported that the caulking compound version was actually a failed experiment in making solid rocket fuel, the more beneficial use being discovered as an accident.[35]

Peter and I were young fellows on Barnegat Bay at the same time, though we never met. However, had we met, I would have been very envious of a young guy sailing such a classic old vessel. In my hands *Lotus* wouldn't have raced, but I sure would have managed to cruise far and wide, far more than I'd been able to in my 15-foot sneakbox!

Paul Smith, shipwright at David Beaton and Sons, boat builders in Mantoloking, has been with the firm for decades. He recalled when Peter Kellogg and his young turks raced *Lotus*. Smith recounts that one afternoon, "They literally exploded *Lotus'* mast; it was all in pieces. They brought the remains in to Dave [Beaton] and left it to be fixed." Peter Kellogg would, I think, appreciate an analogy with the bittersweet 'rite of passage' when competitive skiers break a bone.[36]

Lotus was towed home, and the wait began for Beaton's meticulous repair. Class A catboat masts are not simple balks of white cedar to be spoke-shaved, sanded, varnished, and delivered. They are rather complex, extremely long, carefully spliced, and reinforced boxes that are masterworks of craftsmanship. Remember, the earliest spars of these once state-of-the-art racing boats were built by Pigeon Hollow Spar Company, which made the feather-light elegant wing struts for early experimental airplanes early in the last century.

Despite the eagerness of Kellogg and his buddies to get back to racing their leaky old bucket, Beaton had to complete whatever he was currently working on, acquire the right lumber—often Sitka Spruce from across America—and set up the proper jigs for shaping and gluing a new spar.

The young guys, after an uncertain number of inquiries, were impatient. One night one of them got into Beaton's locked shop, nipped a can of white paint, and emblazoned across the big doors through which all boats had to pass, the burning question "*Lotus'* Mast?" This rubbed Dave Beaton the wrong way and probably likewise most of the guys working for him at the time. Master shipwright Paul Smith, in those years still a kid just learning his trade, recalls Beaton's terse Scottish brogue: "Dave just said 'They won't see THAT mast,' not another word."

The painted sign at Beaton's shop, however, was left there for more than half a century.[37] Peter, by then a true champion of Barnegat's sailing community, had asked pointedly: "Can't we get rid of that?" But the stinging memory of youthful hubris was allowed to persist well into the new millennium. It was finally expunged when the doors were replaced after the floods from Hurricane Irene in 2012![38]

Amazingly in 1960 you could still go up to (long-deceased) Edwin Schoettle's Cross-trees estate and pull out an old spar from the barn to work with. Newt Kirkland (Peter's brother-in-law) recounts Peter and his crew found an old 20-foot sneakbox mast to which the bottom of another spar was spliced. This became their jury-rigged Class A catboat mast. Newt recalls, "It had about five (wire) stays on it" (versus the conventional two shrouds). "They actually won some races with it, too!"[39]

FIGURE 6-12. An accidentally broken Class A catboat mast with its shattered hollow construction is shown here at Beaton's Mantoloking shop in 2013 for a complete re-build.

Kent Mountford photograph

FIGURE 6-13. Inside the great sliding doors at Beaton's shop in Mantoloking, *Lotus'* young owners tried to urge repair of their catboat's mast to no avail. When Dave Beaton found this he simply refused to make the repair; the inscription stayed there for over half a century, memorial to youthful hubris!

Kent Mountford photograph

SILENT MAID FINDS A NEW FAMILY

It is likely that Jimmy Kellogg was continuing to press his agenda of keeping old boats moving into responsible ownership when my father was looking for a catboat. My Dad and his brothers—Mom and I, as well, had sailed a few seasons on the catboat *Osprey* out of Johnson's Boatyard in Bay Head. There was something about the classic, simple rig and that big single sail that really appealed to us. My parents started looking for a boat on which we could summer as a family on Barnegat Bay.

Records are not available on the following brief episode in *Silent Maid*'s life, but Jimmy Kellogg seems to have already moved ownership of the *Maid* to Robert L. Cameron, who lived in the then-rural Lebanon, New Jersey. While Cameron held title to her, he appears to have used his time and sailed *Silent Maid*. He was certainly pleased with her, nonetheless circumstances changed in his life, and he and his family were rethinking how and where to spend their summers. Cameron received a letter a year later from none other than Judson Smith who was now living in Huntington Valley in Montgomery County, Pennsylvania. Poor Jud was again trying to track down and hopefully own the *Silent Maid*. It was in the response to that letter that I have my only record of Robert Cameron's ownership, which appears to have spanned barely a year. He writes "My reason for selling the *Silent Maid* was simply that my family and I have transferred our summer activities to Long Island Sound and the boat was not suitable for those waters."[40] Judson Smith, following up on that letter from Robert Cameron, wrote in September 1954 to Grant V. Bauer, who was yacht broker and manager at the Hubert Johnson Boat Yard in Bay Head. Jud was again enquiring about the availability of *Silent Maid*. He was just about a year late this time; the *Maid* was well embedded in my family by then.

Silent Maid was still tied up in a slip at Bay Head Yacht Club when my plebeian family got a hold of her. At any rate, through Hubert Johnson Boat Yard's broker Grant Bauer, the bill of sale was executed by Mr. Cameron in 1953. Our family's ownership of *Silent Maid* was to change my life irrevocably.

*   *   *

Jimmy Kellogg died in 1980, at just age 65—young in today's terms. He was at the shore in Bay Head when hit by a stroke and passed away in the nearby hospital at Point Pleasant, which ironically looks out at the beautiful Manasquan River. His death notice stated his end was brought about by "coronary thrombosis." Kellogg's fate was shared by many famous people including U.S. Presidents Calvin Coolidge and Teddy Roosevelt, King George VI of Great Britain, and Indian Premier Jawaharlal Nehru.

Jimmy Kellogg's son Peter maintained close ties with the boating community while building his still growing interests in IATRE, the re-insurance business he founded after leaving Spear, Leeds & Kellogg. He has continued saving and benefitting worthy boats through the J.C. Kellogg & Sons, Inc., syndicate. It was he, who in 2003, would acquire *Silent Maid*, and send her safely on her final journey and to reincarnation.

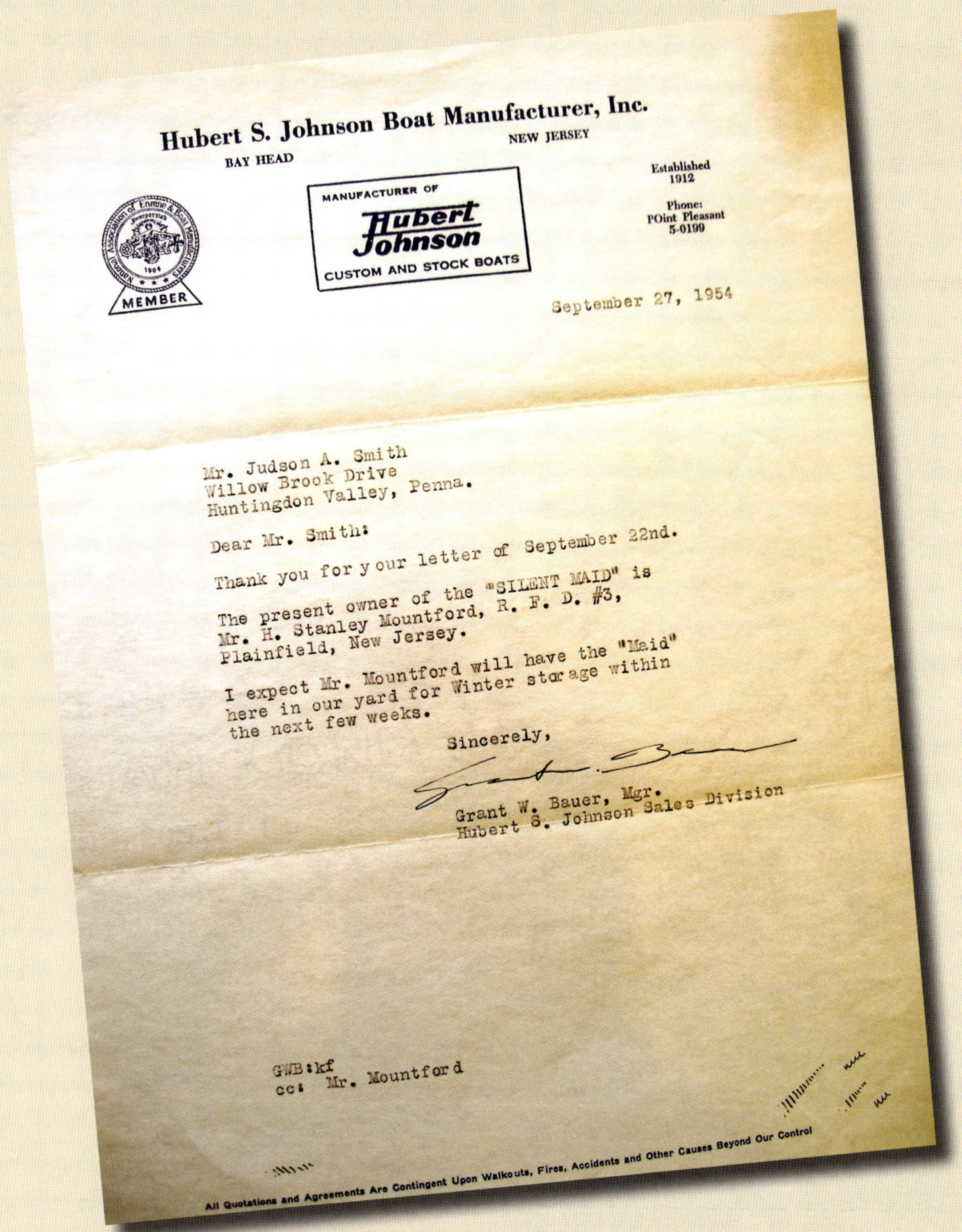

Hubert S. Johnson Boat Manufacturer, Inc.

BAY HEAD   **NEW JERSEY**

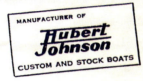

MANUFACTURER OF

Hubert Johnson

CUSTOM AND STOCK BOATS

Established
1912

Phone:
POint Pleasant
5-0199

September 27, 1954

Mr. Judson A. Smith
Willow Brook Drive
Huntingdon Valley, Penna.

Dear Mr. Smith:

Thank you for your letter of September 22nd.

The present owner of the "SILENT MAID" is
Mr. H. Stanley Mountford, R. F. D. #3,
Plainfield, New Jersey.

I expect Mr. Mountford will have the "Maid"
here in our yard for Winter storage within
the next few weeks.

Sincerely,

Grant W. Bauer, Mgr.
Hubert S. Johnson Sales Division

GWB:kf
cc: Mr. Mountford

All Quotations and Agreements Are Contingent Upon Walkouts, Fires, Accidents and Other Causes Beyond Our Control

FIGURE 6-14. Grant Bauer's letter to Judson Smith, indicating *Silent Maid* had again eluded him and had sailed on into new hands . . . ours! The *Maid* in actuality was stored that year at the Winter Yacht Basin in Mantoloking.

Toms River Seaport Society

Peter Kellogg Follows in His Father's Footsteps in Business and Boats

Peter R. Kellogg, Jimmy's second son, was born in 1942. He attended the Berkshire School in Massachusetts and enrolled for a short time at the Babson Institute of Business Administration. Babson, the famous economist, was closely connected with Edwin Schoettle before and during World War II. After Peter's experiment with Babson, he worked on Wall Street in the 1960s and eventually joined his father's firm Spear, Leeds & Kellogg in 1967.

Having grown up as part of his father's mission rescuing classic boats on Barnegat Bay, Peter Kellogg eventually amassed a significant fleet of rescues of his own, including Commodore Edward Crabbe's Stonington motor sailer *Barnegat* and the classic catboat *Myth*. Working through the Independence Seaport Museum's "Workshop on the Water," managed for years by shipwright John Brady, Peter sponsored or helped create new boats to augment the A Class catboat fleet. He also sponsored two classic "sandbagger" racing sloops, not surprisingly named *Bull* and *Bear*, harking to his Wall Street roots. Peter contributed a pair of replica 19th century whaleboats following restoration of the *Charles W. Morgan*, America's last square-rigged whaleship, now sailing out of the Mystic Seaport Museum in Connecticut.

Chapter 9 of this book recounts the long and interesting life that Sally Schneider had with *Silent Maid*. At the end of Sally's tenure, it was Peter who purchased the *Maid* for restoration as a museum exhibit. While the evaluation and restoration work was in progress, he and John Brady worked out a plan for the re-creation of *Silent Maid* as a completely new yacht, designed to be competitive on the classic racing circuit.

FIGURE 6-15. *(Left)* Peter Kellogg at the helm of *Silent Maid*'s successor off Padenarum, Massachusetts. Timo White is on the mainsheet; they are racing against the large classic catboat *Kathleen*. *(Right)* Peter Kellogg listens to speakers at the launching of *Silent Maid*'s re-incarnation in Philadelphia, June 2009.

Kent Mountford photographs

ENDNOTES — CHAPTER 6

1. U.S. Bureau of the Census, Elizabeth, Union County, 1920, 106.

2. "Bluing" is a term unfamiliar to most modern homemakers. Now an ingredient in modern detergents, it was once added to wash water to counteract yellowing of white fabrics and restore them to whiteness. Chemically it is the deeply blue pigment "ultramarine," originally the finely powdered semiprecious mineral Lapis Lazuli from Afghanistan. It has since been synthetically made at high temperature from china clay, sodium carbonate, and sulphur. The intense blue absorbs yellow light reflected from the fabric, yielding the perception of intense white. http://en.wikipedia.org/wiki/Bluing_(fabric)

3. "Spear, Leeds & Kellogg History," FundingUniverse.com, accessed 2013, www.fundinguniverse.com/company-histories/spear-leeds-kellogg-history/

4. Ibid.

5. Thacher Brown, October email exchanges with Kent Mountford, 2013.

6. "Spear, Leeds and Kellogg History."

7. Ibid.

8. Alan Fitts, interview with Jody and Alan Fitts at Mantoloking, January 2, 2011.

9. Ibid.

10. "Spear, Leeds and Kellogg History."

11. Ibid.

12. Benjamin Kracauer, correspondence with Kent Mountford, October 2013. Kracauer is curator of the Bay Head, Manroloking and Lovelandtown Museum and advised Scientology management on restoration of the East Avenue Kellogg House.

13. "L. Ron Hubbard," http://en.wikipedia.org/wiki/L._Ron_Hubbard

14. Ibid. Quoted as saying this about his life as a pulp fiction writer.

15. Ibid.

16. Ibid.

17. Lloyd's Register of American Yachts, 1956, p. 591. James Crane Kellogg 3rd, *White Whale*, 30' keel, auxiliary cutter with Ratsey and lapthorn sails. Auxiliary Universal 16 HP.

18. Russell Manheimer presented this vignette about Beaton's in his blog "Hove to off Cove Point," 2007 (www.Sjogin.com). (*Author's note:* Beaton's shop *is* inevitably messy; they do work there!)

19. Tom Beaton, text review discussion with Kent Mountford, November 27, 2013.

20. Fiddle blocks on larger sailing vessels were used to lower a topmast in bad weather or raise it into position where it was used to set a gaff-topsail, increasing sail area and windward performance in the "age of sail."

21. *White Whale*'s name, incidentally, has been resurrected by Peter Kellogg in the large triple-engined rigid inflatable that Henry Colie and his staff run as tender to the modern (21st century) Kellogg fleet.

22. Peter R. Kellogg, in conversation at Padenarum, MA, 2011.

23. Thacher Brown, email to Kent Mountford detailing the event, October 15, 2013.

24. Thacher Brown, email to Kent Mountford, October 26, 2013.

25. Kenneth L. Kaumeyer, personal communication to Kent Mountford, October 2013. Kaumeyer was a curator, now retired, for the Calvert Marine Museum, Solomons, MD, and during his tenure was largely responsible for a popular, long running exhibit on early outboard motors.

26. Jody Chandlee Fitts, interview with Jody and Alan Fitts at Mantoloking, January 2, 2011.

27. M.W. "Rusty" Kellogg, email to Peter R. Kellogg on this event, November 2013.

28. Tom Beaton, text discussion with Kent Mountford, November 27, 2013.

29. M.W. "Rusty" Kellogg, email discussion with Kent Mountford, December 2013.

30. Alan and Susie (Chandlee) Fitts remained married until Susie's untimely death from cancer at age 32. Jody Chandlee had been a babysitter for the couple some years before, and when re-acquainted with Alan as an adult, they married and have been together over thirty years at this writing; thus references to Jody and Alan Fitts in this book.

31. Alan Fitts, interviewed with wife Jody at Mantoloking, New Year's weekend, 2011.

32. Alan Fitts, emails to Kent Mountford July 19 and 20, 2014.

33. Roy Wilkins, interview with Kent Mountford, 2009.

34. Newt Kirkland, interviewed at Philadelphia Independence Seaport Museum on August 10, 2010, while working on the original *Silent Maid* restoration.

35. Clarence Meredith Leeds told Kent Mountford this origin of an old-boat standard remedy, circa 1956.

36. Peter Kellogg and two of his sons held, and perhaps still hold, a Guinness World Record for number of vertical downhill miles skied in a week. One of the two sons, "Rit," with whom he skied, was killed subsequently in a tragic, though unrelated, backcountry skiing accident.

37. Log *Nimble* records speaking with shipwright Paul Smith, March 7, 2011.

38. Tom Beaton, recounted this conclusion of Paul Smith's account to Kent Mountford, 2013.

39. Newt Kirkland, phone conversation with Kent Mountford reviewing this chapter, October 2013.

40. Robert L. Cameron, letter to Judson Smith, July 27, 1954.

FIGURE 7-1. With *Silent Maid* in the background on a port tack, left is a view of her cabin trunk with peak and throat halyards belayed, the brass fog bell in place, and the tarred manila centerboard pennant coiled. Right, Stan Mountford, the author's father at *Silent Maid*'s helm.

Dorothy Mountford photographs

7

The Mountford Years
on *Silent Maid*

I have provided a very thorough history of each of *Silent Maid*'s families, but regarding my own family, especially my parents Stan and Dorothy (Gordon) Mountford, who brought *Silent Maid* into my life, I, of course, know their histories in greater detail.

Nineteen hundred sixty-five was a watershed year for me. My parents had sold *Silent Maid* at the end of the previous summer, and out in the working world myself, I was struggling with a love affair on shaky ground. My love interest was an intelligent and literate young woman named Martha Fuessel, who was a German national and had returned to Europe to decide where and how she wanted to live her life. I determined to chase her, my first trip as a true innocent abroad. In the process I made way stations on the west coast of Ireland and through the Scottish Highlands; thus discovering my own maternal roots.

* * *

Bal Ellis, the James Kent home, was a late 18th century farmhouse with thick stone walls located in County Wicklow, near the Irish Sea and south of Greystones, a fishing community (and now summer retreat) on Erin's west coast. My great grandmother Jane Evans Kent, among other unknown talents, was a nicely trained pencil sketch artist. Two of her better drawings survive after 160 years and reside today on my bedroom wall. Bal Ellis was, after all, a farm and that work, plus her *fourteen* children, likely took most of her energy in life. It is unknown if she ever painted in oil or watercolors, but it must be in the genes because I have sketched in my own journals as long as I can remember. Jane bequeathed me more than my given first name. A portrait of Jane Kent has survived; she was dour enough in countenance that my wife declines hanging her in our home!

FIGURE 7-2. **Jane Evans Kent** *(left)* in a lightly colored mid-19th century photograph, *(center)* her circa 1840 pencil drawing of weathered ruins near an old Irish church, and *(right)* her mid-19th century dressing case or "casket" preserved to the present.
Mountford family collection

Jane's youngest child, Isabella Maria Kent, was last of the fourteen,[1] born in Kilkool on April 12, 1863[2] while the American Civil War was still being brutally fought and Gen. James Longstreet commenced the siege of Suffolk in southeast Virginia.[3] When Isabella was nine years old, her mother died a widow at Bal Ellis, which would have been in 1872. This created a conundrum for the family: the estate was placed in the hands of the Courts of Chancery and could not be settled until Isabella, the youngest child, reached age 21 in 1884. This Court sat at nearby Dublin and the little Isabella was made a "Ward of Chancery."[4] Her siblings resented this delay—and with cause—because when she came of age in 1884 the estate had dwindled to £500 (approximately $2793[5] in 1870 U.S. dollars). There was very little to go around.

The only heirloom passing from Jane's generation to mine was her lovely mid-19th century dressing case, in those days called a casket (somewhat different from how we take the term!), which came to my mother in the 1950s through her Irish cousin Annie Buckley of Greystones, County Wicklow.

One brother James Evans Kent was an adventurer, off seeking gold in Australia, and nothing was heard of him. One of Isabella's other brothers, I think Sam, was a seaman. Isabella, thinking she might be able to find the missing James, took passage aboard Sam's ship the SS *Sorata*, 4059 gross and 2604 tons burthen. *Sorata* was a Royal Mail Ship run by the Orient Company Line and captained by 35-year-old George F. Dixon. The ship was home-ported in Liverpool, but on her Australia passage she sailed from London on February 6, 1885, then around the English Channel to Plymouth. It's not clear where Isabella embarked. Their passage took them into the Mediterranean, stopping at Naples (what must this country girl have thought of this city and its volcano, Vesuvius?). On July 31, they continued to Port Said, entering the Suez Canal, which after a decade of construction had been open for 16 years.

Sickness broke out aboard and ship's surgeon P.H. Rockforth, 28-years-old at the time, believed it might be smallpox. As Isabella described it, in the exhausting heat, she watched bodies sewn in canvas and a mother and her dead infant slid over the ship's rail in burial at sea. They had hung one fever-stricken man in a hammock (under shading tarpaulins) lashed to the rigging. Other crewmen were cautioned not to go near him for fear of contagion. Rockforth tested Isabella and found she was immune to smallpox, apparently due to being exposed to livestock at Bal Ellis[6] and contracting cowpox as a child. She ministered kindly to the sick man, helping him drink in his fevered state, and thereby saved his life. It is supposed that smallpox was not involved, because at her ports of call *Sorata* was not placed in quarantine.

Her sailor brother proved a poor chaperone, drinking and whoring ashore whenever possible. He ripped the veil from a Muslim woman (perhaps in Suez) and was nearly killed by a mob. He later deserted the ship and young Isabella. The ship's ports of call may be incompletely recorded because Isabella said that she had drunk from the River Nile, and legend said that she'd be fated to return. She never did.

From Suez, *Sorata* voyaged some 1900 miles across the Indian Ocean to the tiny British Territory of Diego Garcia, an atoll with just ten square miles of land area, where a coaling station was maintained from 1881–1888. Here in the Chagos Archipelago, and below the Equator, Isabella saw coconut palms and the thin white beaches of this tropical isle.

Freshwater on Narrow Beaches

Like New Jersey's barrier islands, Diego Garcia was not far from being a desert. In the absence of seasonal rains, seawater, immersing islands or barriers like those on the New Jersey shore, infiltrates through every interstitial space, between every sand grain. When rains come to such habitats, the water either evaporates or quickly percolates below the surface. Once there, it does not simply mix with the salt.

Freshwater, particularly rainwater, is much lighter than seawater and with no wind or waves deep underground, the freshwater floats atop the salt, actually forming a bulge, or what geologists call a Ghyben-Herzberg freshwater lens, lying above the underlying intruding seawater. If one can dig a simple well deep enough one can tap this resource for potable water.

In the case of Diego Garcia, the deep, freshwater reserve was a considerable resource, 40 times thicker than the height of this little atoll above the sea. It held literally millions of cubic meters of fresh water, stored from one rainy season to another. It could yield 560,000 liters (25,454 gallons) a day, enough drinking water to support a population of 3,500 people.

When wells are pumped too hard or fast, however, they begin to suck up the ever-present seawater from greater depths. Geologists call this 'upconing,' from the conical shape rising seawater assumes underground when replacing the removed freshwater. This salt intrusion can ruin the whole game, as it did with over-ambitious development on the New Jersey shore not too many years after Isabella's brief stop at Diego Garcia in 1885.[7]

Sorata arrived in Adelaide, Australia, on September 2, 1885, and at Sydney, New South Wales, on September 7.[8] In Australia, young Isabella's arduous journey turned out to be a fool's errand; her brother James had died on July 26, during the Austral winter of 1882. After all her travel and travail she could only visit his lonely grave. She listed three friends made while in Australia—Cassie Graysoll, Joseph Smith of Sydney, and Elizabeth Smith. Nothing more is known of them.

On returning to Ireland, Isabella and her sister Nellie worked as milliners (making women's hats) with a young apprentice named Margaret Harrison, who helped them. Margaret immigrated to Philadelphia with her family, found employment, and formed connections vital in Isabella's later life.

Isabella, still in Eire was courted by Dr. Colin Kennedy, but his over-use of alcohol frightened her so much that she and Nellie decided to follow Margaret to America in

FIGURE 7-3. A men's velvet smoking jacket label with facsimile of John Wanamaker's signature.

Estate of Edmund M. Sage

FIGURE 7-4. Dorothy Ellinore Gordon at the Gables in 1914 with her middle name spelled wrong.

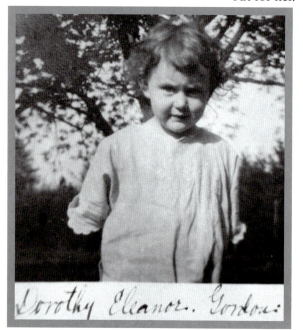

the late 1880s. In Philadelphia, they both were employed by John Wanamaker in his department store as milliners. In my early youth, I never saw my grandmother dressed to go out without a proper hat, quite like Mary Galvan Schoettle (see Figure 2-7).

This was seasonal work, and John Wanamaker, a "true Christian man," helped Isabella obtain work modeling hats and secured her a position teaching her craft at the Young Women's Christian Association (YWCA). The YWCA was known to her in England, where it was founded in 1855 and the organization was in 17 countries by the time Isabella took her job.

I do not know if Isabella ever went to Wanamaker's Methodist Camp at Island Heights on Toms River. This was usually an opportunity for the cash boys and girls in the store, and Isabella was probably too old. She always told us that Mr. Wanamaker had taken a personal interest in her welfare.

Meanwhile, Margaret Harrison, as part of her job, had met David Virtue, a New York City silk and finery merchant, who imported goods for Wanamaker. One of Virtue's sisters, Anna Eliza Virtue, while still in Ireland, had married a young man named Alec Gordon.[9] They had a son and she was pregnant again when, because of anti-Protestant violence in dominantly Catholic Ireland, they emigrated to Queen City (today's Plainfield), in a fertile stream-fed valley at the foot of the Watchung Mountains in northern New Jersey. Alec was a hard worker, having cut peat and firewood as a boy in Ireland, and started farming on what is today urban Clinton Avenue in Plainfield. Unfortunately, Anna Eliza succumbed to tuberculosis and shortly after their infant daughter died too. This left Alec alone to raise his son David Virtue Gordon.

Apparently through merchant David Virtue and Margaret Harrison, Alec found out about the young milliner, Isabella Kent, in Philadelphia. A wife and helpmate was pure economic necessity in 19th century agricultural America. Alec eventually drove from Plainfield to Philadelphia in a horse-drawn wagon to meet, marry (June 20, 1894), and trundle all the way back with his (likely apprehensive) young wife. She had her work cut out for her.

Alec had a milk route drawing upon the production of his small herd of cows, but he was better at delivering milk than collecting the bills. He was widely appreciated in his Presbyterian Church and the nearby community as a "fine Christian man" (he did not smoke, drink, or use profanity and threw coins to small children), but while generous to others, he was penurious to the detriment of his growing family. Alec and Isabella had six children of their own, Maud (who died at one year), Louis, Florence, Margaret, Mildred and the last, my mother Dorothy Ellinore Gordon, born February 16, 1912, when Isabella was almost an unheard of 50-years-old. In March of that year, the Girl Scouts of America was founded and in April the RMS *Titanic* sank, when little Dorothy was just two months old. As the baby, and a surprise at that, Dorothy was doted upon by her father.

The dairy business was insufficient to support so many mouths and Alec took employment as a caretaker at "The Gables," the Fanwood, New Jersey, estate of American Bank Note Company President Augustus D. Shepard. The estate had cottages, a friendly dog (Garibaldi), a pony (Ponce de Leon), a two-wheeled cart, and wonderful memories for little Dorothy. The children all called their father "Pa" or "Papa."[10] This was a valuable position for Alec with all his responsibilities, but fate intervened.

Alec Gordon had a stroke on the job and his resulting disability ended the family's sinecure at the Gables. Alec, who loved animals, tried to keep working as a local veterinarian, which skills he'd brought from Ireland. He died in 1921, when Dorothy was nine, a great trauma for her.

Isabella's son, "Lew" Louis Kent Gordon, the apple of his mother's eye, had been successful in business, and after Alec's death, helped her settle into a comfortable frame house in North Plainfield, New Jersey (a $2500 purchase). Isabella's sister Eleanor, had immigrated in 1885, and married Arthur Tyrrell, a Philadelphia upholsterer and later merchant. He had done well and they had a white clapboard summer cottage at Ocean Gate on Toms River, tributary to Barnegat Bay. They invited Dorothy, and sometimes Dorothy's brother Lew, to summer there around 1921-22, while she dealt with the bewildering loss of her beloved and doting father.

The community of Ocean Gate in the early years of the 20th century was rapidly building along the shoreline where Edwin Schoettle had sailed his catboat *Scat* and nosed ashore on open sandy beaches (see Figure 2-25). Schoettle later rued the solitude lost from development of this cottage community. In those early days of development along Barnegat Bay, he did not consciously make the connection between his industrialist's enthusiasm for growing Island Heights or his participation in construction of the automobile bridge to the barrier beaches with what destructive growth would occur over the following century.

Little Dorothy Gordon experienced the salt waters of Barnegat for the first time while visiting with her Aunt Eleanor. Her brother Lew taught her to jump off the dock while holding her nose and hollering "Kick, Kick, Kick!" thus, after a fashion, teaching her to swim. She was confirmed 'water-rat' for the rest of her life." She remembered the river, boats, and hot sunshine, but most painfully falling over a rowboat on the beach and jamming the horn of an oarlock into her little undeveloped breast. Fifty-five-year-old Uncle Arthur rowed all the way from Ocean Gate to Toms River village and back after securing a liniment from the apothecary to ease the painful bruising; so much for easing the healing of her father's loss.

She would return to the Jersey Shore, to Manasquan, as a pretty, single, and almost 21-year-old girl in 1932, where she would meet....

*   *   *

My father Henry Stanley Mountford was born in 1906 to Thomas Alfred, Jr., and Paulina Amelia (Hicks) Mountford, in Newark, New Jersey. An error on his birth certificate transposed his first and middle names, and since they intended to call him "Stan" anyhow, the family and he maintained the order "H. Stanley" in his signature thereafter.

The first Mountford ancestor traced by my Kentucky cousin Mark Watkins was from Lady Wood, Birmingham, in Warwick County and at the industrial heart of mid-18th century England. The men were machinists, the earliest working in the brass industry and their residence was on Brass House Passage. Other family members would transfer their skills to steel. Great, great grandfather George Mountford's profession was listed as an Engineer on the birth record of his thirteenth child, Thomas, born March 30, 1842.[11] It is assuredly in the genes because all five subsequent generations exhibited unusual mechanical skill and ingenuity working with steel and subsequently precious metals. Those genes have become a little diluted in my case! George was a convivial soul, and it is said that he had a sign outside his business stating that if he was needed, he could be found in a nearby pub.

George's son, the first Thomas Alfred Mountford, sired my grandfather Thomas Alfred Mountford, Jr. The latter claimed to us that the family could be traced back to French nobleman and Albigensian Crusader Simon de Montfort and his son Simon de Montfort, 6th Earl of Leicester (1208-1265). The father had the dubious distinction of leading the brutal Albigensian Crusade against the perceived heresy of the Cathars in Southern France (they espoused, for example, certain equal rights for women). He was killed by a stone thrown, appropriately, by some desperate and resourceful women operating a mangonel (catapult) from the battlements of Toulouse.[12] His son, the English Earl *de facto,* ruled England for about a year, but fell trying to storm Evesham after which angry Royalist opponents dismembered his body.

We modern Mountfords have always suspected that if we had any such heritage, the de Montfort coat of arms (a red lion rampant on a field of white)[13] came down to us *bar sinister*, the heraldic shorthand for bastardy! Subsequent generations, to our knowledge, were all a gentler sort of people following more mundane pursuits, though some died in service to England in various 19th century wars.

The first Thomas Alfred Mountford was thirteenth child in line for any inheritance, himself with three children by his beloved wife Emily. Being that far from the inheriting son, Thomas was certainly left to his own devices. He was thus tempted, when in the 1868, the Canadian Province of Ontario sought to draw settlers to what was then stony, long-wintered, trackless, heavily timbered territory used seasonally by Iroquois tribal bands, who travelled the water-laced Muskoka Lakes District in birch-bark canoes. Family tradition said there were more Native Americans—well, native Canadians!— around than English settlers at the time.

Through the Free Land Grant and Homestead Act,[15] crown land policy ceded at least 100 acres to any man reaching age 18, or 200 acres to any family man who would agree to settle in Ontario. At age 33, Tom Mountford had made two exploratory trips to America before deciding to bring his family across, making the jump to take advantage of the appealing land grant.

In 1876, the Mountfords took passage on Allan Line's sail-steam barque *Circassian* arriving in Bracebridge Ontario via a circuitous route involving rail from Toronto, then on wood-burning lake steamers through the Muskoka Lakes chain, and finally aboard an Indian barge poled to their debarkation site in the frontier outpost at Port Carling.

It was said by grandson Franklin Mountford in 1989 that they camped overnight while their goods were left on the barge. In the morning, they found that the barge had sunk, partially submerging much of their goods, including a melodeon (likely Emily's attempt to hang onto civilization!). The melodeon survived and was later used in the local church. An old steel engraving of Moses survives marked with the waterline from that sinking over 140 years ago: an eerie premonition of a later generation's family disaster in the 21st century.[16] The engraving was of Noah and the Ark, signed W.H. Simmons.

The Muskoka Lakes District is a chain of lovely—and cold—water bodies carved 12,000 years ago by the great North American ice-sheet. Interior lakes abounded throughout the region. The Mountfords had been granted a couple of hundred acres bordering 250-acre Brandy Lake, so called for the color of its waters, tinged with humic substances leached from the surrounding mostly pine forests. They were fortunate that part of the land included several acres of level bottomland, which had good sunlight and would be easily tilled because it was level. No family legends survive that spoke of the terribly difficult job of clearing rocky land by men who were not born farmers. Some

FIGURE 7-5. *(Top)* Thomas Alfred Mountford, wife Emily (nee Antrebus), and offspring Sid, Charlie, and Tom, Jr., in England, obviously anticipating a bucolic life on their future Canadian farmstead. *Undated Mountford family*

(Bottom) Simon VI de Montfort, dismembered by Royalists on the field at Evesham, 1265 AD.[14]

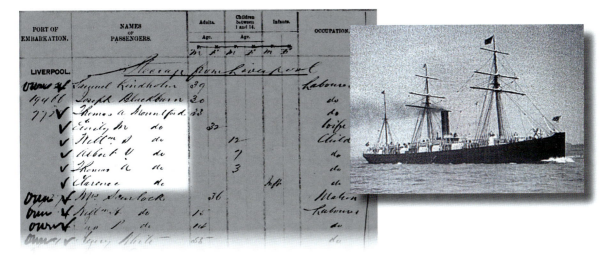

FIGURE 7-6. *(Left)* Detail of Circassian's passenger list detailing Tom, Emily, and their four children. *(Right)* The Allan Line's steam barque *Circassian* bore Tom Mountford's clan to the Canadian Provinces. *Images courtesy of Mark Watkins*

remember that the men and boys would stick to the shady side of the field when plowing under hot Canadian summer sun.

There may have already been a cabin on the parcel; one is shown on the section of Watt County's map outlining Tom's land and two more dwellings on adjacent parcels. One of the conditions of the grant required a habitable dwelling within a certain amount of time. All they had to do then was "farm the rocks" (as many settlers were cavalierly instructed), and the land would be titled to them in perpetuity by the Provincial Government.

Tom, Jr., was three years old when they left Liverpool on the *Circassian*. Shortly after the family took up their land, the toddler rolled off one of the massive glacier-shaped, bedrock outcrops bordering the lake shoreline. He certainly would have drowned, but he was saved by one of the native Algonquian or Huron Indians. Perhaps that's where the Mountford's deep attraction for the water began! These native people were friendly to the settlers and named one of my grandmother's sisters "Wenona" by which she went all her life.

As young men, Thomas Jr. and his brother Charlie moved to Ottawa to better employ their mechanical talents. They lived in a rooming house next door to the Hicks family, who had two daughters—Paulina Amelia and Wilhelmina. The boys fell in love with these sisters, but decided to immigrate to the United States to find more lucrative work so they could support future wives.

FIGURE 7-7. *(Left)* Tom Mountford's land grant on Brandy Lake, shown at the corner of Watt County, Ontario, in the 1870s. *Image Mark Watkins.*

(Right) The rock from which, legend has it, 3-year-old Thomas Mountford, Jr., fell before being saved by a passing Native American. *Kent Mountford photograph*

FIGURE 7-8. As an adult, Paulina (Hicks) Mountford returned to visit the Canadian log cabin of her birth during the 1920s. By then she and Tom had built their own home in Newark, New Jersey, and he was foreman and partner at Blanchard & Company in New York City.

Tom Sr. and Emily eventually moved to Toronto where they died many years later. Mark Watkins, our family historical researcher, thinks the Mountfords had full title to the land in Muskoka by that time and kept it as an investment. One wishes it were still in family hands; Brandy Lake is today ringed with high-end summer and retirement homes worth well into six figures. On Tom Mountford's parcel, local business people Joe and Marina Baker had just finished a large, upscale home in 2012. They looked askance at my wife and I when we came calling that summer, with our tales of a royal land grant to us encompassing their brand new house!

A third brother, Sidney, lived in Newark, New Jersey, and worked for Krementz, a precious metals fabricator and makers of then widely marketed Lohengrin wedding rings. Sidney got Tom Jr. a job with the firm as tool-maker, where he advanced to foreman of the tool room and invented the "V" click necklace clasp.[17] Krementz was not interested in this line of business and sold the idea to a competitor.

Tom Jr. and Charlie separately returned to Canada and married the sisters; Tom doing so at Paulina's home in Ottawa. Both Tom and Paulina lived and worked in the U.S. the rest of their lives, but they remained Commonwealth citizens; subjects of the British Crown until their deaths!

Tom next joined Blanchard & Co. in New York City. Schooling on the far-flung Canadian frontier had been sketchy, and Tom never learned to properly read or write. His skills were such that, despite this shortcoming, he eventually advanced to Shop Superintendent and was made a partner in the firm. In 1911–12, he and Paulina built a new family home for themselves in Newark, New Jersey (which still stands).

FIGURE 7-9. Tom and Paulina Mountford at their Newark, New Jersey, home.

Mountford family photograph

Tom's other siblings were similarly inventive and a search reveals a number of Mountford Canadian Patents, including one stamping mill product for the popular "D" handle shovel, which one can still buy today. There's no evidence this patent was carried to the U.S. market.

Tom and 'Lina, as she was called, had four sons—Sidney, George, Stan, Franklin—and a daughter Pauline. In the early to mid-1920s, they rented and later purchased (for a then pricey $4500) a New Jersey oceanfront cottage with the Manasquan Inlet and River just to the south.

They had just settled in for a couple of years when the Intracoastal Waterway canal from the Manasquan River to Bay Head was dug and Federal money stabilized Squan Inlet, assuring rapid growth and escalating values in what had been a backwater community.

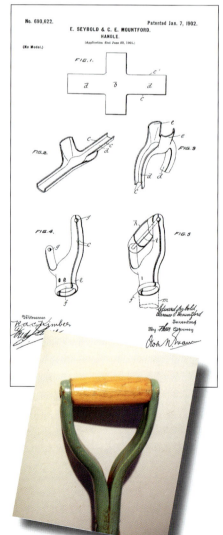

FIGURE 7-10. Edward Seybold and Clarence Mountford's Canadian shovel handle patent, 1902 . . . and an example of a similar finished product, which the author owns.

Kent Mountford photographs

FIGURE 7-11. *(Left)* The first four Mountford children Pauline, George, Sid, and Stanley about 1904. *(Right)* Stan Mountford in the 1920s whose looks were compared with Rudy Vallee, a contemporary heart-throb singer. Stan sang and played the coronet, a small trumpet-style instrument.

Mountford family photographs

FIGURE 7-12. The Mountfords' family home in Florham Park, New Jersey.
Oil, A.A. Heyder, 1934, Mountford collection

Just before the Great Depression, and when sons Sid and George were off from home and working, Tom and 'Lina bought a substantial hilltop estate of a dozen acres[18] in Florham Park, New Jersey (eventually surrounded and its lovely views protected by the golf links of Braidburn Country Club). As a child, I remember counting all the little rooms and alcoves in this mid 19th-century Victorian home, coming up with a total of 21, including the attic servants' quarters.

The oldest son Sid, then aged 29, had been a successful investor, weighted heavily in IBM stock on the advice of his mentor a Mr. Wordley, whom none of us ever met. In 1929, Sid was photographed driving an Auburn boat-tailed speedster. Sid literally "saved the farm" during the Depression by meeting mortgages or expenses when needed. Blanchard, out-voting their partner Tom, folded and went out of business during the crash.

Seeking a way around the Depression slump, the Mountfords began manufacturing wooden-cased electric clocks when these were still a novelty. If there was a power failure, however, you had to manually re-start them by spinning the setting knob clockwise to give the motor momentum. If you spun them in the wrong direction, they would run backwards as well as forward! These Mountford Electric Clocks were not a resounding success, but the small company that morphed out of this, Mountford Manufacturing, continued producing Tom's necklace clasps, the rights to which had been repurchased, in many different designs, which were now covered by a U.S. Patent. Overwhelming the competition, the firm was viable for over 40 years and was finally sold out to another company as the principals reached retirement age.

FIGURE 7-13. The beachfront cottage at Manasquan as it appeared looking westward in a 1971 pencil sketch by the author and in his photo looking seaward in 2006.

Two of the brothers, George and Frank, went on to join IBM Corporation in its early phases. George was a rigorous and upright sales manager and his employees, regardless where they were at day's end, were required to return to the office and log out before going home. A former IBMer, Peter Herrington, recalls, tactfully, that George was a stickler about this stolid, but impractical rule.[19] The youngest brother, Frank, had a significant role in development of the electric and Selectric® ("golf-ball") typewriters, which preceded the computer as a major innovation jumpstarting American office practice.

Throughout the years, thanks to father Tom's forethought and Sid's financial help, the whole family had the Manasquan Beach cottage as a seasonal refuge.[20] The Mountford boys made leeboards and created a sailing canoe for themselves to explore the adjacent river.

Families like the Pearces, who owned a boatyard by the railroad drawbridge, and the Baileys, who owned an entertainment pavilion up Manasquan Beach, built, raced, and sometimes rented boats on the Manasquan River. Sid, George, and Stan, dating some local girls, also rented these catboats, developing a taste for the convenient rig.

* * *

At the end of the 1920s, my mom and dad met on the beach and 'spooned' watching moonrise from the sand dunes directly out from the family cottage. At that time the inlet, not yet stabilized, had been opening and closing with sandbars and moving about since the mid-nineteenth century. Periodically, it ran northwards in front of the cottage location and parallel to the coast, with the sea separated by an ephemeral sand peninsula eastward of the channel. My mother recalled that as a girl her older brother warned her not to walk across to Point Pleasant, which was sometimes possible at low tide, because a small person could be trapped or swept away by rushing tidal currents.

Silent Maid crewperson Gillie (Evelyn) Ogden, who also grew up at Manasquan, said that her family used to walk across the inlet bar at low tide to Point Pleasant, simply out of boredom during an influenza epidemic of the early 20th century, when people were literally quarantined in their villages and enjoined against any significant travel.[21]

In 1931, after extensive local lobbying and the input of Federal funds, the inlet was finally opened and stabilized by the Army Corps of Engineers, with significant effects on the local economy and, unexpectedly, on the ecology of upper Barnegat Bay. Once freshwater, the region around Bay Head was now inundated twice daily with seawater from nearby Manasquan Inlet.

When Dottie Gordon met Stan Mountford, she was a commuter from North Plainfield to New York City where she worked as a typist for a railroad industry trunk line company. Her minimum-budget lunches were from the innovative and once famous automat vending outlet of Horn and Hardart. She always

FIGURE 7-15. Dottie Gordon and Stan Mountford, Manasquan Beach, pre-1933. Unisex bathing suits in those days!

Mountford family photograph

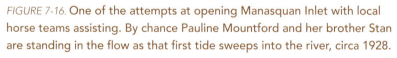

FIGURE 7-16. One of the attempts at opening Manasquan Inlet with local horse teams assisting. By chance Pauline Mountford and her brother Stan are standing in the flow as that first tide sweeps into the river, circa 1928.

Photo from John Wooley, Esq.

looked forward to Wednesdays when the machines dispensed split pea soup with noodles, and she was addicted to their legendary good coffee.

More than two decades later, that percolator-brewed coffee was a daily mainstay from the Primus stove aboard *Silent Maid*. The split pea soup must have a genetic component, because I now make my own version in big gallon-sized batches because of which my wife Nancy calls me the "Soupmeister,"[22] though she much prefers it without the noodles!

Dot and Stan Mountford married in 1933 when Dad was making something like $15 a week. Tight budgets in those days did not stop conventional men from wanting their wives to stop working so they could "support them as was proper." Dot was thus expected to quit her job in New York City. This meant tough going when, surprise, in November 1937 Dot became pregnant—her first and only time—with me! Born in July 1938, I was just a year old when I spent my first summer at Manasquan in 1939. One of my dimmest first memories of the shore was about three years later during World War II when we had nighttime blackouts and heard the 'whump' of what were presumed to be antisubmarine depth-charges offshore.

During the war Dad worked desperately long hours as a precision tool and die maker for Weston Instruments, making aircraft instruments that kept him stateside during that terrible conflict. My memories of that time were being awakened from sleep in the dark so my father could actually see that he had a living, growing child. Uncle Frank, the typewriter engineer, wanting to enlist, was called in by his boss at IBM and told: "You're not going to enlist [just think of] the typewriter as another kind of machine-gun." He was sworn to wartime secrecy and thereafter worked on a military code typewriter.[23]

When the War ended, Sid proposed that Dad join him as a silent partner in Mountford Manufacturing, then bustling along short-handed and in need of the creativity and ingenuity my father possessed. Would he stay and rise at Weston in the post-war years or stop working for someone else and take his chances in the free market?

Scion of a staunch Republican family, he chose the free-enterprise route and his skills opened new design and manufacturing opportunities for the little company, then employing about a dozen. My mom eventually provided services as payroll clerk and bookkeeper.

FIGURE 7-18. *(Top)* Kent Mountford at age 2 in 1940 at Surprise Lake, New Jersey, with a cocktail and his first sailboat. *(Bottom)* In 1943 with David and Steven Graham, he launches one he built himself.
Stan Mountford photographs

FIGURE 7-17. Mountford Manufacturing Company was a major supplier of pierced sterling silver and gold jeweler's findings to the cultured pearl and costume jewelry industry. Two of Stan Mountford's designs are shown.
Kent Mountford photograph

While at the Manasquan Beach cottage each summer during the late 1940s my Uncle Sid would hire an evening charter of Captain Rick Yaeger's *Duchess III*, one of the Brielle offshore fishing boats. This event probably cost Uncle Sid $75[24] a tidy sum and something of a gift to his siblings and family members. A ride like this about 1946 or 1947 through the Point Pleasant–Bay Head Canal was my first experience on Barnegat Bay. My cousin Judy and I, riding in the bow cockpit of the *Duchess,* were so excited we thought we were getting seasick. Captain Rick smiled and asked me if I wanted a sandwich? "Sure!" I responded, and he said, "…then you're not getting seasick." I've come close in awful conditions at sea, but Rick was right, and I've never been seasick since.

Duchess III had obviously been repurposed for her offshore fishing trade. That forward cockpit would have meant foundering in a plunging head sea. But it was amazing for us two kids. You walked through the forward sleeping cabin and opened these two little glass windowed doors (imagine the ventilation they'd give anchored out on a hot night head to wind?) and stepped into the small cockpit forward. For me it was almost neck high, but we were safe, like puppies sniffing out a car window, salt air in our faces as we forged towards the horizon.

Duchess III was one of the large numbers of post-World War II charter boats operating out of Brielle. This was before the advent of fiberglass fishing poles, and *Duchess III* had tall bamboo outriggers that spread lines, lures, and baits far out to either side of the trolling boat. The fishing lines were clipped (like with clothespins) so that when a hit occurred, they released and the fishermen with their poles and fighting chairs would immediately take over playing their quarry.

We ran up the Manasquan River and through the Bay Head-Point Pleasant Canal. In Bay Head Harbor at some point we passed unaware within yards of the Blake

FIGURE 7-19. *Duchess III* heads east through the Bay Head Canal after her foray into Barnegat Bay. The immigrants are (*l to r*) Aunt "Min" (Wilhelmina) Mountford, Dottie and Stan Mountford, their skinny little kid Kent, Pauline, Judy Leeds, (Grandma) Paulina Mountford, and Chick Leeds. ("Min" was Grandma's sister.)

Mountford family photograph by Sid Mountford

Chandlee family's sailing yacht *Silent Maid*! Captain Yaeger intended to take us through Mantoloking Bridge and down Barnegat Bay for my first time on this interesting body of water. It was only a couple of minutes work to lower those outriggers to avoid opening the entire drawbridge. But Captain Rick just blew for an opening—let the bridge tender do the work. No response, more blowing, tempers flared. The bridge operator, gesticulating, said there'd been a power failure, and he could not open the bridge. "Wouldn't open for no God damned bamboo stickers, anyhow!" he hollered. Well, so much for the tender ears of Judy and me standing in that forward cockpit. Today I would wholly agree with the bridge tender, but that evening we navigated back to Brielle our Barnegat Dreams unrealized.

Dad thought (how wisely!) that I should have the experience of a sailboat and not be suckered in by the ease of starting a motor and driving off with no understanding of how the sea, wind, and wood actually worked together. Down near Seaside, where the auto bridge crossed over from Toms River, some guy rented out a bunch of dilapidated old "G" Sloops, jib headed knock-about sloops some 18 feet long. Dad and I rented one of these on a clear morning in the first week of July probably in 1949 when I was an easily bored 11-year-old. I dimly remember that it cost us $7.50 for the anticipated half day.

I was excited, expecting to zoom along at some rakish angle of heel among the shallow thoroughfares, marshy islands and peninsulas that then anastomosed the eastern shore of Barnegat Bay. We started with a light northerly breeze, beating up those narrow channels a few miles from our start. I learned that sailing required thought, planning, and patience.

This light northerly, of course, died away and left us slatting in the calm and heat, a long way from where we'd started. "Don't worry, son, the wind will come back" Dad advised me, but by then I was bored. Nothing was happening. Biting flies may have been involved.

Those old boats were dirty; a moldy piece of manila line lay in the wet bilge with a rusty little iron kedge anchor bent to it. No life jackets were on board, and the effluvia of blown grass from ashore and droppings gave evidence that seagulls had roosted on this boat when she was lying by unused. The sails were grey and misshapen. In the bilge was a cheek block caked solid with green paint. It had likely carried the centerboard pennant before being frozen up and immobilized.

Eventually a light air slid in from the northeast. It almost always does, and I remember the sharp coolness of it on my hot little body. The old bucket began moving again, now enabling a broad reach through the grassy shallows and our speed increased along with the building sea breeze. We sailed back south, a little later than we had expected, but this was a shoestring operation with marginal boats and the guy was likely just happy to have one of them rented out.

I ended up with that block in my pocket, and at home cleaned it and shined the brass lovingly with Noxon™ polish until it shone brighter than it ever had since casting. I still have this souvenir of my first time on a sailboat 65 years ago and suppose I still owe that guy's heirs a dollar, which was what new 'Number-0 Bronze cheek blocks' cost at the time.[26]

The sailing bug had infected the current Mountford generation and was spreading. My uncle Chick Leeds and Sid encouraged each other to buy a boat and together, for $1500, they purchased a boxy little catboat named *Osprey*, which was

FIGURE 7-20. A portion of the wonderful Bronson Map of Barnegat Bay, lifelong project of Addison Woolsey Bronson (1869–1947)[25] showing where Stan and Kent Mountford sailed in 1949–50, before significant development along the Bay Shore.

Courtesy of Bob O'Brien, New Jersey Museum of Boating

FIGURE 7-21. *(Left)* Chick (Clarence Meredith) Leeds. *(Center)* The boxy little catboat *Osprey*, Chick Leeds and his brother-in-law Sid Mountford co-owned about 1950. My cousins Judy Leeds, Tommy Mountford, and I are aboard at Johnson's Boatyard, Bay Head.[27]

Stan Mountford photograph

(Right) Osprey returns to Johnson's in Bay Head after a sail with Sid hanging onto the starboard running backstay (almost all catboats had them!) Judy Leeds and the young author are in the bow.

Chick Leeds photograph, Mountford collection

FIGURE 7-22. Detail from an aerial photo of the Johnson boatyards at Bay Head, adjacent the mouth of the Point Pleasant Bay Head Canal (left). *Osprey*'s slip was among two dozen along the sand road with informal parking adjacent.

Courtesy of the New Jersey Museum of Boating

docked at one of the three Johnson Boatyards in Bay Head. She was 21 feet and unusual in having a carvel planked hard-chined hull.[28] Not much of a sailer in the broad scheme of things, but her catboat rig and generous beam assured stability, an open cabin, two settee berths, drop leaf tables on either side of the centerboard trunk, and a large cockpit for a boat her size.

There were no marinas for common folk in those days, just little rickety plank cat-walks and some light cedar sapling stakes driven in to tie the boats head-in to the quay in some order. Mostly, there was no electric power, fresh water, or security, and certainly no showers or toilets. The rental slips we had access to, going for maybe $37 a season,[29] were tucked off to one side of the Morton Johnson yard's eastern side. The rest of the yard was occupied with large storage and building sheds, where a stream of repair work and new wooden yachts maintained the yard's cash flow.

Osprey's slip was also just a few yards from the Bay Head-Manasquan Canal, separated only by the bulkhead and a landfill road along which we parked, reaching the boat through a screen of tall *Phragmites* reed grass.[30]

The three Johnson boatyards, all independent yet often interdependent, were shown on Henry Horrock's whimsical map of Barnegat Bay in 1938 by labeling that part of Bay Head tongue-in-cheek "Johnsonville." Nearest the Canal was Johnson Brothers; central and abutting the gut where *Osprey* moored was Morton Johnson's or "Mort's;" and on the far, or eastern side of that, across a little canal with a mostly inconvenient small drawbridge was Hubert Johnson's, a son of Morton. Hubert's daughter was married to a crew-cut guy named Grant Bauer, who figures in our family boating life some few years on.

This bridge was closed during the workday so foot traffic between the yards need only be interrupted when boats were moved in and out of the dredged basin behind it. It was kept open after hours though and, if your car or boat was on the wrong side, it was a long walk or a significant drive around, should you be caught.

Osprey's Gray Marine engine assured a sprightly turn of speed under power and made possible regular runs out Manasquan Inlet, when the tides were favoring; these were my first times at sea. My dad would often get seasick on these runs and I (with my cast iron equilibrium, who never felt a twinge) was very concerned for him retching violently over the rail, but my unsympathetic uncles just laughed.

I recall one day an immense glassy sea running 6 feet or more with a 10 or 11 second period. It was sunny, but with a high, thin cirrus web giving a slightly grey look to sky and sea. I later learned that this was

FIGURE 7-23. A loggerhead sea-turtle (*Caretta caretta*) about the size of the one I saw those many years ago.
Kent Mountford photograph, Marine Resources Center, Bogue Banks, NC

the sea and sky telegraphing us a warning on the approach of some distant gale. As we motored many miles offshore, I sat in the bow, legs astride the forestay. The water grew bluer and clearer than I'd ever seen and suddenly beneath me, coursing obliquely across our bow and headed further to sea on some mission, came a young strongly swimming loggerhead turtle. I was stunned and moved, never having seen such a creature. I never forgot that experience.

FIGURE 7-24. Sid Mountford aboard *Osprey* in her slip, with the *Phragmites* behind, September 1953.
Mountford family photograph

Back at the Manasquan cottage and at high tide that night, the surf boomed heavily in characteristic long tempo and the swash hissed far up the beach. We were in for several days of lousy weather. We called them nor'easters then, but they were often near-misses by far more serious storms that today would have us glued to the Weather Channel with concern.

*   *   *

From the end of the 1940s into the mid-1950s, the working boatyards at Bay Head were still a wonderful place to learn about wooden boats. It would be a few years before fiberglass would contest this tradition of shipbuilding.[31] Real craftsmanship and the apprentice system were still strong, and it would have done me good, and likely changed my life, if my parents had nudged me into such a summer job for a few years! While the end of widespread wooden boat building appeared to come within the next two decades, the discipline would have been wonderful for me and would have lent realism to my naive, hard-pursued, but never-realized, aspirations to be a naval architect and yacht designer.

The scrap piles from these yards yielded long strips of mahogany trimmings, clear grained white oak flitches, and stout plank ends that would supply any youngster with wonderful wood for innumerable projects. I remember showing a piece of mahogany I'd varnished to one of the old shipwrights and he snorted at the finish I'd achieved, saying, "When I was apprenticed, the boss would come round when you were done hand finish sanding and if he didn't like it, he'd whack it with a hammer and you'd spend hours working it down flush with a sanding block to get the dent out before he'd even look at it again. You sanded the whole piece true and flat, not just where the dent was!"

The far corners of the three Johnson yards were salted with old wooden boats in varying states of disrepair or decay—maybe awaiting someone with the skills to restore them after a few hundred dollars had changed hands. Maybe awaiting a tractor that

FIGURE 7-25. The young author pumps out *La Boheme*, his first small cruising sloop kept at Beaton's Boatyard in 1963. Bought for $750 from brothers John and Dayton Trubee at Bay Head, this modified 1940s (Abaco) Bahamas dinghy may have looked great, but she sometimes had trouble floating.

Stan Mountford photographs

would haul them to the edge of some marsh, dump soil over them, and encroach the boatyard's limits a little farther into the bay or salt hay wetland.

I remember looking at a graceful old deep-keeled Nat Herreschoff sloop with laid decks, every seam and the kingplank wide agape, for which the yard wanted $700 or $800. That was top dollar at the time and far beyond my woodworking skills to save. There would be a lot of other wooden boats that I would resurrect in the future: I could make them look pretty good eventually, but—as Lachlan Beaton once joshed me—there was no guarantee that they would actually float!

The whole place was nonetheless redolent with the scent of fresh sawn mahogany, oak, Jersey white cedar, and the rigging shed smelt of tung oil varnish and tarred marline. The lofts were hung with dusty old spars, most with their manila halyards, wooden blocks, cast bronze Merriman, and Perko hardware still in place. Many rigs, with their boats beyond repair—or outright gone—would never see sunlight or feel wind again. Over the years, from broken booms, masts, and rotted hull fragments, I salvaged enough blocks, cleats, sail track, and fittings to rig more than one of my own little sailboats. Ingenuity replaced the dollar investments wealthier families could make in the nautical futures of their more fortunate kids.

The hardware, in those days, was simply not valuable enough to be rigorously removed by the yard workers. You could buy a small boat bronze bullet-block from the ship chandleries on Chamber's Street in New York City for less than 70 cents. My friend Alan Van Winkle found a lovely lapstrake Lawley pulling boat (tender to some yacht long gone) and bought her, along with a perfectly functional little outboard of a couple horsepower from one of the yardmen for $10.[32]

One winter I found an old Seabright surf-skiff weathered grey and simply tossed on Beaton's Boatyard scrap heap. She had the traditional box keel and had been built by Willard H. Jeralamon at Galilee on the Jersey Shore. She had light cedar planking, still tightly copper riveted, springy sheer, and flaring topsides. I somehow got her back to the family garage at Manasquan with the hope of restoring her and planned to name her after a young girl I was dating at the time.

FIGURE 7-26. Alan Van Winkle paid $10 for this boat and motor in Bay Head about 1962. He lives on Maryland's Eastern Shore at this writing and (after many repairs over more than 50 years) still owns this lovely skiff.

Not excluding the girl, an enthusiastic companion, there were many things occupying my time. Before the project could get very far, winter had passed and my Uncle Sid told me to get the boat out of the garage so he could park his car there come spring. Sid, oldest of four brothers and a sister, always got to park his car in the garage. With a VW bug as my vehicle, I had no way of moving the boat entire, and she fell to the handsaw—cut into three pieces for the spring garbage pickup. Her bow was so pretty that our neighbor, Tom "Doc" Talon, dragged it off to where it sat for years propped up on the sand in front of his beach cottage. His comely daughters would sit in its lee, working on their nearly all-over tans and enabling them on chilly spring and fall days to shelter from the brisk sea-wind. You could call this loss the destruction of a real treasure, a fate that today I, and most maritime historians, would never permit.

At Morton Johnson's, my Uncle Chick Leeds probably enjoyed his time at the dock as much as sailing. Chick was not a confident single hander, and he was always more comfortable "taking out a party," which meant he would cajole someone to join him to handle lines, fend off, or nurse *Osprey*'s occasionally temperamental gas engine. He would more likely spend the windy afternoons sanding and varnishing cockpit coaming caps, the tiller, a handrail, or just slipping below to take a nap on one of the lumpy and musty old mattresses. He might have been trying to get away from a nagging wife, my Aunt, and their demanding daughter Judy. Spending his time on *Osprey* was the search for a 'silent maid' of his own! Chick still had an elegant sense of boating and taught me some of the ethics, pride, and attention to detail necessary for working around the water that I have carried with me six decades farther on.

FIGURE 7-27. The catboat *Osprey* sailing up the Metedeconk River with me as nearly clueless first mate, September 1952.

Chick Leeds photograph

*   *   *

My dad had sailed with Sid and Chick for a couple of years on *Osprey,* but he was never *in command,* a position for which Sid and Chick subtly vied. Dad was a good mechanic and had a good sense for sailing and running a boat—this likely frustrated him.

So, my dad began looking for a boat of his own. One afternoon, Chick, in one of his visits to the yard, heard about a catboat for sale, over at the Bay Head Yacht Club. My dad drove over to look at the *Silent Maid*, for sale through Grant Bauer, the local broker on behalf of Mr. James "Jimmy" Kellogg. Bauer worked for Hubert Johnson as Sales Manager. (He was the one who'd married Hubert's daughter, but was himself a scion of another part of the Johnson clans round Bay Head.[33] Such was the closeness in that community.)

We knew only dimly at that point that *Silent Maid* had been designed by naval architect Francis Sweisguth for Edwin Schoettle, a Philadelphia businessman. Schoettle had a complex history with big catboats on Barnegat Bay, and Sweisguth had designed other boats for him. *Silent Maid* was to top the list and claimed to be (variously) 33 or 34 feet on deck, 28 feet, 6 inches on the waterline, 12 feet, 6 inches beam, and draft of 32 inches. She spread, Grant told us, 950 square feet in her huge main. It was not clear to us why Schoettle wanted such a big catboat, but one benefit was that she would make a roomy family cruiser, with almost 6 feet of headroom under the coach roof.

Schoettle had contracted with Morton Johnson's Boatyard to build the *Maid,* and it was just several hundred feet from her birthplace that my family found her for sale.

FIGURE 7-28. *(Left)* *Silent Maid* pretty much as we found her in late summer of 1953. Our unsupervised trial sail aboard her would be quite an adventure, but confirmed a lifestyle that would reshape our small world.

Stan Mountford photograph

(Right) *Silent Maid*'s original canvas decks were done in gray-green paint, and were blazing hot for bare feet in the midsummer sun.

Kent Mountford photograph

Dad told Grant that he was interested in this big boat and would like to make an offer for her. However, he really needed to take her for a sail before committing to owning her. The *Osprey* we'd sailed for a few summers was a much smaller catboat. We didn't then know that everything about boats changes with the cube of the length. Grant Bauer, the broker, likely thought: "21 feet . . . well the 'A' cats are 28 and they're bears to sail, these guys oughta know their way around . . ." James Kellogg, apparently, was amenable, and we had no idea that this benevolent man was quietly in the business of passing great boats on to future generations.

So, my father, mother, Sid, maybe one other uncle, and I went over to the Bay Head Yacht Club near noon one late summer day and piled aboard. Grant Bauer sort of pushed us out of the slip as *Silent Maid*'s Gray Marine "Seascout" four-cylinder gas engine struggled with its little offset propeller, trying to move this big boat straight backwards in a rising breeze.

FIGURE 7-29. *Silent Maid* goes into reverse and makes sternway, as always sluggishly backing out of a slip with Sid, Stan, and a watchful Dottie Mountford aboard.

Kent Mountford photograph

The boat, to my wondering eyes, was huge. I could walk completely around her decks like I was on a neighborhood path. The cockpit was four times the size of *Osprey*'s and the cabin seemed as big as the living room at our family beach cottage. What a wonderful feeling of power, spaciousness, and command the *Maid* gave when one stood at her varnished, holly-inlaid helm. Her wake slid out smoothly from under that broad transom, and it seemed as if we were aboard the biggest, grandest thing on all of Barnegat Bay. We were completely hooked, beaming with smiles—wholly unaware what we were getting into for the first time!

We motored south a couple of miles, found the old galvanized fog horn and blew, three times, for an opening at the Mantoloking Bridge. Up she went in a couple minutes. The irony was not wasted on me, because I still remembered having to turn round in *Duchess III* six years earlier. My dad and uncle, accustomed to tiller steering, were getting the hang of how she handled with the wheel. Despite a massive rudder and worm steering gear, her offset propeller made turning to port sluggish, but it was much easier to turn starboard.

Once clear of Swan Point, Barnegat Bay opens significantly and it was time to hoist the *Maid*'s massive gaff mainsail. The boom was 36 feet long and the gaff 27 feet, with seven-parts of hoisting tackle between throat and peak halyards. The heavy canvas main, we later learned, weighed at least 137 pounds by itself, bone dry.

The wind, not surprisingly on Barnegat Bay in summer, was rising from the SSE, and what by early afternoon might be a faint breeze at Bay Head, was a stiffening weight of wind below Swan Point. Hoisting was a significant piece of work. We found that a man forward could gather the falls of peak and throat together in his hands and haul, lifting both ends of the gaff together. Two more people in the cockpit would pull the lines in tandem through deck blocks and across the coach roof to cleats on the aft side of the cabin trunk where they would be belayed. A huge pile of line accumulated on the cockpit sole and atop the engine box. There was a little single action bronze winch atop the trunk to sweat up the last of the peak halyard. After several tries, we learned that the hoist had to be planned to keep the gaff relatively parallel to the boom when going up, until the throat was chock-a-block and it was time to run up the peak.

When we'd hoisted the *Maid*'s main, it was flogging pretty heavily. We got the boom crutch out of its socket and paid off, leaving me with a pile of halyards in the cockpit—a couple hundred feet of 7/16ths manila. I was

FIGURE 7-30. Once south of the marshy peninsula of Swan Point at Mantoloking, the bay widens significantly allowing some serious sailing before one encounters the distant bridges at Seaside.

Kent Mountford photograph

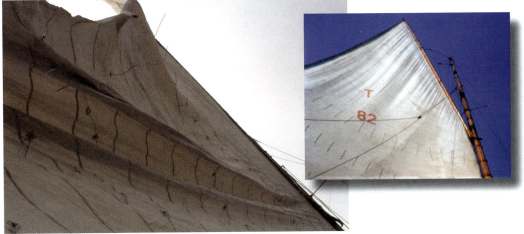

FIGURE 7-31. (Left) Silent Maid's huge main flogs as it is being hauled aloft. (Right) Silent Maid's mainsail, once hoisted, fails to show its full size using the 'normal' lenses of 1954 style cameras. This main, over a decade old, was the last one used by Edwin Schoettle before World War II and when failing health ended his sailing years.

Kent Mountford photographs

scrambling, wisely, to coil it down best as I could to run free and without hockling when it came time to strike sail. The final approach I took after a year sailing her was to Flemish the lines, coiling clockwise out, then in, and out again until the line stood in a stack, several coils deep like whalers coiled their harpoon lines to run out smoothly from a tub. Though without the tub, the line paid out flawlessly every time. I got so I could do this with both halyards in a few minutes and the stacked coils could be slid under the cockpit seats and away from foot traffic. The ease with which they ran out made it a worthwhile task.

The sail was clearly old, bearing *Silent Maid*'s original Toms River Yacht Club number T-82. With mildew and old age aside, it was without tears or significant patches and would get a workout this day! We paid off on a port tack, beating up towards what was then called Seaweed Point.

The *Maid* flew beyond anything we'd experienced under sail. Her running backstay, set on the weather rail, was bar-tight, and as she lay over her lee rail came down to the water and she snored along with the bow wave anything but silent. With a bone in her teeth, foam ran all along the lee side, and the quarter wave chased close enough that it threatened to come aboard on the starboard afterdeck.

The farther we got down bay towards Lavallette, the stronger the wind became. Based on my later long experience, it was getting up to 18 knots or so. Brilliant sunlit whitecaps struck the bow and sent a shower of spray back towards the cockpit. My dad and uncles were at the limit of their self-confidence; my mother was worried and letting them know about it. I was awed, but clueless.

We came about mid-Bay onto a starboard tack, losing much of our way, and thus steerage, so she fell off more than the helmsman had intended. We got the weather backstay tightened, but forgot to pay out the port, now lee, backstay and, of course, could not ease the boom. In this stiff breeze, the big *Maid* lay way over, eliciting rapid criticism from my mom, who was fully aware we did not own this boat. One of my uncles got the hitch off the backstay cleat, and it ran free.

I think it was my father who had the mainsheet and let it run out through his hands to take pressure off her. This could have been a serious skin removal event with a manila hemp sheet, and as it was, his palms got brush burned. (Later Dad found, on the advice of a more experienced skipper, that cotton line would neither burn the hands, nor insert manila fiber splinters into uncallused fingers. The *Maid*'s next sheet was therefore 5/8" cotton. We found cotton line was hard to come by when we tried to replace it some

FIGURE 7-32. (Top) A profile and sail plan for *Silent Maid*, which I drew for my father for Christmas in 1956. Note the two (galvanized wire) bridles Francis Sweisguth designed for the gaff, along which the throat and peak halyard blocks slid with snap-on bronze saddles. This automatically adjusted the lead of each halyard as the sail was peaked, improving angle, and reducing effort. (Bottom) An original 1924 Merriman[34] *Silent Maid* peak halyard block showing how the saddle was rigged on a wire bridle.

Kent Mountford pen-and-ink drawing and photograph

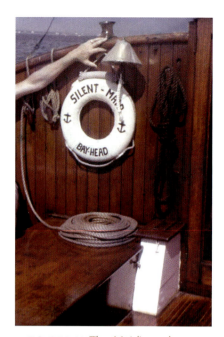

FIGURE 7-33. The *Maid*'s peak halyard flemished down atop the engine hatch in 1958. The coiled centerboard pennant of tarred manila hemp hangs above the aft end of the trunk.

Dot Mountford photograph

years in the future. Though relatively expensive, it was a wise purchase in the years before synthetics took over the entire cordage market.)

The *Maid* gathered way rapidly and, sheeted in, she headed off on the starboard tack. This was just a trial sail and we were not about to try jibing a purported 950 square feet of sail in 20 knots of wind. After getting a feel for her on this point of sailing, the men paid out the long main sheet and put her on a broad reach up Barnegat Bay towards Mantoloking. *Silent Maid* rose to hull speed with her bows nearly buried in foam and the quarter wave almost on deck, breaking almost continually on the port side. I stood at the stem-head, enthralled, looking up at her huge mast bowed forward under the press of canvas and that immense sail towering over me. I could hardly believe this might be our own boat. My future danced before me.

Another large auxiliary, the kind I used to wonder at, passed us going to windward. I suppose our combined approach velocity must have been 12 to 14 knots. Her helmsman took in the amazing sight as our own wonderful vessel swept down on him. "Whot clauss are you?" he hailed in an English accent.

Uncle Sid, beaming, hailed back, "First Class." The Englishman waved and we swept past each other. *Silent Maid* was, of course, the largest "B" Class catboat of her era, unique in her century and certainly first class in every sense of the word.

I don't remember striking sail that afternoon, but on other days to come it was quite an exercise—holding her into the wind, dragging the huge boom down onto its crutch while the main galloped, and making sure the gaff came down in an orderly fashion and all the way down. Many times we dedicated a crewperson to the task of setting the crutch and capturing the end of the heavy, active boom. Mom's sister, Aunt Mildred Du Four, often serving this role, became known as "Boom Crutch Milly" when aboard. Having this simple task done well, added orderliness to the work of striking sail in a real blow.

Two crewmembers were generally used to lower the gaff. It was heavy enough to make the trip down on its own, so long as throat and peak were eased to keep it just a bit jaws-down and relatively parallel to the boom, and the gaff saddle rubbed with a block of paraffin wax. The sail was mostly captured by the *Maid*'s generous lazy jacks, but that much canvas usually meant a big billow of sail was over the helmsman's head, and in front of him as the vessel forged forward into the wind under power. I have great respect for the *Maid*'s early owners who could get the sail down fast enough just bringing her up into the wind.

FIGURE 7-34. "Boom Crutch Millie" Dottie Mountford's sister (Mildred Gordon Du Four) standing next to her "namesake" at the *Maid*'s helm in late autumn of 1953. Her windbreaker logo is for the Municipality of Bound Brook, New Jersey, where she was tax collector!

Polaroid by Stan Mountford

There was usually a swarm of us atop the coach roof with sail stops, getting the main off to one side of the gaff, which was topped up a bit, and then furling all that sail into itself. This was intended to be a tight-rolled harbor furl in the square-rigger's sense—no 'pleating' being done in those days. The gaff was then dropped atop it all and secured with the stops, which were always led through the lacings and atop the boom. We must have done something like that the first afternoon!

Bringing the *Maid* into a slip, dead downwind for the first time was interesting. Since she didn't respond well in reverse, the *Maid* had a hard time stopping, and with the prop offset a couple feet to port, she wouldn't steer either. We likely grazed a couple of pilings coming in, but we got the spring lines on fast enough to stop her from nosing into the Yacht Club pier. There were, of course, many eyes watching surreptitiously as novices presumed to sail one of their member's flagship yachts. Grant Bauer was there politely positioned with his trademark crewcut, waiting to see if, in this now moderate gale, we'd managed to take the stick out of her.

When we got home that week, I immediately wrote in the log of my beautiful little sailing kayak *Suomi* that I would sell my boat to help Mom and Dad buy this big catboat. *Suomi* was a lovely thing, molded in Birch plywood by Stamus Boat Works, Tenela, Finland, and varnished stem to stern. I think I got a hundred bucks for this really beautiful kayak, on which I'd lavished a hundred hours of diligent work. My parents claimed it looked like the top of a grand piano. I sold the kayak to Clem Wibblesman. On a trip to Lake Hopatcong, New Jersey, he inadequately tied *Suomi* to the top of his car, and when he rounded a turn, she launched like a spear, smashing into a roadside guardrail; she was completely destroyed. She'd likely be in a museum today, if she were still extant.

The *Maid* was a classic. My hundred dollars would not have gone very far in what was for those years a major family purchase; but knowing I'd still want a boat of my own, my dad agreed the following winter to help me build an 8-foot Chris Craft pram kit.

Dad, for his part, might have gone back and forth with Grant Bauer a couple of times, but the denouement was that my family purchased *Silent Maid* for about $2800 in cash. In one fell swoop he outclassed Sid and Chick's little catboat forever. I'm not sure if the price had been eased for our benefit, or if the sellers knew something we didn't, but the price was right for our family.[35]

Thus began more than a decade in this fine vessel for our family; years of adventure and exploration in Barnegat Bay. It was curious to me that though Dad had been seasick a few times on *Osprey* and queasy at a sailing party aboard the steamer *Queen of Bermuda* while she was nearly motionless at her pier in the Hudson River, he was never sick once he skippered his own boat, even in the roughest weather.

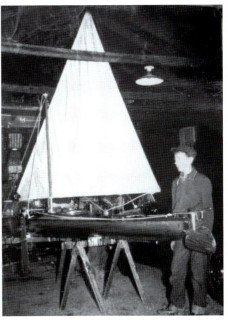

FIGURE 7-35. **The author's Finnish kayak with sailing rig, spring 1952.**
Stan Mountford Polaroid

Bob Reddington Recounts a Disturbing Event

Bob Reddington of Bay Head, who has always been interested in and has continually traded one catboat or another, said that "about 1953" (he can't really reconstruct the date, but it couldn't have been any later) he was thinking of buying the *Maid*, but changed his mind when he observed a disturbing event. He swears this is true and has repeated his story several other places and under stiff interrogation! He watched the crane at Morton Johnson's yard pick up the *Silent Maid* with Paul Johnson at the controls. Paul lost control of a slipping clutch and dropped her to the ground, a distance of about three feet, showing this measure by the spread of his arms. "'CRUNCH,'" Bob said, "then he just picked her up again and went on with his business."[36] Who knows what problems we subsequent owners had that stemmed from those few seconds.

FIGURE 7-36. *Maid* motoring south in Barnegat with my cousin Joan Du Four's head on Stan's shoulder. Kent is towed in *Poor Man's Pirate* with the hat donned daily on arising in cold weather.

Dot Mountford photograph

Dad progressed to be a good, sensible and competent skipper. He had to come a long way following his short stint with a leeboard canoe on the Manasquan River as a kid and his time on the *Osprey*. He and Mom both took the U.S. Power Squadron basic boating safety courses. By serious osmosis and application to a 1950 Chapman's[37] *Piloting, Seamanship and Small Boat Handling*, I learned the basics of boating. More young people today really should have the discipline of solid boating basics—piloting, splicing, whipping . . . and ethics—before being handed their own 30-knot PWC.

In subsequent years, Dad went on to a higher level with the United States Power Squadron and taught piloting and coastwise navigation. In September 1956, he was a charter member of the Watchung Power Squadron. I still have the old skipper's hat he wore when aboard the *Maid*. And I still wear (much repaired) the Navy surplus wool watch shirt he bought on Chambers Street in New York when that was 'chandlery row' for the maritime industry. Anchored out on a brisk November morning, much like many we had aboard the *Maid* that first autumn, that old shirt warms me with its weight as well as the memories it carries woven in its fabric. It warmed me in the Chesapeake cabin of my yawl *Nimble* as I wrote this section in 2011.

In that fall of 1953, we literally lived aboard the *Maid* for a couple to a few days every week, returning home only for work, school, or family business. Therefore, comfort aboard became very important. As the weather cooled, staying warm overnight in the *Maid*'s big, damp cabin was a challenge. This was a time when goose-down sleeping bags were not readily available nor their virtues fully appreciated. I ended up sleeping with most of my clothes on. My parents would later joke that when I got up in the morning, all I had to do was put on my sailor's hat!

The *Maid* was laid out with two "double length" bunks—one each starboard and port. They were wonderful settees capable of seating perhaps a dozen folks below on chilly days or during a rain shower. The *Maid*'s original mattresses were pretty dank. After the first autumn, Dad and I went into downtown New York, around Chambers Street to the old ship-chandlers section, where we found a small business with the pretentious name "Defender Industries"[38] started in 1938 by Shelden Lance. It was operating from an old loft, and Lance sold us new foam rubber for the bunks. Based on butcher paper patterns we'd brought, he cut them out from big sheets of four- or five-inch-thick foam with a vibrating electric kitchen knife set up on a sliding base. Similar tools are standard now, but with foam rubber being a relatively new material in the early 1950s, this Rube Goldberg tool was innovative and effective. It made a clean, square cut along any plan shape needed for a boat interior.

With the new foam rubber mattresses in place, sleeping was more comfortable, especially for my Mother who wasn't sure about all this boating stuff yet. The cabin was also less musty with the new foam replacing what had smelled like dried eelgrass from the bottom of the bay!

This natural material had, in fact, been the vegetative parts of the sea-grass *Zostera marina*. It was collected and used commercially in the early 20th century both as wall and roof insulation, mattress stuffing, and even as the padding of coffins! The 1924 catboat *Spray*, which my then-fiancé Nancy and I bought together in 1971, had just such mattresses. They were lumpy and almost as uncomfortable as the bunk boards beneath and their dampness went up and down with the surrounding humidity! We could afford nothing more at the time.

Years later I found that some people had these eel grass stuffed mattresses in their homes as well, and one older man told me his parents used to shoo him off to bed telling him it was "time to go sleep in the grasses."[39]

Aboard the *Maid*, we slept head to toe with four aboard, or when my first innocent girlfriend was aboard with my folks in close chaperone, the two of us adopted the risqué head to head configuration on "my" starboard berth—the same one I've occupied on all of my own boats for the balance of 60 years!

Despite new mattresses, the *Maid*'s cabin had the odor of old wood, a hint of tarred marline emanating from the ditty bag nearby, some old tarred hemp rope from the Kelloggs' days, and the scent of fresh varnish when we undertook our own maintenance. With all the problems our society has with mold spores and volatile hydrocarbons, I still treasure those odors as part of my youth . . . part of my life. A whiff of them today brings flooding back all those memories. A poignant example later in my life brings this home, I was at Jamestown, Virginia, with archaeologist Beverly Straube examining artifacts dug up from burial at the 400-year-old colonial fort site, and when she showed me scraps of unearthed marline, the odor took me instantly back to the *Silent Maid* of my youth.

The *Maid* had a generous hatch in the midst of her wide cabin trunk, and when this was propped up with a stick, it was a grand aid for accelerating ventilation below decks on hot nights. Had I my druthers, I would have made it 2 to 3 times as large! Also, I would have made it a skylight, so the moon and stars could be seen from one's bunk. My current yawl *Nimble* has one and it defines her cabin space when at anchor or cruising. I still look back with wonder at the *Maid*'s original cabin layout when her galley was at the forward end of the cabin. How poor Sara Schoettle must have struggled with the stove in post-Victorian clothes during a Barnegat summer!

FIGURE 7-37. The life ring, with my early lettering in black. Carolyn MacDonald and Mary Pietro MacDonald flank this work of art sitting atop the *Maid*'s engine box in July of 1954.

Stan Mountford photograph

In the *Maid*'s forepeak under a pile of old lines, I found the wreck of an old sailboat steering wheel. The brass hub and most radii were broken out, but the tarnished brass rim and hand spokes were intact. Delighted, I took it home as my first project on the boat, cutting away the broken stumps level with the rim, sanding and varnishing the wood, and polishing the brass band to brilliance. I was proud of the result. A few weeks later my parents got a phone call from the broker asking if we had found an old wheel. It had great sentimental value, and the Kelloggs wanted it back. My parents, saddened by how much work I'd lavished on the piece, simply decreed that we would return it. I always wondered from whence the wheel had come; surely from Barnegat but I've never found where. Peter Kellogg, Jimmy's son, when asked about this in 2011, had no memory of any such an artifact in his family. I would have kept it in a place of honor to this day.

*   *   *

When I was a little kid, one of my first introductions to maritime affairs was a favorite record (that is, those flat, Bakelite discs played on a turntable) with its companion book *Ahoy Matey*. You played the record with its dialog, foghorns, seagulls, and bell buoys and read along viewing the pictures. One of the icons in that book was a cork life ring (as I recall it said "Matey" on it), and with our acquisition of *Silent Maid* I thought it only right that we should have a life ring. One of my earliest proper lettering jobs was to inscribe "Silent Maid, Bay Head," with a couple of little anchors on a cork throwable ring. For the better part of 40 years, it hung on the aft face of the cabin bulkhead.

That first autumn we had the *Maid* was one we wished would never end. It was such a joy to have our way with this big, exciting landmark vessel. She had solid companionway doors, which Dad first replaced with moveable wooden louvers for ventilation, especially while Mom was cooking. Then as autumn closed in, he made wood framed

Plexiglas "storm windows" that covered the louvered slats—something which with variations I've done on most all my subsequent boats.

With both parents long dead at this writing, I still have the image of my mother, backlit by a cold November morning sun, squirting alcohol into the pre-heat pan of that old Primus kerosene stove. Once the burner was hot, the kerosene valve was opened and fuel ignited. Soon the burners became incandescent and the vaporized fuel burned with a hot blue flame, a peculiar hissing sound and unpleasant odor[40] that would soon be overwhelmed by the smell of frying bacon filling the cabin, followed by the unique carbon-and-caramelized odor of toast made on a small pierced and pyramidal sheet metal rack over the open flame. It was browned and crusted on the outside, still soft inside. It excites me just to think of tasting it again. My wife Nancy suggests this is why I burn my toast so often these days!

Those were some of the most memorable breakfasts of my life. The scents, the light, the cold feet on that cabin floor, are all indelible in my mind. I often relive them on my own boats today, but without the parents who created the warmth and love of the experience for me then, and these days I am usually aboard alone.

Dottie Mountford would usually add preparation of some one-pot, bring-aboard meals as part of her week's cooking chores. This wasn't easy in a time when freezer compartments were the size of a few ice cube trays; she, nonetheless, made sure we had at least two meals to bring with us to the shore.

Full of the excitement of this new boat in 1953, I simply had to have my best high-school friend Kenny Nilsen down for a weekend. He'd never been on a boat before and I was proud after years of yearning to be a real yachtsman and to show this good buddy how the other half lived!

FIGURE 7-38. *Silent Maid*'s galley (September 1953) with the Primus stove atop the centerboard trunk, coffee percolator in place, and a Pyrene (carbon tetrachloride) fire extinguisher left of the companionway door. Our three toothbrushes hang on the side of the dish rack over the sink. The mahogany drop-leaves are raised for a meal, set here for four with simple white Navy-style crockery, but she could seat eight for close company dining.

Stan Mountford Polaroid

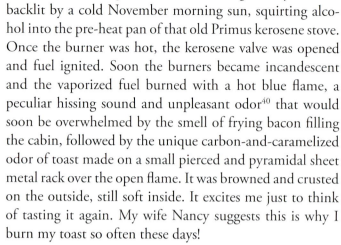

FIGURE 7-39. *(Left)* A pierced metal stove-top toaster, developed late in the 19th century, served us well at each breakfast aboard *Silent Maid*.

Kent Mountford photograph, Ocean County Historical Society

(Right) Looking through the cabin doors to the *Maid*'s expansive cockpit. At right the louvers represent my father widening the original small head compartment so ladies could change clothes in private.

Kent Mountford photograph

Another mouth to feed on short notice was hard for Mom so on Saturday night Dad took us all to Risden's Seafood Pavilion, which must have just about been ready to close for the season. It was cold, rainy, and uncomfortable aboard the *Maid* and the warm restaurant was a treat. It would have been easy to fall asleep at the table after a cold autumn day, which we'd spent outdoors, determined to make a good weekend of it.

Kenny and I felt very adult being part of this big—indeed famous—old yacht, though we were arguably the smallest, youngest looking kids in North Plainfield High School. When the meal was over the waitress came to our table, bending condescendingly over we two young sailors and presented us each with a lollipop. Each had a tag on the wooden stick which proclaimed: "I have been a good child and eaten all my dinner at Risden's Seafood Pavilion, Point Pleasant, NJ." Talk about burst balloons of hubris; we were mortified . . . but ate the lollipops anyway. I STILL have that damned tag somewhere amongst my mementos as a remedy against self-promotion.

FIGURE 7-40. The Freeman family—Bob, father Lew, Mom Jean, daughter Donna—and Dottie Mountford hunker in the cockpit against autumn chill, stretching the season as far as possible.

Stan Mountford photograph

We did not haul out that first year until far into the cold of November 1953; too long delayed as it turned out. As the *Maid* lay alongside Johnson's rigging ladder for the week, a violent coastal storm came through with very high winds and tide. The *Maid* lost her forward hatch. It was only coincidence that someone, finding it afloat among the sheds, recognized what boat it was from and returned it. Dampened bunks, from being open to the weather, was our price; secure hooks—supposedly to be religiously fastened—were the solution. Hinges would not do because clearance between coach roof and boom was too small.

That first winter we kept the boat at Morton Johnson's Boatyard in Bay Head, where she'd been built three decades before. She'd had a traditional spot in one of the big sheds, for which we paid a significant premium. Former owners had simply said "have the boat ready by Memorial Day" and paid the bills, as the boat was brought out, refitted, and launched. We faced doing all that ourselves, naively, in the big shed. I remember sanding the brightwork one Saturday preparatory for varnishing and we were told to stop by a guy named Mr. Clark on a nearby boat, a lovely Herreschoff *Rozinante*. He had already sanded and, dressed in re-purposed old business clothes complete with a Fedora felt hat, was ready to varnish; he was not going to tolerate dust from careless neighbors. We, at the time, were clueless about such a level of inflexibility. I don't remember how that issue was resolved; we only had a few of those Saturdays. Thereafter

FIGURE 7-41. *Silent Maid* being rolled back into a shed for winter storage.

Sally Schneider photograph

we moved the *Maid* to a new home at Winter Yacht Basin in Mantoloking. The *Maid* was stored outside for the next decade under World War II surplus tarpaulins, which we rigged ourselves.

Dad quickly decided the easiest way to scrape the *Maid*'s immense bottom was with a sharpened garden hoe. I thought this crude and unseamanlike; all the old yard birds lay underneath with hand scrapers in those days. My father retorted that any time I wanted, I could get under there with a hand scraper and do whatever quality work I thought appropriate. Dad also decided that lying on his back with a paintbrush, copper paint running up his sleeve, was silly. He would use one of the paint rollers just coming on the market.[41] Rolling on copper paint? The Scandinavian workmen scoffed. They were a tough lot—one guy crawled on the ground to catch seagulls with his bare hands, then cooked and ate them. Their claim was that brushing was necessary to "work the paint into the seams," and the roller would never do. But, of course, bottom paint needed to go on heavy so that its ingredients could persist long enough in ablation from the flowing water to do their job of antifouling. The roller pushed a wave of paint ahead as it was drawn up the hull and did a perfectly fine job.

Today I might well 'tip' my bottom paint with a brush, but I know of no major boat bottoms on which the antifouling paint is not rolled in application!

Some of the *Maid*'s cordage was pretty old manila, long in the jaw, as it was said. Stan Mountford bought a lot of rope in the early years, figuring out how much was required, reeving the peak and throat halyards, so that when it was all raised up with the newly varnished mast, everything led correctly. Dad had quickly acquired a copy of Edwin Schoettle's classic book *Sailing Craft*, where the then only known copy of the *Maid*'s plans was available. His notes are still penciled inside the front cover of that volume, totaling out at 750 feet of cordage. The peak halyard alone was 171 feet of half-inch line.

The mast was a bear to handle, certainly the largest stick any of us had been around. It was 32 inches in circumference at the partners (where the mast wedges were driven) and this was pretty much average for a telephone pole of the period. When the mast was unstepped and set on several saw horses, I could just about lift one end of it the first year

FIGURE 7-42. *(Left) Silent Maid* stored for winter with her massive mainmast alongside.

Kent Mountford photograph

(Right) Stepping and unstepping *Silent Maid*'s big telephone pole of a mast was always an interesting event, requiring calm conditions. George Roome handles the butt, as Stan Mountford watches anxiously.

Dorothy Mountford photograph, 1964

FIGURE 7-43. *(Left)* The Ostrander family—Dicky, Artie, Dot, and Art—join my parents (center) aboard *Silent Maid.*

Kent Mountford photograph

(Right) The Ostrander's Dachshund ready to call "hard alee!"

Dot Mountford photograph

we owned the boat, the flexibility of the spar keeping the bulk of it flat on other horses. As I grew and matured, by the end of our twelve seasons with the *Maid*, Dad and I could just move the spar from one set of sawhorses to another as we did maintenance. Basic training in the U.S. Army physically did me a lot of good!

The interior of the *Maid*'s coach roof had been finished bright by the Schoettle's years before. The resulting old, dark varnish, plus mildew and peeling, made for a dark cabin. Wooding it using a blowtorch and toxic paint removers in the closed cabin was a session that would give fits and starts to today's OSHA. It was a terrible job, which years later my wife to be and I repeated with our own old 1924 catboat. Sanding it and repainting in brilliant white made a much brighter environment below decks. However, with cracks in the canvas top and tiny resulting leaks in future years, it was prone to blister and mildew.

Dad's eventual solution, supported by Mr. Lance at Defender Industries (who sold polyester resin!), was to strip and fiberglass the cabin-top and waterways along both sides. The choice, after having withstood burnt feet on decks that had been traditionally painted over canvas with a light green, was to go for a completely white gelcoat. Pure white has been my choice for decks ever since, and aboard seven of the nine boats I've owned and cruised.

This decision on the *Silent Maid* left the cabin leak free during the subsequent decade of our tenure. However, in the long scheme of things, we understand that sealing water out by sealing the wood usually means sealing water in—that's a long-term formula for trouble. It took a lot of work and was a prolonged source of profanity for subsequent owners to undo!

Silent Maid literally changed my family's life. My parents' golf-centered weekends, evening parties at friend's houses, and multi-family picnics pretty much faded away. During the warmer months, *Silent Maid* was very much the center of our lives. I don't think my parents ever realized during my restive "difficult" years, how much bonding with *Silent Maid* contributed to our mutual family fabric. This may have been true briefly for the Schoettles until world events overtook them, but I don't think any previous owners had made the *Maid* so central to their lives.

Silent Maid also altered social arrangements among our family and friends. People either came to or were interested in the boat, or they were somewhat sidelined. The parade of old friends coming aboard nonetheless was extensive. Who wouldn't want to be made a part of this famous yacht and her doings? But, new friends also were made focused around *Silent Maid*; people whose lives intersected ours around Barnegat Bay.

Families I had known all my life had their first experience on the water aboard *Silent Maid*. A few, before long, actually moved to the shore to make this way of life part of their own heritage. I'm not sure we did either Barnegat Bay or the coastal ecosystem any

FIGURE 7-44. *(Left)* U.S. Coast and Geodetic Survey Chart 825-SC (1953) shows marsh creek and coves unspoiled since the 1920s Bronson Map (Figure 7-20). *(Right)* The Curtis and Dutchmans Points development as it was by 1977. (National Ocean Survey Chart, detail.)

Kent Mountford photographs

favors in this regard. One couple, Hazel and Bill Cameron, built their home (and spent the rest of their lives) at Curtis Point, just south of Mantoloking, where a wonderful section of shore and salt marsh was land-filled, pierced with a labyrinth of canals and bulkheaded, a process ending forever their ecological function.

Of course, after this "development" had run its course, no one can ever, in a thousand years, have the same experience I did sailing down that once-pristine thoroughfare on sunny mornings. Today's enthusiastic call to "Save Barnegat Bay" thus rings quite hollow to me. The Barnegat Bay I knew six decades ago is long past.

* * *

There was still the young boy wanting to go off on his own—explore, set his own schedule, pick his own destinations—and Dad realized this was necessary. In our "cellar" in North Jersey during the winter of 1953-54, we cooperated in building a Chris-Craft® 8-foot pram kit bought for $69. I put cellar in quotes since our little home was at that time about 135 years old, and the cellar was not much more than a cavity, lined on the outer wall with big rounded glacial boulders and with a dirt floor. During a particularly wet period, the cellar flooded above the gravel base that my dad had put in (by wheelbarrow!). My new pram first floated right there in the cellar! By the time she was launched, we had put together her sailing rig for an additional $42. *Silent Maid* had a dinghy, and I had my own sailboat.

At that point in high school, I was determined to become a naval architect. It was still the era of wooden boats and unsatisfied with a simple cat rig, I created a raffee topsail with a parrel at the base of my forestay and thus about doubled the little boat's sail area. Though it was triangular, like a spinnaker, the sail was set square to the centerline of the dinghy, and technically it was a 'square sail.' Thus I dubbed my pram "the world's only one-masted brigantine" and named her *Poor Man's Pirate*. The strain of all this extra force made the little boat twist when I hiked out. Therefore, the next modification was to double her gunwales with a stringer on each side stood off neatly with white painted wooden blocks and that solved the problem. She was an immaculately maintained little boat. Of course, for an eager explorer, she would be a satisfactory personal yacht for a very short time!

FIGURE 7-45. The author ties up newly launched *Poor Man's Pirate* in the slip next to *Silent Maid* in the spring of 1954

Stan Mountford photograph

One weekend about 1954, a boat named *Chaser I* suffered a gasoline explosion north of the Mantoloking Bridge and burned to the waterline; her hull drifting ashore on Herring Island. I sailed up in *Poor Man's Pirate* a few weeks later and picked through the charred remains, which had been abandoned and were mostly underwater. I hauled out all kinds of bronze remains, piles of screws, cleats, clamshell vents,

FIGURE 7-46. A gasoline explosion sent *Chaser II*, a similar boat, to the bottom off Barnegat's Herring Island, where the author salvaged some badly heat-damaged fittings.

Kent Mountford photograph

throttle levers and a couple of oval port lights from which the glass had been shattered by being plunged in salt water at incandescent heat. All the hardware was severely compromised by the fire, but much could be cleaned up with wire brushes. I probably *still* have some pieces from her in my huge inventory of maritime junk!

One of the nearby boats at Winter Yacht Basin was owned by a character named J. Everett Nestell, who was a promoter of many schemes, and who called himself a 'marina consultant' in a time when marinas were just boatyards. He promoted, among other things, Sea Sleds as the powerboat of the future and a line of coatings called Day-Glo®.[42] He had painted his whole boat a vivid phosphorescent green with the stuff. He saw all the salvage I was bringing back from the wreck and negotiated a barter agreement with me to take items he wanted in exchange for tools, electric drills, wire brushes, disc sander, etc., that he had no use for and of which I had none.

I, thereafter, fancied I would start the American Marine Salvage Company of New Jersey with a high school buddy Rod Barr and imagined an immense cash flow would soon follow. Of course, it never did, but near the end of our sailing season–exactly on September 10, 1954—I was sailing *Poor Man's Pirate* across the channel towards Mantoloking Beach and saw a submerged shape floating ahead in open water. Inspection showed it to be another 8-foot pram, stove in one side, sunken to the gunwales, and in dilapidated condition. I towed her back to the boatyard. Bailing the wreck and getting her ashore on the beach at Winter's, I found she was a McKean Pram. She was obviously a tender to some yacht because she had bronze breast-hooks for davits bow and stern. The boat had mahogany seats and chine planks, good bronze oarlocks, and, though in poor repair, had been a much more substantial boat than my Chris-Craft® kit pram.

My parents made sure we put out the word (as thoroughly as possible for those pre-web and Internet times) to try to find her original owner. She sat with a sign on sawhorses in front of the boatyard office for weeks before I was permitted to start restoring her. The proviso was that when one boat was finished, the other would be sold. *Silent Maid* was not equipped to handle *two* tenders simultaneously!

I called her *Wake* since she would follow in the *Maid*'s wake. Loyal, tough *Wake* would also follow each of my own boats for the next 40-odd years. I eventually sold her to Dr. Lowell Sick, and she would go on to live still more years on an estuary near Charleston, South Carolina.[43]

FIGURE 7-47. *(Top)* *Silent Maid* headed to windward in late summer of 1953 with family and friends aboard. I am atop the cabin trunk. Some fishing was done that day and from the forestay flies a "skunk flag" left over from Blake Chandlee's ownership, indicating we had no catch and had been "skunked."
(Probably) Dr. Sam Wilde photograph

(Bottom) Stan Mountford at the helm, Fred MacDonald on his left.
Dot Mountford photograph

FIGURE 7-48. *(Left)* Kent towed behind *Silent Maid* in *Poor Man's Pirate*, sans sailing rig off Island Beach in lower Barnegat Bay.
Stan Mountford photograph

(Right) Kent's view of *Silent Maid* lit with autumn gold, on a very long tow astern in September 1954. Sid and Stan with their peajackets on; Dottie and guest with a windbreakers and hoods.
Kent Mountford photograph

Wake, the McKean Pram

Robert B. McKean was described in 1968 as the first Friendship Sloop builder of the modern era. An article in the December 1939 issue of *Yachting* magazine described the sloop's construction. It is interesting that the Kelloggs, former *Silent Maid* owners, saw a Friendship Sloop around Nantucket and subsequently had their own version built in New Jersey during the middle 1950s.

McKean sold the Friendship Sloop he'd built, which was then renamed as the well-known *Peggoty* that sailed at least into the late 1960s. He used the proceeds of this sale to set up a dinghy-building business at Port Washington, Maine, constructing mahogany and plywood sailing prams.

McKean also built a 14-foot racing sloop called *Ghost*, which became the prototype for the "Blue Jay" Class. A man of eclectic tastes, McKean also sold a purported asthma cure based on an old, secret family recipe that he stirred up in multi-gallon lots in the shop while the varnish was drying on his latest boat.[44]

Wake was one of McKean's prams, already old and a near-derelict when I rescued her on Barnegat Bay in 1954. She

FIGURE 7-49. Kent and Sid Mountford clown around in *Wake* while *Silent Maid* lies anchored off Island Beach State Park.
Stan Mountford photograph

had no sailing rig and was clearly a dinghy to a larger yacht, with nice cast bronze knees with lifting rings bow and stern where davits hauled her up aboard. When my new wife Nancy and I were planning our move to the Chesapeake in 1971, I could not bear to leave Barnegat without owning a sailboat, so I designed and put together a rig for *Wake*. Bob McKean passed away about 1956, two years after I found *Wake*.

FIGURE 7-50. (Left) *Wake*, the dinghy that followed *Silent Maid* for a decade after 1954, gets one of many refits at Winter Yacht Basin in 1958.
Dr. Sam Wilde photograph

(Right) *Wake* with the sailing rig I built for her from salvaged parts at Beaton's Boatyard in 1971.
Nancy Mountford photograph

When the *Maid* was hauled in 1954, Dad looked into a new sail and found it would cost well over $1000, which was more than a third of what he'd paid for the boat. Well, that would have to wait. When the sail was unbent, its size and weight became a reality. It took three of us to get it into the family station wagon for transport. We hauled the huge thing home, dingy and gray from years of use and abuse, spread it out in the yard behind the house in Warren Township and washed it with soap, scrub brushes, and the garden hose.

I am not sure if we made any significant improvement in the sail (which nonetheless carried on well over another decade), but we made our yard look as if a quarter acre of snow had fallen!

FIGURE 7-51. *(Left to right)* Kent presumes to haul the *Maid*'s immense sail down the dock at Winter Yacht Basin, Stan secures the gaff and boom for haul out, the *Maid*'s spars are stored against Winter's largest shed for winter, and *Silent Maid*'s mainsail in 1954, stretched over our lawn at home on Stirling Road in Warren Township, New Jersey, makes it look like a late summer snow had fallen.

Dot and Stan Mountford photos.

When *Wake*'s over-winter restoration was complete, I had an amazingly sound, very high-end dinghy. She would henceforth follow *Silent Maid*, and I put *Poor Man's Pirate* up for sale in front of the boatyard.

I soon had $150 burning a hole in my pocket after selling *Poor Man's Pirate*. Not long after, I used $125 of this on an old 15-foot Perrine sneakbox named *Skeeter*[45] found in adjacent Beaton's Boatyard. After a lot of restoration, I also added a rafee tops'l to her and mounted a small black powder cannon on her cockpit coaming. This project diverted an unfair amount of my attention and maintenance help from Dad and Mom aboard *Silent Maid*.

I used *Wake* to row back and forth from Winter's and the *Silent Maid* to Beaton's and *Skeeter*. I gained a great deal in upper body strength, since the prevailing southerlies were frequently strong and a heavy chop rolled in from Swan Point almost every afternoon.

FIGURE 7-52. *Skeeter* runs downwind with her raffee 'square' topsail off Mantoloking in the summer of 1956.

Photograph taken from Silent Maid *by Stan Mountford*

FIGURE 7-53. A commercial grass shrimp fisherman operates in the lower bay off Island Beach.

Howard and Betty Height photograph (1980s) given to Diane Bennett Chase

Rowing along the marsh edge, I began to recognize the extraordinary life on small scale that this rich estuary harbored: fish feeding on the peaty edge of the *Spartina alterniflora* sedge, thousands of ribbed mussels (*Geukensia demissa*) that inhabited the rhizomes of this dense spongy turf, and it was thronged by almost completely transparent little shrimp *Palaeometes septemspinosa*. I had no idea such resources existed in the bay, though as bait there was already a commercial fishery for the tiny shrimp!

In 1956, friend George Roome and I sailed my Perrine sneakbox, *Skeeter* down a meandering thoroughfare with the centerboard up. I stood in the bow as we ghosted before the wind with George at the helm. The water, calm and unruffled, was as clear as air beneath my boat, and I literally flew over the widgeon-grass beds carpeting the bottom.[46] Crabs and small fish scattered as the threat of *Skeeter*'s advancing shadow passed over them. This was a defining moment in my life; one of the insights that eventually turned me towards marine science as a profession. Ironically, that very day, I remarked sourly at the development that was occurring at Chadwick, nearby on the barrier beach; development that would obliterate this entire little ecosystem.

*   *   *

My high school friend Rod Barr and I were headed towards careers in engineering and naval architecture in those days. I had already worked my way through Howard I. Chappelle's *Yacht Designing and Planning* and could turn out a faired set of lines by age 16. I entered Rutgers University's College of Engineering in the fall of 1956. At our first assembly, Dean of Engineering Elmer Easton lectured us on what a tough road lay ahead. Dean Easton said, "Look to your right and left. At the end of the year, neither of those men will be here." He said "men" because there was only one girl in the entire

The Rutgers Toilet Bowl Debacle

My college roommate George Roome and I were pretty tame fellows, but we got into trouble just once together. Someone had left an empty can of lighter fluid in the shower room, and we joked throwing it back and forth between stalls[47] while our eyes were full of soap. I tossed a little too hard and it landed in one of the toilets. When I got out of the shower I found the toilet had been used. Damned if I was going to fish that out from amongst somebody's turds, so I flushed.

The toilets were what are called siphon jets with a gooseneck curve cast into the porcelain, and when the lighter fluid can hit that snake bend it stuck. We had no idea this had happened, but when the next guy used the toilet it overflowed and the janitors, trying to "snake" out the obstruction, jammed the can in harder and harder until the toilet broke.

There was hell to pay, and a great uproar followed. At first we didn't understand what had happened, but a few days later in the Rutgers University College newspaper a headline shrieked "Toilets Roaring in Hardenburgh Dorm!" The Dean decreed that unless the miscreants came forward, everyone in the dorm would be assessed a fee for the broken toilet bowl. I recall the total cost was about $65. To lend a little perspective to that cost, I ate five days a week on a budget of $10 and tuition was then $250 a quarter.

I was terrified and eventually sucked up. I put on my suit and tie before marching down to the Dean of Men

Cornelius B. Boocock's office. He glared at me across a massive desk in his huge office, accepted my apology and my $65.

"What do you do in your free time, young man?" he roared (imagining that I threw lighter fluid cans every day). "I'm a sailor, sir," I quavered.

He immediately softened. "What kind of boat?"

"My family owns a catboat, sir, the *Silent Maid*."

"Ah!" he slapped his thigh, rolling his big chair round the end of the desk. "Look at this!" pulling up a pant leg to display a big scar on his shin. "I got this racing [with Edwin Schoettle] aboard the *Silent Maid*! Slipped on a wet deck and went right under one of those long cockpit seats. Do you still have them?"

"Sure do!" I replied, relaxing now.

"Well, come see me in Mantoloking when you're down this summer."

I did go see him, crossing the big covered porch on what appeared to me to be a mansion. The Boocock's had owned the famous 1900 catboat *Vim* and they had been in Mantoloking for many decades. He was cordial. I was shy and a fool not to invite him out on the boat and build a relationship with him. Who knows what it might have done for my then-uncertain career plans. Dean Boocock is long dead now, but I have to wonder!

engineering school! I was clueless and certain I would be a yacht designer. I looked left and right with confidence, but George on my left would graduate as an electrical engineer and Larry on my right would be gone . . . but so was I!

At the end of the first year, overwhelmed by physics, chemistry, and calculus all at the same time, I changed my major to business and economics, eventually being pretty well grounded in psychology and personnel administration. I never regretted the more liberal education I pursued, but still thought I wanted to be a yacht designer.

My friend Rod, on the other hand, earned a full scholarship to Webb Institute of Naval Architecture, went on to get his Ph.D. and started his own company called Tracor. In addition to large amounts of design work for the U.S. Navy, Tracor's tow tank eventually did top secret model tests for a couple of America's Cup defender syndicates. The company also undertook troubleshooting for the mechanical shark "Bruce" (from the movie "Jaws"), later animated for Universal Studios' theme park. It was fun visiting him and seeing the shrouded, 20-foot, scaled down cup defender hulls and the "Bruce" effigy lying there vacant-eyed with its mouth open!

In the required freshman English course, reigning Professor Ayers mandated that we write a term paper and, he warned, "If you misspell anything I will fail you." Simply put, I did and he did. I'd written an ecstatic essay on the marine life I'd discovered in Barnegat Bay, pouring my heart into it. When he gave me a solid failing grade, I was so incensed that I was determined to write a book on the subject in spite of him. There followed throughout my college career a series of papers/essays that led me into the economics, environmental, and historical roots of Barnegat Bay. A few years later, all this serious research came together as my first book manuscript *Closed Sea*. Rutgers Press (in cahoots with Dr. Ayers, no doubt) declined to publish it. Eventually it was published in 2002, has been through two printings, and by 2014 was still muddling along in paperback.[48]

＊　＊　＊

One October, I rowed out from Beaton's, where my sailboat hung on her mooring and joined *Silent Maid* as she headed down bay. *Wake* always followed *Silent Maid,* and we sailed on down to Applegate Cove, where we anchored for lunch. With *Wake* I could go ashore and explore, always looking for some way to expand my knowledge of the bay. That afternoon, I found a small rivulet draining into the cove with water the color of Pine Barrens cedar creeks. The forest then—more than half a century ago—was more extensive and has since been killed back by intruding saltwater as sea level has risen significantly. I nosed *Wake* ashore and walked through marsh to where salt-tolerant plants graded into upland woods. A band of bayberry (*Myrica carolinensis*) grew there and the bushes were full of 3/16 inch waxy fruits. I recalled that colonists in the Americas had made candles from this wax, and I picked my bailing scoop full and stuffed my pockets with them.

Yes, you can make real bayberry candles, but on a home kitchen stove, melting the wax is inefficient, messy, and to my mom's alarm, it can catch fire right in the abused saucepan. The wax did not float to the surface when a pile of berries was boiled to be skimmed off as folk tales claimed. The resulting candle, cast in a little paper tube with string hung down the middle, was all of a half-inch diameter and three inches long, though it did emit the expected delightful pungent "bayberry candle scent." All I can say is, there must have been a lot of very large bayberry bushes in Colonial times, and harvesters must have been on their toes to beat the migrating birds to them each fall!

＊　＊　＊

FIGURE 7-54. **We enjoyed making** *Silent Maid* **our home so many weekends each year. In hot weather, the cabin was pretty close, but Dad quickly got an extension cord aboard and rigged a couple of oscillating fans, which helped a great deal. There were also frequent, impromptu showers on deck with running water available right at the dock.**

Dr. Sam Wilde photograph

Folks in most boatyards form an eclectic pick-up society. In the 1950s and 1960s, Winter Yacht Basin was no different. My parents made friends with an amazing variety of people from different backgrounds. Dr. Constantine Illides was a north-Jersey physician who went by his nickname "Illy" in a time when doctors were aloof and treated with deference by their patients. Captain Bill Evans and his wife Vera were frequent guests in the *Maid*'s cockpit. Captain Bill had skippered an oil tanker for one of the major oil exploration firms. He told us about having a collision with a barge in close quarters. "You heard and felt nothing with a ship that size, but when we ran forward, there was a 30-foot gash in the hull!" He and Vera lived in Philadelphia and said that some years earlier (in the 1940s) one of the neighborhood girls came 'round selling Girl Scout cookies. So cute, they recalled. Her name was Grace Kelly, and she grew up to be a beautiful actress and Princess of Monaco.

FIGURE 7-55. **Sun over the yardarm friends gather in the** *Maid*'s **cockpit at Winter Yacht Basin. George Atkins, Vera Evans, Stan Mountford, Capt. Bill Evans, and Helen Atkins, ca. 1955.**

Dot Mountford Polaroid photograph

FIGURE 7-56. **Martha Neary (carrying my logbook) and I walk up the little beach at Winter Yacht Basin in 1958.** *Wake*, **black hulled, is at right. The** *Maid*'s **big mast is far background and dark widgeon grass is windrowed at the water's edge.**

Dot Mountford photograph

Silent Maid in her time with us barely escaped destruction on more than one occasion. The first was a tornado that swept over Beaton's Boatyard and Winter Yacht Basin on Friday the 13th, 1958, at about 6:30 pm. From my Logbooks:

"I was at Manasquan when the holocaust occurred and missed the excitement, but three friends witnessed the whole thing. The roof ripped off Beaton's big shed and the *Maid*'s forward hatch again gone. The Atkins cabin cruiser, just a couple of slips away had the deck house torn away. Dr. Sam Wilde, whose boat was down the pier from us, said he'd been aboard in his pilot house and grabbed the latches on his windshields to keep them from flying off, and felt his entire 40-foot cabin cruiser lifted in the dock as the vortex came over. His bridge canopy was torn to shreds.

"At Beaton's, most of the boats moored in Jones Tide pond were capsized; several ashore were jumbled together and damaged or flipped over in place. My mentor Jim Odea's boat rolled (her mast jammed into the mud of the harbor bottom) and my friend Len Schwartz's old G Sloop lifted bodily over my dinghy *Wake*, over a mooring pile 50 feet through the air, and she landed with her mast splintered atop someone else's skiff."

FIGURE 7-57. The results of a tornado that swept over West Mantoloking on Friday, April 13, 1958.

Kent Mountford photograph

Boats 20 feet from my sloop *Surge* were flipped, but my boat, just launched after months of work, was unscathed. I lived on such a thin financial shoestring that this was truly good luck.

Captain Evans at Winter's stood incredulous as the funnel went over the water and formed a spout. He said that water was rising and falling at the same time. In Mantoloking, across the bay from us, TV antennae were lost, a chimney blew down, a roof was torn off, and some kind soul, half a mile distant, eventually found, recognized, and returned the *Maid*'s hatch! No TV coverage in those days; we all picked up and went on with our little lives. The *Maid*'s second brush with disaster will be recounted a little later.

*   *   *

Winter Yacht Basin's docks in those years formed a right angle embayment at the apex of which wave action built a small sand beach. We all swam off that beach in summer. There were no sea nettles in Barnegat Bay then, and I kept *Wake* pulled up there when she was not at Beaton's, which was about a quarter mile row away. No thought of an outboard for me.

However, there were vast underwater meadows south in the bay towards Lavallette where the bottom was totally covered with widgeon grass (*Ruppia maritima*), one of the bay's most valuable ecological resources. These are rooted plants, just like those ashore, but they grow, flower, and set seed underwater. They are indispensable as food for migrating waterfowl each winter and provide protective habitat for fish crabs and countless smaller life forms.

In late summer, however, the long, stringy vegetative parts of these plants are shed naturally as part of this species' life cycle, and these plant parts—also spreading seed in the process—float up the bay or wherever wind and currents take them.

It sometimes seemed that most of them ended up sloshing around in the embrace of those two bulkheads at Winter Yacht Basin. We all swam in them anyway, accepting them as part of our summer environment.

By late July, Barnegat Bay is as warm as a bathtub, and one dark moonless night I pushed *Wake* into the water, preparing to row over to Winter's.

FIGURE 7-58. The dense widgeon grass beds off Lavallette with the flowering structures of these valuable plants, Barnegat Bay.

Kent Mountford photograph

FIGURE 7-59. Captain Bill Evans emerges like King Neptune, festooned with bay-grasses from a summer swim off Winter's dock, right in front of *Silent Maid*'s south-facing slip.

I literally gasped out loud to see her enter a bath of fire as a dense bloom of phosphorescent plankton was disrupted. This luminescence was more than I had ever seen and I rowed out to my "mooring with a twinkling glowing swirl about the blade of each oar . . . on *Skeeter* I struck the mooring cable and was astounded as the whole thing glowed from surface to bottom . . . to me a scientific revolution. Quite a display was given [rowing] all the way to Winter's until the dock lights outshone the glow. On the *Maid* I interested all present by passing a crab net through the water, whereupon the whole thing glowed like a sub-sea will-o-the-wisp. Captain Evans (aboard as a guest) said that during World War II, the porpoises, coming through tropic waters made them hold their breath, as they appeared so much like torpedoes."[49]

Luminescent plankton, thereafter, became an attractive mystery I was determined to follow. Without my realizing it, this urged me another notch along the road to a career in marine biology. My first understanding of the phenomenon came from a seminar to which I was invited at Sandy Hook Marine lab by Dr. Frank Johnson. He essentially said that bioluminescence is in fact a "cold light," not heat producing like incandescent light bulbs. It may have been an evolutionary leftover from cells trying to get rid of unneeded energy without the damaging heat.

What I saw in Barnegat came from luminescent dinoflagellates—minute, actively swimming, single-celled plants that often "bloom," developing populations so dense they color the water amber. These blooms occur in estuaries where too much nutrient material is leaking in from human activities on the landscape. I was unaware at the time that this was a sign that humans were beginning to overwhelm Barnegat Bay.

FIGURE 7-60. My first microscope kit, bought on a lark for under $7 from Lafayette Radio and Electronics in 1961. *Insets:* Plankton organisms, each a fraction of a millimeter in diameter, which contribute to luminescence and red tide blooms in Barnegat Bay. A. *Gonyaulax spinifera*, B. *Noctiluca scintillans (miliaris)*, C. *Polykrikos hartmani*.
Kent Mountford photomicrographs

One of the blessings of being a really skinny little kid in high school was that in gym class, I became one of the few guys who could scurry twenty feet up the big climbing ropes hand-over-hand like a squirrel, and this talent was carried aboard the *Silent Maid*. It was not long before I could shin up the halyards to the crosstree spreaders and thus reach fittings at the very truck. This was a source of wonder around the boatyard; this skinny fellow flying aloft as no one else could. I suppose I could get up to the spreaders and truck in 30 seconds and did that sometimes with my little camera taking pictures of what passed for aerial views around the bay at the time.

Long after we sold the *Maid* in the mid-1970s, her subsequent owner Sally Schneider asked me to fix something aloft, having seen me scurry up many times in my youth. By then I'd been in and out of the Army where I routinely had to do 10 pull-ups before each meal. I hardly thought twice about going aloft for Sally. No problem I thought, but it had been 20 years away from *Silent Maid* since I'd tried that, and I thought I might die before I got to the spreaders, shaking like a leaf when I finally gained their security. My head, after all, was now over 40 feet above the water! My modest "bulking up" in U.S. Army Basic Training meant more body weight and I barely had the strength to get up. I'd not try that again without a bos'un's chair!

FIGURE 7-61. *(Left)* Kent Mountford climbs *Silent Maid*'s mast. Feet on the spreaders, one's head was about 41 feet above the water. In July 1963, fasteners holding the iron spreaders carried away almost costing the author's life, but a second climb with tools repaired them securely.[50] *(Center)* An aerial view shot from *Silent Maid*'s masthead of mosquito-ditched salt marshes near Reedy Creek, south of Swan Point in October 1953. This area is now public lands, part of the Edwin Forsythe Wildlife complex, and managed by the U.S. Fish and Wildlife Service. *(Right)* *Silent Maid* shows her wide decks and large cockpit in this view after climbing her mast.

Kent Mountford photographs

The *Maid* went to sea quite a few times, most often so my dad and uncles could fish when the blues were running or simply for an exciting sail. With her small engine and offset prop, it was not a trivial exercise to motor through the Bay Head-Manasquan Canal, but when the tide was with you, it was a fast trip . . . as long as the Rt. 33 and Lovelandtown bridge operators were awake. This was before VHF radio, and 'short wave' was uncommon aboard inshore sailboats. So, the bridge guys relied on hearing the old brass-reed, mouth-blown foghorns then in use. Blowing one today reminds you how feeble they were and how much lung power they required to get any volume out of them.

At any rate, running with the tide meant an over-the-ground speed that could approach 9 knots. Turning, with all the completely inconsiderate powerboat traffic around you, when a bridge tender was sluggish, was a risky operation, replete with blue language. One of the few improvements in New Jersey coast boating today is the

FIGURE 7-62. Old mouth-blown fog horns were the small boat sailor's means of opening bridges and protecting against collision in low visibility. They were not very loud, even when considerable lung power was applied.

Mountford photograph, collection of Dr. Ralph Eshelman

FIGURE 7-63. Stan, Kent, and Sid Mountford off Manasquan Inlet on *Silent Maid* in the summer of 1955.

Dot Mountford photograph

prompt, courteous way these two bridges now operate. It benefits both highway and water traffic alike.

Manasquan Inlet was not much better than the canal for underpowered auxiliaries, especially when heavy fishing boat traffic was headed out in the morning or, more hazardously, inbound when an ebbing tide flowed against the prevailing late day southeasters turned the inlet mouth into a washing machine.

Conditions in Manasquan Inlet were sometimes dangerous due to infrequent dredging of the channel in those days. Shoaling of the inlet, where sand was transported by northward-flowing along-shore currents and swept around the Point Pleasant jetty, built a bar across the mouth that tended to break in heavy weather and became literally impassable in major nor'easters. Some of the U.S. Coast Guard Auxiliary training films of the time showed boats broaching to and hitting the rocks in Manasquan Inlet, and that reputation stuck for a long time.

My father made it a point of pride to sail through the inlet when conditions permitted. It was also a grand show for family members not aboard to watch for the *Maid* approaching and coming up the inlet. They would run down to the esplanade and wave to the incoming crew (our oceanfront family cottage was just three doors away). In those days this pumped up both waver and wave-ees!

Despite her great beam (12 feet 6 inches), the *Maid*'s mast was so large and so far forward that she thrashed and yawed fiercely in confused cross wakes. With *Silent Maid*, you did much better carrying sail through the inlet, which steadied her greatly, but there was then the hazard of coming 'round into the wind to drop sail in all that thoughtless traffic before reaching the railroad drawbridge. You worked it out. One lovely day, after a fine sail almost out of sight of land to weather outbound and broad reach back to the Manasquan sea-buoy, Dad anchored just outside the surf line and in front of all those sweet young girls I never got to date. I dove overboard, swam ashore through the breakers and walked nonchalantly up to the cottage . . . as nonchalantly as a skinny kid of 16 or so with significant acne can be! The *Maid* weighed her big Danforth and headed back through the canal to Mantoloking.

* * *

FIGURE 7-64. *Surge*'s pennant on the author's yawl *Nimble* in 2013.

Kent Mountford photograph

In August 1957, I visited Beaton's Boatyard where my old friend Captain James O'Dea was showing a sailboat "suitable for restoration" to a wary prospect. O'Dea was a creaky-voiced senior who spoke with an Irish lilt. He sailed a lightly built little red cabin sloop named *Curlew*, which was my ideal as the next boat to own. I could actually sleep aboard such a boat. Jim O'Dea was a supremely kind and supportive mentor to me during my youth at Beaton's.

Captain O'Dea, showing the defective boat for sale, said the owner only wanted $100, and my ears perked up. The boat was an 18-foot Crosby Seagull Sloop and twice the vessel my 15-foot sneakbox *Skeeter* was. All she needed was a new centerboard trunk. I sought advice from Dave and Lally Beaton, and they thought that my dad and I could do the job. I would name the boat *Surge* for her stalwart bow wave and designed myself a pennant that would be my personal burgee for the next five decades. We built the trunk that winter and bronze-bolted it in place the following spring.

Stan Mountford's Bethabara Fishing Pole & Meiessleback Reel, 1915–16

With *Silent Maid* replacing *Osprey* as platform, the Mountford boys still went to sea fishing mostly for bluefish, but they would take any errant bite from fluke, striper, weakfish, or black bass and play it for sport. There was also dinner at the old beach house, of course.

Dad's fishing pole—he had just one through much of his life—went to sea along with them, though it was built many years before as a nine-foot surf pole. The pole was of Bethabara, as my Uncle Sid described it, saying that it was "an Egyptian reed." My research many years later shows otherwise!

Aside from good old American hickory or native giant cane (*Arundinaria gigantea*), there were at least three exotic woods sought after for fishing rods when my dad was a boy. According to English chronicler Lord Henry Charles Howard in 1911,[51] these three woods were lancewood, then grown in Cuba; greenheart, from British Guiana on the northeast bulge of South America; and, the most expensive, reportedly called washaba (several alternative spellings follow!), also from British Guiana.[52]

This latter wood proves actually to be the timber-tree Hakia (*Tabebuia serratifilia*, [Vahl] Nicholson) with local names wassibi or washiba (translated as "Bow-wood"). It was described as very resilient, and a fine piece, then quite hard to come by, could be worked very thin towards the tip allowing a light pole, which weighed just 5 ounces.[53] A walking stick made from washiba was "almost unbreakable."[54] The genus *Tabebuia* has about a hundred species, some of which are marketed today as expensive "ipe" for decking and boardwalks.

When first imported to the U.S., washaba was christened Bethabara by Malcolm Shipley—the manufacturer claiming to have made up the name. He later tried to copyright it as a trademark, taking one usurper of the term to court,[55] but failed because the name Bethabara was already widely used. It was at that time established as generic. Oddly, whatever Shipley said, the name was clearly—by accident or design—derived from an historic place in (modern) Jordan, so named since the 6th century AD, where John the Baptist immersed those seeking salvation.[56] By 1962, Frank Longwood, a USDA botanist, put Tabebuia together with the name Bethabara.[57]

A significant investment for a young fellow, my dad apparently got his Bethabara surf-casting pole and its accompanying reel when quite young; he fished with it for decades. His reel was a free-spool, surf-casting model, serial number 1559, made by A.F. Meisselbach & Bro., in

FIGURE 7-65. **Stan Mountford's Bethabara surf-pole and Meisselbach reel, circa 1915, which fished from *Silent Maid* when she went to sea.**

Kent Mountford image

Newark, New Jersey, sometime between 1915–16,[58] when Dad was about 10 years old. It is a nicely made piece of German silver and a little brass, crafted with "hard" rubber end plates and a full 100 parts in the assembly. At this writing, it is perfectly functional after being fished in salt water for over 70 years and having survived flood and burial during Hurricane Sandy in 2012.

This was the pole that went to sea aboard *Silent Maid* from the early 1950s until the mid-1960s. It usually 'lived' in the Manasquan beach house, where Dad or his brothers could grab any of several poles available and dash down to the surf if a run of bluefish came alongshore.

My father was an excellent surf caster. His only concession to technology was a leather thumb guard that allowed him to feather the spool and avoid "bird's nests"[59] while casting. The old Bethabara pole also made many trips in rental rowboats, bottom fishing for summer flounder in the tidal Manasquan River. To this day the only finfish I really enjoy is flounder, fresh caught, and unadorned—simply dredged in bread crumbs for pan frying in a little butter or oil—the way Grandma did it at the old cottage.

I remember Dad replacing a guide on the pole that had come loose, long before I was handy with any such detailed work. I watched how he lashed its arms to the pole using a technique sailors call "common whipping" with a long, perfectly wound strand of maroon thread, securing his work at the end with a couple of coats of spar varnish. These repairs still hold perfectly after more than half a century.

FIGURE 7-66. The old repurposed building where the Mountford Manufacturing Company once resided. This winter view is the only picture remaining and demonstrates Stan's courageous commute following a 1950s blizzard.

Stan Mountford photograph

FIGURE 7-67. With her Vincent Kanser Dacron® main drawing well, *Surge* roars along on a broad reach off Mosquito Cove. The author's then-girlfriend Kathy Pultz and cousin Don Collier are aboard. The omnipresent dinghy *Wake* trundles astern.

Stan Mountford photograph

FIGURE 7-68. My Grandma, Paulina Mountford, celebrates her 80th birthday on September 19, 1958, at the *Maid*'s helm. She wears a *Cattleya* orchid corsage.

Stan Mountford photograph

My first summer job during college (netting me one semester's tuition at a dollar an hour) was working as a foot-press operator and general helper at Mountford Manufacturing Company. One of the local merchants near the factory was V. Kanser Cover Company, which produced awnings and tarpaulins. Dad and I became friends with Vincent Kanser, just two years older than my father. Like many people in the post-war years, Kanser had ideas of entering the burgeoning boating industry. Cruis-Along was building its successful line of powerboats to reach a middle-class market. As bait for those considering an entry to boating there was Topper. A Topper ad in 1950 read: "Are you havin' any fun? If not, you need a Topper."[60] They sold a little 18-foot cabin cruiser for about $1995. You bought your own 7.5 HP outboard and became a yachtsman.

Kanser began building sails and boat covers of nylon and Dacron.® The company made a Dacron®—then a newly developed fiber—mainsail for *Surge*, which cost $65. Kanser had developed a new technique for making the roach stand out thus increasing sail area, while holding shape. It was a solid, serviceable sail that received many favorable comments and stood a lot of stiff Barnegat blows.

Vincent Kanser had designs for low weight sailboat hardware items that were to be stamped and formed from stainless steel stock. Familiar with my father's skill at tool and die making, Kanser told him he was looking for a manufacturer to produce them at competitive cost. Sid, Dad's brother, had no interest in deviating from the path he had taken for Mountford Manufacturing Company, so those ideas never bore fruit. I often wonder what would have happened if Dad had been free to explore and innovate. Race-Lite, a manufacturer of similar sailboat hardware had not yet entered the business. Its current revenues are from $2 to $5 million annually.[61]

With constrained resources in a very small company, my Uncle Sid still described my father in good humor "as a genius with a bit of wire and string." He was always coming up with ideas to do things better. Before they were ever marketed elsewhere, he invented the toothpaste tube key that got all the product out. He also designed bars of

soap with a pigmented company logo die-cut and machine-extruded into a form from which individual bars were cut. The logo in each bar was always visible down to the last sliver.[62] He never filed or held a patent, though his artistic embossing and precious metal piercing designs for the company were copyrighted.

*　　*　　*

On September 26, 1958, Dad corralled Uncle Sid, Uncle Chick, and me to set off on a couple day's sojourn to lower Barnegat Bay. This was well before modern, almost real-time NOAA weather information and projection of tropical storm tracks. The U.S. Weather Bureau on September 27 reported the eye of Hurricane Helene at 36.5 N, 76.2 W and maximum winds at 135 mph. I'm not sure we ever even heard that forecast. The storm skirted the North Carolina coast, doing what was then $11 million in damage ($72 million in 21st century values) and reckoned worse than Hurricane Hazel, an earlier severe storm. Her course was recurving, as these storms mostly do, east northeastwards and out into the north Atlantic.[63] Local forecasts suggested it was a good bet we would be OK for our weekend cruise; so off we went.

Our four and a half hour run down Barnegat Bay was uneventful and mild. My dinghy *Wake* followed quietly on her painter. We were unaware that an arm of that storm, which was interacting with a frontal system from the U.S. interior, was also approaching. We anchored off Harvey Cedars and out of the channel east of red "Nun" 6, between Sandy and Long Beach Islands.

I rowed *Wake* across to Sandy Island and went ashore looking for specimens to feed my burgeoning interest in marine biology. It was not long, however, before I looked up to the north and east and saw a white squall, spreading like a snowbank across the horizon and tumbling at a great pace, much as a waterfall pouring through hell-black clouds into even blacker water.[64]

The prospect of this monster riveted my attention as I rowed furiously back to *Silent Maid* and resulted in a pencil sketch made later, showing the red nun and a waterman's garvey running for shelter . . . as I was! I barely made it back to the boat before it hit and

FIGURE 7-69. **Part of Hurricane Helene, September 27, 1958, approaches Harvey Cedars and** *Silent Maid* **at 3:00 pm. Barnegat Light is on the horizon to the right.**
Kent Mountford pencil sketch

FIGURE 7-70. **A Perfection kerosene heater identical to the one we used on** *Silent Maid* **though** *never* **underway!**

Kent Mountford photograph

pulled out our Danforth anchor. We set it again inshore, but had to run into a harbor at the Cedars for the night. The squall had been the 'nose' (actually an outer rain band) of Hurricane Helene (then over a hundred miles at sea), and we had a good storm the rest of that day and all night. I nearly froze whenever I went out in a bathing suit and parka . . . for any reason. It cleared and was windy and cold by 6:30 am. Later the U.S. Weather Bureau summaries suggested about three inches of rain had fallen over that part of Barnegat Bay during the storm. I emptied my nearly full dinghy.

The cabin was warm thanks to an old Perfection[65] kerosene heater we had aboard, and Dad cooked us breakfast of bacon, eggs, toast, and coffee on the hissing Primus stove. The men mulled over when it would be best to leave as the wind was now howling down the bay directly against our course for Mantoloking. I suspect our departure was delayed in hopes the blow might pipe down, but for me, it was an opportunity to row ashore, land *Wake* at Harvey Cedars, and explore.

After breakfast I went for a four-mile hike (on the ocean front of Long Beach Island) picking up trophies, including some from a boat wrecked during the night.[66] This had been a light cabin cruiser, her true fate never revealed. I recall dragging back a door with chromed hardware and pieces of nicely varnished mahogany. I'll bet my dad and uncles were chafing to get underway by the time I came back with my salvage. We motored out through Barnegat Bay's narrow and winding channels until, off Gunning River Marshes and Gulf Point, we could lay a course up-bay. Here the fetch was very long and the chop had a long time to consolidate into short, steep, and white-capping seas, which occasionally and randomly sent unusually big waves forward.

The *Maid* though travelling slowly, hammered very hard into this chop, and off Barnegat Light my log recorded "really cracking down painfully hard on some big waves." We were all tired by the time we tied up at Winter Yacht Basin. The men headed back to their work weeks, and I returned to college classes in New Brunswick.

More rain came during the week, but by Saturday morning we drove down to the boat with Jimmy Djeu, one of my best college buddies and a novice to boating. Jimmy was a native of Shanghai, but an expatriate now living in Buenos Aires, Argentina, whence his parents had fled with their business from Mainland China's post World War II dislocations. Argentina, however welcoming the current government had been, was not the pacific refuge the Djeu family had anticipated. Jimmy told me when he was in school one day, brass machine gun bullet casings began falling among his playmates at recess. They looked up to see an aerial dogfight—another South American *coup d'etat* was underway. And so Jimmy was being educated in the U.S.

When we arrived at *Silent Maid* that weekend, it had been six days since we'd tied up following the violent weather around Hurricane Helene. When we opened the cabin doors, we were stunned by the sharp odor of kerosene and the sight of water, 18 inches deep, over the floorboards. Atop all floated the scum of used motor oil flooded out of the *Maid*'s engine crankcase when the dipstick went under water. The kerosene had all floated up and out of the Perfection oil heater, which had been sitting on the cabin sole. If there had been anything lucky about this mess, it was that water had not reached the height of our bunk mattresses. We had to sleep there that night!

The *Maid* had an automatic bilge pump. I always thought it a good design, built as things in America used to be built. The manufacturer, PERKO, placed the pump motor inside a housing made with two 3/16" heavy brass plates screwed together with stout brass legs and surrounded by heavy brass mesh cage with an area of about 80 square inches, which made stoppage from debris in the bilge highly unlikely. Nonetheless, the

pump's hard work had long since flattened the common six-volt storage battery trying to keep up with the relentless influx of Barnegat Bay.

Dad fairly flew over to Rudy Winter, the boatyard owner, and in a short time the *Maid* was warped around to the railway and hauled out. A plank butt had let loose on one of those hammering waves down by the Inlet, and was letting the bay flow in unimpeded. We were lucky she had not gone to the bottom.

The butt was properly screwed home and the disturbed seams re-caulked, payed with Dolfinite®, and daubed with bottom paint. The engine was flushed, new oil topped up, the distributor and points made right, and she ran fine. Amazingly, thanks to Rudy Winter and his workmen, all was put to rights the very same day. Unlikely that could have been done in the present era.

My mother was widely known for keeping an immaculate house (and boat), so with whatever detergent and sponges were available, the cabin was put to rights again. Save the lingering odor of that kerosene, we were back in business, and we all spent the night aboard. Jimmy and I actually got to go sailing in my little Crosby Seagull sloop *Surge* after bailing a lot of rainwater from her bilges. Jimmy manned the tiller most of the way home, which he greatly enjoyed.

The next day, October 5, we headed undaunted (well, not actually—we were pretty shaken) down the bay again. There was "just a waft of kerosene in the cabin," said my logbook! After all, we had an engagement to keep!

Uncle Chick's brother Everett Leeds kept his big, old Elco cruiser *Go Go* at Forked River and had given us coordinates for an anchorage he said was locally called "Clearwater." Today's charts show this just south of Tices Shoal as a wedge or cut of deeper water reaching inshore almost to the edge of Island Beach and thus allowing close approach from the bay's main channel. Centuries ago, this must have been the site of some former inlet, the tides from which had scoured the bottom this deep, where elsewhere there was barely a foot or so of water inshore.

The *Maid* nominally drew 32 inches, board up, and could come quite close to the beach here. *Go Go*, fairly towering over me in my dinghy, was already at anchor with her crew relaxing. While they heard the *Maid*'s adventure story, Jimmy and I took my dinghy ashore. We rowed in over dense dark eelgrass beds, the richest in all Barnegat, with small sand patches occasionally showing as bright spots in the water.

If you snorkeled over these beds, much like flying over an underwater meadow, you passed over those occasional sand balds, where no vegetation grew, and would find them scoured out significantly deeper than the surroundings. These bright patches often had pretty Atlantic bay scallops (*Argopecten irradians*) that sat on the bottom with their shells wide open like mouths as they filtered their plankton food from the water. On close inspection the interior mantle of each scallop was lined around the edge with tiny blue eyes, and if they saw your approaching movement, the shells would slam shut. Using the water as jet fuel, they would 'clap' their shell valves, squirting out a seawater jet, and go zig-zagging into the eelgrass. In those days, over a half-century ago, New Jersey had a commercial fishery for these succulent little shellfish. In 1956, 56,000 bushels were harvested in New Jersey, mostly from this section of Barnegat Bay. By 1974, this had fallen to 2,700 bushels and thereafter to almost nil.[67]

We rowed very near shore then waded the rest of the way in. The water was as warm as a bathtub, and the whole bottom was bare sand. I later learned that the really shallow places were scoured of their eelgrass by massive, wind-driven sheets of bay-ice during

FIGURE 7-71. *(Top) Silent Maid* on emergency haul out for a failed plank butt below the waterline.
Dot Mountford photograph

(Bottom) Shown on another old boat, this is how the *Maid*'s plank butt fasteners failed.
Kent Mountford photo at IRIS, Newport, RI.

FIGURE 7-72. Kent Mountford snorkeling next to *Silent Maid* while anchored off Island Beach at Clearwater.
Dot Mountford photograph

FIGURE 7-73. Ice sheets coming ashore at the Clearwater (A-7) site, February 18, 1968. The mounds of ice at right have been wind-driven right over the shore plowing up a berm of dead eelgrass and sand. These forces downed many shoreline trees in the maritime forest.

Kent Mountford photograph

winter freezes. Where the water was just a few inches deep—and dewatered at low tide—the sand had a brilliant pink-colored crust, much like the colored coral sands on parts of Bermuda. In this case, the color was from dense colonies of sulfur bacteria, subsisting largely on the energy of bright sunlight and nutrients from the decomposing bands of eelgrass driven ashore each year.

My logbook from October 4, 1958, provides this account:

> "We pulled the dink up on a small beach almost covered by *Hudsonia tomentosa*, the poverty grass Henry David Thoreau wrote about in *Cape Cod*. Pushing inland we followed a none-too-well defined trail, crossing the road [paved and maintained by the State] to the dunes spotted by *Hudsonia* in near acre patches. [The dunes] are also well stocked with rabbits and other small life. Pieces of some old lumber schooner [a 19th century shipwreck] presented themselves at frequent intervals in the form of keels, joiner work and spars.
>
> "At an old shack [owned, I found later, by NJ U.S. District Court Judge Richard Hartshorne[68]], I found two whale vertebra one small and the other a foot in diameter [I believe they were from a sperm whale, *Physeter cataodon*, which is in range off New Jersey]. . . . Jim [who had a foot problem] was none too enthusiastic about the sojourn and stopped near one of the wrecks to soak his feet in seawater. . . .We lost the trail through the scrub on the on the way [back] to the bay."

On our return, it was blowing pretty hard, we found that the *Maid* had parted the old manila rode for her storm anchor and lost the hook. This (my memory is unclear) was probably the big folding-stock yachtsman's kedge, which had been aboard since Edwin Schoettle's time. My parents had set the big Danforth instead.

Discounting that loss of ground tackle (and our near-sinking!), it had been a wonderful day for me, one which allowed me to become closer to this wonderful barrier island habitat, otherwise inaccessible to the general public. Island Beach would not become a true public resource for some years. My parents were likely a little less sanguine about the weekend, and my friend Jimmy had sore feet, scratched legs from the brush, and with no sea boots, wet feet to take home with him that night.

FIGURE 7-74. The Judge's Shack at Island Beach still stands 55 years after I viewed it as derelict in 1958.
Kent Mountford photograph

Inset: Judge Richard Hartshorn at right.
Newark Sunday News, May 25, 1952, provided by Diane Bennett-Chase, 2012

Commissioner Erdman (left) and Judge Hartshorne examining one of the many different wild flower plants which have survived time and the elements on Island Beach. At right, they are shown viewing the scenery from lookout tower of station abandoned by U. S. Coast Guard.

FIGURE 7-75. *(Left)* The sand dunes on Island Beach at what is today called the A-7 Fly Road as they appeared in 1958 just at the end of a rude trail leading from the Barnegat Bay to the sea. *(Right)* A broad swath of *Hudsonia tomentosa* (poverty grass) covers some dunes, accumulates windblown sand, and prevents erosion.

Kent Mountford photographs

On October 12, a clear and cold morning, we took the *Maid*'s sail off for the season. The failed plank butt had shaken us severely. If the week's rain had continued, and we'd not come to the shore, *Silent Maid* could well have gone to the bottom.

It was only a few Saturdays later that Dad and I drove into New York City (you could actually drive to lower Manhattan in those days and park on the street!) to the ship chandleries down on Chambers Street near the Battery. We bought boxes of 2½-inch Everdur bronze screws to largely refasten *Silent Maid*. As I recall, they were about $2.65 for a box of 100; today the cost would be over fifteen-fold more than that!

When the *Maid* was hauled that month, Dad accomplished the task with a combination drill he made himself—drilling pilot, clearance, and countersink holes in one operation—and, with a good eye and steady hand, he could drive the slot-head screws home in one long thrust with a Stanley mechanical screwdriver. Thus armed, the two of us re-fastened everything below the waterline with the screws Edwin Schoettle had actually wanted to use 34 years earlier! In our ignorance, we failed to understand that mixing bronze with the iron would again be a problem someday down the road.

At the end of her sailing life when *Silent Maid* was restored for exhibition at the Philadelphia Independence Seaport, one of her workers, Newt Kirkland, and I found the very plank that had failed. I counted in that single, troubled, 80-year old butt joint some 41 fasteners, driven in desperation over the decades trying to hold the poor thing together.[69]

Trips like this, down the bay to Clearwater and Barnegat Inlet, became important experiences that always drew me away from my own boats to join *Silent Maid*, and my logbooks recorded some of the amazing times one could have in and around Barnegat Bay a half century ago. It was still only after we had sold the *Maid* that I realized she had led me inexorably into my real future as a marine biologist.

FIGURE 7-76. *(Top)* The plank butt that failed almost sinking *Silent Maid* in 1958 eventually had 41 fasteners screwed into it. *(Bottom)* Newt Kirkland in 2010 trying to patch up the old girl for exhibition.

Kent Mountford photographs

Plagues of Biting Flies

In August of 1959, we made one of those coveted trips to Island Beach aboard *Silent Maid*. It was a really hot day with a hot and dry southwest wind. We came down the bay on a single point of sailing, and were absolutely driven mad by the black stable-flies blowing aboard. They were in a feed and breed frenzy—biting legs, arms, and ankles.

FIGURE 7-77. **A *Stomoxes* stable fly lands on my arm, and I tough it out long enough to take this photo. Note the piercing mouthpart inserted in my skin!**

Kent Mountford photograph

Female *Stomoxes calcitrans* need a blood meal—in this case our human blood—to get sufficient energy to mate and produce eggs, which are laid above tide level in the marsh grasses and along the bayshore where a wrack-line of dried eelgrass accumulates. On an offshore breeze, they are blown out over open water and seek refuge on any large object that passes. Males were buzzing around frantically mating with females that had just bitten us, often through socks or tee shirts. Males were even mating with dead females we had swatted to the cockpit sole.

We were at them continually with flyswatters, hands, anything to kill them, and often had the satisfaction of getting one or two mating pairs with a single blow. But kill though we did, leaving scores—hundreds—dead all over the cockpit, there seemed to be more coming aboard all the time. You did not see them fly in to the boat; they just appeared; from where was always a mystery.

It was only on a subsequent day, when I happened to look over the leeward side of *Silent Maid* and there, on her white topsides, were hundreds of black flies, like raisins stuck to the hull, awaiting their chance to come aboard . . . in a continual stream of tormenters.

For *Stomoxes*, we have only our forbears to blame. It seems their eggs were brought in with livestock manure as horses and cattle were sailed trans-Atlantic, centuries ago. They are a terrible plague upon livestock in Africa.

FIGURE 7-78. An American Export Lines three-island "break bulk" freighter (probably the *Exeter*) offloads a cargo of stacked (cattle) hides from Spain—fodder for America's leather industry at Hoboken, NJ, 1960.

Kent Mountford photograph

Near the little beach at Winter Yacht Basin, one of the slips was occupied by Mr. and Mrs. Walter Holmes. It took a while for me to realize he was Personnel Director for the American Export Steamship Lines, which ran the large cruise ships *Independence* and *Constitution*, and four, now long-obsolete, "three Island" freighters that plied the world's oceans to ports on the Mediterranean and in Africa.

International maritime trade in those years was still carried on 'break bulk' ships, where cargos of incredible variety were loaded in casks, on pallets, or in bales directly into the vessels' deep holds, as they had been for thousands of years. Loading was a slow, expensive, and creative process where the weight of each cargo parcel was carefully—and manually—calculated to maintain the ship's stability, and the scheme of stowage was designed for orderly and quick removal of each item at the correct port.

If you came into Mombasa, Kenya, for example, with the required load of tractor tires incorrectly stowed deep in the bilge, everything else had to be off-loaded to access the needed items. The same went for bales of odiferous raw steer hides or huge barrels of wine headed from Spain or Portugal to Hoboken, New Jersey. Thievery and damage were rife on the docks, here and abroad, as longshoremen handled isolated bits of valuable cargo in a rushed, often chaotic, environment. Things were always rushed. Ships in port earn their owners no profits!

When I graduated from college, with a business and personnel background (not naval architecture), Mr. Holmes hired me for my first full-time job as a passenger reservations agent working in a 'fishbowl' office at 666 5th Avenue in New York City. This was a wonderful experience, and I learned a great deal about the trade. I also ate frequent lunches at the nearby Horn and Hardart, as my mother had 30 years before. The commute was long and arduous, but my workmates were knowledgeable and good-humored, training me up in the trade, with occasional irresistible pranks on this greenhorn. Booking for the passenger ships, we often had requests to place a client on the 'commend list.' I received such a call one day from an apparently eccentric gentleman with clipped English accent, who offered to donate a "selection of his books" to the ships library. So, I put him on the commend list, and one day this small, parchment skinned man walked into our 5th Avenue office to thank me. It was thus I met John Dickson Carr (1906–1977), one of the 20th century's renowned mystery writers.[70]

Mr. Holmes later made the mistake of promoting me to Personnel Assistant for American Export, just when the company entered a period of financial stress and bitter negotiations with a union attempting to organize the staff. As a naïve young man, I was totally out of my depth in this hard-fought time with high stress, secret negotiations, and my boss using the early pharmaceutical tranquilizer Milltown® to keep his sanity.[71] The job at American Export did not work out well for me and now, even American Export is gone.[72] I did learn a great deal about how tough business life could be!

A career-guidance counselor at Rutgers University had also set me up for an interview with a 1955 start-up, marine interests company called Sea-Land Corporation, but I had the job with Walter Holmes. I have often wondered where I might have ended up had I taken the other fork in the road. Sea-Land pioneered containerized shipping, which ended shipping in older break bulk cargo ships. Containers now dominate world ocean trade moving millions of tons every month.[73]

Through my darkest, most hassled hours at American Export—and everywhere else—*Silent Maid* was a refuge and a stable place to recoup and bond with the estuary that I loved. I also lost a girlfriend during this stressful time, but the *Maid* was there, providing the opportunity to meet and become involved with the daughter of neighboring boaters at Winter Yacht Basin. Kathy Pultz was too young to be serious about just one boy, and her mother far too vigilant to let her get umm… *really* involved, but out on the bay in my little sloop *Surge*, I did learn a lot more about life and what then passed for love in teenage girls! We both went on with permanent, but minor scars, to very successful lives!

FIGURE 7-79. (Top) Kathy Pultz at 16—almost 17—on the little Beach at Winter Yacht Basin. (Bottom) The *Maid* approaches some anchorage with George Roome, Kathy Pultz (readying the anchor rode), and Kent by the mast.

*   *   *

While the *Maid* was hauled during the 1961–62 winter, there was a disastrous several-day northeaster, which took several lives and wrought havoc on the coast. Hundreds of homes were destroyed or damaged. *Silent Maid* slept through this mayhem on blocks ashore, while not half a mile eastward, 100-year-old houses tumbled into the sea. The Mountford cottage in Manasquan was virtually unscathed, making this terrible storm an object lesson we failed to take seriously.

FIGURE 7-80. This home on the oceanfront in Lavalette was one of hundreds that succumbed to the "Great Storm" of March 1962.

Kent Mountford photograph

The historic drought of the 1960s was all around us, and coincided with preparing our boats for launching. On April 19, 1963, while the *Silent Maid* and my own boat *La Boheme* (Figure 7-25) were still fitting out, both had a very close brush with disaster. Coming into Beaton's Boatyard and Winter Yacht Basin, we were aware that woodland fires were burning perhaps a mile to the west of us and that the mild southwest wind was rising and forecast to blow really hard. I payed (caulked) bottom seams with compound all morning. In my logbook, I recorded that Richard, one of the boys in the boatyard, had run up to report the fire to me.

" . . . fire had broken out of the pines and hit the marsh, which was tinder dry after winter. The wind was roaring terrifically and the flames raced at an unbelievable rate jumping through the air like a demon towards the north end of the boatyard. . . . I cannot describe the wind and its intensity, bearing a choking yellow pall of smoke at speeds (according to an anemometer at Winter Yacht Basin) up to 52 miles per hour. The fire reached the main road and began burning across wind towards the boats. Richard and I jumped onto the sedge, up to our ankles in water with the flames sizzling angrily across the grass tops at about a yard every five seconds. We beat it out with sticks as far as a mosquito ditch and thus preserved a small unburned rectangle in front of the first rank of boats [which faced westward along the marsh edge].

We stumbled through the smoke half choked and blinded, with buckets in case our rectangle caught fire. Someone tried to get a hose going [to wet down the boats] but the power lines to our west had burned through. [We had no water pressure. I remember Richard standing there holding the hose, which was ineffectually dribbling while the flames came at him.]

Fire had by then broken out of the Pines farther south and hit the main marsh. It was difficult to see anything with the wind driven smoke, but we could hear it roaring along just over the creek from us. As the main body of the fire came abreast of Beaton's, we had a trifling wind shift that in all probability saved the yard by preventing flames from jumping the channel and creek. . . . The fire raced on at walking speed clear out Swan Point, setting a barge grounded there afire.

The wind shift had come too late for it to stop the jumping of Beaton's road thus exposing Winter Yacht Basin and the *Silent Maid*. . . . I hiked out the road to see for myself what was happening. I cannot re-create the fiendish impression thus gained. Every other house I passed was either completely in embers or in the process of blazing collapse. The wind was so strong that for hundreds of yards you could feel the spray from fire hoses, and pieces of heat-shattered light bulbs were blowing along the street. The old Brick Presbyterian Church [now a construction company building] had collapsed, crushing a truck inside, the naked shell of which [vehicle] could be seen. A cabin garvey next to it burned merrily on her blocks. A home lay in a smoldering heap while fifteen feet away, unscorched laundry still blew on a clothesline in the back yard. . . . Weirdly, across the street, a house was flattened, the next one to it totally unscathed; next to that a garage in rubble. Farther up the road a fuel tank exploded with a report that echoed over the bay and at the same time, leveled a dwelling. A propane tank burned a bright torch against the setting sun. I counted in all sixteen homes [others report 22] and two garages over a span of two miles totally beyond any repair or salvage whatsoever.

[A mile or so farther down-Bay, fire again left the pine woods] . . . preceded by a vast rolling pall of white and gray smoke, a storm of flame was dancing across the marsh towards Havens Cove a mile distant. With binoculars I could see great pieces of naked fire breaking loose and dancing through the air to connect with new rising tongues ten feet high and blowing like unconnected spirits in union for the destruction of all before them. Behind was only black marsh and a slithering white shift of vapor, punctuated by agitated sentinels of still blazing matter . . ."[74]

At the end of the day, *Silent Maid* and all the boats at Winter Yacht Basin and Beaton's Boatyard were undamaged, though we worked the rest of the day under a constant aerial rain of ash, like falling *Lapilli* from a volcanic eruption. My logbook continues, "I drove to Manasquan under a sky blanketed by great plumes of smoke from almost uncounted fires all across the state. You could see them glowing after dark like so many nuclear fire storms, exhausting holocausts as far as the eye could see."

It took several days for exhausted firefighters across the state of New Jersey to get control of these fires. One estimate was that 13% of the state's forests had been affected. This was an amazing experience for me, having fought part of the blaze myself, and the impression has lasted over half a century. My boat *La Boheme* painfully dry from the extremely low humidity sank as soon as she was launched.

The *Maid* did a little better. On the last day of May, we were finally sailing again. Anchored at Clearwater, and looking under the boat, we were astounded by the "vast number of blowfish in the eelgrass at the bottom. . . . We had some rolls left over from lunch and we began luring them to the surface with scraps. It was quite an experience seeing so many fish respond to hand feeding in salt water. We could have scooped up a dozen in a crab net, had we one."[75]

This visible abundance was never repeated in my years on Barnegat Bay, but when these blowfish spawned, it was not long before the water was full of tiny babies. They could inflate just like the adults, and you could hold several in your hands like a bunch of peas. I took a few to my little aquarium at home, but they did not thrive in my primitive setup. I learned, but they, poor little things, died.

*   *   *

On the dunes in June, the *Hudsonia* is profusely in bloom and very fragrant in the quiet swales. Few people visiting Island Beach encounter this abundance because this grayish, ground-hugging plant only blooms for a short period and does so well before the major rush of visitors to the shore. In June of 1963, my then (German) girlfriend Martha Fuessel found a tiny horseshoe crab, no more than an inch across, in the shallows. I took

FIGURE 7-81. A (deflated) blowfish (*Sphaeroides maculatus*) from Barnegat Bay, imaged at the public aquarium at Island Beach State Park, 2005.

Diane Bennett Chase photograph

this critter to my saltwater aquarium at home, and he lived long enough to shed his exoskeleton, so my tank appeared to have two in residence.

"Crossing the barrier island at Clearwater, I waded into the surf for a swim, and I was astounded to find myself surrounded by a vast urgently moving school of young bluefish. They were sweeping by in the thousands, a few side-stragglers zipping inshore of me and the main horde veering but slightly in their course; a weird feeling to be so outnumbered in the unquestioned domain of another life form.

We returned up the beach and observed surf fishermen taking the little blues two to a cast with silver squids [a popular fishing lure]. The fishermen had to close the trunk of their wagon to keep their still active catch from jumping out onto the sand."[76]

As summer progressed, Martha's family joined *Silent Maid* for a very heavy weather sail, dealing with an unusual early July northwest blow. In all the hubbub, I managed to dislocate a toe very painfully. The relationship however was getting serious, and it was time for the parents to meet, though hers spoke limited English.

On previous trips to the lower bay, Dad had found what we called the "back channel" out to Barnegat inlet which had extremely clear incoming ocean water and a strong current from the inlet's fierce tides. We anchored there one afternoon with my girlfriend Martha and Dee and Bob De Nicholas, a couple from my workplace, who were excited at all the warm water ". . . and the sand bottom perfectly clean and white. We lay at anchor streaming two lines off the transom quarters so that those tired (of swimming) could hang on. All of us totally enjoyed the experience with hundreds of blowfish, striped sea robins, starfish, gastropods (snails, and delicate) Ctenophores or 'comb jellies.'" Bob was a shining star in our office, handsome and totally in control, but on *Silent Maid* he was completely blown away by the deluge of totally novel experiences. Many people were similarly amazed and, in delivering such surprises, *Silent Maid* excelled.

"The sand bottom in the back channel . . . was thrillingly crystal clear. It was totally like being in the Bahamas! Water a pale aqua, current swift and sparkling, breeze cool, water full of life with *Ctenophores* (sea walnuts, a non-stinging luminous 'jellyfish') and the red-belled jellyfish, *Cyanea capillata*, gracing the view. Martha dove with a mask for the first time and was thrilled. She surfaced burbling after the first foray, eyes a sparkle behind the face plate: 'The sun is shining downstairs!'".[77]

FIGURE 7-82. *(Top)* The Ctenophore *Mnemiopsis leidyi* is abundant in Barnegat Bay, feeding on minute plankton organisms, harmless to humans and brilliantly bio-luminescent at night. *(Center)* A large red-beard sponge (*Microciona porifera*) about 6 inches in diameter from Barnegat Bay. *(Bottom)* The red tinged 'lion's mane' jellyfish *Cyanea capillata*, common through springtime in Barnegat Bay.

Kent Mountford photographs

FIGURE 7-83. (Left) The unusual egg cases of the 'Channeled Whelk' (*Busycon canaliculatum*)—a large snail.
(Below) Individual egg capsule of a related species (*B.carica*) opened; and the minute baby whelk snails inside each.

Kent Mountford photographs

FIGURE 7-84. *(Left)* The *Maid* anchored in the back channel to Barnegat Inlet in August of 1960 with a light sea fog obscuring Island Beach. *(Right)* My mom swimming on a hot afternoon.

Stan Mountford photographs

I was down there with my snorkel and fins too, just as enthralled as she was. Snorkels in those days were Rube Goldberg devices with re-curved upper ends where a caged ping-pong ball was supposed to float up and stop water from entering the snorkel tube when you dove. They did not work very well either!

I could jump off the *Maid* and ride the current aft, tailing on the bitter end of the trailing line then pulling myself back. A whole new world of marine biology opened before my eyes. Across the brilliant white sand a snake-like egg case of a channeled whelk *Busycon canaliculatum* tumbled along on the current. Brilliant red-beard sponges were on the bottom and some abandoned clamshells were coated with a thick, bright, yellow boring sponge (*Cliona celata*). I'd never seen or experienced anything like it and, for me, Barnegat Bay would never be the same.

*   *   *

The year 1963 was difficult for my family. Mom at age 50 was beginning to struggle with menopause and the resulting emotional ups and downs led her to spend more time in church than on *Silent Maid*. This put more of the work of maintaining, and in fact using, the boat on Dad's back than he had in the previous decade. I was too focused on my own life at that age to recognize how stressful this was for him.

Then one day at our home in Warren Township, trucks pulled up next to our woods and while my mother watched from the porch, men drove stakes and fired off explosive

Still a Wanna-Be Yacht Designer!

It was still possible in the late 1950s and early 1960s to enter the field of boat design despite the lack of an engineering degree. So, years after college and a stint in the military, I took some of my boat designs to naval architect Gerald Taylor White who ran Westlawn School of Yacht Design. He thought (or at least said) I had a good eye for it. I did not have the brains at the time to connect Mr. White as one of Edwin Schoettle's contributing authors in the book *Sailing Craft*, which my family owned as part of our *Silent Maid* kit.

With Mr. White's encouragement, I paid my money (10% of my annual income at the time) and signed up for Westlawn's correspondence design course. Trying to do this part-time, while immersed in another full-time career, I never finished the courses. However, continuing with feelers in the field and showing my designs around, I eventually got a job offer from Sparkman and Stevens as a draftsman in its design section. By then I was fairly well established as a nascent professional—doing the hiring and job placement, rather than out there looking for employment—and I was too conservative to jump at the opportunity.

seismic charges with window rattling reports. Not a word to the owners until Mom hurried out and asked what the devil they thought they were doing. She was told there was to be an Interstate Highway—Route 78—through here and they would be condemning our 135-year-old home under eminent domain. She was in shock until Dad and I arrived at the house, then simply distraught. The government's cavalier action made front-page news in the widely read *Plainfield Courier News*, but there was no misunderstanding, no appeal. This would all come to pass within the year.

Dad had also developed a hand tremor, a problem where the ability to do extremely fine work had been a hallmark of his skills. That was affecting his work, and our family physician Albert Misko finally did some definitive tests and determined that it was Parkinsonism—a terrible sentence for a man whose defining skills had been linking mind and hand throughout his life. I will always remember the afternoon when I was in my home office and Mom came in to tearfully tell me this. In this time before Internet information and local support groups, neither she nor I, nor Dad for that matter, had any understanding what this affliction would mean to our lives at the time. It meant, for one thing, that Dad would soon be unable to handle maintaining the *Maid* alone. My logbook records that: "The beginning days of April found my father also making a decision. After 12 years—12 sailing seasons at least—he deigned to consider an offer to sell the *Silent Maid*."

FIGURE 7-85. **The fire-destroyed facility at Winter Yacht Basin in 1964.** *Stan Mountford photograph*

In 1964, the *Maid*'s final brush with doom on our watch came while she was hauled and completely uninsured—or as my father described it "self-insured." Evoking shades of the Class A cat *Tamwock* burnt at Island Heights, a fire broke out in Winter Yacht Basin's nearby largest shed. The building was completely destroyed together with a then-astronomical loss of $3 million in stored yachts. Rudy Winter said after that, he never wanted to see such an event again. We certainly agreed, and I looked at the wreckage, wondering whatever would we have done if the *Maid* had been in that conflagration?

During those cold spring weekends in 1964, my parents made it clear that if I had the guts, and resources for it, *Silent Maid* could become my boat! I thought about this opportunity, but fully recognized that I was not willing to undertake the work and expense of this big boat by myself. My job, my modest income, and a turbulent love affair in progress made all that abundantly clear.

Because Dad increasingly needed the help of a physically fit son, we commissioned the *Maid* mostly working together. What I could not fully grasp was that this would also be the last time my father and I would be able to share such a major project as adults; the last time I'd be able to absorb his skills and inventiveness first hand. I did my share of work, but my attention was elsewhere—for the young man burning with testosterone and the thirst for independence, this was an opportunity wasted.

Dad had kept that letter from Judson Smith received years before about seeking to purchase *Silent Maid*. Dad dug it out and wrote to him on the off chance he might still be interested. We'd had only that one enquiry from him and no idea of the long history of him chasing *Silent Maid* across almost two decades.

Jud waited a month to reply to Dad's letter, clearly thinking about his response at some length. While he missed this chance to be the *Maid*'s skipper yet again, amazingly, he was not yet done interacting with her, though the next time would be 45 years later.[78]

The *Maid* hardly needed to be put on the market. Having long been an icon on Barnegat Bay, quite speedy negotiations led to her being bought by a young man named

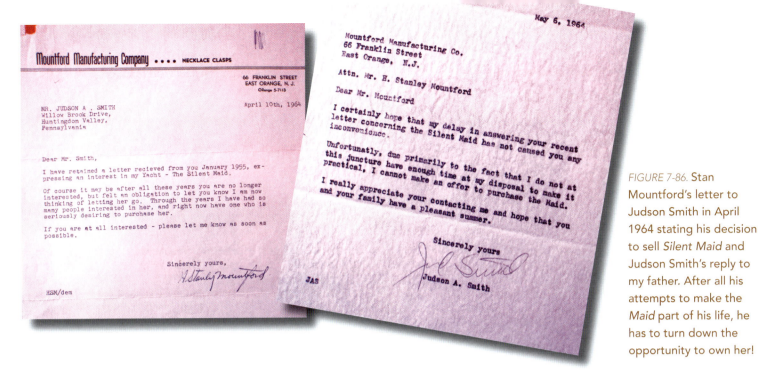

FIGURE 7-86. Stan Mountford's letter to Judson Smith in April 1964 stating his decision to sell *Silent Maid* and Judson Smith's reply to my father. After all his attempts to make the *Maid* part of his life, he has to turn down the opportunity to own her!

FIGURE 7-87. *Silent Maid*, off Mantoloking in Barnegat Bay, sails away from my family and on to yet another incarnation.

Kent Mountford photograph

Clifford Hogan, of Mantoloking. Hogan was not the only person who had their eyes on the *Maid* during the years we docked her at Winter Yacht Basin. Winter's Drop Anchor Snack Bar, where my family had eaten often was also frequented by Sally Schneider, a Summit, New Jersey, schoolteacher. She just missed purchasing the boat when Cliff Hogan concluded his dealings with my father. The cash price of $3500 was a strong barrier for Sally on her modest teacher's salary!

Dad was a reluctant seller; the boat had become part of my family's life. My parents wanted her to be with us for one more summer vacation, and we rigged her out so they could use her during Dad's annual July vacation at the shore. With my German girl-friend sometimes aboard (and with whom I was in the throes of a very disruptive and exciting relationship), we experienced our last times together on the *Maid*. As my log-book recorded on Saturday, July 11, 1964, we had "a dandy final run down to Mosquito Cove and back. I will miss that old gal dearly. She has been an eye-catcher wherever she went, and we have been unceasingly proud of her over the years we have sailed her since

FIGURE 7-88. Despite Barnegat's problems, subsequent generations had the wisdom to acquire one side of Mosquito Cove, and the bluff I mentioned, as public lands. This feature, called "Yellow Bank" on the Bronson map, along with nearby Applegate Cove is preserved today as part of the popular Cattus Island Park.[79]

FIGURE 7-89. My college roommate and lifelong friend George Roome looks out on Mosquito Cove (Silver Bay) with *Silent Maid* anchored far off amongst a busy weekend fleet.

Kent Mountford photograph, 1956

FIGURE 7-90. **Stan Mountford in 1974 at the helm of his son's 1938 wooden yawl** *CEMBA* **sailing on the Chesapeake Bay. Stan passed away from side effects of Parkinson's disease in April 1981, 16 years after diagnosis.**

Kent Mountford photograph

August 24, 1953." I might have said something like that about the girl-friend, with whom I essentially broke up that fateful weekend.

During her time with us, the *Maid* had hosted scores of friends and visitors from China, Canada, Sweden, Germany, and Argentina. The old times were ending, but for *Silent Maid* and me, new times were just beginning.

FIGURE 7-91. *Silent Maid*'s cockpit as it appears today, where she is stored at the Philadelphia Navy Yard prior to exhibit at the Independence Seaport Museum.

Kent Mountford photograph

ENDNOTES — CHAPTER 7

1. Dorothy Mountford-Sage, notes on family genealogy found in the papers of her estate, 1980.

2. Isabella Kent (Gordon) was two years old when Abraham Lincoln was assassinated; she died just days before her 86th birthday in 1949, when the author was eleven.

3. Civil War Timeline /Chronology, April 1863, http://blueandgraytrail.com/year/186304

4. Notes from the family Bible record this as presented here.

5. The value of one U.S. dollar in 1870 was 0.1790 British Pounds Sterling, http://www.Measuringworth.com/exchangeglobal/

6. Lew Gordon, about 1955, told the family that at his visit to a somewhat rough-edged Bal Ellis the previous year, a calf had wandered into the house through an open door, and the dog had come into the hall and pissed on the base of the grandfather clock. In 1965, I found more normal housekeeping conditions and a cheerful, enthusiastic farmer.

7. http://en.wikipedia.org/wiki/Saltwater_intrusion and http://en.wikipedia.org/wiki/iego_Garcia#fresh_water_supply

8. Shipping Intelligence, *Sydney Morning Herald*, September 7, 1885. Reported the itinerary, arrival, detailing Master, crew and passenger categories for RMS *Sorata*. Isabella Kent was not listed on the manifest, perhaps because she was in steerage and had her passage pre-paid for her.

9. Dorothy (Gordon, Mountford) Sage, handwritten family history, 1990. Alec's father was born in 1798 and lived in three centuries, dying in 1900 at age 102. Ethnic violence (his brother-in law?) was ambushed and stoned to death by a mob and the King's Sheriff murdered) and a boycott against Protestant goods, stimulated Alec's emigration to America with his family.

10. Florence (Gordon) Ottinger, letters to her brother Lew Gordon on genealogy provided much detail on the family's history, 1953.

11. Birth certificate of Thomas Alfred Mountford, March 30, 1842, Brass House Passage, Ladywood, Birmingham, Warwick Co., Great Britain.

12. The author, attending concerts of the Washington (DC) Choral Arts Society came to know Count Marc and Countess Anita d'Anselme. When this supposed ancestry of mine was mentioned, Marc blanched and said "Then your ancestor **massacred** my ancestors." We were still friends!

13. Katherine Ashe. Katherineashe.blogspot.com/. Simon, 6th Earl of Leicester, 1208-1265, fell on August 4 in the Battle of Eavesham, England, fighting against Royalist troops, after which he was dismembered. He wore his coat of arms both on his breast and shield, a red lion rampant on a white field.

14. "Simon de Montfort," http://en.wikipedia.org/wiki/Simon_de_Montfort,_6th_Earl_of_Leicester

15. "Early Settlers," http://www.visitmuskoka.com/history.htm

16. The family beach cottage at Manasquan on the New Jersey Shore was destroyed by Hurricane Sandy in October 2012; an uninsured loss of about a third of a million dollars.

17. Thomas A. Mountford, U.S. Patent 1.814,486, July 14, 1931. Necklaces are usually joined with some kind of clasp that can (sight unseen) be fastened behind the wearer's neck. The clasp Tom invented "clicked" when fastened and later models were called "safety" clasps because, if they became accidentally unfastened, the springy "click" end to which the pearls were attached had a "V" shaped hook that still captured the end of the necklace, so it could not fall off unnoticed. This design was widely adopted in the pearl necklace industry for natural, cultured, and costume pearls. While the idea was initially sold to the Schick Company, when my grandfather Tom and Sid entered the business they filed a patent and were able to beat most competition with their efficiency.

18. Professional Appraisal Associates, Summit, NJ, 1980. Following Sid's death, an appraisal of the property for potential subdivision detailed 15.79 acres, plus two proposed roads, valuing the land (Block 62, Lot 8), at $320,000 to $352,000.

19. Peter Herrington (docent at the Bay Head, Mantoloking, Lovelandtown Museum), interview with Kent Mountford at Bay Head, NJ, 2009. His memories of George Mountford's bull-headedness were guardedly unpleasant!

20. This refuge continued in the family for 90 years until Hurricane Sandy destroyed it during the storm surge on October 29, 2012. The author began rebuilding a home on this site in January 2014.

21. Evelyn "Gillie" Ogden, interview with Kent Mountford at Point Pleasant, NJ, 2010.

22. Dr. Mountford's split pea soup with ham: 1 lb dried split peas, 12 cups water, three large carrots, 2 large ribs celery, one large yellow onion (all finely chopped), ½ lb lean smoked ham shredded, and four bouillon cubes. Bring to a boil, then simmer covered for hours, adding more water if required for desired consistency! Break a 1.5" diameter handful of vermicelli pasta into ½" lengths, pre-boil 3-4 minutes, drain, and add to soup. Serves many, tastes good, and freezes well for quick cold-weather shipboard lunches. The noodles are better when freshly made and added just before serving.

23. Franklin Mountford, interviewed at Ft. Meyers, FL, January 2005.

24. Thomas Alfred Mountford, III, discussion at Manasquan with cousin Kent Mountford, when we reconstructed these annual charity voyages, October 2013.

25. Frederick B. Colie, *An Exercise in Nostalgia* (Morristown, NJ: Compton Press, 1970). Addison Woolsey Bronson, 1869-1947, crafted this hand-drawn map recording all the islands, points, and coves with their "original" historic names. He sailed the Bay most of his life in a small sloop exploring and recording. According to Bob O'Brien, NJ Museum of Boating, 2010, the U.S. Coast and Geodetic survey borrowed one version of his map when it was formally charting Barnegat Bay.

26. William H. Whiting Company catalog, Pratt and Gay Streets, Baltimore, MD (1935), p. 125 Cheek Block.

27. Gail Mountford, 2014. The author's first cousin was also a usually happy sailor on *Osprey*. The wildly spinning flywheel of the *Osprey*'s Graymarine engine was unenclosed behind the cabin companionway ladder, and the toe of Gail's sneaker was caught in it and sheared completely off, but her toes were undamaged. What a tragedy this would have been for this prettiest of my cousins had luck not intervened.

28. Carvel planking has the edges matched and caulked so that the surface of the hull is smooth and can be painted so as to appear without discontinuous planks. The frames in hard-chined boats are made of multiple pieces or futtocks, and where they are joined the cross section of the boat has hard spots or "corners" called chines and visible from the outside.

29. Thomas Beaton, discussion on slip rentals with Kent Mountford, May 23, 2014. "When my grandfather (David Beaton, Sr.) was alive we figured that the rental of a few slips (in Brick Township, NJ) took care of the taxes. Then it got to where the rental of slips on one dock went to pay taxes. Now the revenue of all our slips barely make the tax bill, and (during Hurricanes Irene and Sandy) we both lost so many slips (to storm damage) and the number of boaters coming to rent fell so much, that we go seriously in the hole from this revenue source. The taxes never really go down." The author, for one slip during summer 2013, paid Beaton's $2700, versus the $32 he paid for his first mooring about 1955.

30. *Phragmites communis* is known as common reed grass, an introduced subspecies of the Genus probably brought from Europe with the colonists. It is a very aggressive invasive plant, growing to a height of 6-10 feet, which has overwhelmed hundreds of thousands of acres of native salt marsh vegetation in the United States. Eradication programs have generally been unsuccessful.

31. Lynn Tidwell, personal communication, July 2006. As we sailed aboard the *Victory Chimes*, one of the nation's oldest wooden schooners, Tidwell of Charlotte Harbor, Florida, told me that fiberglass boats had their genesis with a chemistry graduate student at Ohio State University named Raymond Green, who had the idea you could bond together resin and flexible glass fibers, making a wonderful hull—rigid when

cured and exactly the shape you wanted. He started a manuscript, but his advisor said "don't use the term 'boat' or people will blow you off. You've got to couch it in dull engineering terms such as an 'architectural form' or something." What he built, terminology aside, was *New Horizon,* a 26-foot sloop with shoal 3-foot draft. *New Horizon* still exists, Tidwell said, though she was damaged in Hurricane Charlie in 2004.

32. Alan Van Winkle, personal phone communication, 2010. Van Winkle, who lives on Maryland's Eastern Shore, told me he still has this skiff 47 years later—refinished and refurbished more than once.

33. Thomas Beaton, personal communication to Kent Mountford, log entry on July 3, 2007.

34. Merriman Brothers (Boston, 1898-1995), produced excellent pulley blocks and marine hardware with a trident trademark. When the company was being "restructured," Frank Merriman, Jr., watched the "bright young men," who were then in charge, take all the wooden casting patterns to the dump and where they burned them. http://www.forum.woodenboat.com/archive/index.php/t-19771.html

35. In perspective, four years earlier, my parents paid $10,000 cash for our modest home, garage, pump house and 1.5 acres of mostly wooded land. The *Maid*'s purchase was another significant investment!

36. Bob Reddington, personal discussion with Kent Mountford at Beaton's Boatyard, and later in the presence of Marie Darling, who initially dismissed the story, 2012.

37. Charles F. Chapman, *Piloting Seamanship and Small Boat Handling* (New York: Hearst Books, 1950).

38. Stephan Lance (President, Defender Industries), email exchange on his father's founding the company, October 2013.

39. David Wolfe, personal communication at Mystic, CT, February 2014.

40. Subsequently, this was recognized as formaldehyde gas, the formation of which was catalyzed from vaporized alcohol by the metals in the stove. Years and many tears later (from stinging eyes), I found this release even more pronounced and persistent in full-blown alcohol stoves, gravity or pressurized, whether burning methylated spirits or pure grain alcohol... any of the latter that was subsequently "spirited" out of my laboratory was for the STOVE not consumption, should the Bureau of Alcohol, Tobacco and Firearms still be interested!

41. "Paint Roller," www.Wikipedia.org/wiki/paint_roller. The paint roller was invented in 1940 by Canadian Norman Breakey, who was unable to capitalize on it. Richard Croxton Adams, who worked for Sherwin Williams Paint Co., filed the first U.S. patent also in 1940.

42. Day-Glo Color Corporation, Cleveland, OH, are now a world leader in manufacturing these pigmented coatings.

43. Lowell Sick, PhD. Previously at the University of Delaware, Sick moved to South Carolina and changed his professional name to Sycke for the sake of his kids, who were then in grade school. He used *Wake* for years, sailing out to harvest local "coon" oyster reefs.

44. John Riesman, MD, *Friendship Sloop Days* (Yearbook of the Friendship Sloop Society, 1968), 27-28.

45. *Skeeter* was built by J.H. Perrine before World War II at Barnegat, NJ. *Skeeter*'s former owner indicated she had been her Class B champion one year, racing at Bay Head Yacht Club. Runyon Colie, a world-class Barnegat sailor, distinguished in Penguins and later "E" Scows, tells of being asked by her owner to sail *Skeeter* in a race while he was home on leave from the Navy Yard late in WW II. The wind was westerly and the fleet was off Goodluck Point at the mouth of Toms River. Colie saw, glinting in the water out by Seaside Park, the first hint of the incoming southerly and tacked to go out and anticipate it. What could have been a brilliant gamble seemed not to be. The wind came up stronger still WSW, and he was far from the fleet. But, he could see the front of the southerly wind still coming and the boats, now a mixture of two classes racing for the same mark, would surge out in the cat's paw, then lose the wind, while the rear boats, moving faster in the stronger rising wind, were piling up behind the leaders. Colie, who had come about again, was clear of the pack as it turned into a remarkable jumble of several score boats. Someone took a picture of that tangle of boats, which he climbed up the spiral staircase in his home to show me—the moment preserved for 60 years. *Skeeter* was **not** in the picture; Colie having slipped home, clear and ahead of the tangle, in what he said was the sweetest victory of his long sailing career.

46. Kent Mountford, Log *Skeeter* , October 13, 1956. "I was delighted to stand forward with G at the helm. And gaze through the shallow waters their Eelgrasses waving, providing a remarkable illusion of free flight."

47. Lighter Fluid was the weapon of choice for dormitory "vandals" (make that jokesters) in the late 1950s. The university required each room have a nameplate on the door; ours stating "George Roome, Electrical Engineering and Kent Mountford, Civil Engineering." We made nice cards, neatly lettered, with color logos, and each time some dorm wag would light them with a cigarette lighter we had to replace them. Having enough of it, we laminated two (ornately labeled) 3" × 5" cards and glued a layer of homemade gunpowder between them. Next week we were quietly studying when "WHUMP!" the space around our entire door frame shone a bright flash. Running and cursing was heard in the hallway. We never had the problem again, and of course WE never faced any discipline!

48. Kent Mountford, *Closed Sea: Manasquan to the Mullica* (Harvey Cedars, NJ: Down the Shore Publishing Company, 2002).

49. Kent Mountford, Log *Skeeter,* July 20, 1957.

50. Kent Mountford, Log *La Boheme,* July 2, 1963.

51. Lord Henry Charles Howard, Earl of Hadley and Berkshire and Frederick George Afalo. 1911. *Encyclopedia of Sport,* p 55. Lord Henry, in the English manner, called reels "winches."

52. "Tackle," www.overmywaders.com/index.php?stjohnrod1

53. Denis Boyles, *How to Catch a Pig* (HarperCollins e-books, 2009), p. 72.

54. L.S. Hohenberk (Forestry Officer), "British Guiana Timbers," *Journal of the Board of Agriculture of British Guiana*, (1916): 163.

55. *U.S. Trademark Register*, Vol. 10, 1909. Cases argued and determined 1920, pp 255-56. Bethabara:"Shipley…used this name for fishing rods for many years (after 1880) and sought exclusive rights in 1920 charging trademark infringement (*Trademark Reporter*, Vol. 9. p 294). This wood had been imported from England 40 years earlier, in 1880, and some was sold then to F. D. Divine, rod maker, in Utica, NY." It was characterized then as the most expensive wood used in rod making.

56. "Bethabara," place of crossing; a ford, likely a stream flowing into but not the River Jordan itself, so identified on the *Madaba* map (as the Greek "BEOABAPA"), and also in the Talmud. (httm://Wikipedia.org/wiki/Bethabara)

57. Franklin R. Longwood in *Present and Potential Commercial Timbers of the Caribbean, Agriculture Handbook 207*, Washington, DC (1962): 2.

58. Phil White. (www.oldreels.com), and personal correspondence with Kent Mountford, 2013. "Gus Meisselbach fished at Ocean City, NJ, until his retirement in 1919, and passed away in 1927.

59. When casting, the free spool reel will continue running out line as the momentum of the lure and/or sinker declines, and fishing line will pile up in a looped mass (or "bird's nest") around the reel's frame, unless the spool is delicately slowed by dragging a thumb (feathering) on the spinning spool. With dry line the friction of doing this can burn and blister your thumb; hence a leather flap was added to prevent injury. In old reels before mechanical friction devices like Star-Drag were developed, you could also slow a running fish using this flap and hard thumb pressure.

60. Topper Boat Company (Baltimore, MD), full-page magazine advertisement, 1950.

61. Race-Lite South Coast. http://www.manta.com/race-lite-south

62. This concept was decades later adopted (I'm sure independently conceived) and such clever glycerine soaps are marketed today by Primal Elements Company, Huntington Beach, CA.

63. Hurricane Helene, September 21-29, 1958. http://en.wikipedia.org/wiki/Hurricane_Helene_(1958)

64. Kent Mountford, Log *Surge*, September 1958.

65. Perfection® kerosene heaters came into use after John D. Rockefeller introduced kerosene lamp oil into the domestic whale-oil fueled lantern market. He thus possibly, by that single market decision, saved the world's whale populations from extinction. The use of kerosene in heaters started about 1892, but in 1901 Rockefeller started manufacturing a lightweight, pierced metal space heater with integral fuel tank through a company called Perfection. (http://farmhousefollies.com/2011/12/20/the-government-wont-mind-if-you-freeze-to-death/)

66. Kent Mountford, Log *Surge*, 1958.

67. Clyde L. Mackenzie, Jr., "The Bay Scallop Argopecten irradians, Massachusetts through North Carolina: Its Biology and the History of its Habitats and Fisheries," *Marine Fisheries Review* 70:3-4 (2006): 1-79.

68. Richard Hartshorne, 1888-1975. Descendant of an American Revolutionary War veteran, once partner in a Newark law firm with my old friend Runyon Colie, whose sailing and historical expertise is elsewhere cited in this volume. During World War II, Hartshorne wrote the seminal pamphlet "Venereal Disease; Saboteur of War Manpower."

69. Kent Mountford photo, August 10, 2010 at Philadelphia Independence Seaport, Philadelphia, PA.

70. John Dickson Carr, www.en.wikipedia.org/wiki/John_Dickson_ Carr

71. Sea Land Corporation founded by Malcolm McLean in 1960, later became part of A.P. Moeller-Maersk. It now operates under a modified logo as Horizon Lines, Inc. (http://en.wikipedia.org/wiki/Sea-Land_Service)

72. American Export Lines was acquired by shipping magnate Jakob Isbrandsen and was for a time the leading U.S.- flag shipping company between the U.S. east coast and Mediterranean. The company declared bankruptcy in 1977. The assets were acquired by Farrell Lines, New York.

73. Kent Mountford, "Past as Prologue" (environmental history column), *Bay Journal*, 2011. (www.bayjournal.com)

74. Kent Mountford, Wellsprings, personal journal for this year, 1963.

75. Kent Mountford, Log *La Boheme*, May 31, 1963.

76. Kent Mountford, Log *La Boheme,* June 13, 1963.

77. Kent Mountford, Log *La Boheme,* August 16, 1963.

78. Peter Kellogg brought the brand new replica *Silent Maid* to the Chesapeake Bay in the autumn of 2009 for the schooner *Sultana*'s Downrig Weekend. I had located Jud Smith, still active, and living in Easton on Maryland's Eastern Shore and told him he simply *had* to visit the *Maid*. On a lark, he drove up that Saturday to finally get aboard this boat that had eluded him for so long. That was exactly when skipper John Brady (with me aboard) was summoned by the festival organizers to get out on the Chester River for a dramatic sail-by with the rest of the fleet, including the historic reconstruction of the square-rigged ship *Kalmar Nyckel*, the topsail schooner *Sultana,* and several other sloops and schooners. We were a mile down-river when Jud, walking along the shore at Chestertown, saw no sign of *Silent Maid* and after two hours gave up and drove home! Next time, Jud.

79. Cattus Island Park was named after the family who formerly owned surrounding properties. It was likely some of their relatives who chased George Roome and me with a shotgun on one of our hikes ashore there! I always thought the bluff was the site of fabled "Indian Hill," and over the years I found a midden, giving evidence of Native American habitation. I found turtle and mollusk shells in the 2000s eroding from the bank, which I turned in to the nature center there with an admonition that the site should be excavated and conserved.

FIGURE 8-1. A Hogan family Polaroid of *Silent Maid* ghosting along south of Mantoloking with Cliff at the helm and Nancy looking over the cabin trunk. Note the T-82 is missing from the *Maid*'s sail. *Inset:* The Hogans sailing the *Maid* before a south wind, just north of Seaside Bridge, off Mosquito Cove.

Hogan family photographs, ca. 1965

8

Silent Maid's Hogan Years

*T*he Hogan family built their home at Mantoloking in 1945 just after the end of World War II. When son Clifford Leo Hogan was seven years old, they moved to the shore from Newark, New Jersey. Cliff attended Bay Head Grammar School starting in the third grade and was in school with Priscilla Beaton, whose uncle Dave Beaton had been a boat builder at Morton Johnson's yard where *Silent Maid* was built—a coincidence lost on Hogan at that age!

Being part of the community fabric gave young Cliff good access to Barnegat life-ways. As a boy, he loved to hunt waterfowl and walk through Slade Dale's Bay Head Yacht Basin, then row down to Herring Island, or sometimes through the Mantoloking Bridge and out to Swan Point and shoot ducks. He also sailed on boats in the 18-foot range, and his boating skills were thus further honed. He worked for a while with one of the local marine construction companies and the pile driver guy taught him how to splice three-strand line. Some Saturdays, with friend Tom Royal, he would tie up to the Mantoloking Bridge piers and haul a seine for spearing (a popular New Jersey choice for bait; see Figure 8-2) or whatever else nature provided.

With Cliff's adulthood came one of the United States' international military adventures: young Hogan's war was the controversial Vietnam conflict during which he served in the U.S. Navy on a demolition crew and aboard the USS *Sioux*, a 206-foot ocean-going tug and salvage vessel. His service involved not only demolition jobs, but also seven slow trans-Pacific passages at a sluggish ten knots, sixty-four days each way. The skipper sent Hogan to several navigation courses, and he became the ship's navigator, as well. The crew's task was hauling damaged vessels back to the States for repair and refit.

FIGURE 8-2. **Spearing (*Menidia sp.*), a popular bait fish for New Jersey surf fisherman.**

Kent Mountford photograph, 2010

Thus, Cliff anticipated future cruising on boats he'd yet to own. Later in San Diego, he taught celestial navigation. One of his acquisitions during this effort was a big old Navy compass salvaged from an aircraft carrier in the mothball fleet, which followed him home to New Jersey, along with a new sport—SCUBA diving—which he pursued with his brother.

A good looking, well-built young man able to network his local credentials was a hot ticket in 1950s' Mantoloking and, according to former schoolmates, Cliff had little trouble attracting girls. It was a good time for him. He'd just been freed from the Navy immediately after one of those 64-day Pacific transits and had driven four days across country, arriving at Mantoloking at what turned out to be the perfect time. Cliff's younger sister Lucille had brought her roommate, Nancy Carlson, down to the shore. It was pure coincidence, because Nancy had just finished her summer job and had a short break before her next semester started. She had grown up on Lake Erie and cut her teeth water skiing behind small, fast outboards.

Not missing the fact that she was really cute, Cliff, who was just on his second day free of the Navy, took her water skiing. During the afternoon, the story is told, "she did three somersaults and lost her bra: the whole top, in fact." During Cliff's time in the Navy, the water skiing rules had been changed to require two people in the tow boat. It was just Cliff towing Nancy, and she'd no sooner fallen than a cabin cruiser full of male and female Coast Guard Auxiliary volunteers came up to brusquely advise Cliff of his transgression and "ordered that woman out of the water. No way was she coming topless out of the water with THAT audience."

The rest is history. By November 2014, they'd been married 51 years.

After his discharge, Cliff took advantage of his post-military education rights and attended night school at Rutgers University. He earned an accounting degree and became a tax accountant—a profession he still pursues.

With their marriage, Cliff and Nancy's circle of friends and relatives widened, which brought an increasing flow of visitors to the family's Mantoloking beach house. As Nancy candidly described it, "I would have to feed them all breakfast, after which they'd disappear for swimming. I'd barely cleaned up the breakfast mess when they'd all come in sunburned, tracking sand, and looking for lunch."

Nancy and Cliff began talking about a boat of their own where they could get away from all this. Each had his or her own concept of what this boat would be, but failed to share it clearly with the other. "I, on one hand, was thinking," says Nancy, who'd not yet let go of water skiing, "of a fast, comfortable cabin cruiser, *not* a sailboat, especially an old one!"

Cliff, according to Sally Schneider, was familiar with the *Silent Maid*, and had either sailed or might have briefly chartered her in 1951.[1] Maybe this was where the idea had been incubating for over a decade!

That's where *Silent Maid* came into the marriage. Cliff was with my father on a trial sail aboard the *Maid* and about to strike the deal; his wife, incidentally, was in the cabin—five months pregnant with daughter Kimberly—and frantically signaling "NO!" Nancy did so to no avail and a second 'marriage' of three years' duration was about to take place. As Cliff recalls it, *Silent Maid* changed hands for $3500, which as I recall, meant that after twelve seasons' hard maintenance, paying slippage, and making hopeful improvements, my father elevated his family finances by seven hundred bucks. In any event, the escape from a crowded beach house would be dubious, given the Hogans' penchant for entertaining.

Thus, Cliff Hogan begins spinning the tales about his years with *Silent Maid*. "I'm Irish," he cautioned me, "and, a good Irishman never lets the truth get in the way of a good story." I've done my best in these pages to keep him honest, and though I make no warranties, I think all that is printed here is truth, if painted in the colors Cliff wanted!

The Hogans at first kept their new boat at the same Winter Yacht Basin slip where she had been for a decade. They launched right in with an autumn cruise taking *Silent Maid* into waters somewhat distant from Barnegat Bay. Leaving Manasquan Inlet, the *Maid* beat north and into New York Bay. Cliff intended to sail up the Hudson River and past the dramatic Palisades. It was a cold autumn trip against strong Northwest winds, and their course past the Statue of Liberty was a rough one, with waves dashing over the entire cabin top. A guest, aboard from Texas and naïve to sailing, was soaked even while sitting in the *Maid*'s usually sheltered cockpit.

Making a late arrival at Weehawkin, New Jersey, they moored alongside a Sea Scout barge after dark with a camel (low, fendered float used for maintenance) between them. Adjacent was a break-bulk freighter that had just arrived from the tropics loaded with a cargo of coffee. The smell was alluring enough for the *Maid*'s windblown crew to briefly think about moving aboard.

It was 1964, the year of the New York World's Fair, which was located on once-meadows in Flushing, New York. The next day still with northerly winds, the Hogans and their crew rounded the tip of Manhattan Island into the East River, timing their passage to benefit from the tide change at Hell Gate.

They had strong head winds, sweeping around the great funnel of New York City's skyscrapers and the *Silent Maid*'s big sail gave her a lot of weather helm. In a passing situation in these narrow straits, a heavy gust overpowered the wheel, and she rounded up, catboat fashion, and went bonk into a big steel tanker underway in the East River. No damage to either party was documented, but this was not a light wind passage.

To keep the old cotton sail set properly, the peak halyard was set tight and, in the midst of all this close concentration, the line chose this moment to part. The tip of the *Maid*'s big gaff fell down like a scimitar until it hit the boom, enveloping everything in billowing folds of old canvas. They had just an hour and a half to make the tide through Hell Gate! From my own experience, this is not an easy condition under which to get the gaff—or that huge sail—down while the peak halyard and gaff jaws are awkward! Lowering the gaff in heavy weather, securing it to the boom, and tightening up on the topping lifts, however, was an old emergency strategy fused by sailors in the Bahama Islands, and they had a name for it: scandalizing or the Bahamian reef.

"Very frightening," Cliff recalls, "so with our very first Bahama reef in place, we continued to the Fair!" At the end of that busy day, *Silent Maid* anchored, at rest for the night, under

FIGURE 8-3. *Silent Maid* docked in front of the elder Hogan's 1945 Mantoloking residence. Cliff has sketched the Maid's sail to show someone its advertised size.
Hogan family photograph, ca. 1966

FIGURE 8-4. *Silent Maid* at the Hogan family pier in 1965, not in her regular slip. Nancy, now with longer reddish hair—her natural color—stands watch.
Hogan family photograph

FIGURE 8-5. *(Top)* Cliff, sailing the *Maid* with three adult crew and two babies. His electric halyard winch is atop the cabin trunk. *(Bottom)* His old Navy compass is mounted as a binnacle, here with its lid on just ahead of the helm.

Hogan family photographs

the not very relaxing flight path of jet airliners taking off and landing at La Guardia Airport.

The World's Fair was a pretty cool experience for that generation, which had never experienced such an exhibition. Cliff and I are age mates and I certainly recall wandering those international pavilions with great interest. With their visit completed and a stiff land breeze still in progress, the *Maid's* passage down the East River was either across or before the wind. It took them first past Governor's Island into New York Bay, then coastwise into the lee of Sandy Hook and the Jersey Shore, which sheltered the zooming *Silent Maid* from any developing wave action. This passage—with a wet sheet, a flowing sea, and a wind that followed fast—took them all the way to Manasquan Inlet in a single afternoon.

Leaving her long-time slip at Winter Yacht Basin, the *Maid* sometimes occupied a slip at the family home across Barnegat Bay on Mantoloking Beach. Cliff loved being at sea and, probably the next year, *Silent Maid* was docked in Brielle, just on the ocean side of the Route 35 Bridge, alongside some year-round charter boats. It was the end of the sailing season, and Cliff decided she could spend the winter afloat. With high salinity, there was little danger from ice damage, and he had rigged a toilet float to the bilge pump against any unexpected leaks.

Before shutting down entirely for the season, he took some friends to dinner at The Ferry, a once posh restaurant, which was a huge, genuine-retired ferryboat then moored nearby alongside the Manasquan River. This floating Brielle establishment hosted jazz artists like saxophone and clarinetist Kenny Davern.[2] As Cliff said, "beverages may have been involved," and after the meal he piled ten people into the *Maid's* cockpit, cast off the lines, and put the engine in gear. A stream of mud flew out from under the transom. She was sitting on the bottom at one of Manasquan's extreme autumn ebb tides—that put an end to the after-dinner cruise.

Cliff liked to sail in the ocean and to do so, while mooring at Brielle, each trip to sea required two trips through the old, late-19th century Bascule railroad bridge, while entering and leaving the river. This bridge, still operating after over a century, has only a three-foot vertical clearance when closed. It is usually open, but closes for each passing train, and with huge overhead counterweights to get moving, the opening is pretty sluggish. Boaters in this strong tide-way often race to be first through, lest a train unexpectedly blocks their way. On one passage by *Silent Maid*, a powerboat accelerated and passed her in the draw, which is only 48 feet wide at water level.

Because the bridge only opens to about a 60-degree angle, only half the width of the draw opening is available to boats with tall superstructure or masts. *Silent Maid* was forced south, towards the low side of the raised bridge. When the interloper's wake started the *Maid* rolling, it was a nasty few moments with her tall mast whacking into parts of the railroad trestle. So much for courtesy and awareness about fellow boaters.

The next spring, Cliff took *Silent Maid* up the Metedeconk River where he could do spring maintenance and some re-thinking. One of the changes he made was to install a house battery-operated winch drum atop the cabin trunk. We traditionalists thought this out of character for the *Maid*. However, Cliff makes the cogent argument that when handling the boat alone it was impossible to keep her into the wind if you were up forward hoisting throat and peak halyards together: point taken. He also built a serious binnacle box that was mounted ahead of the *Maid's* helm. It housed the compass he'd brought home from his sea duty in the Pacific and was his way of introducing serious navigation to the *Maid*'s routine.

Cliff's competitive side made him eager to race *Silent Maid* whose history as a bay-wide champion of note he wished to amplify. He signed up for a summer offshore race, south from Manasquan Inlet. There was a pre-race evening meeting at Bay Head Yacht Club for participating skippers. Proud and outspoken schooner owner Walter Flower stood up and said relative to *Silent Maid*, "I wouldn't take that catboat out in a swimming pool on a calm day." That dismissive challenge was all Cliff Hogan needed. I'll let him tell it in his own words:

> The next day at the start of the race, we were *allowed* to race, but were instructed to start last. There were 50 or so boats in the race. Very quickly we started to overtake the fleet; everyone was heading up-wind. The *Maid* was moving so fast I just gave her the wind and we blew by, leaving one at a time in our wake.

> We passed the first five-mile mark and eased to a reach towards the east with a stiff south wind setting in. On the first tacking leg we [had] passed half the fleet. Pretty impressive! A reach! My entire body was smiling. With 18 knots' wind on a reach the rest of the fleet was mine. Shortly, on this leg, I spotted Walter Flower in his salty schooner ahead. The *Silent Maid* did her thing, blowing past him as though he had an anchor out. Daughter Kim [one year old] was all smiles swinging in her hammock below decks.

> About this time I was informed that Nancy was in the head and she couldn't get the door open. I had the word sent down that we'd just passed Walter Flower and wanted another five minutes, at which time I eased the main, the door opened and out came Nancy none the worse for wear!

> [*Silent Maid*, showing her very advanced age, had literally twisted from the strains of racing under sail, and the warped doorframe had locked Nancy on her unwilling seat of ease!]

> Not long after, [with] Flower well behind, [and] with only two or three boats still ahead of the *Maid*, the Committee Boat caught up to us and stated that someone (it turns out an old eastern dragger, trawling) had stolen the outer mark. Everyone behind us already knew this and had [changed course giving them] a much shorter run to the finish, but we still beat most boats to the line, including the salty schooner.

> I don't think Flower ever talked to me again!

Summer sailing on *Silent Maid* was fun and, on one Saturday night party trip, the Hogans were returning up Barnegat Bay with about a dozen people aboard. Modern racers have downhauls, but most owners of the *Maid*, when the boom was swung well outboard, have let people sit along the boom, butts in the bight of her mainsail, thus flattening the sail. Returning to Winter Yacht Basin with a southwest wind behind, "I was trying to work past Swan Point [off Mantoloking] and there were people all over the boom," as Cliff tells it. "When I went a little too far and —oh shit!—very slowly the boom came over in a jibe." It was pitch dark, so imagine the result for yourself. It was all sorted out and with everybody dried out, the matter was closed.

FIGURE 8-6. Nancy Hogan riding *Silent Maid*'s boom, ca. 1965, probably at the mouth of the Metedeconk River.
Cliff Hogan photograph

FIGURE 8-7. *Silent Maid* leading Walter Flower's schooner in an offshore race about 1965. Brother-in-law Walt Davis is at right.

Hogan family photograph

In light air, the Hogans enjoyed running a line out about 50 feet astern. Guests would walk gingerly to the end of the boom, which swung far out to leeward, and they'd jump off and swim to the line. Sailing offshore opposite Lavalette in a pretty stiff southerly, an English boy aboard decided to try this trick. As the *Maid* rolled, her boom jerked and the boy's foot slipped through one of the bridles holding the sheet blocks. He ended up hanging upside down for about a minute, dunking into the sea at each roll, until those aboard could haul in the sheet and straighten him out.

It wasn't long before a Coast Guard skiff zoomed up to enquire about a report received by phone from somebody ashore that they were trying to drown someone and that a "body" was hanging from the end of the *Maid*'s boom!

Silent Maid was comfortable enough that she was a natural live-aboard when Cliff Hogan wanted to go duck hunting in the lower bay. He had a friend who owned part of the Gunning River Marshes just below the village of Barnegat.

He built a blind there and anchored the *Silent Maid* in sheltered waters while the hunt went on for three or four days. A local came by about midnight on one dead calm night and being already under the influence, thought nothing of waking Cliff to find out what was going on. With true Irish hospitality, Cliff offered him a few more libations and they became friends. By that time the fellow was pretty befuddled and Cliff's surname "Hogan" became "Fogan." On subsequent trips when the *Maid* arrived, she was routinely greeted with the nighttime hail of "Hey, Fogan!"

FIGURE 8-8. Gunning River Marshes. The *Maid* was probably anchored just above Gulf Point (at the arrow) and the visitor likely came out from behind Conklin Island, which has since mostly eroded away.

U.S. Coast and Geodetic Survey Chart, 1924, Paul Smith

FIGURE 8-9. Gulf Point Marsh and the Gunning River area in December. The remnant of once much larger Conklin Island is in the foreground at the mouth of Double Creek, Barnegat. *Inset:* Working block decoy for the lesser blue bill or Scaup *(Aythya affinis)* carved by Bill Beardsley (1890–1966) and shot over on Barnegat Bay during Hogan's time.

Kent Mountford photographs

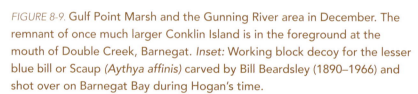

FIGURE 8-10. The 19th century Bascule railroadbridge, crossing the Manasquan River near where Hogan docked *Silent Maid* for ocean access.

Postcard, ca. 1950, Robert Jahn, with permission

On one expedition down the bay, Cliff's companions Ted Keefer and a third man brought "Asher," an extensively trained Labrador Retriever. Asher would make it much easier, they anticipated, than wading or rowing out to fetch downed waterfowl. Sent after the first bird shot, however, Asher swam out and eagerly retrieved a decoy. One can imagine how Asher smelled, wet and panting, inside the *Maid*'s steamy cabin that night!

For ducks like bluebills, which flew high and farther away, Cliff carried three or four shotgun shells with heavier #2 buckshot.[3] These, intended for larger game, had heavier lead pellets than normal bird shot shells. On a subsequent hunting expedition aboard the *Maid*, they were to play an interesting role.

In December, probably of 1966, Cliff and Leon Slack, his barber from Lambertville, New Jersey, went down Barnegat Bay to shoot some birds including Brant geese. It was during the workweek, and they were to shoot from a blind Cliff had on Island Beach, then a relatively new state park. The blind was about 1.6 miles south of the original park office—and the Governor's house—and well north of Tices Shoal, where a popular deeper water anchorage is found pretty close to the beach. They had a sneakbox, but it was already ashore at the blind, and Cliff, having anchored the *Maid* in as close as possible to the barrier island, remembers a very cold wade ashore to get it! Cliff says they saw red foxes ashore, the same population that ekes out a living there today, but they looked disheveled enough that he thought they might be rabid.

FIGURE 8-11. The foxes on Island Beach still look pretty mangy despite clandestine (and illegal) visitor feedings!

Kent Mountford photograph, 2011

The *Maid*, however, had been anchored very close in to enable Cliff to wade in, and with tide and wind she got aground. They put the anchor out in a deeper spot and used the electric winch to warp her off and safely afloat, but Cliff says, "We also managed to grind up the winch and run the battery down far enough it couldn't crank the engine." Six-volt batteries did not have the cranking power of modern 12V high amperage versions, and this battery had been sitting two days discharged in chilly December weather. Remember this was also before cell phones and VHF radios. They were really on their own out there.

"We hunted for two days," Cliff recalls, "and slept aboard." Cliff thinks it would have been Saturday, when they were ready to leave. The wind had come up southerly and was rising. "This wind was what we called a 'blue bird day' and it meant poor duck hunting. We had a hard time getting the anchor up and were tired by the time we got underway." I remember well that big Danforth anchor, a wide and heavy piece to shorten up and break out of the bay bottom once well set.

FIGURE 8-12. Cliff built a sailfish from a $67 kit while at the U.S. Navy Post Exchange in San Diego. He still owns it! Here he used the sail as an impromptu "jib" to move (slightly!) the massive *Silent Maid.*

FIGURE 8-13. Nancy Hogan's father Herb Carlson with granddaughter Kimberly Hogan, properly life jacketed.

Hogan family photographs

No matter about the engine, they thought; while Leon was not a sailor, Cliff was, and his vessel was one of the best sailboats around. They would simply sail home. They started with *Silent Maid*'s full main hoisted, and she roared off like a banshee. They were headed a bit north of west towards a small cottage, painted red, alongshore and south of Goodluck Point, which juts out below the mouth of Toms River. A chop was up by now, and there was too much wind to safely jibe. The *Maid*, however, was hard to tack with so much wind and sea, slowing too much from the waves as they attempted to come through the eye of the wind. They managed it, but as Cliff recalls, so close to shore that "our long boom nearly took the roof off that red cottage!"

It would have been good to power into the wind and tie in a couple of reefs, but without the engine there was no way they could keep her up long enough, especially with just one experienced man aboard. The boom was swung out to port now and they squared up on the narrow channel aiming for the draw of Route 37's Thomas A. Mathis Bridge. Cliff immediately began blowing his horn, three long blasts, which in those days was the proper request for a bridge opening. They saw no response and the *Maid* snored closer to the draw.

Cliff was blowing hard on the *Maid*'s original, old galvanized fisherman's horn with a brass mouthpiece and a thin brass reed soldered to and facing the mouth end. Blow and the reed vibrated, with the horn amplifying the animal-like bleat, which might or might not be heard for a quarter mile. The Freon canister horn (now compressed air) was not patented until 1990.[4] Cliff started sounding four blasts for danger. Since it was probably Saturday, Cliff recalls, there might have been a football game on the radio or TV, but in any event there was no response from the bridge tender. Who would be out there on a blustery December afternoon, anyhow? *Silent Maid* was, and she was coming fast.

Rut rather than smack the bridge head on, Cliff spun his helm to starboard; he knew navigable water would end, but he didn't know where . . .

"At that point we went aground—hard. The boom and sail [were] flailing off to port and [we were] listing to port. The centerboard was hard aground and would not raise." [The board had been bent to starboard by the pressure of bottom and sails; all the old iron drifts run edgewise through the planks and had distorted permanently!] "With 40 knots of south[erly wind], we slid [sideways] bouncing towards the bridge."

Apparently when the bridge was built across shallow Barnegat Bay (this span, one of three over time, was opened in 1950)[5], an access channel was dredged for tugs, pile drivers, and barges parallel to the course of the bridge and running easterly towards Pelican Island. The *Maid* had struck some side-cast material from subsequent dredging of the draw and broke loose into this channel and started roaring along parallel with the roadway above her. "With the tip of her gaff just skinning the bridge piers 'whoosh, whoosh, whoosh!,' Hogan said "we shot on towards Pelican Island."

Cliff knew he had to bring the *Maid* about. Cleverly, he recounts: "I sent the barber [Leland Slack] forward to flake out the anchor rode, belay it, and on command drop the Danforth overboard. Whip! Out went the line and it came taut with a hum, exactly as I spun the helm. She was pulled about in a moment and off we went the other way!"

He had his crewmate haul in the line as fast as he could as they sailed back westward, and just as they passed the now set anchor, Leland was instructed to snub the rode short on the *Maid*'s big bow cleat. Out came the anchor, and the boat was now on the other tack.

Hogan grabbed his shotgun (an Ithaca Pump, which he still owns). "I fired three shots, blasts that is, the signal to open the bridge. Three shots at the bridge tender's office [and the] #2 buck loads took the window out." This was, Hogan muses "probably the only time *Silent Maid* was used as a gunboat!"

One can imagine the bridge tender, cautiously peeking, Kilroy-like, over the window ledges, then ducking down again: "You want the bridge open?" [he hollered down]. Hogan, frustrated and in real trouble, screamed at him (apologizing to my wife who was with me when we heard the story first hand) "OPEN THE F-----G BRIDGE!"

They then were sailing west, past the draw, boom out to starboard. One can imagine the *Maid*'s huge main half drawing, half wildly flagging. He considered (another) Bahamian reef (dropping the peak of the gaff to be lashed to the boom, resulting in a sloppy triangular sail), but he was afraid that with the wild thrashing gaff—26 feet long, hundreds of square feet of flogging canvas and a combined mass of 3 to 400 pounds—they might take off the cabin top.

There was "a small open area, and with lots of way on and the *Maid*'s super-large rudder, we came about." "Try tacking," Cliff recalls, "with the bridge 20 feet away and 40 knots blowing." (They were then headed east again, approaching the draw.) Then try turning "sixty degrees to run through the bridge opening." The *Maid* just managed to make that turn and get through the draw, her boom whacking one of the bridge piers, the transom clipping the other side.

The familiar upper bay now lay before them with Mantoloking dimly on the northern horizon. Cliff and the shaken barber got home free. Cliff said, "I had a lot of small boat experience before the *Maid*, and I knew how much to allow for carrying to a pier and I just sailed the *Maid* into the opening of Winter Yacht Basin's breakwater."

The chain of events thus triggered, however, was far from over. Hogan soon received a letter threatening a lawsuit from the state of New Jersey. Being accustomed to arguing tax litigation in court against the government, Cliff fired off a suit of his own. A state trooper, by happenstance, had been stopped in traffic on the bridge and witnessed the whole thing, and Hogan wanted to be sure he would be a witness. The affair lingered in the courts for some time. Cliff thinks it was December of the next year, when one morning he got a handwritten letter torn off a yellow pad from the bridge tender himself. He said that he was a disabled man to begin with and if this decision went the wrong way he would lose his job, and he had six kids to support. Out of compassion, Cliff dropped his lawsuit and the state never pursued its threatened litigation.

Over the years, especially before VHF hailing on Channel 13, I've had troubles at this particular bridge as well, mostly in heavy weather. Once when we couldn't get it to open, the wedding anniversary we'd planned to spend secure among friends in Mantoloking was spoiled, leaving my young wife in tears. Another time a powerboat crowded us at the draw and her wake sent my dinghy crashing into our stern, cracking her bows, a wound never quite healed, though I still own the wonderful dinghy four decades later! I, too, once had to call the police, trying to get an inattentive bridge tender's attention. In the early years of this new millennium, things have been far more responsive, and certainly talking one-on-one with the tender on VHF or cell phone makes misunderstandings much less likely.

Once inspected after her ordeal and the damage known, Cliff took the *Maid* up to the head of the Metedeconk again. He had her hauled and placed atop two ranks of 55-gallon steel oil drums set on end to give high enough head space for the

FIGURE 8-14. *Silent Maid* sailing a more tranquil passage through the Route 37 Seaside Bridge in August 1995. By this time, the tender could be hailed by telephone!

Photo courtesy of Marie Darling

repairs. The first discovery was that the ancient centerboard pin, exercised repeatedly since 1924 (by then 40 years) had worn almost through. When finally worked free of the hull, *Silent Maid's* old centerboard lay distorted on the ground beyond hope of straightening.

Cliff decided, after trying the idea on a respected local boat builder, that he would make a major change in the centerboard's shape by truncating it to a near-triangular profile. Also, inside the boat, he would lower the forward end of the trunk almost level with the sole. He would lose the *Maid's* big traditional mahogany tables on each side of the centerboard trunk, but gain walk-about room at the cabin's forward end. He replaced the pin with a robust stainless steel version, which served for the *Maid's* remaining 38 sailing years.

Likely at the same haul-out in 1966, *Silent Maid's* old Gray Seascout was replaced with a newer (but still used) Atomic Four engine. Maybe the incident off Island Beach had a role in this decision. Hogan is silent on the matter, but the engine replacement is enumerated as an upgrade in a later 1980s survey.[6]

The rebuilt centerboard trunk, however, could not compensate for the old girl's ancient garboards and softening frame heels. Nor could it rectify inherent flaws and past damage to the keel. A lot more expensive, creative woodwork would be necessary to nurse her through her long remaining life.

Cliff and Nancy say the boat really served as their private summer cottage, reporting that while they owned her, they virtually lived aboard four months of the year. Little Kim spent her nights—and naps—in a hammock hung athwartships from the coachroof coamings.

Cliff and Nancy enjoyed life, and enjoyed love too! They smilingly tell of making love one afternoon in the *Maid's* cabin when some untoward noise interrupted them. Cliff leapt up to look out the cabin's forward hatch, left open for the breeze, and knocked himself nearly senseless against the unyielding overhead coaming. In the spring of 1968, the *Maid* was in commission one mild April weekend. That's when, both partners are sure, son Justin was conceived, first such known event in the *Maid's* history. *Silent Maid* owners, start to finish could say . . . "no children to speak of."

FIGURE 8-15. *(Left)* Justin Hogan still figuring out what being aboard *Silent Maid* is all about during his first summer. *(Right)* Nancy's mother Betty Carlson holding granddaughter Kimberly in *Silent Maid's* cockpit, ca. 1965, at the Winter Yacht Basin slip. Note the bank of electric meters, this being just when marina owners began charging separately for utilities.

Hogan family photographs

Nancy Hogan, still imagining more comforts of home aboard, really wanted to have a shower. Sure, the family's shore home was just across Mantoloking Bridge in the village, but that was hardly convenient. The useful hanging Sunshower would not be invented until 1985,[7] leaving Nancy with a washbasin or a dock hose in the cockpit.

Wider issues also intervened: "…we wanted to sail to the Bahamas; we needed to go to sea (and be able to) take a knockdown and come back up!" Cliff also recognized that a boat with an inside shower would keep his pretty wife in the game! Putting *Silent Maid* on the market was a straightforward process. She was an easy boat to sell because her once-disappointed "next owner," had been watching the *Maid* and waiting, with an eye to ownership from the snack bar at Winter Yacht Basin since 1964, when Cliff literally bought the boat out from under her nose. Cliff remembers that the *Maid* was put up for sale at $7500, but paperwork following indicated he didn't get his asking price. Sally Schneider, nonetheless, gave the deal all she had and more.

Cliff and Nancy were soon sailing their new big yawl around the upper bay in preparation for wider horizons, though still unused to a boat with greater draft than the *Maid*'s 36 inches. I recorded a footnote to Cliff Hogan's time with *Silent Maid* in my logbook aboard *La Boheme* on October 15, 1967:

"A true October prism day temp[erature] mild. . . . Hogan's new yawl aground off Curtis Point; beautiful photography of *Maid* lost; out of Goddam film." That was one of the early trips the new owner Sally Schneider and her friends took on *Silent Maid* and it was not long after that they passed the Hogans again on Barnegat. Cliff's wife Nancy shouted across to Sally: "This boat has a fine shower, but she's not half the boat *Silent Maid* is!"

The Hogans, 45 years later, were settled in North Jersey, wintering in Florida on Hobe Sound and kept their big, comfortable 50-ft motorsailer in front of a waterfront condominium on upper Toms River.

ENDNOTES — CHAPTER 8

1. Log *Nimble*. Notes on interview with Sally Schneider while sailing aboard *Silent Maid*, July 16, 1998.

2. Few references remain about this venue, here's one: http://njscuba.net/reefs/site_nj02sg_cranford.html

3. Shotgun pellets are sized inversely to the designating number with smaller #6 pellets typical for upland game, #4 or #5 for ducks and #2 for the largest game birds like Canada goose. http://www.shotgunworld.com/ammo_s042002.html

4. The multitone Freon horn was registered as Patent #4970983, November 20, 1990. Freon, a refrigerant gas (compressed and liquified in the canister), was thought environmentally safe. This was not the case and modern versions use compressed air. Chlorofluorocarbons, liberated widely for decades, are believed to deplete Earth's protective ozone layer, which shields the planet from some forms of extraterrestrial radiation.

5. Thomas A. Mathis Bridge, with a bascule draw, was completed in 1950 by Ole Hansen & Sons, a company founded in 1929. It replaced the wooden bridge opened in 1915 (originally privately funded and a toll crossing) that had crossed the Bay parallel to and a little north. Sources say Ole Hansen managed that construction project before forming his own company. Another source says the Shinn family did this work. Remnants of the old bridge can still be seen along its alignment on the western side of the Bay, with the timber strongbacks slanting southward, where they were intended to break up wind-driven winter ice floes. The Hansen Company also built the subsequent high span (J. Stanley Tunney Bridge) in 1973, parallel to the Mathis Bridge. (www.olehansen.com/Accomplishments.html)

6. Marie Darling, 1967. Copy of the impromptu marine survey she did to bind Lloyd's of London insurance coverage for *Silent Maid*. Philadelphia Independence Seaport Museum.

7. The "Sunshower," marketed most recently by Stearns, was patent #4520793i registered in 1985.

FIGURE 8-16. *(Top)* The Hogans' yawl *Slainta* (cheers in Gaelic), which replaced *Silent Maid*.

Cliff Hogan photograph

(Bottom) Cliff and Nancy Hogan with their trawler in background at Toms River in April 2011. As of that year, he had owned 13 small boats!

Kent Mountford photograph

FIGURE 9-1. *Silent Maid*, Barnegat Bay (ca. 1968).

9

Sally Schneider's Story

The "Perle Mesta" Years

A post-WW-II flyer from the Little Egg Harbor Yacht Club patronizingly referred to a women's event as a "Skipperette" function. Women's liberation had not yet been achieved. A woman was incomplete unless partnered with a suitable man, and women, clearly the "weaker sex," were usually in the shadow relative to the manly sport of yacht racing. The War had brought fundamental changes to women's roles in the workplace, and they were ready to branch out across other aspects of lifestyle and work. They would not be denied these changes any more than suffragettes were to be denied their vote after the 19th amendment.

*S*onja Virginia Schneider, born in 1936, was known to all as Sally. She grew up to be a woman who worked hard building friendships all her life and demonstrating the folly of any restrictive or elitist view of femininity. Her friend Evelyn "Gillie" Ogden says that Sally would have been the last to consider herself a "women's rights activist," but she was clever and just never accepted limits on what was right for her or her circle of friends.

Of the *Silent Maid* years Gillie recalls, "After all, we had [as role model] Mrs. [Louise] Colie, who was then over seventy, rowing out in her skiff to sail her boat off moorings. She had broken the mold if anyone had, showing up at the Bay Head Yacht Club in 1915 with her all-woman crew in bathing suits and going on to win races. Why, it just wasn't done!" Gillie mused further that those awful woolen bathing costumes might well have been more uncomfortable than women's light summer dresses of the time![1]

Sally Schneider started out from infancy in difficult straits. The trail is unclear and those who know the whole story have remained silent and inaccessible to me, but Sally's birth family's name was Schwallback. Her mom was described as a striking woman of Scandinavian extraction. Sally and her brother John looked markedly different from their other three sisters. Sally was blond, naturally blond her whole life, and of shorter stature, though never overweight.

Sally's father was estranged and never parented her; he and Sally's mother were splitting up about the time Sally was born. Sally's friends describe her in infancy as becoming a ward of the state, and though brother John stayed with his birth family, Sally was placed in foster care with the family of Josephine and Frank Schneider.[2] Frank never tired of his "little blond" and doted on her. The Schneiders received a

Feminist Role Model Louise Edgar Colie

Louise Edgar Colie was the wife of a Newark, New Jersey, attorney and later jurist. They were early Mantoloking settlers. They came there via the railroad after renting in Bay Head with their latest (colicky and loudly crying) baby Runyon, thinking that having their own place would be easier than worrying about troubling other guests. Louise, in 1915, with her all-woman crew won an overnight race in *Frolic*, a 20-foot sneakbox. The course was from Bay Head to Waretown and back, part of which was reportedly sailed in 40 knot winds.

Her children, corrupting Louise, called her "Weed" rather than Mother. All the Colie offspring went on to make names for themselves in the panoply of boating history. Inducted into the Barnegat Bay Sailing Hall of Fame in 2012, her son Runyon, trained as a Naval Architect at Stevens Institute, was International Penguin champion 1947–50 and 1952, 1954, and 1962. Sixty years later he won his 18th BBYRA Championship in the E-scow *Calamity*. Runyon's son Henry Colie manages the fleet of boats owned by Peter Kellogg, who built the re-creation of Edwin Schoettle's original *Silent Maid*.

Louise sailed into her nineties and was a tough woman. When quite elderly, she fell overboard one night, was unable to board, and stayed in Jones Tide Pond until the morning. Mike Lee noticed her, launched a small boat from his pier, and made the rescue.[3]

FIGURE 9-2. **Louise Edgar Colie, 1915 Ladies BBYRA Champion racer.**

Bay Head Mantoloking, Lovelandtown Museum photograph

FIGURE 9-3. **Louise Colie sailing out of Beaton's Boatyard in 1970.**

Beaton's Boatyard photograph

FIGURE 9-4. **Skipper Evelyn Ogden and Diana Robinson aboard Ogden's catboat *Vim* during the Toms River Classic Boat Show, July 1998.**

Kent Mountford photograph

state allowance for their work raising Sally, and at eighteen she was adopted, and she took their family name.

Sally graduated from college with a New Jersey teaching certificate[4] and began as an instructor in physical education and coaching women's athletics, first in Bernardsville, New Jersey, then at West Essex. One of her students was Janet Jessel, who became a lifelong friend and later a frequent sailing companion.

Sally later earned a Master's Degree and eventually taught until her retirement from the Summit, NJ, school system having at some point added Driver's Education to her teaching repertoire.

Sally attacked her job with verve—well, some describe her as a rabble-rouser with respect to school administrations—but I am quite certain the number of young women whom she started on an open-minded, self- aware course in life was legion. Sally's career was stable, respectable, socially useful work, but it was not the highest paid profession; and not the best situation for a socially active young woman to amass money for a sailing yacht.

Sally, always gregarious, started an after-hours volleyball league for single women and moms looking for outside companionship. It was there that she met another life-long friend, Marie Darling, then living in North Jersey and married with children. After volleyball, the original plan was to go out for ice cream; it wasn't long before the participants agreed that they'd rather go out for a couple of drinks!

Sally's adoptive mother in her later years lived on one of the Barnegat Bay west-shore lagoons in Brick Township. When Sally visited her mom she had a taste of being near the water where everybody seemed to be having fun. Maybe that was the trigger that started her boating or was it just in her genes? Rumor had it that her birth mother had worked on boats out of Brielle, and her natural brother in adulthood was also a boat owner.

Like many of us with little money and an interest in sailing, Sally found her way to the legendary David Beaton and Sons Boatyard on Jones Tide Pond in West Mantoloking. At Beaton's, Sally quickly came under the instructive wings of several wonderful boatyard residents.

Sally's first boat was an old Comet, which she purchased from Beaton's. Comets were designed by C. Lowndes Johnson in the 1930s as a trailerable version of Francis Sweisguth's famous Star Class, and there were many hundreds sailing when Sally bought hers. Evelyn "Gillie" Ogden owned a similar one-design Snipe there at the same time. She had known Sally casually since 1961 or 1962, though not in a boating context. Gillie, who had learned to sail in Girl Scouts as a Mariner, went on to summer sailing camps, and eventually became an instructor. While an undergraduate at Douglass College (then the Women's College of Rutgers University), she was a competition swimmer[5] and on the Rutgers Sailing Team.

With Gillie at Beaton's, Sally learned to sail and became acquainted with Tom Mount, well-known scion of an old Bay Head family. Mount Street is a thoroughfare in the town, and Tom's house was nearby. Tom had to drop out of Columbia University at the time of the 1929 stock market crash, but he was there long enough to get some knowledge of wise investing, a practice that carried him through into the future.[6] Tom eventually wanted to marry Sally, but she declined that entangling alliance. Tom sailed well into his 90s and always had a girlfriend, his last was Ginny Glasby. She was a younger gal, then into her 80s.

Sally's other mentor at Beaton's was easy-going Ben Benham, who owned a dilapidated old catboat with a history.

FIGURE 9-5. *Silent Maid, Barnegat Bay (c. 1968).*
Sally Schneider image

FIGURE 9-6. (Top) **Ben Benham drying sails on his catboat at Beaton's, September 26, 1970.**
Kent Mountford photograph

(Bottom) **Catboat, moonlight, and Clark's Landing on the Manasquan River.**
Edward C. Boulton, ca. 1880

Ben wore hearing aids, and what he assumed was his faint voice was always the loudest lecturer in any gathering! Both these guys, Tom and Ben, loved to party and were never above welcoming a suitable beverage. Marie Darling says they taught Sally a lot about sailing, and eventually Sally bought a new fiberglass Columbia 'Islander' sloop[8] that gave her personal live-aboard space and larger boat experience.[9] Symbolically, she named the boat *Rebel*. Sally's first houseboat opportunity arrived about this time, a motorized version with a fiberglass hull and shared with friend Lynette Fassano.

Tom Mount bought what is believed to be the second fiberglass (Brett) Marshall Catboat on Barnegat Bay. I was struck by this new boat in town when Tom, in flat calm, sculled her easily into Beaton's, late one September evening in 1967. Immensely practical, handy, and low-upkeep boats, they quickly developed reputations as good family cruisers and smart sailers. A robust racing community developed, which would engage Sally's attention even after *Silent Maid* entered her life.

* * *

Sally had her eye on *Silent Maid* in the years leading up to 1964 while my family owned her and because we kept her docked at Winter Yacht Basin in Mantoloking, Sally was familiar with our comings and goings. Rudy and Millie Winter leased out a little summertime snack bar at the water view end of their marina's main building. It was the most convenient place around for nearby boaters to grab a coffee, burger, or a sandwich. Sally clearly remembered sitting "there at the [snackbar] counter, just looking and drooling at *Silent Maid*, not a hundred feet away. The *Maid* would be perfect for her lifestyle; room on deck and below to entertain and for many guests to flop down or pile in to spend a crowded night. The boat was a symbol throughout Barnegat Bay and had been so for over four decades; that mainsail was the largest piece of canvas flying at the time. Sally was interested if the boat was ever again for sale. She might have mentioned this to me when we met at Beaton's, but I have no recollection, which meant she didn't find out in time and literally missed the boat when Cliff Hogan bought the *Maid* in 1964. Sally was nonetheless ready when the *Maid* came on the market again a couple of years later.

Cliff Hogan had been keeping the *Silent Maid* in Brielle on the Manasquan River as his account tells it. This was where Janet Jessel and Sally found her in 1966, just possibly for sale again. The *Maid* was in a slip above the Bascule railroad bridge on the Manasquan's north bank almost under today's Route 35 Bridge and adjacent to the then-popular Ferry Boat restaurant.[10] Brokerage for the sale was Hubert S. Johnson's Boatworks in Bay Head, and Sally negotiated through them. There are a number of figures on the bill of sale. It seems Cliff Hogan was trying to get $5300, Sally offered $4600, and, after some undisclosed flaws were accounted for, the final price seems to have been $4250 plus New Jersey's sales tax, thus setting her back $4257.

As the sale neared completion, Sally went to her credit union and said, "I need a loan to buy a boat." "How much is the boat?" the manager asked her. "$5000," she replied. "How much of that will you need to borrow?" he asked. "$5000," she said.

"But," Sally continued, "when I mentioned *Silent Maid*'s name, he said, 'Oh yeah, I know that beautiful boat,'" and she got the loan. Before very long she would want to borrow *another* $5000 to make necessary (surprise) repairs, which a more sophisticated buyer might have anticipated![11]

Sally and her friends were unaccustomed to the Manasquan River's relatively large tidal rise and fall of several feet—compared with upper Barnegat Bay's average six inches! The *Maid* was bought in the cold months accentuating tidal amplitudes with seasonal storms and frontal systems piling up or blowing out the water.[12] They once hopped aboard with early winter snow and ice all over the dock and decks, got involved in some project, and, upon coming out, found the *Maid* fallen down with the tide and the dock was virtually at head level. With everything frozen and slippery, that made it pretty challenging to get up or down again.[13]

The *Maid* immediately drew Sally's friends and while still at Brielle during the early winter of 1966–67, they piled aboard during one of those remarkable west-to-northwest blowouts that characterize New Jersey weather. While they partied, smoked, and drank, the tide fell lower and lower until suddenly someone smelled gasoline. They checked and it wasn't the *Maid*, but they looked overboard and found she had settled squarely into the mud and was immobilized. Around them, though, were a number of charter boats, fuel tanks properly topped off to prevent over-winter water vapor condensation, which had also settled. Some round-bilged boats had rolled port or starboard taking on a large angle of heel, and the fuel was siphoning out through their tilted overflow vents. Rivulets of raw gasoline were running down the hulls, across the exposed river bottom

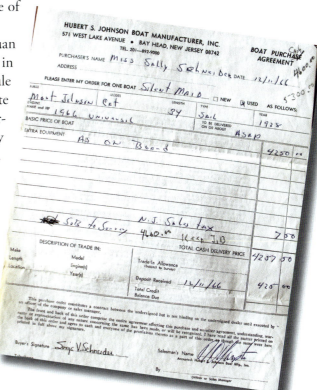

FIGURE 9-7. Sally's bill of sale for *Silent Maid* dated December 11, 1966.
Toms River Seaport Society archive

and into the Manasquan River's ebbing tide stream. The *Maid* was instantly evacuated, lest they incinerate the entire fleet with a stray spark.

Sally and her friends moved the *Silent Maid*, by then a 42-year-old boat, through the Bay Head-Point Pleasant Canal and down to Beaton's Boatyard.[14] Tied up at Beaton's, *Silent Maid* inspired Sally to name her houseboat the *Silent Butler*, which was moored adjacent. *Silent Butler* serviced *Silent Maid* as road hotel until about 1981, when *Silent Butler* left with Lynn Fassano.[15]

This was roughly about 1967 when Sally and her friends began to look gratefully for support to Beaton Boatyard's neighbor, the remarkable Mike Lee. A bachelor, Mike's recreation up to that point had been going to the movies with Tom Mount, and he thus welcomed the friendship of this bunch of offbeat, independent women, together with the other couples that were part of their circle. It was not too long before he invited the boats, one after another, to move over to his side of the Pond. Mike would get his tenants on the land and then have the Swenson brothers, also tenants, to drive a few piles for the new boat and maybe a few more when owners bought different boats.[16] Mike was as strong a character in his own boatyard as these women were headstrong in *their* lifestyles and opinions. The balance struck was dynamic, but pretty stable—disagreements often ending in a big 'family' dinner.[17]

Mike Lee and His "Family"

Adjacent to Beaton's Boatyard was a land parcel created by filling in the salt marsh, and owned by Mike Lee. Mike was born about 1925, and as a youngster worked for the Singer Sewing Machine Company. In 1942, however, at age 17, Mike enlisted to participate in World War II and became a "SeaBee" (CB was for Construction Battalion). While on active duty he served with the Marines and then with the Navy. After the war, he was a civilian machinist at the Lakehurst Naval Air Station. Lee was skilled at doing almost anything and was the perfect guy to solve mechanical or structural problems with boats or buildings. At Lakehurst, he had access to all manner of excess and salvageable materials. He'd lost his wife to cancer in the 1950s[18] and lived alone on a big houseboat barge, which was eventually a permanent installation facing out on Jones Tide Pond.

The barge had been a mobile office and work crew residence for the New Jersey Bureau of Navigation in a different time and economy when transportation and commuting were less easily managed. This vessel stood two stories high, with supervisor's quarters and offices topside and a balcony at one end commanding dramatic water views wherever the barge was towed to maintain New Jersey's waterways. At hull level aft, were mechanical plants delivering steam heat and water to all compartments and a mess room and galley that fed the whole operation. Along an amidships corridor were showers and two rows of small two-bunk cabins for the

working crew, each with a radiator and washbasin. At corridor's end, egress was up a few steps and through a door to the forward deck.

Lee shared his waterfront property with the Swenson brothers, Les and Harvey, who were marine bulkhead and pile driving contractors. This was a rapidly growing business in those days of marsh and shoreline exploitation. The Swensons were extremely strong guys. When the vintage 1900 catboat *Vim* needed an engine, the two of them slung it from a stout beam and shouldering the load, walked out the dock, onto the boat, edged around her shrouds, down the deck, and lowered it into place on the engine beds.[19]

Strength discounted, the Swensons were useful partners for many of Mike's projects, but also brought unwelcome visitors when Hurricane Flossy threatened at the end of September 1956. On rising tides, a tugboat brought in two Swenson-clan barges, with cranes, tanks and a large amount of cable and steel rubble to shelter from the storm. When this extraordinary tide later went down, I sailed over in my sneakbox and the tug's skipper (Les Swenson' father)[20] told me the whole mess was hard aground.[21] Decomposing over the subsequent half century, their remains are still there mostly submerged hazards blocking part of the harbor.

Sometime after the barges arrived, Mike, using his own equipment, dredged a slip in the salt marsh large enough for his houseboat to float into, leaving a temporary land

At the boatyard, Sally held court for her widening circle of friends, whose partying and lifestyle persisted for almost four decades. The *Maid*, in many ways, filled and framed her life. The folks flocking to her boat created what her friends called "Sally's new-found family:" an expanded circle denied her as a little girl. It became routine to have from 13 to 14 people aboard for an afternoon sail.

Sally's birth family had been far from her mind for a long time, but one day in the 1980s on the Garden State Parkway she and friends saw her natural brother John Schwallback's work truck in traffic. Sally said, "Oh, that was my real last name. She had never had contact with the family, and as they passed the truck, Sally was shocked to see her own spitting image, her brother, driving it! One of her friends wrote down Schwallback's phone number, through which she made contact. Opening the past was probably therapeutic for all, and she found she liked them. Still, when on invitation, everybody [the whole family clan to hear it told] showed up at the boatyard one day, they were such an overwhelming bunch, that she later quietly told Tom Beaton that it might have been just as well to let sleeping dogs lie!

Sally, in the first years I knew her starting in the early 1960s, was almost never seen without a cigarette in one hand and a mixed drink in the other, no matter the time of day. Friends say she was always the same welcoming person, regardless of cocktails

FIGURE 9-8. *(Left)* Mike Lee's houseboat barge, a former New Jersey Bureau of Navigation workboat, installed at Jones Tide Pond in the 1950s, was until 2012 Marie Darling's home. *(Right)* Barges floated into Jones Tide Pond during Hurricane Flossy about September 29, 1956, and stranded there permanently! Lee's houseboat, still free-floating, is visible left background. *Kent Mountford photographs*

bridge between this and the tide pond. He aligned this huge houseboat/barge up against the bank and one day when winds were down and the tide exceptionally high, he dug out the land bridge and floated the whole thing into position.

Land-filled all 'round, this once free-floating vessel was still there decades later eventually serving as Marie Darling's comfortable, eclectic home. It still floated—or attempted to—and during major floods and hurricanes, it sometimes required 24-hour-a-day pumping to keep water levels below those destructive to the utilities. In October 2012, Hurricane Sandy overwhelmed attempts to protect the machinery. The entirety of the vessel has since been demolished and the dent in one-time salt marsh filled. The Darling family rebuilt a new residence on long pilings, well above storm tides.

consumed! Still, in those early years her parties were a wonder for the outsider to behold, some continued over several days and nights without respect to a weekend. Sally decided in the 1970s that alcohol was counterproductive in her life and simply stopped drinking—typical, say her friends, of her commitment to any goal. Coffee, thereafter, occupied that free hand.

* * *

In 1972, Marie Darling and Mike Lee, inspired by the success of Tom Mount's boat, bought a Marshall fiberglass catboat kit. Together with Sally, they finished the assembly, rigged the new boat out, and named her *Lee Marie*. Sally was soon skippering and Marie crewing among the growing fleet of those popular one-design boats.

I never thought of Sally as a racer, but Tom Beaton (grandson of the yard's founder) says she was an aggressive competitor on the water while the fleet was still young. "She was good," Tommy Beaton said, "not afraid to take chances to get around somebody." He speculated that in later years she lost her nerve, was less reckless, and won fewer races.[22]

Tom paused, "Of course, the fleet was a lot larger" in later years, with a wider field of competitors.[23] (Beaton's at one point wintered about 50 Marshall catboats). Sally's friends dispute Tom's suggestion. Maybe Sally just felt she'd proved her point, though Jan Jessel says losing her nerve stemmed from an incident aboard *Silent Maid*, a story to be recounted here, in its turn.

Regardless, Marie Darling recalls that Sally, together with herself, Bob Sayia, and Jack Harding were responsible for starting the B Class catboat fleet within Barnegat Bay's Yacht Racing Association. In 1974, with Sally skippering and Marie as crew, they campaigned the *Lee Marie* successfully.

Sally's friends recall the camaraderie of these times as Sally's "Pearl Mesta" years, echoing the legendary New

FIGURE 9-9. *(Top)* Tom Mount's sculls his Marshall cat, second on Barnegat Bay into Beaton's Boatyard on Jones Tide Pond at dusk in September 1967. *(Bottom Left)* Part of the Marshall catboat row, Beaton's Boatyard, Mantoloking, 2010. *(Bottom Right) Lee Marie*, Marshall cat, lunch-hooking in Applegate Cove in October 1999.

Kent Mountford photographs

The Lee Marie, a Sanderling catboat skippered by Sally Schneider with owner Marie Darling of Normandy Beach Yacht Club, has won two of the three races to date in the new Barnegat Bay Yacht Racing Association B Cat class. (Press Photo)

FIGURE 9-10. Sally and Marie Darling race *Lee-Marie* and win in a BBYRA sanctioned competition in July 1974.

Asbury Park Press photograph

York and Washington, D.C., hostess.[24] Sally never thought badly of anyone, says friend Gillie Ogden, and her gatherings drew in an eclectic crowd of all persuasions. Gillie said, "If you had just arrived in the boatyard, were new or misplaced in the yard, had a problem to solve, or were just looking for a friend, Sally was there to say 'Come on over!' and you were part of her circle." People with all manner of professional associations from Catholic priest to welders and carpenters were swept in and became a resource for Sally to skillfully draw upon!

One of Sally's friends during this time was Marie Darling. She was a working mom, coming to the bay on her days off with her energetic kids—a real handful as each felt their oats and tested limits. Her then-husband Gerald would come sometimes, but this was not his choice of lifestyle, and it was just plain uncomfortable on small boats, especially when weather didn't cooperate.

Marie on the other hand, loved the lifestyle and took responsibility for doing a lot of the work around *Silent Maid*—assistance Sally found indispensable. This included working with carpenter Ed Lowe replacing some of the *Maid*'s structural work, and doing lots of homemaking duty—services not always fully appreciated by those receiving them. One evening with 15 or 20 folks partying on the *Maid*, she was accosted by new visitors coming down the dock in search of Sally. "I'd invite you aboard," Marie recalls, saying with some frustration, "but I don't know who any of them are!"

Marie prepped food for those aboard on a subsequent sail, and left clean up to Jan Jessel, who took the expedient method of simply rinsing the plates in Barnegat Bay. Marie, who was accustomed to soap and hot water in the sink, said: "I was appalled, but they all dried, we ate off them again and nobody got sick!" I've often done the same to conserve fresh water from the boat's limited tanks.

There were always a variety of kids around the *Maid*. Russ Manheimer and his two sons Jeffrey and David summered at Beaton's on their knock-about sloop *Caprice* about 1981–82. His children often visited *Silent Maid* with age-mate Patrick Fassano, who more or less lived on Mike Lee's parcel of land. With a bunch of other youngsters, Jeffrey, David, and Patrick played the card game Spoons while aboard. Jeffrey said by watching the other kids excited about bidding on the cards in their hands, he learned to sneak a spoon into his lap, so he was never odd man out—without a spoon—when the game ended! He was also bitten, though not seriously, by one of Sally's succession of pet dogs! [25]

Lorna Shinn was one of the casual visitors who is nostalgic about these times saying, "I remember being drunk at one of Sally's parties, dancing around the *Silent Maid*'s huge cockpit." Dancing in the *Maid*'s cockpit has been one of her urban legends, confirmed here by at least one participant![26]

FIGURE 9-11. *Silent Maid* with 15 aboard in the summer of 1982 westbound for Silver Bay (Mosquito Cove!) above the Seaside Bridge. *Inset:* Sally at *Silent Maid*'s helm in the summer of 1983 off Mantoloking.

Karen Palmer photographs

Lorna Shinn and Sneakboxes

Lorna (Chadwick) Shinn, aged 85 in 2010 when I interviewed her by phone at her home on Maryland's Eastern Shore, came to Beaton's with relatively recent husband Joe Shinn[27], and a little Scandinavian styled double ender with, as she recalls: "A name I still can't pronounce *Sjogin,*" which was concocted of scrambled letters from her husband's name. Russ Manheimer owns Lorna's old boat, and the boat was still sailing out of Beaton's in 2014, after being wrecked and sunk in Hurricane Sandy in October 2012.

Lorna "married sneakboxes" at the shop of legendary J.H. Perrine in Barnegat, New Jersey. Her first husband, John Chadwick, was Perrine's adopted son, who took over the business after the shipwright's death in June 1956. The shop built the boats and Lorna Chadwick made sails for the 15-foot sneakboxes and for "Dusters," an Owen P. Merrill design, which they built to order. It's likely that *Skeeter,* my own Perrine 15-foot sneakbox (owned while I was crew aboard the *Maid*) had a gaff head cotton mainsail built by Lorna.

Though Perrine apparently held a patent on elements of his designs, he felt there was business enough out there for others. Dave Beaton's son Lachlan (Lally) said that in later years the Perrine shop was open about sharing its designs. Lally and his father went down in the mid-1940s and, with Perrine's blessing, took measurements of the boats and offsets from the molds. The Beatons built their first sneakbox *Frisky* in 1946. Rebuilt in 2007, *Frisky* is still sailing.

FIGURE 9-12. *Sjogin* in October 2005 at Beaton's with owner Russ Manheimer, furling sails while on his cell phone. *Insert:* Lorna Chadwick Shinn's fine marlinspike seamanship shows on the head of *Sjogin*'s original canvas jib.
Kent Mountford photographs

FIGURE 9-13. *Frisky,* Dave Beaton's first 15-foot sneakbox, being rebuilt in 2007 after 60 years use. *Inset:* David L. (Pop) Beaton building a 12-foot sneakbox duckboat in May 1974.
Kent Mountford photographs

After Sally Schneider's houseboat *Silent Butler* left Beaton's, the ever-resourceful Mike Lee somewhere found her another floating residence—an old, leaky barge on which was placed a mobile home that had been shingled over to conceal its true identity. Sally used this from 1981 to about 1984, years before she retired from teaching. It was almost untenable in winter, having just an old wood-burning stove for heat. Eventually, it was moored out in Jones Tide Pond until sold to a couple of clammers. They thought it a great place to go drink and carouse between fishing trips. They had it towed over to nearby "Pleasure Cove" north of Mantoloking Bridge, where in those years many old, crumbling boats went to die. There the erstwhile houseboat-trailer sank in a canal.[28] This site, subsequently acquired with public funds and cleaned up at great expense, is today a community access facility.

Once the second houseboat was gone, summering on *Silent Maid* was pretty cramped when Marie and her kids joined Sally during summers off from teaching. Marie eventually found herself a small houseboat up on the Metedeconk River, which offered them all more space to spread out. Mike Lee offered her a spot on the Tide Pond. When the gals got the old houseboat underway towards Mantoloking a rising wind overpowered their weak motor and making no headway, they found themselves wallowing in the middle of a Sunfish race. A volunteer U.S. Coast Guard Auxiliary boat on patrol saved the day, giving them a tow to their destination![29] No $250 minimum commercial towboat charges in those days: boaters simply helped each other out of a jam.

When just acquired, Marie's houseboat had been owned by an artist and looked at first glance like it was painted with zebra stripes. On closer inspection, the stripes were a collage of fanciful animals and elongated nudes in black and white. Eventually, all this artwork was covered by more sedate cedar shakes, stained gray, which remain to this day.[30]

Mike Lee came to the rescue again when the houseboat roof needed replacing. The Navy was decommissioning old dirigibles (lighter than air blimps) and the fabric covering their skeletons was excess, top-quality rubberized material. Mike hauled some of that back to the boatyard where it was nailed in place and lasted for decades. Other salvaged material included rubberized canvas gussets, edged with brass grommets, which had served as internal, roughly trapezoidal baffles reinforcing fabric walls inside the dirigible's huge helium gas bags. These were loose around Mike Lee's place for years. I inherited some of these, and they served as little tarpaulins aboard several of my small boats as late as the 1990s.

FIGURE 9-14. *(Left)* Marie Darling's original houseboat at Mike Lee's headed for Jones Tide Pond

Janet Jessel photograph

and *(right)* covered with more sedate cedar shake shingles in April 2012.

Kent Mountford photograph

* * *

Marie's son "Jay" (for Gerald) Darling (born 1954 and now a well-known New Jersey attorney[31]) grew up on the *Maid*. Marie talks fondly about him on an early trip, so excited, but not yet in command of nautical terminology and asking "Can I go up in the beginning?, meaning the *Silent Maid*'s bow! Jay grew up fast, partly with Mike Lee's tutelage as surrogate father figure, and he was soon a competent sailor.

Jay tells of night sailing on the *Maid* when he was a teenage boy aboard with large parties of Sally's mostly inebriated, or at least well lubricated, friends. He recalls:

"Now, don't ever breathe a word of this to my mother," he said, but, of course, I did and between the mother's and son's memories a tale emerged. "I was in my mid-teens and we went sailing sometimes every night of the week. There were some serious drinkers aboard in those days and I did much of the actual sailing. [In darkness] they would throw [my brother] Billy overboard—he was ten or eleven— and then I'd have to sail back and try to find him. He was allowed to holler to us, but no lights." Obviously they always did find him. Marie's side of the story explained that, "we always made sure he had a life jacket on."[32] Other participants on these evening sails describe these heavings overboard as planned man-overboard drills, but I accept the edge that Jay puts on his story. Go argue with him; he's the lawyer!

FIGURE 9-15. *(Top)* Silent Maid in her first slip at Mike Lee's in October 1967. Note her transom, painted since the Chandlees owned her in the late 1940s, and the name board made by Stan Mountford in the early 1960s. *(Bottom)* Jay Darling "at the beginning" then a seasoned sailor at about 15 off Mantoloking.

Kent Mountford photographs

FIGURE 9-16. *(Left)* Michael, Billy Darling, Patricia, Sally, Marie Darling, and Jay Darling, Beaton's 1968. *Jan Jessel photograph*

(Right) Gerald (Jay) Darling, Esq., at his daughter Kelly's wedding aboard the replica *Silent Maid* in the summer of 2011.

Darling family photograph

Sally and her crews found *Silent Maid* to be a remarkably stable and forgiving vessel. In moderate winds, friction in the steering gear would hold even her huge barn-door rudder steady, and they could walk away. One participant recalls, "The *Maid* sailed herself. You could leave the helm and go make your coffee."[33] That, however, failed to compensate for 'driver errors.'

One day above Seaside Bridge, when all aboard (including Marie Darling and Mike Lee) were relatively new to the *Maid*, they sailed into one of the small channels to the east side of Barnegat Bay. These are narrow and marked with thin white cedar saplings driven hard into the bay's soft bottom and held there tenaciously by suction. Atop each is a nailed wooden lath triangle or square, depending which side of the channel it is on. Heeled hard to port in a strong breeze, the *Maid*'s leeward running backstay snagged one of these and as it came taut, the *Maid* slewed around port, increasing the pressure

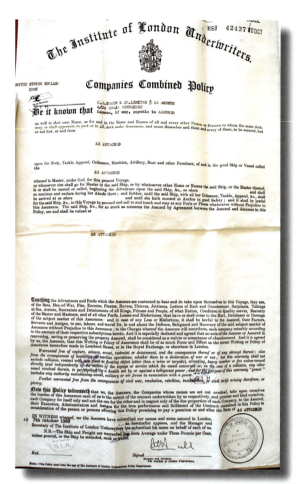

FIGURE 9-17. *Silent Maid's* original policy.

"Be it known that (name of Company and Sally) … in their own Name … doth make Assurance … upon the Body, Tackle, Ordnance, Munitions, Artillery, Boat and other Furniture of and in the good Ship or Vessel called [space for *Silent Maid*] whereof is Master, under God for this present Voyage … and until she hath moored at Anchor in good Safety. …Touching the Adventures and Perils which the Assurers are contented to bear and do take upon themselves in this Voyage, they are of the Seas, Men of War, Fire, Enemies, Pirates, Rovers, Jettisons, Thieves, Letters of Mart[36] and Countermart, Surprisals, Takings at Sea, Arrests, Restraints and detainments of all Kings, Princes and People, of what Nation…, contact with any fixed or floating object (other than a mine or torpedo),…stranding or heavy weather…Further warranted free from the consequences of civil war, revolution, rebellion, insurrection or civil strife arising therefrom, or piracy."

Philadelphia Independence Seaport Museum

on her sails and threatened to put her rig at risk. Marie yelled (in her strong voice) "CUT IT!" and Mike Lee who had a sheath-knife, pulled it out and did so. Someone re-spliced the Manila hemp backstay and the *Maid* went on to complete her afternoon sail. A lesson learned, one of many to come.

Gillie Ogden and Jan Jessel recall a pivotal moment for Sally Schneider when the *Maid* took a knockdown while she was at the helm and there were "a lot of people aboard." The boom hit the water and dragged aft, effectively keeping the boat close-hauled. Catboats, even big ones, *can* be capsized and this time the boat went over far enough for the side decks to go under and for water to pour over her high cockpit coamings. Jan Jessel said, "The portholes were under water, the alcohol stove went flying and everything below that wasn't secure went adrift.[34] With the *Maid's* rudder virtually flat on the water, she wouldn't respond to the helm. Only a lull in the wind let the righting moment of her lead keel slowly pull her back up. This was also a terrific strain on a boat of *Silent Maid's* age, then close to half a century. This seriously shook Sally[35] and Janet Jessel believes this was when happy-go-lucky Sally Schneider lost her nerve. With so much invested, financially and emotionally in the big boat, she was thereafter considerably more reserved in her sailing.

* * *

Work on *Silent Maid* was unceasing. In October 1968, Sally needing a loan for more repairs (and perhaps because of narrow scrapes like that just recounted). She also sought someone to appraise the *Maid* and evaluate her for insurance coverage. There were no takers, Marie recalls, and without a survey there would be no policy.

Mike Lee had his trade name Bayview Boats and Marie says, "Well, I took that name and wrote it [the survey] myself. . . I had absolutely NO idea what I was doing, and Lloyds of London took it! I guess I can say that now and nobody will care!" The insurance policy was something in itself, written complete with coat of arms for the Institute of London Underwriters. This organization was formed cooperatively with Lloyds of London in the 19th century and the wording, long and laboriously tested in Admiralty Courts, was precisely that: 19th century. The assured amount was just $5000, probably what Sally would owe after the repairs, and constrained with a six-month navigation period for a premium of $57.

The perils insured against are a delight to read. Sally must have found the Ordnance and Artillery coverage especially comforting.

* * *

Sally networked all around Barnegat Bay, making friends with the Neilsons, who owned an Island Heights boatyard where (under other owners) *Silent Maid* had been hauled during her halcyon days. The Neilsons owned *Vim*,[37] a vintage 1900 catboat that had raced with *Silent Maid* during her early years.

Gillie Ogden proudly brings up a 1924 reference in BBYRA's archives in which *Vim* roundly beat Ed Schoettle, who, sailing *Silent Maid* in that early race, finished last! In 1971, Sally, sensing the Neilsons were wearing thin on *Vim's* heavy maintenance requirements, suggested that Gillie make an offer, which they accepted. *Vim* thus, with a few more of the Swenson's pilings driven courtesy of Mike Lee, joined the fleet at Beaton's.

Vim and her crews became part of the extended family, but also like Mike Lee, one of the buffers for shifting interpersonal relationships around the yard. Gillie Ogden recalls with good humor the time during one dynamic phase when she and Jan Jessel "… actually bought, and flew, the Swiss flag, to maintain neutrality while the rest of the group worked things out!"[38]

In 1976, when Sally had owned *Silent Maid* for about a decade, Mary Schoettle Mitchell wrote a history of her father Edwin Schoettle's boat, and expressed great pleasure that Sally and the *Maid* had found each other. "She and a friend, Miss Marie Darling, have worked together restoring the boat, mostly doing the work themselves. I hope someday they write the story of all the love and care they have put into this restoration."[39] Marie bristles a bit at Ms. Mitchell's choice of words, preferring today's widely accepted "Ms.," but "Miss" is what was what Mrs. Mitchell published. Perhaps this chapter will fairly tell the story Sally was unable to write herself!

*   *   *

Silent Maid was not spared threat of storm, because summer sailors on Barnegat Bay always bear the risk of thunderstorm and squall lines. Sally was at the helm one afternoon, everyone facing up-bay towards Swan Point and home, when a guest aboard, Karen Palmer, chanced to look behind, the sun just occluded by the blackest cloud she can remember. Instantly she called to head into the wind and strike sail. The gaff came down and in what Karen says was no more than 120 seconds, a few sailstops were thrown on just as the gale hit. "It was like another knockdown without sails," Karen said, and she was surprised how far the *Maid* heeled from just the windage of her mast and rigging.[40]

At that stage in *Silent Maid*'s career, the real heavy repair work was just beginning, and the cashing in of chips from friends entertained was already long underway. Karen Palmer was to provide much needed help in that regard.

Sally met Karen Palmer in 1984 and invited her down that winter to see her boat. Karen had sailed with the Girl Scout Mariners and gone on to teach kids sailing, as well. She was underwhelmed to see *Silent Maid* under her winter tarpaulins one cold day. "I could see only this huge *blimp* under all that dark canvas," she said. But Sally lifted the covers, and Karen crept under to be astonished by the size of the cockpit. "It was like a ballroom" she recalled, "and the *wood*—all that varnish. I was hooked."[41] Twenty-seven years later she beamed, and her eyes still sparkled at the memory.

In 1985, Karen bought a relatively large "Genesis II" houseboat. It was towed north and moored at Mike Lee's against new pilings with a pier alongside. It was a natural for Sally to move aboard and Karen was interested enough that she began helping Sally fund more of the *Maid*'s restoration work. Karen said that as she began working on the *Maid*, Mike Lee would help her, saying, "I'm going to have to train you to be our mechanic. You know, I'm not going to be here forever!"[42]

This was about the time when Sally retired from her teaching career. Karen and Sally were to share the houseboat as roommates for almost 20 years, and the two of them struggled to keep up with the aging *Silent Maid*'s demands for time, work, and money!

One of their early projects was to wood down *Silent Maid*'s interior coach-roof and return it to a bright (varnished) finish. They thus undertook re-doing what my mother, working alone twenty years before, had attempted. Karen says they worked for weeks using heat guns. However, the smoke and fumes from the heat guns (and from the

FIGURE 9-18. Sally's friend Karen Palmer in at May 2008 photograph at Bay Head.

original 1924 lead paint!) made working in the cabin very unhealthy. Every now and then, one of the peels of paint coming off would catch fire and have to be stamped out. They tried every technique known from sanding, bleaching, and scrubbing with wire brushes—all to no avail. The white lead wouldn't come out of the grain. The job "ended up being another nice coat of white paint," Karen conceded.[43]

The Atomic Four gasoline engine Cliff Hogan had installed around 1966 was already used equipment when put in service aboard the *Maid*. Karen's brother was aboard once and the transmission simply wouldn't shift to get her out of the dock. He was mechanical enough that he opened the transmission case and tightened the bands to get it working again. It continued making pretty terrible noises and soon one of their friends, Walter Shoffer, came by with two cans of some miracle transmission stuff and dumped them into the transmission. Nothing happened at first, but then suddenly, as Karen Palmer reports, VAROOOOOM! It took off and a great clot of goop flew out of the transom. Problem fixed . . . temporarily!

One day Sally invited me to join a sail aboard *Silent Maid* and (why was I surprised?) the old gasoline engine refused to start. Thus passed a grand Barnegat summer morning with a cool breeze coming up east and clocking slowly around to southeast. Bobby Wescott, welder by trade, was to be another guest that day for this relaxing day on the bay. He was, I thought, a particularly rugged and handsome fellow, but Marie said he was even then working through the chemical cocktails necessary to adjust his body after a kidney organ transplant. Folks said this had changed his personality, but he was, the whole time I knew him, an especially gentle and generous man.

Bobby spent that "sailing afternoon" hanging head down in the *Maid*'s bilge. I hung over his shoulder the entire time, hoping some of his way with engines would rub off on me as he adjusted and cajoled the updraft carburetor (dripping raw gas), tweaking plugs, wiring and distributor until the old engine finally fired with another belch out the transom and revved up smoothly. It was by then far too windy for the old *Maid* to go head-to-head with the whistling southerly blow. Bobby, good soul, was pleased enough that, for the moment, the mechanical problem was solved.

One of their other friends, Charlie Williams, had come highly recommended and worked on Karen's little motor launch *Tootsie* (her mother's nickname). He eventually was spending so much time working on the *Maid*, mostly after work at his day job that he would arrive in the evening to start the struggle announcing to Sally and Karen: "Hey, honeys, I'm home!"

The *Maid*, as an aging lady, had few opportunities to race, but the Marshall Catboat fleet was growing rapidly around Barnegat Bay, and the old vessel had a major and enjoyable support role in advancing this fleet's success.

When Marshall catboat racing was on the upswing, Sally piled a bunch of people aboard *Silent Maid* and towed the 18-foot Marshall down to Little Egg Harbor, southern extremity of the Barnegat Bay watershed system, where races were held. Four kids, Sally, Marie, and sometimes others would somehow arrange themselves around that cabin and sleep aboard. Once (Marie Darling says "probably") at Brant Beach Yacht Club, they slipped in between two big motor yachts. The gentlemen aboard the yachts were in their club attire and jackets. Cocktails were being served and they looked with some disdain at this "mess of ragamuffins" as she collectively described their group. Who knows what they thought when the *Maid*'s crew began pouring out their own libations and got into the swing of it!

The *Maid*'s crew left after dinner and sailed down to Little Egg Harbor Inlet, where on a previous voyage, they'd found the blowfish abundant and tasty. It was too late on

Mosquitos and Development

Marshall cats on Barnegat started with *Priscilla* sailed in the lower bay by John Van Orden. Like most sailors he was an independent spirit and recognized that the pesticides then being aerially sprayed over New Jersey marshes were inherently detrimental to their ecology. The story was that he bribed—or tried to bribe—the pilot, one Bob Murphy, to replace the mosquito larvacide in his aerial spraying rig with salt water, at least around Van Orden's neighborhood! Of course, he failed, and so did the real pesticides as far as making a serious dent in the mosquito problem.

Mosquitos have challenged human visitors since colonial times. Swedish colonists sent to settle a colony on the New Jersey side of the Delaware River were defeated by these frustratingly abundant, bloodthirsty insects. This long-known reality had not lessened the pressure for shoreline development during the mid-20th century. Large dredged canal systems removed a number of ecologically critical salt marshes, much to Barnegat Bay's detriment.

At Van Orden's end of the bay, Mystic Shores off Little Egg Harbor was one of the projects of widest impact. Others like it were later prevented, but in Barnegat Bay proper this took a long time. Skippers Cove, its dredging completed by 1962, was billed as "the Venice of Barnegat Bay." Curtis Point and its adjacent marsh peninsulas were completely built over in stages from the mid-1950s to the mid-1970s. While these developments were legal at the time, because of misguided and inadequate state and federal laws, the profound effects on Barnegat Bay's ecosystem are probably irreversible.

FIGURE 9-19. *(Top)* Skippers Cove development near Waretown 1962, from a postcard owned by the author. *(Bottom)* Contract bi-planes spray DDT on marshes, Beaton's, and all over *Silent Maid* in August 1969. DDT was banned in 1972.

Kent Mountford photograph

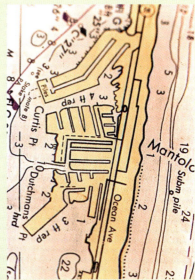

FIGURE 9-20. *(Left)* Curtis Point, Mantoloking, in 1956 when the development process was just beginning. *(Right)* Curtis Point, Mantoloking, in 1977 when all the natural marsh had been buried and the shore bulkheaded.

U.S. Coast and Geodetic Survey SC Chart, NOAA

that busy race date for such an adventure, since the markers even today are confusing in the dark and the area beset with swift tidal currents. They decided about 2200 hours to simply anchor and wait for morning. *Silent Maid* never had a depth sounder and thus unaware they awoke hard aground and sat many frustrating hours awaiting the next rising tide.

The *Maid* had another encounter with the bottom—on a day sail just north of the Seaside Bridge. Having been inattentive to the acute—and well marked— turn of channel, they ran her well up onto the adjacent flats. Sally's friend Ben Benham with his more shoal draft catboat came up and sailed delighted rings around the immobile *Maid*! Marie Darling says that they were there for hours trying to get loose.

Sally was still willing to adventure with the *Maid* occasionally, and with Marie and others aboard, they sailed her out of Little Egg Harbor into the Atlantic. This broad inlet has many shoals about which seas break to port and starboard even in moderate weather, but they kept to the channel and were OK. There was a significant sea running outside, however, and they became concerned when the *Maid*, rolling deeply when beam to the seas, began to trip her boom in the water. They wisely came back inside, and Sally's heart rate, remembering her knockdown in the *Maid*, came down to normal levels.

Northbound from Little Egg Harbor, they stopped, probably late season in 1981, at Beach Haven on Long Beach Island, and while the *Maid* was docked, an inexperienced sailor blundered out of the harbor and snagged the end of the *Maid*'s long, overhanging boom. He ripped the *Maid*'s mainsail near its clew, effectively meaning *Silent Maid* could not sail home. The guy just stupidly sailed on his way, but Marie and her son Michael jumped into the dinghy they had with them, cranked up the little outboard, and chased him down. They dragged the clueless man back and made sure they knew where to file a claim against him for damages.

FIGURE 9-21. *Silent Maid* aground north of Seaside Bridge with Janet Jessel (dark hair) pushing the bow. *Inset:* The *Maid*, this time sailing around Ben Benham's anchored catboat.

Photographs courtesy Janet Jessel

But then, what to do with the disabled *Maid* on a Sunday afternoon? They went ashore and walked from store to store on Long Beach Island until they found one that had a supply of iron-on patches. Marie heated up a heavy old sad-iron on the *Maid*'s cook stove, and getting the clew down in the cockpit, they sealed on the patches well enough to get them home. There were, Jan Jessel muses, many such patches applied repeatedly over the subsequent years!

Silent Maid was widening as well, her hull loosening with the passing years. She was again re-fastened at some point; nobody remembers the year. While she was out of the water, Beaton's replaced her old transom with a new one of mahogany, a project funded by Karen. To get fastenings into sound wood for this project, the *Maid* was actually shortened by 1½ inches, reducing her total length slightly.

Lally Beaton, Dave's son, offered me the original 1924 mahogany transom, which wouldn't quite fit in my car. Lally saved it for a while as I reconsidered, but I foolishly let the opportunity slip away. It probably ended up sawn small enough to fit in the boat shop's wood stove that winter. What a wonderful cocktail table it would have made, with the name *Silent Maid* still faintly visible across the center!

* * *

FIGURE 9-22. Sally had at least 13 of her "new family" aboard on this sail.

Kent Mountford photograph

FIGURE 9-23. **At Mike Lee's in the latter 1980s,** *Silent Maid'*s **home for almost 40 years. Note her transom had been replaced with new mahogany by Beaton's Boatyard.**

Sally Schneider photograph

FIGURE 9-24. **Mike Lee shown in the mid 1960s in his permanent garb standing by Jones Tide Pond.**

Marie Darling photograph

Marie Darling continued to live adjacent to Sally and Karen's houseboat in Mike Lee's compound. Her profession was as a licensed drug and alcoholism counselor in New Jersey, and she had an intermittent stream of clients. Her office was aboard her houseboat, which was heated in winter by a small cast iron Cannon heater or pot-bellied stove. I always thought that environment was near sufficient counseling by itself. Just being in that space with sun streaming in, the houseboat's subtle movement there imparted a sense of calm and intimacy that's kept us good friends for decades. It was hard for me to visit her sometimes because when cars were parked near the houseboat, they were often her clients working out their problems and that demanded privacy.

It comes to each of us, but eras sometimes don't end smoothly. Mike Lee had little trust in doctors. As he got older, joints began to cause pain and he would stand up from the table exclaiming "Creak, Creak!" The only remedy he accepted was horse liniment a friend had given him. In late winter, some 11 years after Sally bought *Silent Maid*, Mike Lee fell ill. They'd had dinner with him one early March evening and he was ailing, but with usual stubbornness he initially refused medical treatment. Over a few days though, he worsened quickly. A friend who was a physician looked at him, and they finally got him to the hospital.[44]

There had been a tipping point, however, and to the surprise of all, he died—as Jay Darling recalls—"from some sort of pneumonia." Those in Mike Lee's circle were stunned and suddenly they were all in a power vacuum without the "yard patriarch." He was a central character in life adjacent to Beaton's. As a machinist, he had the skills and equipment that ran not only his personal business interests and the complex piece of waterfront property, but provided creative mechanical support to Marie Darling, her family, and Sally's never ending needs for maintenance and salvage. Mike had held definite views and made peace reign on his property, where with many personalities, free-style organization, and people running in different directions, things could easily have gotten out of hand. Jay Darling says he will never forget that Mike passed away on St. Patrick's Day 1987, an event that still saddened him after a quarter century.

The fate of the place, its people, and the boats were all temporarily in limbo. There were difficulties and inevitably relationships among people changed. A status quo was reached, however, and when Mike's will was read, appropriately aboard one of the houseboats, he had made arrangements that meant that the lifestyle for Sally and the *Silent Maid* could go on for another 18 years.

*   *   *

Sally's commitment to women enjoying their freedom of expression was widening. She and her friends started a recurring series of all women's sails that might each involve over 20 friends and a few boats.[45] These were all competent sailors, or could take direction from those who were, and strong camaraderie was a hallmark. At day's end, or for a mid-day picnic, the boats would raft up abeam and people would swim, sun, and move freely about boat to boat, passing food, drink, conversation, and whatever other enjoyments were available.

The All Women's Sails went on for over 20 years and are still fondly remembered by the participants. People of all persuasions and levels of competence joined in these events. Anna Domingues was remembered for her ebullient enthusiasm and confidence. They had brought Karen's Dyer sailing dinghy, named (appropriately, Karen says) *Scullery Maid* and folks were tacking all around the anchorage. Anna, with no sailing experience, said "Oh, I can do that!" and set off, slowly losing ground downwind until she

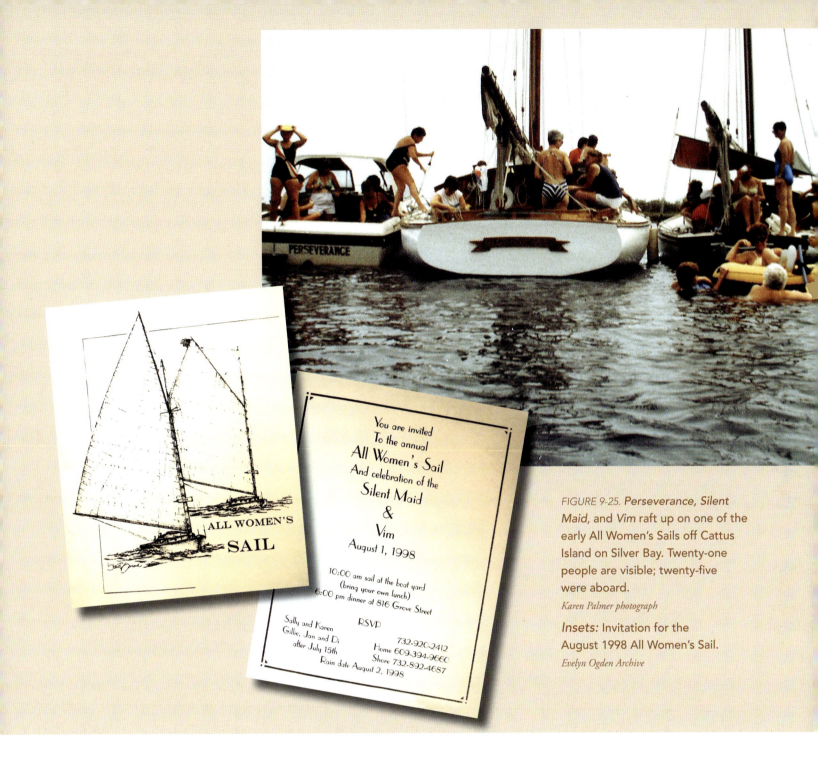

FIGURE 9-25. *Perseverance, Silent Maid,* and *Vim* raft up on one of the early All Women's Sails off Cattus Island on Silver Bay. Twenty-one people are visible; twenty-five were aboard.

Karen Palmer photograph

Insets: Invitation for the August 1998 All Women's Sail.

Evelyn Ogden Archive

You are invited
To the annual
All Women's Sail
And celebration of the
Silent Maid
&
Vim
August 1, 1998

10:00 am sail at the boat yard
(bring your own lunch)
6:00 pm dinner at 816 Grove Street

RSVP

Sally and Karen
Gillie, Jan and Di
after July 15th

732-920-2412
Home 609-394-9660
Shore 732-892-4687
Rain date August 2, 1998

ALL WOMEN'S SAIL

was against shallow flats far to leeward, and someone had to row down and recover her. More laughs than troubles.

These were good times, when Sally's strength and energy kept activities like this going on and on. After her pre-retirement carotid artery clearance her health remained good—save that cigarette cough one could sometimes hear echoing across the harbor on quiet summer mornings. Her circle of friends—men, women, couples, and singles— was still widening.

Sally had a soft spot for critters in distress and the number of dogs and cats in residence around *Silent Maid* escalated as the years went by. Some grew old, some might have a bout of summer mange. One tiny kitten fell into the bay crying piteously, paddling

FIGURE 9-26. *(Left)* Marie Darling sailing the *Maid* down Barnegat Bay in 1998.
(Right) Sally, George and Jane Matsuda, with Marie Darling on the houseboat, ca. 1990.

Marie Darling family photographs

furiously, but headed under *Silent Maid*'s dock where in a few more seconds nobody would be able to reach him. I happened to be nearby and Karen Palmer hollered for help. Still youthful and limber, I flattened myself on the dock, and with a lucky long reach, snared the poor terrified kitten squealing and all claws deployed. I'd not visited Sally for what seemed a very long time, but the first thing I asked about was the fate of that tiny bedraggled thing. She pointed with a smile towards the then full-grown bruiser tomcat that weighed in at 18 pounds. He had, it seems, prospered after his dive.

Sally also seasonally fed a massive (and in its later stages, unhealthily dense) flock of 'marina mallards' from *Silent Maid*'s dock. Many indigenous waterfowl collected around the edges of this flock as hangers on: canvasbacks, scaup (the Bluebills of Cliff Hogan's hunts aboard *Silent Maid*), coots, and gallinules to enumerate a few. I recall one winter stopping by to say hello, while the waterfowl were all busily feeding on the huge cast of corn the gals had put out. I approached casually, but with no stealth and was suddenly startled by wind and a shower of feathers as a couple hundred birds burst up from next to the houseboat.

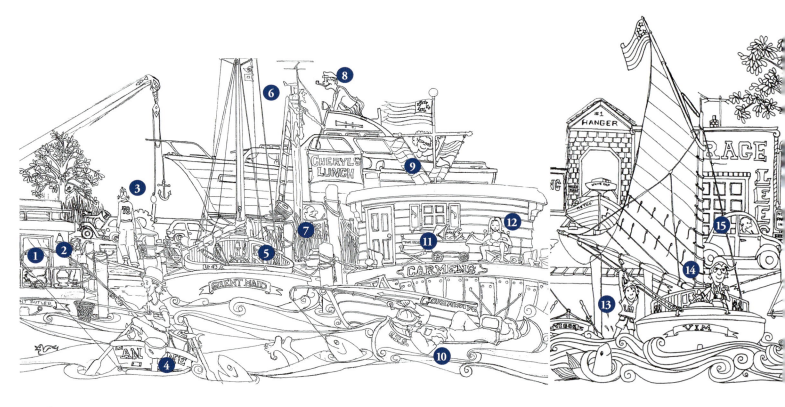

Sally dabbled in watercolor painting and was always sketching and cartooning. In 1982, she made a huge—and humorous—several-foot-wide cartoon (see Figure 9-27) showing the whole panorama across Mike Lee's place, with all the boats, characters, and activities played out in detail. It is a comprehensive archive of the times, and the few reproductions made have been jealously guarded by those fortunate enough to possess one! Inspection reveals projects and yard characters shown in dozens of activities and there are four Mike Lee images as he struggles to control Marie's exuberant kids.

It is no exaggeration to say that a small book could be written just expounding the stories of all the characters in this drawing. There are few alive today who could tell all those tales with authority, but someone—not me, thanks—should do it!

* * *

Annually, Sally called in favors from her friends to help fit out the *Maid* for the upcoming season. She was adroit at doing this, usually with no ill will or feeling of exploitation from the victims. Sally was perfectly capable of laying on a good coat of paint or varnish, but for any serious carpentry, rigging, or mechanical work she was content to supervise! She would often be ready to start a job herself when some visitor arrived and she would be diverted into greeting or inviting them "Tom Sawyer fashion" to join the fun.

There were often observers of work on the *Maid* full of wonder or interest as the huge mast, laid out on saw horses was sanded and varnished right at hip level where its size could be readily grasped. People would stand at the rigging ladder, heads back, as the spaghetti of lines and shrouds was untangled to make her ready for the season's sailing. One yard character, a strangely suspicious fellow on a neighboring boat (we were all strange in our own ways!) watched Janet Jessel hoisted to the masthead in a bosun's

FIGURE 9-27. Changing
Scenes of Bayview,
1981 by Sally Schneider.
*Courtesy Evelyn Ogden, Janet Jessel,
and Karen Palmer, 2012*

Key:
1. Tippy, Sally's Yorkie
2. George Matsuto
3. Jane Ross
4. Jeff Skona
5. Sally Schneider
6. Patrick Fasano
7. "Mac" MacKenzie
8. Bill Howie
9. Nancy Howie
10. Ed Skokna
11. Annie Monaco
12. Cheryl Monaco
13. Janet Jessel
14. Evelyn "Gillie" Ogden
15. Michael Darling
16. Carman Monaco
17. Marie Darling
18. Peter, Sally's dog
19. Mike Lee (3 places)
20. Billy Darling
21. Patty Darling
22. Nancy Ramsberger
23. Jay Darling
24. Peter Kellogg
25. One of the boys
26. Jerry Norris
27. Barbara Norris
28. Howard Rogers

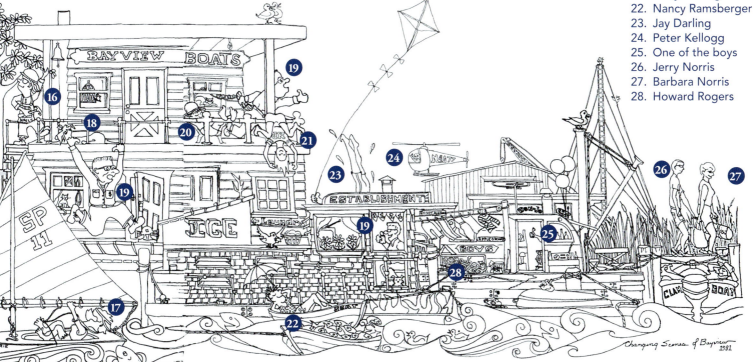

Sally Becomes Award-Winning Waterfowl Carver

Sally was offered a sabbatical by the school system after carotid surgery, but before her retirement. She thought carefully and decided to pursue a long-held interest in carving waterfowl, once the distinct province of *male* baymen. She had dabbled in finishing and painting machine-lathed decoy blanks made by Charlie Birdsall of Bay Head and Lovelandtown.[46] She learned to burn feather impressions using a hot metal nib with unusual skill, having a fine sense for capturing the appearance and personality of waterfowl in three dimensions. She sold a few at a local outlet called The Cranberry Scoop.

Being serious about carving led to another dimension of her craft. For two years, starting in 1987,[47] she made weekly trips to the Michael Veasey Studio in Delaware and learned the art well. She never rushed a carving or its painting, and this was later reflected in her teaching the craft to others. Her first entry of a bufflehead drake at a Toms River competition was judged third best in show.

Sally and Karen acquired an old house trailer, and it was set up a few yards north of the houseboat. There, they each had ample workshops for their pursuits. Karen said that Sally sharpened her tools beautifully, but she was left-handed and honed the edges for a left-handed user and that left them unsuitable for Karen, who is right-handed, to use effectively.

Sally soon had students coming to learn from her. They showed up regularly on agreed days, and she taught them what she knew. I remember during a visit I watched one of her older students bring up a duck he had carved. In sketching plumage and details to be carved permanently into the wood, he was trying to pencil in the eye. She instantly saw his error and I watched her turn the bird over in her hands a few times. "No, this is not right, look here, the eye is . . . like this . . ." and with the tip of a pencil brought its eye to life. She turned the bird again, sighting the alignment perfectly and did the same with the other eye.

Sally was more and more recognized, receiving awards, and was featured in multipage newspaper articles. When Sally passed away, her waterfowl carving students took over, and moved the trailer to a spot provided by Tommy Beaton. Under a varnished sign stating they were still "Sally's Carvers," a core group of them met each Wednesday to carry on the work and enjoyment to which she'd introduced them. Their mentor, however, was gone. For women carvers, a growing community among what was a solely male profession 100 years ago, there is now an annual award given the New Jersey Wildfowl Carvers Association in Sally Schneider's name for a superior decorative shorebird.

FIGURE 9-28. Sally's work table in the trailer in February 4, 2005. *Insets:* One of Sally's carved waterfowl heads (note the eye) and a finished Sally Schneider mallard hen, ca. 2000 (Evelyn Ogden collection).

Kent Mountford photographs

FIGURE 9-29. *(Left)* Stepping the *Maid*'s mast spring 1982 *(l to r)* Dwayne, Don Burke, (unidentified), Karen Palmer, Craig Schoffer, (unidentified in hatch). *(Right)* After sorting out that spaghetti, the *Maid* was ready, viewed from the crane at Mike Lee's.

Sally Schneider photographs

chair one time and when she came down on deck he allowed that he'd better be careful from now on with her up there spying on him.[48]

In at least one spring, Karen recalls the gaff halyards, peak and throat were reeved incorrectly by someone, so that needed mechanical advantage was lost in hoisting. It took eight people to set sail in that configuration, four people forward hauling the halyards, two aft tailing in the cockpit one—usually Sally—at the helm, and one getting the boom crutch out and handling the sheet. Edwin Schoettle and his moderately sailorly wife used to do the whole thing alone and with no engine to keep the *Maid* into the wind!

Karen says that she was lucky to have three of those eight people with any knowledge at all of sailing, and recalls one time in the midst of hoisting, one of their woman crew just threw down the halyard and said "I can't do this." Asked how this was resolved,

FIGURE 9-30. The *Maid* departs Jones Tide Pond, hoists her great sail, and progresses towards Swan Point.

Marie Darling photographs from her houseboat, August 1994.

Karen shrugs and looks knowingly. I vaguely remember Sally asking me if my dad's copy of Edwin Schoettle's book *Sailing Craft* had the proper leads for the halyards we used. I don't recall the answer I gave, but the problem with the spaghetti of lines was eventually straightened out, and making sail again became straightforward.

* * *

The *Maid* was not immune to other accidents. Karen Palmer remembers one day when she took the helm, and the wheel suddenly just spun free. Inspection under the helmsman's seat revealed that while the old worm gear was OK, one arm of the steering quadrant had—after 60 years' service—simply sheared off. Mike Lee, the machinist, fabricated a new one, and the same day they were sailing again.

One day south of Mantoloking in upper Barnegat Bay, the *Maid* was struck amidships by another boat, an impact sufficient to crush a length of plank and pierce her hull. There was not much to do about it immediately and since the wound was above the waterline, they duct-taped over it and made their way home to Beaton's. Then in another freak event, part of the Beaton's yard's equipment struck and pierced a *second* plank on the opposite side while she was being readied for haul out. Repairs that time, alas, were done at some considerable cost.

When the Philadelphia Independence Seaport Museum wooded down the old *Maid* in 2010 to restore her for exhibition, Newt Kirkland, who did the job, showed me two short Dutchman planks put in to heal both these injuries some three decades earlier.

The *Maid* got her revenge on other boats one time following this event while sailing inside Swan Point off the Mantoloking Yacht Club. A Lightning sailor had come out and crossed *Silent Maid*'s bow. The *Maid* had her main out to port on a starboard tack and could no longer see him, but assumed him moving farther a-lee. The Lightning, however, tacked, which put him on a port tack with his own sails blocking any view of the *Maid*. He was thus crossing her bow unexpectedly a second time and was hit hard and square amidships. Perched on the *Maid*'s bow, the smaller boat—deeply indented—was pushed sideways until she could be freed. The Lightning's deck was partly crushed and at least one plank splintered. The skipper readily admitted he'd been the burdened vessel, but it was an unfortunately expensive accident. The *Maid* was essentially unharmed.[49]

* * *

The *Maid*, after her early campaigning, was increasingly weakened over the decades. Mike Lee replaced her stem-head early in Sally's ownership. Local craftsman Ed Lowe and Marie Darling replaced her king plank around the same time. Eventually the garboard planks were replaced, those key and leak-prone components on either side of the keel. The job was done by Russ Manheimer during a year when he worked at Beaton's.

The technique for taking out a very old plank was clever. A small-diameter hole-saw was run through the wood at the site of each fastening, leaving (in the *Maid*'s case) the hopelessly corroded iron nail, and supplemental screws in place. The intact plank was peeled off and, with edges, bevels, and length intact, could be used as a near perfect pattern and fastening guide for the replacement board.[50]

FIGURE 9-31. *(Top)* Dutchman plank repair of a 1970s injury to the *Maid*. *(Bottom)* Newt Kirkland who uncovered this repair at Philadelphia Independence Seaport Museum, August 2010.

Kent Mountford photographs

The fastenings, problematic as they might be, were each isolated and undamaged so that, in the case of a screw, it might be backed out, or a nail pulled without undue damage. The shipwright also knew exactly the position of each old fastener and could avoid driving a new one into a location where it would have no holding power, further weakening frames with shakes (splits) or "iron sickness."

Sally's friend Carmen Monaco, one of the crowd assembled around the *Maid* and her problems, had been a rigger and splicer for a sailmaker as a teen. On the *Maid* he once stepped through a rotten spot in the cockpit sole, which had already been replaced once in the past. Carmen, with Karen Palmer and Walter Shoffer (who lived in an old bus on Mike Lee's land) undertook removal and rebuilding of the *Maid*'s cockpit sole and framing. Carmen's payment was really just the pleasure of being part of this community and having his young wife Cheryl and their little daughter more or less grow up living part-time at the yard.

In another work session, while the centerboard trunk was being restored, Karen Palmer found a small porcelain yacht sink and brass hand pump at a yard sale. As things were being put back together, this amenity was installed against the aft head bulkhead, a nice touch that became a permanent feature aboard the old boat.

Water seeping in for years around the boot—where the mast passes through the deck and its reinforcing (wooden) mast partners—eventually took out the king plank again and had let rot progress much too far for a simple repair. The result was a massive and expensive rebuild. Sally commissioned Beaton's to do this work, and it involved all the skills young Tom Beaton and others could apply.

Silent Maid was out of commission for a year and a half, and informal bets were made around the yard whether she would ever sail again.[51] In the yard's big shed, a chain hoist was employed and the entire cabin structure was carefully unfastened and lifted off.

There were more and more problems as the job progressed. Knees in the bow had rotted. The bill mounted to tens of thousands of dollars[52] and when Beaton's presented a summary at the end of the job, it seemed far too large and was a great shock to Sally and Karen.

Negotiations eventually worked it all out, but the impact was great on the gals' perception of how much they could continue to afford in preserving this old vessel. Karen Palmer said, "I found this had made a large hole in my inheritance!" Reflecting years later on the multiple surgeries to which *Silent Maid* had been subjected, Karen shakes her head and intones "poor baby." She recalls a fitness survey done at the time (which

FIGURE 9-32. Carmen Monaco and Karen Palmer in the *Maid*'s cockpit.
Karen Palmer photograph

FIGURE 9-33. *(Left)* Silent Maid with her cabin removed for rebuild. *(Right)* The cabin coach-roof suspended by chainhoist.
Marie Darling photographs

FIGURE 9-34. (*Left*) Tommy Beaton working on *Silent Maid*, 1987. *Marie Darling photograph*

(*Right*) Rebuilt mast partners shown in 2010, when exposed at the end of the *Maid*'s sailing life at the Philadelphia Independence Seaport Museum. *Kent Mountford photograph*

FIGURE 9-35. Kent Mountford and Sally Schneider aboard the *Maid* on September 5, 1983. Notice the then-inevitable cigarette in Sally's right hand. Sally's little sailing dog behind the wheel is Tippy.[54]

Nancy Mountford photograph

has not been preserved) indicated that to restore the *Maid* to true sea-keeping fitness would cost $200,000.[53]

But, the *Maid* still would be sailing again for a few more years, against all those bets. Despite a significant investment, the *Maid*'s very spine was still unsound and Sally was always wary pushing her under sail. I sailed with her a few times, and she was pretty conservative, slipping below to listen for the bilge pump; how frequent? How long did it run? When I was at the helm, eager to have the *Maid* perform as I remembered her from a decade or two before, I'd see Sally wince as I began to let her heel into the southerly!

The *Maid* couldn't perform largely because her shape was changing—like all of us! The rig was also softer, distorting under pressure, and sail shape wouldn't let her point as well as I remembered from my youth. Something was different about the hull that would not be fully clear for more than two decades when John Brady would try taking off her lines.

At one of the Toms River classic boat rallies in the 1980s, Sally pushed me to be skipper in a short antique boat race. While I never have been a racer, I was appalled how poorly I was able to do in this big, one-time bay champion. Sally still took prizes at the Toms River Yacht Club that afternoon for the maintenance, presentation, and love for her old classic. In this competition she was usually vying with her friends aboard *Vim*, a 1900 catboat survivor, at Toms River and at the Toms River annual classic boat show.

At these exhibitions someone would always come up and say "I sailed in this boat . . . ," "I varnished this umpteen times. . . ," or, in the case of Suzie Mitchell Davis with her grandkids, "This was their great grandfather's boat . . ." and the little ones would each be photographed at the helm as a keepsake.

Janet Jessel, longtime crew aboard *Vim* as well, muses that with all the investment in repairs made aboard the *Maid* some of the tackiest patch jobs lasted for years. Once she went below to use the head and found the original old 1924 soft lead intake pipe had split and was leaking. She grabbed what she recalls as a Wonder Bread wrapper and securely coach-whipped it in place with marline. The leak was cured and the repair was allowed to stand, lasting for many years.

The Wonder Bread wrapper withstood a lot of use Jan recalls, like the summer night's sail with many friends aboard when one person noticed the striking bioluminescence of plankton flashing in the toilet bowl as it was pumped. "Of course," Janet said, "everyone aboard just HAD to go down and pump the head to see this. I've never seen luminescence so bright since."[55] This was, of course, in years before there were laws or even concern about discharging untreated sewage into Barnegat Bay. It is a different world now, but one wonders how many old boats are still out there with manual flush, straight to the seacock toilets.

Sally was wonderfully cordial to my mom Dorothy who had been twice widowed in her later years. We brought Mom several times to visit the *Maid* in and out of the water and to visit Sally on the houseboat. She was always greeted in full voice as *"Mom! Come on aboard!"*

In July 1998, I was at the boatyard one cloudy morning and bent on all of the *Maid*'s mast hoops for their season's duty, tying up those completed with a sail stop till they were all securely whipped with waxed twine, and the sail properly furled. My reward was to join that afternoon for the shakedown cruise. Sally said I could invite whomever I wished so my mother, in-laws, the Kirks, and little niece Elisa Boyd joined my wife Nancy and me. My mother had been Dad's first mate on *Silent Maid* during all our years aboard her, and it was poignant to get her sailing again after being away from the boat for 34 years! My logbook[56] recorded the day:

FIGURE 9-36. *(L-R)* Vim, Silent Maid, and *Lucy*—three classic catboats being judged at a Toms River Classic Boat Show on the water at Huddy Park after year 2000.

George Chase photograph

". . . two forward on the halyards, two tailing in the cockpit, boom crutch, sheet and helm manned, two at switching the backstays. Quite a grand sail on this old lady, now in her 74th year. My mom enjoying it quite a bit in her 86th year. She's pretty game about it all and was very glad she came. [Mom took a trick at the helm and beamed the whole time.] The *Maid* sailed well, as always not admitting to be pinched at all to windward but given her head she schooned along at six knots. A good sail, clean bottom and enough rail meat[57] to make a difference with 12½ feet of beam.

"Wind up to 15–18 knots and we really over exercised this big machine. The scuppers were down on the lee side and took water into the cockpit, from whence it waterfalled into the cabin through an unclosed join in the cockpit sole! The pumps clogged with woodchips from the two years' rebuilding (Sally had just completed) and we ran off downwind from Lavallette to Mantoloking. Once ashore I made Sally flaps for the scupper thru hulls and soaked the leather in copper bottom paint. Corks for the scuppers I made from two crutch tips, contributed to the ship."

The following day *Silent Maid* was to transit to Toms River and be on exhibit for the annual classic boat show. My log continues:

". . . to the *Maid* in a deluge, streets curb-full in Point Pleasant, but not a drop in Mantoloking! Departed about 1415, making sail off Swan Point with some expertise now, but a slow trip south. Seaside Bridge was very sluggish responding but the wind slightly increasing sou'east gave a slow reach up Toms River. Struck sail and motored up to Huddy Park. What goes around, comes around… This is the most sailing I've had on the *Maid* since WE owned her."

FIGURE 9-37. *Silent Maid* at rest in the big shed at Beaton's, April 28, 2001.

Kent Mountford photograph

I had hoped to repeat those flashbacks to my youth, but some of the last years Sally and Karen managed the *Maid* she remained on blocks in Beaton's big shed. With my mom's falls and the increasing infirmity that so often pursues the very elderly, we were not able to revisit that afternoon before she died at 91½ in 2003.

* * *

Sally and Karen eventually decided to try selling *Silent Maid*. Their expectations were high; six figures were rumored, reflecting in their minds the history of this grand old boat. Ads were placed in *Soundings*, in *Salty Dog*, on Craigslist—everywhere they could think of. People did not flock to the houseboat with open wallets.

Peter Kellogg, known for his repeated interest in preserving classic boats, thought *Silent Maid* a classic that really must be preserved and quietly negotiated with Sally, at first without success. He offered her an annuity, but she knew her own health was not good, and she wisely sought a shorter-term solution. Kellogg eventually made clear to Sally that he was not purchasing an *asset*, but rather a *liability*. She eventually sold *Silent Maid* under a private understanding, with assurances of a bright future for the *Maid* and her concept as a racing yacht. That, he would amply deliver.

Sally thought about getting another smaller boat, one she could pilot and relax aboard without the challenge of leaking seams and a thousand square feet of sail! There was Karen's classic wooden runabout *Tootsie* and that was convenient and fun. Her friends Gillie Ogden and Janet Jessel, who owned the somewhat older 1900 catboat *Vim*, took Sally out sailing, but these women were equally tired of the annual mainte-nance bills.

Vim's surprise sinking was another source of worry. A plug driven into a former shaft log boring, long thought to simply be a knot in the deadwood, popped out one night. Salt water does wonders for marine engines, but all was patched up again after the shock was over. Gillie says, however, that she knew *Vim*'s days with them were num-bered "when my crews were showing up walking with **canes**! There was no way I could ask these friends to climb atop the cabin and furl that mainsail in a blow." She and Janet decided to sell *Vim*.

Sally was in declining health, diagnosed with adult-onset diabetes. She recognized how smoking had contributed to this and from two or three packs a day, she quit overnight, cold turkey. This did not arrest her struggle with poor circulation in her extremities. I was unloading one of my boats alongside the houseboat one afternoon, chatting with Sally and Karen as I shuttled off and on with armloads of gear. I managed to accidentally step on one of Sally's feet, already painful and swollen, and it hurt her terribly. It was a few minutes before the pain subsided and she regaining her composure. I felt very sorry about this, but could do nothing but sympathize. It brought home to me her delicate condition.

The winter's cold on the houseboat was becoming untenable for Sally. Karen says "every winter [despite insulation] the water supply pipes would freeze and I'd be out there with a blow-torch thawing them out in the coldest weather." Stairs, even the few steps on *Genesis II*, became a painful struggle for Sally, so Karen bought a condominium in tree-shaded, nearby Brielle to ease things for her. They would just winter ashore then summer as always on the water. Sadly, in the summer of 2005, they spent only one night on the houseboat.

Sally had been to her cardiologist on Friday, September 30, 2005, and was given an OK, actually glowing, bill of health. That evening she went out and enjoyed dinner with friends,[58] a regular engagement during which she was, as always, good, engaging company. She went to bed with no premonitions, but when Karen awoke and sought to rouse her Saturday morning, she found Sally dead. She had quietly slept away without a sound, an ideal passing that all of us would like to emulate, though terribly hard for loved ones around her. She was just 69 years old.

That Saturday the A Class catboat fleet (which the *Maid* had mastered in the 1920s) contended for the Beaton Cup (memorial to David L. Beaton). It was awarded for the best of three circuits around a course south of Swan Point, but in some sense the race was also a tribute to Sally and *Silent Maid*.

FIGURE 9-38. *Vim, Silent Maid*'s antique dock mate, sank one day by surprise. *Marie Darling photograph*

FIGURE 9-39. The Barnegat Class A catboat fleet contends for the annual Beaton Cup trophy the morning after Sally Schneider's death. *Kent Mountford photograph* (Right) Sally aboard *Silent Maid* with a cup of coffee. *Karen Palmer photograph*

ENDNOTES — CHAPTER 9

1. Evelyn Ogden, personal interview with Kent Mountford, April 10, 2012.

2. Marie Darling, personal interview with Kent Mountford, April 10, 2012.

3. Karen Palmer, reported to Kent Mountford during interview, May 19, 2012.

4. Ogden, 2012.

5. Marie Darling, personal interview with Kent Mountford at Mantoloking, 2009.

6. Palmer, 2012.

7. Eveyln Ogden, personal communication to Kent Mountford, May 10, 2014.

8. Janet Jessel provided length and name, 2012. See also www.columbia-yachts.com/history.html.

9. Maureen Molz, one of several editorial comments on draft text received April 2012.

10. Natalie Holmquist, "History of Brielle," in *Early Hotels and Restaurants,* 2007. The Ferry Boat Restaurant, opened in 1965, was owned by jazz trumpeter George Mauro, who bought the Jersey Central steam ferry *Cranford* (1905) and tried to get her through the Manasquan River bascule drawbridge, then operated by the New York and Long Branch RR. The company's structural engineers refused to open the bridge until Mauro's crew and Capt. John Boyle had chopped off a total 13 feet of beam from her extended port and starboard sides, which timber was burnt to fuel her boilers! She still hit the draw with her superstructure, scaring the wits out of by-standers and temporarily halting train traffic over the Manasquan. After clearing the drawbridge it still took the *Cranford* six attempts to jam her way into the intended slip where customers were soon served and danced to Mauro's popular band. He operated the facility for seven years, covering the time when *Silent Maid* was berthed nearby.

11. Mark McGarrity, "Dreamboats," *Asbury Park Press*, August 17, 1998, 59-62. Article quoted Sally Schneider.

12. Marie Darling, personal interviews with Kent Mountford, December 7-8, 2009, and subsequently into 2012 at Mantoloking, NJ. Marie helped reconstruct the sequence of events and much of Sally's history.

13. Ogden, 2012.

14. Marie Darling says this move was at the beginning of the following season (1967), when her daughter was two years old. Her daughter was 42 at the time of our interview.

15. Palmer, 2012.

16. Ogden, 2012.

17. Marie Darling, re-interview by Kent Mountford on draft of this book, May 19, 2012

18. Palmer, 2012; Janet Jessel, personal interview with Kent Mountford, May 2012.

19. Ogden, 2012.

20. Karen Palmer, states the barges were abandoned by Les Swenson's father, a tug skipper, 2012.

21. Kent Mountford, Log *Skeeter,* September 29, 1956.

22. Marie Darling, notes in proof to Kent Mountford, April 10, 2012.

23. Thomas Beaton, interview plus discussions with Kent Mountfourd throughout about Sally, the *Maid*, and the boatyard, 2012.

24. Perle Mesta (1889–1975) was an American socialite, political hostess, ambassador to Luxembourg, and early women's rights activist. She was known as the "hostess with the mostest" (sic.) and noted for lavish parties with the brightest stars. Born Perle Skirvin, m. George Mesta 1916–25. (http://en.wikipedia.org/wiki/perle_mesta). Perle Mesta was in Brielle, NJ, for the town's 50th anniversary celebration in April 1969, which might have stimulated the analogy with Sally!

25. Jeffrey Manheimer, interview with Kent Mountford at Manasquan, November 24, 2013.

26. Lauren Shinn, telephone interview with Kent Mountford, 2010. She was referred to me by then Independence Seaport Museum Librarian John Weiss. Shinn and her second husband owned *Sogjin*, a lapstrake sloop, now at Beaton's Boatyard, skippered by Russell Manheimer.

27. New Jersey Courier, 1902, July 17, Contractors Shinn and Hyde built the early Mantoloking drawbridge in 1902, funded by the Ocean County Board of Freeholders. Microfilm Ocean County Public Library, Toms River . Shinn was an old South Jersey Name according to Tom Beaton. The depression era bridge, successor to the 1902 draw was always in sight and sound from Beaton's Boatyard.

28. Palmer, 2012.

29. Jessel, 2012.

30. Evelyn Ogden, 2012, Ibid.

31. Darling, 2012.

32. Gerald (Jay) Darling, at launch of the *Silent Maid* replica on June 14, 2009.

33. Palmer, 2012.

34. Janet Jessel, interview with Kent Mountford, April 27, 2012.

35. Ogden, 2012.

36. "Letters of Mart," more commonly letters of marquee, were documents issued to mariners by a government authorizing them to take hostile action against enemy vessels and to profit from the sale of goods captured = sanctioned piracy!

37. Henry Colie, 2014. Brochure at launch of the rebuilt *Vim* (aboard which his father Runyon sailed in 1937) records that Robert and Gloria Neilson owned *Vim* from 1969 to 1971, when Evelyn Ogden purchased her, owning the boat until 2007.

38. Ogden, 2012.

39. Mary Schoettle Mitchell, "Nostalgic Photostory of the Catboats of Edwin Schoettle *Scat, Scat II,* and *Silent Maid*." *The Catboat Association newsletter* (c. 1976): 10-18.

40. Palmer, 2012.

41. Palmer, 2012.

42. Palmer, 2012 (quoted Mike Lee in these words).

43. Palmer, 2012. (No OSHA regulations were violated [or known] that long ago.)

44. Palmer, 2012.

45. Evelyn (Gillie) Ogden, Janet Jessel, and Karen Palmer, interviewed by Kent Mountford at the Ogden home, Point Pleasant, NJ, 2010.

46. Artie Birdsall, Charlie's nephew, is the 4th generation carver in the family. Eugene Birdsall may have started decoy carving at Toms River in 1883 before moving to Lovelandtown (Bay Head) in 1890 (http://decoymag.com/features/tidbits/wildfowler/3.htm).

47. Palmer, 2012. Karen remembers Sally starting in 1985, Veasey opened his studio in 1987, specializing in airbrush painting techniques.

48. Jessel, 2012.

49. Jessel, 2012.

50. Russell Manheimer, discussion with Kent Mountford, 2010. Manheimer worked on the *Maid* for Beaton's Boatyard.

51. Palmer, 2012.

52. Palmer, 2012. In May, Palmer estimated with bills of $10K and $40K that the aggregate was at least $80,000 invested in the *Maid*, including prolonged storage and handling of the boat.

53. Palmer, 2012. Palmer reports there was more than one survey made; only one, the last, was preserved.

54. Palmer, 2012.

55. Jessel, 2012. Bioluminescence of varying intensity is often observed in Barnegat Bay. It is the result of agitating microscopic plant plankton cells called dinoflagellates, which emit bluish sparkles of light upon being disturbed. The author's amateur study of this phenomenon starting in 1964 formed the start of his 40-odd-year career in marine biology

56. Kent Mountford, Log *Nimble*, entry #532, July 16, 1998.

57. Rail meat, sailor's shorthand for using human ballast along the high side of the boat to counterbalance the heeling moment of the sail, flattening the boat, and making her carry sail better.

58. Karen Palmer, interview with Kent Mountford at her home in Brielle, NJ, and elsewhere, 2010.

FIGURE 9-40. Silent Maid, picture of grace, and the level of courtesy shown her by some modern power boaters!

Aerial photo by O. Kanzler, 1983 with permission

FIGURE E-1. Reincarnated *Silent Maid* competing in the 2014 Elf Classic race from the Eastport Yacht Club finishing at the Chesapeake Bay Maritime Museum, St. Michaels, MD.

Susan Vianna photograph

Inset: John Brady, builder of the reincarnated *Silent Maid* in 2009 and then-shipwright at the Philadelphia Independence Seaport Museum on the Pennsylvania side of the Delaware River.

Kent Mountford photograph

Epilogue

Sally Schneider, *Silent Maid*'s final sailing owner, sold her beloved boat in 2005. It was an act intended to offer a new lease on *Silent Maid*'s life. However, her condition, with flaws from keel to the end of her gaff, made this impractical, and she was taken by her new owner Peter R. Kellogg to the Philadelphia Independence Seaport Museum, leaving Beaton's Boatyard for the last time aboard a significantly oversized highway trailer.

There, at Penns Landing on the Delaware River, shipwright John Brady at his "Workshop on the Water" began a thorough assessment. He took a table of offsets— hundreds of measurements—off *Silent Maid*'s old hull, and when he drew them out on paper, attempting to make a fair reconstruction of her lines, he found the structure seriously warped and hogged. There was no practical way that the original vessel could be strengthened for serious hard and competitive sailing.

Kellogg, well aware of this conclusion, put a program together with some friends to sponsor a complete reincarnation of this old classic. Shipwright John Brady, with his largely volunteer crew at the Seaport Museum, built an entirely new *Silent Maid* based on her original plans and objective. Faithful in appearance, she was launched in June of 2009, but once afloat and fitted with the finest modern sailing and racing gear she was competitive among 21st century yachts.

Under the hands of Brady's qualified volunteers and, let's be frank, embalmers, the original 1924 *Silent Maid* was carefully refinished and preserved to be an exhibit. She still sits at this writing in a sunlit warehouse at the old Philadelphia Navy Yard (where Edwin Schoettle worked during World War II), but hidden from sight of visitors. I went aboard her there and found the experience an eerie reprise of my youth, sitting at

FIGURE E-1. *Silent Maid*, restored as a future museum exhibit, waits in a warehouse at the old Philadelphia Navy Yard.

Kent Mountford photograph

the helm, on my old bunk, and walking her wide decks. One hopes someday she will have a space at the museum large enough to make her available to the public. She will impress all comers with her size and grace and beside her some visitors can relive the many insights presented in this book.

Preserving old boats, reminiscent of a way of life long past, is not a new idea. Our world in the new millennium has hundreds of them, lovingly nursed along, boldly restored, or created anew. I think sometimes we have rescued too many boats to ever maintain them all over the long run of years in a shifting economy. The elegance of this indenture—salvaging old vessels—comes in selecting what boats to preserve and in how one executes the concept. Everything can't be saved from a longed-for past, but one can select and save symbols and role models for how things were and perhaps should be done. The commitment, following thereafter, comes in keeping a boat to standards that allow her to sail as she was designed to sail, and then putting her out to do that work.

Peter Kellogg, with a vacation home in Bay Head, New Jersey, has since joyously campaigned the reborn *Silent Maid* with several crews and skippers along the northeast and mid-Atlantic coasts with remarkable results. While a brand new boat, this new *Maid* has undergone an almost constant stream of sophisticated changes, adaptations, and top-flight engineering advances that have repeatedly escalated her capabilities. This work clearly delighted the boatbuilders at Beaton's in Mantoloking and at Bill De Rouville's shop on Toms River.

Silent Maid's design, creation, commissioning, and Brady's delivery of the *Maid* to Toms River and Bay Head are exciting tales on their own. Her race record over the ensuing years would make any sailor smile. The *Maid* attracts interested, committed crews from among the region's best sailors. She grows faster, more powerful, and decidedly more complex with every season she sails. I hope another author takes on the task of writing a history of this amazing vessel.

Appendix
Sex and the *Silent Maid*

At the book launch party of Jobson and Wilkins' wonderful account of the A class catboats, which contains no salacious material whatever, Peter Kellogg came up to me amidst the din of several hundred people, laid a hand on my shoulder, and said, "When it got around I was buying *Silent Maid*, a guy I know came up to me and said 'Peter, why are you buying HER? Don't you know that every woman north of Lavalette's gotten laid on that boat?'"

Peter looked expectantly at me (who'd spent my most-testosterone stressed teen years aboard), but I could only report that sadly I'd never (biblically) known any of them. Peter introduced me to a bystander and moved on to his next conversation. As long-time sailing friend, Russell Manheimer, described it, I'd had my Peter Kellogg moment and Peter slipped out of the hall.[1]

But, with my ignorance, where were all those fortunate men and women with their carnal needs gratified in the *Maid*'s spacious cabin? Frankly, it would not, I contemplated, be the most comfortable place to make love. While generous for one, the berths running fore and aft, head to tail were pretty narrow . . . unless the preliminaries had been assured elsewhere, and people were positioned, so to speak, two-deep. And then, being under the *Maid*'s wide waterway decks, under which *both* berths extended, meant constrained positions for enthusiastic lovers, nor was there very much headroom upon rising from one's carnal labors. There was also no hot water or shower aboard . . . nor a holding tank; what you hand-pumped down the head came immediately out a fitting at the waterline and into the bay-water where you might covet a refreshing post-coital swim.

FIGURE A-1. Evidence of casual love amongst the dunes on Island Beach almost a century ago. Aluminum cases like this contained three condoms and were marketed during the first third of the 20th century.[2] I've found these twice walking through secluded swales. The three widows (on another tin) were named Agnes, Mabel, and Becky.

Kent Mountford photograph

I for one was certifiably virgin my entire agonized youth aboard *Silent Maid*. The most passionate of my youthful romantic objects were strongly under observation of my vigilant parents, their parents, and a vengeful God, and should any of the forgoing have lacked vigilance, there were any number of my parents' boating friends. Some were docked bordering the boatyard parking lot and the rest constituted a gauntlet of at least 16 pairs of watchful eyes stretching out to *Silent Maid's* slip, which lay third from the end. I would have had to move any young woman smuggled aboard through all these obstacles. The *Maid* herself was always under floodlight scrutiny day and night by Rudy and Millie Winter, the marina owners.

It was only long afterwards that, reminiscing with the one girl from those times who was most aware of her own sexuality, I found *she* was just as disturbed after what for me were agonizingly chaste evenings. With an unmistakable clarity of memory, she assured me that we never even *made out* aboard the *Silent Maid*.

We did a little better on the narrow 14 inch slat-seats aboard my own little sailboat at the time, but the young lady left me for Archie, who was "a better kisser," and sundry other boys. She was with Archie at this writing half a century later.

When, in my life, the God Priapus was finally relieved of his curse, it was in the embarrassingly cramped cabin of my tiny cruising sloop *La Boheme*[3] or in more comfortable environs ashore. Both trysting places were kept far from watchful parents, themselves still wedded to pre-marital abstinence. Neither of the partners from that distant reach of my life ever made love with me in the *Maid's* welcoming cabin.

I will state here, categorically, that I regret to this day that great deficiency in my youth.

The A class catboat fleet had a wider reputation. Roy Wilkins recounts that a certain unnamed woman (of legendary face and figure) was ritually tied topless and facing forward to the mast of an A cat sailing south of Mantoloking Bridge.[4] Symbolically bound, I expect, but nonetheless a titillating figurehead had one intersected her course that night, splitting the winds with her lovely bosoms.

Silent Maid, in her earliest decades, is also mute about carnal endeavors. Most revealing though is Jack LaFleur's recollection that Edwin Schoettle and his wife Sara, both committed sailors, would go overnight down Barnegat Bay just the two of them.[5] I hope at least that this culminated many times in intimate pleasures for them both.

Edwin's son Ferdinand, according to his son Andy, could have contributed significantly to this brief and indefinite chapter of the *Maid's* history.[6] Since Andy himself is now sadly deceased, and unable to amplify on his own behalf, this hint is all you're going to get!

Sex in my youthful early years turning from the fifties to the sixties was not easy for boys, and was extremely risky for girls, when even securing a condom was embarrassing and difficult. People took whatever opportunities they could find for intimacy, even at the risk of being inattentive.

FIGURE A-2. Sara and Edwin's young daughter Mary Schoettle (later Mitchell) standing just ankle deep at water's edge, smiles beautifully, and is reflected in the varnish of *Silent Maid's* varnished planking.

Kent Mountford photograph

A friend in Bay Head told me of two lovers in a Hubert Johnson's lapstrake sea-skiff. In the dark of summer's night, they were inattentive with their passion while roaring down the Metedeconk. The unpiloted powerboat smacked directly into the stout, driven piling of a New Jersey state navigation day-mark. None of the participants emerged unblemished from that encounter.

This informant himself conducted a promising date afoot to the sandy Atlantic beach in Bay Head, where no lights would interrupt his attempts on her defenses. "She lay on the blanket," he said, eyes misty, her glorious breasts finally exposed to his touch, "as I came over her to kiss, from the sea, behind us, the entire beach was suddenly illuminated by brilliant floodlights." Priapus failed in an instant. "A military transport," he said, "was on his final downward approach to McGuire Air Force Base next to Fort Dix, and had simply turned on his landing lights." My friend went on to marry the young woman; a union that has endured over 50 years.

My pretty cousin Joan DuFour, then just married to Jack Campbell, reported that they spent part of their honeymoon aboard the *Silent Maid*. Indelicately, for this portion of the book, I asked, *"And, did you get laid?"*

"I suppose so," she said, "it WAS our wedding night." Now in her 83rd year, she is a little uncertain about that minor occurrence long ago. It had been my dad's idea that they use the boat; she and Jack spent two nights aboard as she recalls, but she clearly remembered waking to the halyards tapping on the *Maid's* big mast, as some early morning June wind swept along the Bay way past half a century ago.

Their marriage ended decades ago, but their children, John and Jill, are strong, stable, and successful with families of their own. Both Jack and Joan went on to other marriages, and are both widowed. *"We're good friends. I still keep in touch with him,"* she muses.

Clifford and Nancy Hogan, who owned *Silent Maid* directly after my dad, are pretty certain one of their children was conceived aboard her, but who's interested in sanctioned marital sex anyhow? Well, they were an attractive couple, and he and Nancy both recall making passionate love one afternoon when they were interrupted by something outside. Cliff, bounding up to look out the forward hatch, missed his aim and almost knocked himself senseless on the hatch frame. "Thump!", as expressed by Cliff and Nancy, was no way to end or interrupt any romantic encounter. Nancy, furthermore, publically lamented the lack of a shower aboard *Silent Maid* and that was contributory to Cliff selling the boat after a couple years.

During Sally Schneider's time with *Silent Maid*, she was a certifiable party boat. Sally was known as the "Perle Mesta" of Jones Tide Pond at Beaton's Boatyard, and the numbers of people male and female who came and went were legion. One of Sally's students, a willowy girl named Liz, caught the eye of Mike, one of the Marshall Catboat crowd at Beaton's. I thought she was pretty nice too, but Mike was there first, and made a number of overtures to her. I remember seeing them one morning after she'd been aboard the *Maid* overnight standing together sort of downcast in serious discussion. Mike never made any major inroads with her and by summer's end she had decided to go off in another direction, and I never saw her again. Mike, incidentally for whatever reason, never married and would still revisit Beaton's at least until a few years ago.

The "All Women's Sails" certainly put a lot of females around the decks of *Silent Maid* and her companion vessels. On other weekends, there were usually some guys, like Mike Lee, Tom Mount, and Ben Benham, who were regulars, Also, there were

FIGURE A-3. My cousin Joan's daughter Jill Campbell at the wheel of *Silent Maid* about 1958.

casual visitors or people Sally had sweet talked into contributing some mechanical, electrical, carpentry, or muscular strength to the *Maid*'s survival. Certainly the alcohol and good fellowship escalated as the sun went over its proverbial yardarm (remember Marie Darling's meal for 15 to 20 people, many of whom she'd never met before).

Certainly parties often seem to be what they are not and often are amplified in memory as time passes. Most of the girls and guys I've known, if reasonably drunk, were never likely to be very enthusiastic (or effective) sex partners.

Is it thus that a reputation grew? Discreet inquiry among those dwindling participants who survive (even Tom Mount is now gone, dying in Point Pleasant at near 100 years of age) elicits smiles and the response: "Oh, let's not go there!"

Let the legend continue, and by all means contact me with the prurient evidence YOU, dear reader, might have! These insights will all be published at my death as an "Unexpurgated Carnal Appendix."[7] *Silent Maid* herself will, of course, tell no tales at all. Her old seams have been zipped up for all time.

ENDNOTES — APPENDIX

1. Roy Wilkins, interview with Kent Mountford, December 3, 2009. His account of the A catboat book production and subsequent book-launch affair.

2. www.collectorsweekly.com/getting-it-on-the-covert-history-of… The Comstock Act of the 1870s effectively made condoms and all birth control illegal in the United States. By the early 20th century, marketers and manufacturers were beginning to find ways around the bans and the taboos.

3. *La Boheme*, a 17-foot pocket cruiser, built on a 1946 (Abacos) Bahama dinghy hull, formerly owned by brothers John and Dayton Trubee, also Barnegat sailors in their youths from about 1949-1961.

4. Wilkins, 2009

5. Jack LaFleur, written correspondence to Kent Mountford, January 4, 2010.

6. Ferdinand (Andy) Schoettle, interview, July 16, 2010. Andy Schoettle, an internationally known legal scholar, Olympic sailor, and later yachtsman's advisor and instructor, sadly passed away in November 2010.

7. Roderick A. Barr, 1956. Mr. Barr, a lifelong friend, recommended that my logbooks, always crafted with an eye to eventual public consumption, should be accompanied by such an Appendix, which over 60 years would, indeed, make shocking reading, while I am still here and subject to libel and lawsuit.

Glossary

abaft: Aboard a vessel, this means behind something (e.g., abaft the beam); behind the central widest point of the hull.

anchor rode: The rode is the rope or line to which the anchor is attached and to which the vessel rides while at rest.

athwartships: Crosswise on a vessel.

backstay cleat: When a large catboat sail is set to go downwind, the wire shrouds do little to support the mast and thus on the windward side (opposite swung-out the boom) a wire stay and tightening tackle is set up to a fastening T-shaped cleat to take up the strain. When the boom swings to the other side, the backstay must instantly be loosened to allow the boom passage and the opposite backstay set up.

ballast: Ballast, or weights placed aboard a ship, helps keep a boat upright and can be stowed inside the hull or attached to the outside.

batten: In *Silent Maid*'s time, a batten was a wooden strip tied in a pocket along the leech of a sail that is set at 90 degrees to the leech. A line of battens helps the roach stand out smoothly in the same plane as the sail, maintaining its shape as an efficient airfoil, making the boat faster in theory.

beam reach sailing: Sailing with the wind blowing towards the side of the boat, usually the fastest point of sailing for most boats, as opposed to having the wind coming from towards the bow or from behind the vessel.

benthic species: Organisms (as described in this book) that live on or burrow in the bottom of Barnegat Bay. These life forms process organic materials in the sediment and form the lion's share of food supply for many fish, crab, and shellfish species of interest to humans and vital to the ecosystem. There are as many as several hundred such species in Barnegat Bay.

binnacle: A protective, and sometimes internally lighted, housing to protect the ship's navigation compass.

boom crutch: A portable wooden support upon which the weight of the boom and its attached sail rest when lowered for stowage. On *Silent Maid*, the upper end was cut with a semicircular curve and resembled the top of a crutch.

bowsprit: A spar to support sails and rigging that projects out from the bow of the boat, permitting a vessel to carry more sail, since it extends beyond the hull, and which also moves the overall center of balance of the sails forward on the vessel.

catboat: Strictly speaking, a sailing vessel with one mast, stepped far forward in the bow and spreading one fore and aft sail of any sort—gaff, Marconi, loose-footed, or wishbone.

clew: The lower outer corner of any sail, usually strengthened with multiple layers of cloth reinforcing, set with a large metal grommet for securing and with a rope edge sewn in place.

clipper bow: A particular shape given to the bow of a vessel in which, from the waterline, the hull structure sweeps up and outward in a concave curve, usually ending where a bowsprit projects forward. This was a traditional form usually associated with 19th century clipper ships, hence the name.

coachroof: The top of a boat's cabin.

coamings: Coamings are the finish planking, often curved in catboats, which surround the cockpit where passengers sit, separating it from the deck and outer edge of the hull and prevent water splashing on the deck from entering the seating area.

double-block: A double block ("pulley") has two rotating sheaves for two lines to run through. With a single-sheave block below to which the bitter end of a line is attached, the line threaded through makes four trips up and down the mast. The final part in its descent is called the "standing part." This arrangement is one version of a "tackle." To pull a heavy load (e.g., a gaff and sail) aloft, you must haul all those four lengths of line through the blocks, but gain a 3:1 mechanical advantage (pulling only a third as hard, but creating a large pile of rope!)—a great help in raising heavy sails and spars.

E scow: A racing class of light, shallow-draft, sloop-rigged boats capable of planing (skimming over the water) at high speeds with substantial winds. They are characterized by dual bilge-boards set on each side of the hull and small dual rudders operated by a conjoined tiller system.

Flemish the lines: A variety of techniques exist for coiling long lines so that they will run out quickly and without kinking or tangling. Flemish here represents coiling a line in concentric circles so it forms a flat coiled mat and, sometimes, a second and third coiled mat atop the first.

flitches: The thin strips of wood, usually with the bark still on, cut from a round log as it is shaped into square timbers by a sawmill.

forepeak: The usually triangular space forward of the mast behind which the stem and planking come together; in smaller boats it is used as a storage space for sails and lines.

forestay: A wire rigging cable running from the top of the mast to the bow of the boat, tightened with a rigging screw or turnbuckle.

gaff rig: Any boat carrying a gaff sail, as opposed to the Marconi or jib-headed sail, usually seen on modern boats.

gaff sail: A four-sided, approximately trapezoidal sail that is run up the mast, stretched back along the boom at deck level and with an angled gaff at the top, which is usually hauled tight with a tackle until it points upward at a pre-determined angle. This sail permits a larger area of canvas to be carried higher in the rig; fine in light airs, less satisfactory in a blow; thus reef points are provided.

garboards: The keel is the key and central structural member of a wooden boat upon which the frames are erected like a whale's ribs.

The garboards, on either side, are the first planks adjacent to the keel, followed upwards by all the others. As the lowest point for debris and moisture, even when the boat is hauled for storage, they are subject to strains, sometimes tend to leak, and often rot.

gooseneck: A device, attached to the mast, that serves as the base of a pivot for the boom so it can swing to port and starboard as the sail is differently set.

hockling: Most rope used on ships in the past was laid by twisting together three thick strands of manila hemp. Rope thus naturally coiled clockwise without twisting. When rope was forced to coil the "wrong" way and put under strain, permanent kinks, or hockles could develop in the line irretrievably compromising its strength.

jib-headed main: A mainsail, as in the Class A catboats, which comes to a point at the top, as does the common headsail called a jib.

jibe: Sailing downwind, if care in steering to prevent this is not taken, the wind can blow on the back side of the sail, and swing the boom across the other way. With wind force applied, the sail and boom gather momentum and can sweep people overboard to their deaths and slamming to the lee side have power enough to dismast a vessel.

kedge: A traditional type of anchor built with a metal shaft or shank from which two arms curve outward ending in flukes, or flattened areas that dig into the bottom. To assure the flukes dig in, a metal or (once wooden) stock is set at 90 degrees atop the shank, causing the anchor, when dragged on the sediment, to turn the flukes downward. This is an old cumbersome, but effective, pattern of anchor.

kingplank: The centralplank of a vessel's forward deck, usually wider and sturdier. In catboats, the mast often pierces this member.

knees: Angular (close to 90 degrees) timber reinforcements placed in areas where bending, twisting, or crushing forces occur in a ship's hull, such as where the deck is joined to the frames and hull at their outer edges, or in corners around which the mast pierces the deck and requires strengthening.

lapstrake: A manner of attaching planks to a boat's frames in building, where the lower edge of the plank above partially overlaps the plank below. The boat's fastenings hold both rigidly to the structural frames.

lazy jacks: A set of light lines passing in a "U" shape around the boom at two or more points and carried up to some attachment on the mast. Lazy jacks (so-called after sailors in the past) help gather and control a billowing sail as it is lowered.

lead pigs: Simple cast bars of lead of a size that can be stored correctly inside the ship's hull and are of a weight that can be managed by hand. Lead weighs a bit over 708 pounds per cubic foot!

leeboards: Like a fixed keel or a centerboard, leeboards mounted along either side of the hull, help a sailing vessel avoid slipping sideways as she moves through the water to windward. They can be raised or lowered to allow sailing into shallower or deeper water.

leech: The outer (rear) edge of a fore and aft sail, usually forming a curved line from the end of the boom to the head of the mast or the tip of the gaff.

lever arm: The mechanical advantage gained by prying a load against a central point or fulcrum, such that a proportionately small force at the end of the lever can move a much larger load. Here, the multiplied strain on structure from forces applied at the outer side of a vessel's hull.

LOA: Naval architect's abbreviation for length over all: the total length of the hull, stem to stern.

lubber line: An imaginary line down the center of a vessel from bow to stern that is exactly the direction of travel and should agree, therefore, with the ship's compass

luff: The forward or leading edge of a sail, as where it is attached to the mast or wire stay. This, when a sail is improperly trimmed, is the first place where the shape of the sail is spoiled by the wind buckling or "luffing" the sail.

LWL: Naval architect's abbreviation for length (on the) waterline: that is the total length of the hull immersed in the water floating at rest. When a boat sails, this dimension, by virtue of wave dynamics, effectively limits the speed of a vessel. This limit does not apply to high-speed boats, which plane across the surface.

mast plumb: A term to describe how a mast is set and secured in a boat exactly vertical when viewed from the side.

parrel: A fitting at the junction point of a mast and spar that allows it to pivot around the attachment point.

pound nets: The pound net was a New England invention subsequently exported down the Atlantic coast. When fish swimming along the coast encountered an obstacle (in this case, a line or leader of long tree-trunk stakes driven into the bottom with fish net strung continuously), they would instinctively swim offshore and there encounter more net strung to more long pilings. Then a heart-shaped baffle would funnel them into an enclosed pocket where they would accumulate and be harvested by men lifting a fish-net floor upwards and ladling out the catch. These nets set several hundred feet at sea off the New Jersey shore were once a fabulously efficient nonselective fishery. All kinds of fish were caught from sea robins and skates (considered trash fish) to striped bass, mackerel, menhaden, and occasional large and destructive sharks.

raffee: A triangular sail set crosswise to the centerline of a vessel, with a transverse spar or "yard" holding its corners out sideways to gather wind.

ratlines: A series of ladder like steps secured to the main supporting rigging of a mast that enables sailors to climb aloft.

reef points: A line of short cords passing through brass eyelets in a sail for reducing sail area in strong winds. The sail is lowered and all the lines are gathered around the furled portion, thus shortening the sail. *Silent Maid* had five sets of reef points allowing about a 75% reduction in sail area during a severe blow.

roach: A curve built into the leech of a sail that allows it to "bow" outwards towards the stern, giving shape to the sail and adding some additional sail area.

sailstops: Small lengths of line of rope or cloth webbing that are passed around a furled sail to keep it in place when not in use. On gaff-rigged vessels, they are usually passed over the gaff, around the sail, and through the space between boom and sail. Secured with a reef knot, which is half a shoelace bow, the hitch is secure, but, like the shoelace, can be released with a single yank on the free end.

sand balds: Bare areas appearing in an otherwise dense, unbroken turf of vegetation.

scarph: A long, diagonal join made between two pieces of structural wood to create a longer member and preserve its longitudinal strength.

scuppers: Tubular drains in the corners of a vessel's cockpit so that water introduced by waves or rain can be drained out of the hull through fittings, usually closeable with hand-operated valves called seacocks.

seine: A fish net with floats on the upper edge and small lead weights along the bottom. Small seines have a wooden pole securing each end and, when pulled through the water, gather fish and other organisms for fishing.

shrouds: Shrouds are cable supports attached to the rail of a vessel and running (in this case) to the top of and resisting bending strains on, the mast. To compensate for stretch and give the shrouds a better purchase in their support role, spreaders or struts are often attached well up the mast, which push outwards on the shrouds.

skeg: An extension of the vessel's keel, where the rear portion of the hull rises up to the stern or transom. This structure strengthens the hull, gives an attachment member for the rudder, and stabilizes the vessel's steering qualities as she slips through the water.

spiral flax packing: In the traditional bronze stuffing box, where propeller shaft pierces the hull a leak-seal was accomplished using a square, lubricant impregnated length of braided flax plant fiber material, formed into a spiral around the propeller shaft inside the cylindrical bronze stuffing box and compressed by tightening a large bronze nut.

spritsail rig: A quadrangular (four-sided) sail attached to the mast and held out to the wind by a single diagonal spar (the sprit), which runs from the base of the mast to the sail's uppermost outer corner.

stem-head: Planking of a hull in the bow of a vessel is brought together and fastened to the stem timber, a major strength member. The top or head of the stem is where the forestay is fastened, usually to a metal strap that is fastened to the outer edge of the stem.

stuffing box: A tubular fitting used where the propeller shaft pierces the hull, designed to allow it to spin at high speed without admitting leaks of seawater into the hull (*see also* flax packing above) .

throat and peak halyards: The two lines (ropes) and their tackles used to raise a gaff sail's upper spar to sailing position. When raised, the forward end of the gaff is the throat and the after end or "peak" is usually raised sharply using the second halyard, thus stretching the sail to its proper shape.

topping lifts: Lines attached near the end of a boom, which bear its weight and prevent it from crashing to the deck when the usually supporting sail is lowered.

windage: The resistance or friction, caused by a ship's structures, hull, and rigging, all of which increase difficulty of handling and slow the vessel down while sailing.

windlass: A rotating drum, either horizontal or vertical, around which an anchor rope or other line is wrapped for mechanical advantage, and which is operated by a lever (or in modern boats an electric motor) providing a very powerful pull, as in recovering an anchor deeply embedded in the bottom.

wire bridle: On a very long gaff of boom with large bending strains applied, strength is preserved when the force is spread out over two or more points by using one or two wire bridles, to which the force is then applied.

wung out: Sailing with wind behind the boat "running downwind" catching all possible wind, the boom is swung out as far as possible at 90 degrees to the centerline.

Index

Page numbers in italics refer to photos and illustrations; page numbers with "n" refer to a numbered entry in chapter endnotes.

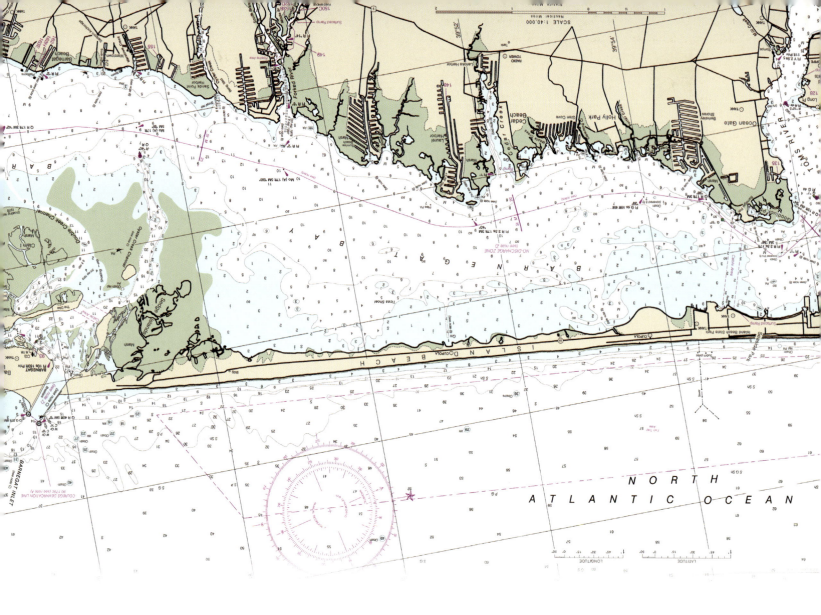

ABOUT THIS CHART

The National Oceanographic and Atmospheric Administration (NOAA) is heir to the role played early in the last century by the U.S. Coast and Geodetic Survey. NOAA maintains up-to-date versions of Barnegat Bay charts on several scales, showing relatively recent shorelines, existing wetlands, bottom topography, and aids to navigation—that is, buoys, lights, and fixed structures current at the time a paper chart is published. Aids and other features change frequently, and it is the responsibility of the navigator to track these changes in frequently posted Notices to

Mariners, and then make these alterations directly on the chart. Most of us rarely do this . . . and this human failing has led NOAA to suspend publication of paper charts; a decision lamented widely in the boating community. NOAA will continue to make these charts available electronically and private vendors will still print you out a "paper" version, even a waterproof one, at significant cost.

Compare this modern chart and its countless differences with the 1924 version presented on the inside front cover. Note especially the intense and generally